Legend In
MISSOURI

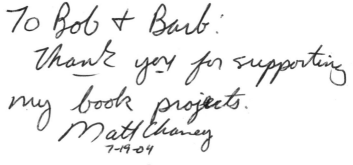

To Bob & Barb:
Thank you for supporting
my book projects.
Matt Chaney
7-19-04

Matt Chaney

featuring passages from writers
and witnesses in history

Editor: John R. Stanard
Page Composition: Diane Schoenbaum
Cover Design: Amy Richardson, Minit Print Inc.

Four Walls Publishing
PO Box 904
Warrensburg, MO 64093-0904

Permissions for use of special passages in this book were granted by:
    The Ulysses S. Grant Association, Southern Illinois University, Carbondale, Illinois; and
    The University of Oklahoma Press, Norman, Publishing Division of the University.

Printed and bound in the United States of America by Walsworth Publishing Company, Marceline, Missouri.

2 3 4 5 6 7 8 9 10

ISBN: 0-9639316-3-6

For John Kendall, a great friend

Acknowledgments*

This book qualifies as a surprise, and pray it does not read like one. A year ago, when relocating to Warrensburg, this book was not on my list, and Laurie and I did not commit to producing it until March of this year. Much of the research and writing, however, began several years ago.

Missouri has endless topics in both history and the present to fascinate and challenge us. Some of the subjects in this book are famous, some not; all are extraordinary. I note I have written previously about these subjects in other mediums, particularly in a newspaper series published by weeklies in Missouri.

I am so grateful to the editor, John R. Stanard, Poplar Bluff, and Diane Schoenbaum of Bella Vista, Arkansas, who performed tasks from page composition to fact-checking. Both went beyond the call, which is necessary for anyone involved with or caught in a Four Walls production. Laurie, of course, was very courageous in the struggle.

Thanks go out to the organizations, writers, and others key in research for this book. Copyright permissions were provided by the Ulysses S. Grant Association, Southern Illinois University at Carbondale, and the University of Oklahoma Press, Norman. Authors, journalists or researchers, living and deceased, who must be cited here are: Bruce Catton, Fritz Kreisler, Ulysses S. Grant, Louis Houck, Jay Monaghan, John Joseph Mathews, Victor Tixier, Louis F. Burns, Willard H. Rollings, Alex Cooper, and James Leon Combs. Thank you to the publications, publishers, and others who supported those writers.

Individuals who provided integral assistance were Tracy and Tami Edington, Kerry Glasco, Doug and Angie Jackson, John and Cathy Kendall, Ted Inurie, Edward "Bud" Fellows, Joe Combs, Herb Schoenbaum, and my parents, Louis and Lillian Chaney.

Family collections of data for research were provided by Larry Fisher and Paul Hauck. And, of course, I thank the libraries and reference centers visited and consulted across Missouri and beyond, foremost the following: Kent Library, Southeast Missouri State University; Ward Edwards Library, Central Missouri State University; State Historical Society, Columbia; and City Library of Poplar Bluff.

Read about Missouri.

Matt Chaney

Reprinted from first edition, 1997

v

FRONT COVER PRINT
Le-Soldat-Du-Chene, "Soldier of
the Oak," An Osage Chief, 1804

BACK COVER PRINT
Mo-Hon-Go, An Osage Woman and
Child, 1830

Stone lithographs with original hand-
coloring (watercolor), from *History of
the Indian Tribes of North America*,
McKenney & Hall, 1836-44

TORNADO

"I could just see a big black cloud and it was
rollin'. It was really rollin'. And it seemed to be
right on the ground."

Cecil Hackworth

Sam Flowers could not have known the peril that lay ahead
when he left Ellington, Missouri, during the noon hour on
March 18, 1925, and began the familiar walk to his farm five
miles northeast of town.

Flowers did know he was probably walking into a storm.
Heavy, dark clouds swept across the Reynolds County sky
from the southwest, fast as any train could travel. At
Ellington, a remote town high in the Ozark Mountains, the
clouds appeared to fly low enough to touch trees on the ridge
tops.

But Flowers was a hearty middle-aged man who worked
a hard-scrabble homestead about five miles northeast of
town. He had made the trip hundreds of times before, in
wagons, automobiles, and on foot. And he had made it day
and night, year-round, through every kind of weather the
volatile skies of southern Missouri could bring.

Or so he must have thought. But the gathering storm
was no ordinary weather event. It would become catastrophic.

Flowers walked the gravel highway, Route 21, through
woods toward the tiny county seat of Centerville. Black
clouds rushed overhead, massive and just above the tree-
tops, it seemed. Winds snapped tree limbs back and forth,
and rain began to pelt the road. He moved over to the rim of
the west ditch, where the woods broke the big drops somewhat, but footing was tricky with the red clay turning wet
and slippery around the stones.

A Model T rattled by, headed south, with top down and
the driver soaking wet. Flowers might have considered
turning back, but he pressed on, still not overly concerned
about a rainstorm. He stayed alert for old, heavy timbers
that might crash down, and he watched for rocky banks to
shield him if the storm worsened. He figured he would be all
right in getting home to his wife and children.

In these minutes, a massive storm boiling 50,000 feet
into the sky topped a 1,500-foot peak near the Current River

and, on the downslope, hit ground along Logan Creek west of Ellington, heading northeast.

Three miles north of Ellington, Flowers came down a hill into Dry Valley. The rain was a torrent, blue lightning bolts exploded all around, and winds came in powerful gusts that almost swept him from his feet. The road crooked northeast, and hundreds of yards ahead lay the path up and over a short ridge into Spring Valley, leading to Flowers' place near the village of Redford.

But Spring Valley seemed a million miles away. Flowers could hardly see. The rain was blinding, and the valley had been enshrouded in a huge shadow, dark as night. Flowers had to look down with lightning flashes to see he was still on the road.

Suddenly, hailstones the size of small potatoes beat from above, and Flowers panicked. Too late, no shelter could save him. An ungodly rumble, like some flying earthquake, rushed up from behind as incredible winds sheared through the valley, tossing large trees. Flowers felt uttermost terror — then he was struck in back of the head.

What would become the deadliest tornado in American history had claimed its first human life: Sam Flowers.

I

Averaging about 55 mph, the storm — rated a rare F5 on today's Fujita Tornado Intensity Scale — flew on a beeline into Iron County, showing no deference for the rugged Ozarks topography, whether peak or plain. Its width hugging the ground was a quarter- to a half-mile and destined to expand. Any tree or wooden structure in the storm's path was subject to destruction; any living being was in mortal danger.

In the twin mining towns of Annapolis and Leadanna, 20 miles northeast of Ellington, 700 citizens did not know the largest breed of tornado was on its approach.

Lunchtime had just ended. At the school, more than 200 students were back at their desks; downtown, people were back at work. Darkening skies had thundered and rained during lunch, so a storm was expected. But when huge hailstones hit a few minutes past 1 o'clock, people took real notice. Adults gazed anxiously to the southwest, up the valley heading out of town. Schoolchildren fretted when the light outside dimmed rapidly, turning their classrooms dark.

Still, there was no funnel cloud visible from town, just a thick, dark fog rolling over the hills — "like a huge column of very black coal smoke," described one witness — covering everything before it. Many people began dashing for cover, while some lingered a moment or two longer before the spectacle. Then a roar like multiple freight trains burst through the valley, and 300 mph winds blasted Annapolis.

In a rare benevolent act, the tornado damaged but did not destroy the two-story brick schoolhouse, sparing the children inside. At a house nearby, a terrified housewife clutched her small son, unable to move because plunging air pressure had sucked the front door shut on her dress. That house was left standing too. But save for a handful of other structures, Annapolis was leveled in seconds. All three churches and the most of the business district were destroyed. Loaded railroad cars were thrown off tracks and dumped, automobiles were lifted and hurled.

On street after street, houses blew apart around cowering victims. Adults were swept up by wind and launched, landing with injurious thuds, while the small bodies of babies offered no resistance whatsoever against the force. One infant was carried hundreds of yards before being laid down unharmed, but another was seriously injured in a long flight.

The air was full of debris: glass, splinters, metal, bricks, timbers, even chunks of buildings. A young teamster, Raymond Stewart, was struck and killed instantly. Nearby, an airborne wooden beam stabbed through two brick walls.

Annapolis, sitting on a hillside sloping south and west, had been swallowed in the storm's path. On the ridge top above town, tombstones in the cemetery scraped a pile of trees and wreckage from the tornado's gut.

The next valley beyond — also in line for a direct hit — was site of the lead mine and Leadanna, a community of mining families in about 30 houses and tents.

The home of Osro and Nell Kelley sat on a west slope in the Leadanna valley. Osro had been predicting "a twister was coming," and he and his wife each held one of their two small daughters. A hailstone crashed through the dining room window, and when Nell looked out she saw the garage flattened atop their new Chevrolet car. Instantly the house itself was picked up and thrown, launching the family backward. Osro flew against a tree stump near a creek, striking his head and killing him; Nell landed unconscious, covered in debris and nearly dead from injuries through her shattered body. The winds had yanked the little girls from their parents' arms, 4-year-old Lucille and 2-year-old Wilma. But they landed *clasped together* in the creek, bruised and cut but not injured seriously. Lucille held her baby sister's head out of the water until help arrived.

Every other house in Leadanna was blown down, and the mine was wrecked at surface level, ruining the crusher mill and other heavy works. The tipple tower above the shaft was mangled, ruining the cage hoist and cutting off electrical power. Seventy-five miners stranded 450 feet underground would have to climb up a ladder to reach the surface.

The terror had lasted barely a minute before the storm screamed off at great speed on a virtual straight line northeast — 21 degrees north of east, the same general bearing it had flown from the start.

Within minutes, the sun was shining over the sudden chaos of Annapolis and Leadanna. This storm left its devastating signature with two communities flattened in a straight track. The ground was strewn with wreckage: boards, bricks, broken glass, twisted automobiles, bolts of store cloth, clothes and household goods. One home stood oddly intact amidst the ruins, but fire broke out nearby and flames spread unchecked to engulf the house and force out the elderly occupants.

Bleeding, dazed survivors roamed the town, some cradling maimed children. Screams shot from under piles of rubble, where rescuers dug urgently to reach the trapped victims. Two lives were lost, Stewart and Osro Kelley, and more than 100 were injured. Seven hundred people were left homeless, virtually the entire local population.

About 10 miles northeast of Annapolis-Leadanna, the storm crossed into Madison County to demolish rural homes, farms, orchards and timber. It plunged into the deep St. Francis River Valley, then mowed back out with no change in course. Two country schools were destroyed south of Fredericktown, but both were unoccupied. Missing Fredericktown, the tornado struck near Cornwall Community, hurling three men. They landed without serious injuries, however, which reflected the miraculous outcome for the area. Properties lay wrecked along a 25-mile path through Madison County, but no one was hurt beyond scrapes and bruises.

The tornado had traveled 50 miles in under 60 minutes of life and expanded to three-quarters of a mile wide, dwarfing the specifications of an average tornado. Already a ferocious freak of its kind, the storm was only growing in intensity. Shooting past a 1,300-foot mount above Marquand, it swooped down off the eastern Ozarks Plateau toward the Mississippi River Valley. With all telephone and telegraph communications destroyed in stricken areas, no warnings could be forwarded ahead.

Next in line was Bollinger County, where the tornado began its penchant for killing children.

A few minutes before 2 o'clock, people in the town of Patton gaped at the sky to the north: gigantic black and blue clouds rushed eastward, seemingly stacked up to heaven itself. The tornado was passing a few miles above Patton. Farther north at the Bollinger County line, the view southward was even more spectacular. A man and his daughter watched curiously, wondering whether this was a tornado — then they saw a large tree swirl through the clouds like a wisp of straw. But no one saw a funnel vortex extending down from the mass.

The tornado crossed Whitewater River and bore down on Conrad School, which sat less than 100 feet up the east slope of the valley. Before teacher Oma Mayfield and the pupils could react, the little frame building was splintered, and everyone was blown and scattered into the hillside. Mayfield and at least 17 children lay injured, some seriously.

The storm topped the ridge and rode a mile through dense timber, cutting trees like blades of grass. At a farm directly ahead, Christina "Grandma" Fellows was tending to baby chicks when she saw the blackness coming. She went back into the house, where her husband, a son and daughter-in-law, and three grandchildren were enjoying each other's company.

"It's a storm a comin' up," said Grandma, which did not alarm anyone. Everyone continued talking, for whether a rain shower or worse was on the way, Grandma always said, *It's a storm a comin' up.*

There came a sudden roar outside and the two-story farmhouse lurched sideways, jolting against an incline to the east. Then it lifted back up, whirled around, and blew apart. Seven people, from infant to elderly, spiraled through the air with debris smacking against them.

When teen-ager Ann Fellows came to, she was sitting upright near the crown of the hill. The wood stove had landed nearby, and she could feel the heat of smoldering blocks. Above her the barn lay flattened, and a trapped horse nickered in distress. A trail of debris led back to where the house had been. A pair of Model T touring cars had their canopies torn off, but were otherwise undisturbed — the only objects around that had not moved or disappeared.

Ann could not stand up; one of her ankles felt like it was broken. Grandpa and Grandma were on their feet, and Uncle Ernest and Aunt Rosie rushed to pick up their baby son; but the 18-month-old, Harley Fellows, was dead from a deep gash in his skull. Ann's brother, 14-year-old Perry Fellows, also perished in the wreckage.

After the storm passed the Fellows farm, it ripped through Henry Bangert's property, destroying two barns and a house, and firing dozens of tin roofing sheets into a stand of 75 oaks. The metal wrapped into those trees like aluminum foil, and it would not be removed for 70 years.

Lixville village was hit next as people dove for shelter, including one man who found himself in a pipe under a road. The Lutheran Church slid off its foundation, Loberg's store was lifted and twisted, and two barns and a blacksmith shop were destroyed. More than a half mile away, the northern span of the tornado severely damaged the new concrete home of Judge Louis Lix, leaving strands of straw impaled in the mortar sides.

The F5 funnel remained hidden, covered in the cloudy black fog that continued to roll over the land at speeds approaching 60 mph. Elevation of the terrain had dropped more than 200 feet in the last 10 miles.

At Garner Schoolhouse east of the Lix home, about 20 pupils and a teacher were preparing for a music program when someone screamed to get in the middle of the room, away from the windows. In seconds the roof flew upward, followed by the wood stove, and then everyone was airborne, spraying across a field outside. Several were unconscious with head wounds, including the teacher, Miss Sidonia

Bangert, and 10-year-old Trula Henry, who died a week later.

Less than a mile beyond the school, young farmer Will Statler was running and not looking back, fleeing from the roar he instinctively knew could kill him. Reaching his father's house, he dove past one of the four stacked-rock supports holding the structure. The din was deafening; dirt, leaves and sticks pelted Statler in the crawl space, but he did not hear or feel the house come apart. Quickly the winds were quiet, and he was optimistic in emerging from underneath the house. But all he found was the bottom floor stripped clean of walls, furniture, rugs — everything but the kitchen table, which stood in place with plates still set for supper. He shuddered, realizing the house could have easily fallen on him.

The tornado smashed every building on Louis Clements' farm, where his baby daughter, Irene, was killed while clasped in her mother's arms. At Schuemer Springs, 24-year-old Grant Miller died in a barn that was leveled, marking the fifth death within four miles, including four children.

In 1925, Biehle was a busy village of 100 in heart of the band of small, picturesque German-American communities stretching from Bollinger County east to the Mississippi River. A key railroad stop, Biehle was in Perry County less than five miles northeast of Lixville, perched on hills over looking Apple Creek Valley.

At 2:10 p.m. on Wednesday, March 18, several men conversed in front of the Biehle general store. Local mechanic A.H. Kirn took notice of the unusual cloud formations in the southwestern sky, and remarked, "I believe we are in for a storm."

The *Southeast Missourian* newspaper had this account:

> As (Kirn) spoke an observable change took
> place in the nature of these clouds. Originally
> dark, but loose-flung and scattered, they seemed
> to gather in their garments, growing denser, lower
> and more black. This process of assimilation
> continued as the clouds drew nearer to Biehle.
> Then as they cleared the horizon . . . the clouds
> had become one lowering nimbus.

Kirn, realizing *tornado*, shouted the warning and dashed across the street to scoop up his daughter in front of his garage. The Kirns made it to cover, but down in Apple Creek Valley, farmer Joe Blechle was out in the open.

Blechle had seen the mass rolling over the 100-foot ridge from Schuemer Springs, where it had ravaged the Miller farm. And now the 35-year-old was in a death race, sprinting for his house on a knob hill beside the creek. There came a bright flash of blue lightning, a thunderclap, then a tremendous roar. Blechle had less than 30 seconds before the tornado reached him.

The *Southeast Missourian* continued:

First the twister, with its deadly stride, cleaved a path several hundred yards in width over the wooded hilltop. Uprooting beeches, elms, and maples and snapping like twigs the trunks of 14- and 20-inch oaks. True to its course, as though steered by a mariner's compass, it next descended upon the valley and the prosperous farming estate of August Lappe. A mule, caught in the open, was lifted high into the air only to be hurled with a sickening thud, a lifeless mass, to the earth some hundred yards ahead. Three horses, two pigs, and dozens of chickens met a similar fate. Two of the horses were found literally wrapped about the trunk and limbs of a fallen oak, while the other was hurled amid a denser portion of the wood to where its cumbersome body never could have penetrated in life.

The neat, two-story home of Lappe was cut in half diagonally, the severed portion scattered in bits far from its original site. The barn merely vanished, while a gang-disc plow was twisted almost beyond recognition. Long lines of lathe and split-rail fences were shattered and thrown, in tangled heaps, as the tornado, gathering impetus, advanced to its next attack.

Blechle reached his house and got inside, only to have it picked up and thrown 75 feet into the creek. The farmer lay dead across a tree trunk in the creek; his wife landed hundreds of feet away, in the bottoms across the water, injured seriously but alive.

The tornado swept from the valley into Biehle, strafing the town with flying livestock and timber. Shaving through a short stand of woods, it came upon the Catholic church and school, where priests, a teacher and children huddled in terror, praying. Debris crashed through the rear wall and roof of the church, and falling rock demolished the altar. The steeple was ripped from atop the front and thrown down beside the school, its tip spearing seven feet into the ground. Incredibly, the school was spared as the storm flew over and past. Up on the roof of the damaged church, just behind where the steeple stood, a thin wooden cross swayed but remained fixed in place.

More properties were destroyed around Biehle, including a Gieringer farm where a woman had to be dragged from the burning wreckage of her home. The tornado rushed forward on its line of travel, staying 21 degrees north of east, a bearing in which the Mississippi River was less than 20 miles away. Every farmstead and community in between would become devastated similarly.

Would this storm ever die? It was now 80 minutes old on a run exceeding 70 miles from its start in the Ozarks. Crossing what is now the modern roadbed of Interstate 55, the amorphous mass of clouds carried its obscene baggage, seemingly without effort. Chunks of houses and buildings rolled along the ground like milk cartons in a breeze. Roofing sheets swirled about like tissue paper before being draped over tree lots that would resemble surreal laundry lines for decades to come. Horses, cattle and hogs were blown through woods with impact severing them to pieces.

Nine lives had been lost in Missouri thus far, and hundreds more had minor to serious injuries. People in the path remained in peril, regardless of the shelter they could find. No one was safe unless completely underground.

Five miles east of Biehle, Apple Creek was a hillside community facing west. At 2:20 p.m., a priest at St. Joseph's School gazed out a second-story window creaking against the winds. The day had grown menacingly dark under the approach of puffed-up, jittery clouds that resembled blackberries from a distance. The priest turned back to his religion class comprised of grade-schoolers, concern etching his face.

"We better say a prayer," he said. "It looks like a real bad storm is coming."

The children obeyed, and the F5 continued northeast, missing Apple Creek and striking the other side of the ridge to cross Route 25 (present-day Highway 61). At the farm of Theodore Unterreiner, the top story of a log house was blown off, leaving a single timber balancing unsecured over a lower wall. A little girl was rolled up in floor linoleum, but unhurt. The barn was demolished and 200 chickens were killed, with some blown clean of feathers.

The twister tore through more hardwoods and farms along ridges and creeks, including five consecutive properties that were "battered down as if a giant roller had passed over them," according to one newspaper account. People were injured but none killed. A well-known physician in the area, Dr. Theodore Estel, was enroute to a house call when he was caught exposed on a road. Leaping from his car an instant before winds smashed it, Estel was knocked to the ground under a barrage of debris. He was struck in the head, impaled in the back by a piece of timber, and he absorbed a blow that fractured a hip. But he held on to the ground and was not blown away. He would survive.

Racing in excess of 60 mph with 300 mph winds, the tornado was six miles from the Mississippi. More would die in Missouri. On a farm near Brazeau village, 63-year-old Crittenden Bull and his sister, Annie Bull, sought cover in their house. But it crashed down and trapped them, and a fire spread quickly from the broken stove. Neighbors saved them from burning to death, but Mr. Bull never regained consciousness and died four days later.

At an estate north of Frohna, the tornado surprised Judge Claus Stueve and others. The big house literally exploded before anyone could react. The judge's widowed sister-in-law, Martha Kaempfe, was in her upstairs room when the walls disintegrated; snatched and launched almost 100 yards, she was found dead.

The hilltops were tighter together as the storm closed upon the final village before the river, Ridge. Sitting atop the tallest point was Ridge School, a two-story brick building that once had been a church. Twenty-two students and a teacher were inside on the bottom floor when flying objects began rat-tatting against the walls and breaking windows. The back door flew open and a pupil rushed to close it. Then the building slid forward 10 feet, and the brick walls crumbled. The wooden interior went high up, flew across the road and over trees, then crashed roof-first down a ravine, strewing human bodies the entire way. Bricks and boards rained down on the victims, but the intact floor fluttered down on air currents, dropping gently enough that those it covered were not crushed.

No one from Ridge School died, and only a few debilitating injuries would last among the students from that terrifying afternoon. This extraordinary case of schoolhouse survivors will always be cited in studies on tornadoes.

Leaving Missouri, the strange cloud appeared to be breaking up in the Mississippi River bottoms. The black fog began dissipating, but that only unveiled twin funnels moving side-by-side. Plowing across the water, the storm shrouded itself in fog again, and 500 people in Gorham, Illinois, had no idea what was coming.

Gorham was two miles off the river in the east floodplain. A resident, Judith Cox, would later describe seeing a mammoth front approach "that seemed to be black smoke," driving a white wall of water vapor before it.

Cox was standing in front of Wallace's Restaurant. "My God!" she cried. "It's a cyclone! And it's here!"

"The air was full of everything," Cox recalled for the *St. Louis Post-Dispatch*, "boards, branches of trees, garments, pans, stoves, all churning around together. I saw whole sides of houses rolling along near the ground."

The winds struck like a giant fist, punching Cox backward through the front door of the restaurant, followed by an airborne brown-and-white cow. As the building collapsed, the cow's body saved Cox from being crushed by supporting the heavy beams that fell.

Across Gorham, clocks stopped at 2:35. A house lost its roof as a young mother, Wanda Mattingly, clung desperately to her small children while grasping a staircase banister. But the walls blew away. Mattingly's infant daughter was sucked from her arms, and her 3-year-old boy was stabbed in the head by a darting piece of wood.

In the darkened 8th grade classroom at Gorham School, an upward rush of air through the floor's heating vent sent straw, feathers and leaf bits swirling about, amusing the students. But giggles turned to shrieks of panic when they looked outside and saw tall trees bend over, come back up, then go flat to the ground, uprooted. Fourteen-year-old Clara Mattingly — Wanda's sister-in-law — rushed for the door. Reaching the hallway, Clara heard screams ringing through the school, then the whole building collapsed into rubble, burying her and 200 other students.

On the east side of town, railroad tracks were ripped out of the ground and wadded up like chicken wire. Grass was stripped from the ground by the roots, as if taken up for a sod sale. A frame house was lifted 30 feet high and tossed into a great elm tree, its branches crashing through windows to hold the full structure in brief suspension. The house began splintering and cracking, a wall blew out, and the elderly couple inside, Paul and Alice Tomure, were drawn into the air. They landed in a cornfield behind the tree, side-by-side. Alice looked over to see a railroad spike driven through her husband's lip.

"I'm dying, Alice dear," he said, and the couple prayed together a final time.

II

Amidst the normally tranquil setting of southern Illinois, the weather phenomenon to become known as the Tri-State Tornado quickly established its murderous reputation in history. The state's official death toll was listed at 606, although some survivors still doubt whether that fully represents the actual number killed. A fact for their argument is that in the storm's immediate aftermath, stricken communities had to conduct burials almost around the clock — often without ceremony or funeral facilities — to properly dispose of the multitude of dead bodies. Some of the deceased were taken straight from ruins to a cemetery.

Almost 2,000 were injured in Illinois, and many hospitalized survivors did not get the chance for a graveside goodbye to loved ones or friends killed.

Gorham was only the first Illinois community to suffer the carnage. Averaging about 12 deaths *per minute* through this coal region, the Tri-State Tornado made direct hits on a virtual straight line of towns and villages, including Gorham at 2:35 p.m.; Murphysboro, 2:45 p.m.; De Soto, 2:50 p.m.; West Frankfort at 3 p.m.; and Parrish at 3:15 p.m.

Statistics conflict among sources, but the following fatality numbers are generally accepted for four of the communities: Gorham, 34; Murphysboro, 234; De Soto, 72, including 38 pupils at the school; and West Frankfort, 148. In the 40 or so minutes from when the tornado entered Gorham and left Parrish, at least 541 lives were lost. In the next 45 minutes, before the storm crossed the Wabash River into Indiana, at least 65 people died across the counties of Hamilton and White, largely on farms.

In Indiana, three principle communities were hit — Griffin, Owensville and Princeton — before the Tri-State Tornado ended in a cornfield at 4:18 p.m. The published fatality figures for Indiana range from 71 to 102.

Estimates of property damage in Illinois alone approached $15 million. Once railroad tracks were cleared of wreckage, travelers were shocked and horrified by the scenes. In St. Louis, reporters merely waited at Union Station for witnesses arriving on trains from southern Illinois. A Tennessee woman gave the *Post-Dispatch* this description of Murphysboro at 4 a.m., March 19:

> The whole town seemed to be on fire. The flames, leaping up into the blackened sky, made a lurid picture. We could distinguish many buildings in the ruins. The headlights of a number of automobiles were turned on the remains of one building and men were frantically digging in the ruins for bodies.

A report in *The St. Louis Star* stated only one building remained standing in De Soto, and contained a "tale of desolation" from the town's railroad agent, M.J. Mulconnery:

> (He) described scenes there as pandemonium. He went through the town at 2:15 p.m., before the storm. It was peaceful and quiet. At 6 p.m. he returned to find it in ruins.
> "The dead and injured were being put in refrigerator cars and trucks and taken to Carbondale," Mulconnery said. "Men and women half clad and muddy thronged the streets where there were no houses. There were fires, and fire engines, but no water or lights. There was nothing but confusion."

The story's headline was "Refugees From Tornado-Torn Area Tell Graphic Stories of Adventures." For days, national media capitalized on the sensational narratives culled from storm-ravaged southern Illinois.

The entire path of the Tri-State Tornado is stated to be 219 miles, excluding a few miles in Reynolds County, Missouri, that appear to have been overlooked. For 200 miles the swath was practically a straight line. The storm's timespan was three-and-one-half hours, with speeds averaging 57 mph in Missouri, 59 in Illinois, and 68 in Indiana. The average speed between two points in Indiana was 73 mph. The breadth of the path spanned one mile at its widest point.

There have been larger, faster, or longer tornadoes, such as the storm of May 26, 1917, which traveled a continuous path of 293 miles from Louisiana, Missouri, to eastern Jennings County, Indiana. But none have traversed a more direct route as far as the Tri-State Tornado — nor has one been as lethal. The official death count from Missouri to Indiana stands at 689, the most ever by a single tornado documented in America, and a figure that, again, may be too conservative. Given the modern technology of radar detection and advance warning systems for storms, it is plausible to declare this gory record as untouchable.

The Tri-State Tornado stands legendary among experts. They are at a loss to fully explain it. Tom Grazulis of the Tornado Project in Vermont labels it as perhaps a 500-year event, possibly a 1,000-year event. "There is no meteorological explanation for it. A super-cell thunderstorm as we understand it . . . can't do that. It just can't produce a 200-mile path," Grazulis said in *Wrath of God: Tornado Alley*, a film documentary by Towers Productions that appeared on the cable History Channel.

Several studies have developed specifications of an average tornado, data that further illustrates the excessive, rare nature of the Tri-State Tornado. The average tornado lasts 13 to 20 minutes over 6 to 10 miles, takes an irregular path less than 400 yards wide, and moves at a forward speed of 30 to 40 mph.

III

In Missouri on Sunday, March 22, 1925, Annapolis and Leadanna were invaded by 6,000 automobiles loaded with sightseers gawking at the devastation wrought by the Tri-State Tornado four days earlier. All along the storm's path into Indiana, survivors experienced intrusion upon their grief. In Murphysboro, Illinois, where half the town was destroyed by winds or resultant fires, city officials pleaded through media for outsiders to stay away. But this was the heyday of "Sunday driving," long before the public's ghoulish curiosity for tragedy could be satisfied by television images.

Most survivors, obviously saddled with more pressing concerns, ignored the visitors. Many themselves, after all, were likely to do the same thing when others suffered misfortune. In addition, sightseers were prone to make relief contributions as a sort of admission to disaster scenes.

But there have been few disasters on display anywhere like the Tri-State Tornado. Besides astronomical human casualties, the storm left over 10,000 homeless and caused more than $16 million worth of damages in period currency. In Missouri, wrecked properties included the Annapolis lead mine, a relatively new $750,000 facility that would eventually be abandoned. After the tornado, the mine never again functioned for worthwhile profit.

Newspaper accounts and photographs of the aftermath, with headlines like "Enormous Destruction," gave graphic details that are mindful of hurricanes or warfare. Such was the violence of this most infamous tornado. While death and injury statistics contrasted greatly between Illinois and Missouri, the type of demolition did not. Much like De Soto, Illinois, newspaper stories and photos of Annapolis portray a razed community.

"We feel wholly incompetent to adequately picture the destruction we saw," the *Farmington News* stated of Annapolis. "It beggars description."

"On viewing the wreckage one could not help but wonder how it was possible for so many to escape without injury," reported the *Greenville Sun*. "In the face of the awful havoc wrought by the fury of the storm it seems almost miraculous that hundreds were not killed."

The journalistic perspective was relatively the same farther east along the path. The *Perry County Sun* stated:

Persons visiting the devastated homes, will stand and gaze at the ruins in wonder and astonishment — Wonder how it is possible that entire families escaped without apparent injuries, and astonished how entire families covered up under the wreckage were not killed. Then you leave the places of destruction, incapable of describing the horror and devastation.

The *Perry County Republican* offered this poignant summation:

Suffering and utter desolation followed in the wake of the storm, which swept down with fury upon the peaceful farming country here, leaving a trail of blood and misery and converting beautiful homes and well-equipped farms into a scene of disorder unimaginable . . . the wind spared few things in its path.

A public issue arising in the aftermath, disaster relief, was addressed by the weekly newspapers of southeast Missouri. The *Wayne County Journal-Banner* commented:

The big task that remains, after the dead and injured are cared for, is the rehabilitation of families and individuals who have lost all their worldly possessions. In this work, the Red Cross expects to take the most active hand . . . (Like in) aftermath of the war, it will seek to rebuild the future for those who cannot help themselves.

The *Greenville Sun*, with its masthead proclaiming "The Home Paper," questioned how firm a commitment existed to aid the state's victims. The Missouri legislature had appropriated $25,000 in disaster funds, compared to $500,000 approved by Illinois lawmakers for their stricken areas. Journalists focused primarily on Illinois, even in reports generated by Missouri's major media outlets. Some Missourians, particularly in the southeast region, believed there was a slant in priorities toward Illinois which affected the agendas of relief agencies and charity groups. Editors at the *Sun* expressed a concern:

Owing to the greater loss of life and property in sections of Illinois, the metropolitan papers have naturally devoted most of their attention to reports from these devastated sections and have not given much space to the situation at Annapolis. While the loss of life at Annapolis was fortunately very light, the property loss was as great as in any community.

The Red Cross did get favorable reviews from many citizens of Annapolis, but the agency was criticized by people in the high-casualty areas near the Mississippi River. One week after the tornado, the *Perry County Republican* commented under the column sub-headline, "Conditions Still Bad":

While a fund of nearly a thousand dollars has been raised by business men of Perryville to provide food and clothing for the sufferers, and local doctors and Red Cross nurses from St. Louis have been in the field every day since the storm, the condition in dozens of homes is pitiful. With all their buildings gone and with not a vestige of property except the clothing upon their backs, family after family, bruised, cut and sick, has been separated and the members are being cared for by neighbors. In several homes, both in this and Bollinger County, four or five (people) are down. A dozen or more have been taken to hospitals and several more will be sent today. . . .

The victims are still stunned, few of the property owners have made any headway in clearing the wreckage. So many families have injured members that little work can be done toward rehabilitation of the stricken area until wounds heal and fever leaves. All furniture and kitchen utensils having vanished in the wind, housekeeping is out of the question until new equipment is bought and some sort of shelter erected. And in the meantime many farmers are quartered several miles from their own property. Some are walking three or four miles morning and

evening to feed their stock, while many are
scouring the woods reclaiming the hay caught
there by the trees.

The Salvation Army was the savior for at least one group suffering in Bollinger County. When Peter J. Statler's house was blown away near Lixville, his family moved in briefly with that of his eldest son, Daniel. A much larger family, that of Louis Clements, gained longer refuge with Daniel Statler. The Clements were neighbors who lost the baby girl, Irene, during the tragic demolition of their home.

Between the Daniel Statler and Clements families, at least 14 people were living under one roof, with several injured physically and practically everyone traumatized.

The immediate needs were food, medical supplies, bed linens, blankets, cots, and clothing, especially for the children. Daniel bought a 100-pound bag of flour, which provided enough food sustenance for about the first week, and everyone prayed for help to arrive. The Red Cross did not show, but the Salvation Army came through on time, bringing adequate supplies for every category of concern, and improving the outlook dramatically around the homestead of Daniel Statler.

Thereafter, the family's staunch loyalty to the Salvation Army passed through succeeding generations, including to a great-grandson of Peter J. Statler, Edward "Bud" Fellows — who is also a great-grandson of Fritz Fellows, whose farm was likewise destroyed, killing two boys in the family.

"According to my mother, the Red Cross didn't do anything to help them," said Fellows. "That's why she always insisted I help the Salvation Army, and I always have."

IV

In many places, a signature of the Tri-State Tornado was its element of surprise upon victims or entire towns. But many people of Annapolis, Missouri, apparently had time to seek shelter, and at least some predicted "a twister" was approaching.

In southern Iron County on March 18, 1925, there had been intermittent sunshine during the morning. But as the noon hour passed, people began seeing darkening, raining skies framed by the jutting, narrow ridge lines. This was a time when human instincts for severe weather, developed through daily observation, had to serve as advanced warning. In Annapolis and Leadanna, folks could feel the humidity and unseasonably warm temperature at ground level; they could see the clash of cold air aloft in the jumpy clouds, and figure something bad could happen.

Nearing 1 o'clock, the weather was coming to dominate discussions along the streets and backyard fences.

Cecil Hackworth was a 16-year-old who was not in school that afternoon; he was downtown, where he encountered some highway workers pointing upward and talking. "They said, 'Just look at that, it's bound to be a storm. It's got to be a storm!'" Hackworth recalled.

Probably by that time, in Reynolds County to the southwest, Sam Flowers had been overcome by the monster tornado in Dry Valley.

"So after I stood there just a little bit, they wanted me to watch some teams (of horses). They were buildin' a highway," Hackworth said during an interview in June 1997. He declined the men's request. "I went on home to see about my mother, but I didn't stay there. . ."

Hackworth's mother was not home, but he knew she earlier had been at the house of banker Vincent Sutton, which faced the railroad tracks down in the creek valley. The teen hurried there, a decision that likely saved him from injury, if not death. Just as hail fell and the notorious "black fog" came into sight, rolling toward town, Hackworth arrived at the Sutton residence, a nice brick home with an Ozark rock wall in front. The winds were starting to come in forceful puffs, people were scattering, and Hackworth got down in the yard behind the wall. Three young men dove in on top of him.

"I heard one of 'em curse and say he'd lost his hat," said Hackworth. "Another one told him, 'Shut up. If that's all you lose, you'll be lucky.'"

The roar hit, and Hackworth saw a large telephone pole had blown down to straddle the wall directly overhead — merely a foot above where the men were piled together. "That was too close to count," he mused.

Hackworth said the storm lasted but a few minutes, and he remembers being more worried about his mother than fearful for himself. He left the Sutton yard and raced to the last place he knew to look for her: a house a few blocks away with a storm cellar. He found a small crowd around the spot because the house had careened on its side like a cardboard box, covering the cellar door that survivors were banging on from underground. Fires were breaking out as a man wielding an ax chopped through to the cellar, and Hackworth was waiting to reach down first for his baby sister, then to his mother.

Rescues were in progress across the flattened town.

The memories are still chilling for lifelong resident Clara Brown. She considers herself fortunate for living on a farm outside Annapolis that fateful Wednesday. Brown did not see the storm, but the cause of black skies and roaring winds was unmistakable, and she rushed into town with family members. "And that's when we saw all that had happened," she said softly, shuddering 72 years later.

"It was just . . . *chaos*. It was just terrible. Leadanna was devastated too. They did try to work the mine after that, but it didn't last very long.

"You just can't *imagine* how we felt, all the tears and crying," said Brown.

Injury reports from Annapolis-Leadanna ranged from 35 to 150, with the variances due mostly to the degrees of severity. Practically everyone was left homeless, and hunger set in immediately; one report stated citizens "stormed" a relief train arriving in Annapolis that first night. For a day or two, until the Red Cross delivered tents, people took whatever shelter they could find, including the school, rail cars, and standing parts of wrecked structures. Bedding and blankets were luxuries. Many men just slept outside, huddled around fires in the streets, joking sarcastically that firewood was plentiful, at least.

Bernice "Peachy" Jones was a 10-year-old in the Annapolis School during the tornado. The school was a two-story brick building brushed by the left wing of the storm, and it proved to be the safest structure in town, sustaining minor damage. "It seems like it just got dark outside, then light, then it was over," said Jones.

She remembers some panic among the 200 pupils inside the school, but none were really hurt. Teachers, horrified at the town's sudden disaster, tried to restrain anyone from leaving the building. But the oldest students included a pair of brothers already maturing into brawny young men. "They were pretty rough characters," recalled Jones, "and they wanted to get home to see about their mother.

"Those boys just pushed open those double doors and ran off. And when they went, why, all the other kids just scattered."

Jones recalls that even children who were not injured were disoriented by the overwhelming experience. Jones, for example, did not go straight to her home, which had been destroyed.

Her mother had been injured while her father was underground at the lead mine, one of 75 men stranded 450 feet below after the tipple tower and hoist were mangled. Electrical power in the shafts was cut off, and the miners had to use helmet lamps to see. Most had families and property "up top," and, knowing a tornado had passed, their anxiety was excruciating. But they had to wait turns to climb an iron ladder up the vertical shaft, pausing for rests along little foot platforms placed at section intervals. Only one man could be on a section at any time to prevent the ladder from collapsing.

Jones' father finally got to the surface, and he rushed through Leadanna, only able to glance at the tell-tale destruction across the valley. No one was around when he reached the spring hollow where the little family home had stood. "When my father saw that house laying flat, that was about all he could take," said Jones. "He didn't know that we were all alive."

Her mother nursed a gaping back wound for months afterward. The family, like most who stayed in town, had to live in tents provided by the Red Cross until they could rebuild their home. There was talk Annapolis would cease to exist, what with the future of the lead mine in doubt.

"It was a real trying time," said Jones. "A lot of people had to move away."

The lead mine did eventually close, Leadanna disappeared, but Annapolis persevered. Today the community is 126 years old with proud assets like the South Iron School District and a granite mill. The population, however, is about the same as when the Tri-State Tornado struck long ago.

The storm ingrained itself in the community character. "It changed the town," said Brown.

Sixteen-year-old Ann Fellows did not want to leave home that afternoon. The roads and fields were muddy in northwest Bollinger County, and it was starting to rain when her brother, Perry, decided he wanted to visit Grandma and Grandpa Fellows on their farm three-quarters of a mile away. Perry did not want to go alone, and he persuaded Ann to come, although she grumbled down the lane from their farm.

"There was a tree stand, and that's where I wanted to turn around and go back home," Ann (Fellows) Blechle recalled 72 years later. "And Perry said, `Oh, no, let's go on.'"

Their grandparents' place was indeed a fun spot, even on rainy days. There were horses and other animals in the barn, and always plenty of family members in the house, visiting or otherwise. Uncle Ernest and Aunt Rosie Fellows lived there at the time. They were a young couple with a growing family, starting with a cute 18-month-old boy, Harley, while Rosie was eight-months pregnant with their second child.

The men were home that afternoon because of the muddy farm, and once Ann and Perry arrived, there were seven people on the ground floor of the spacious two-story farmhouse. Grandma had just come in from the chicken coop, uttering her seemingly innocent remark, "It's a storm a comin' up," when Ann's world changed instantly.

"We never saw anything or never knew anything," said Blechle. "That tornado picked the whole house and shoved it into that incline leadin' up to the garden. And from there it was nothin' but a whirl. It just kept spinnin' the house as it was flyin' apart, and I was just spinnin' myself. I could feel stuff hittin' all over me."

Ann blacked out a few moments, then found herself sitting upright near the top of the hill and the barn, with the injured horse crying out and "all kinds of clutter around." Down where the house had sat seconds before, there "was *nothing* left," she said. "Nothing . . . Nothing."

The bare house pad sitting a few feet from the pair of touring cars, undamaged but for the canopies ripped off, is an indelible image in the woman's memory. And, of course, she remembers the still bodies of her dear little brother, Perry, and the baby, Harley. They were buried together in one casket at Whitewater Presbyterian Church, the same cemetery where other young storm victims were interred. A few weeks later, Rosie gave birth to a healthy baby boy who was named Perry, which pleased Ann and her family. But her intense pain of grief, she confessed, remains.

"I can live it yet today," she said. "Oh, it's been a long time ago. But I can live it yet today."

The energetic great-grandmother maintains a beautiful home and lawn, and oversees her farm not far from the old Fritz Fellows place. Blechle is a charming woman who likes to laugh. But the western hills and skies look much the same as on the land where she grew up. And in daytime when storm clouds fly massive and dark from the southwest, or at night when thunder and winds begin, she cannot rest.

She is haunted by the strange, powerful, unforgiving force she knows can appear so suddenly.

V

In stories and studies from 1925 to present, from academic content to mainstream, the primary themes of the Tri-State Tornado have been Nature's power, the record death toll, and mass destruction.

But the *survivors* should be better known for the messages they offer, especially those who overcame the worst suffering. Countless people endured the terror's physical and emotional brutality, but resolved themselves to live on with purpose. Their courage, which most of us doubt we possess until made to summon it, stands for life.

The human will became manifest all along the storm's path, starting at the first communities struck, and beginning in the very young. As the tornado blew through Annapolis-Leadanna, 4-year-old Lucille Kelley was thrown into a creek with her 2-year-old sister, Wilma, below the mine.

The people who reached them found the two girls crying and clinging together, with Lucille struggling to keep her sister from drowning. Nearby lay both parents: the still body of Osro Kelley, who had been the hard-working, loving man smitten with his girls; and the young mother covered in timbers, Nell Kelley, unconscious with severe wounds from head to her feet, but holding on with a pulse.

The family had been blown from the hill where all that remained of their comfortable home was a smashed garage and car, and the woodpile stacked straight like Osro had left it, not a stick disturbed.

Lucille has long forgotten the incident, and today can relate only what she has been told: "Daddy was holding me (in the house), Mom was holding Wilma, then the tornado blew us both together" — she clapped her palms — "and separated them."

That day Osro had been saying, "A twister's coming," then his productive, promising life was snuffed out at 34. One of the first employees of the lead mine, Osro was in the company's upper level of job status and pay. A talented man, Osro was the powerhouse engineer. He was also one of the first car owners in Annapolis-Leadanna, and was recognized as perhaps the best mechanic around, a vocation he performed in addition to his mine work.

The family's lifestyle had been one to envy in the area, but with Osro's death, his wife and daughters were thrust into a fragile future. The immediate hurdle was Nell Kelley's survival.

Three hours after the tornado, she was finally loaded onto a train bound for St. Louis, one of three injured people deemed critical enough to require hospitalization that night. But Nell, as the *Globe-Democrat* stated, was the "most tragic case of all." She had deep head lacerations and bone fractures from her shoulders down, including a broken hip, crushed left femur, and both feet turned around backward. The girls were left behind with the mine doctor and relatives, while Nell's parents accompanied her on the train.

The 111-mile trip out of the Ozarks took at least five hours as Nell's blood soaked her stretcher and ran onto the floor of the passenger car. At Union Station in St. Louis, ambulance attendants started to switch her to a stretcher that would fit their transport. But after pulling up the sheet to view the broken body, they shook their heads. She remained on the long stretcher, and the ambulance door was left open to accommodate it on the drive to St. Luke's Hospital. At least one newspaper reporter, meanwhile, wrote 23-year-old Nell Kelley was "not expected to survive." At the hospital, doctors told her parents they would start work on her if she lived through the night; they did not think she would.

But she did, beginning an ordeal in the hospital that exceeded six months. The physical trials for Nell while hospitalized included two months in traction; the insertion of a plate in her left thigh to set the femur bone broken in 13 places, a surgical operation which gave her blood poisoning; four months in a body cast; and a bout with pneumonia worsened by the city air, toxic with coal smoke. Emotionally, the suffering was as great. It was some time before Nell learned her husband was dead, and longer before she could see her children, which caused her to fear they had died too. She was, however, a good patient who appreciated her doctors.

Allowed to go home to Annapolis in the fall, Nell was determined to make a home for her family, "the girls," as she always called them. But she was not sure how to accomplish that. Life without Osro was a supreme challenge.

"I never lived hard until after the tornado," Nell recalled in an interview seven decades later. "My husband made good money and he was a good provider. He provided too good." A native Ozarker, Nell said her life had been so innocent, "I didn't know what a twister was."

After leaving the hospital, Nell initially had to use a brace or crutches to walk. All her household items were gone with the tornado. "I had to get a place to live," she said, voice cracking. "I didn't know what to do. I didn't have so much as a dishrag. I didn't have one thing. We had our furniture insured, and I had a little money. Not a lot, but a little."

The family rented a house for a few months, but in that time before government relief, the mother had to find a way "to keep my table up," as she recalled in Ozark dialect. Lucille added, "There wasn't such as thing as (assistance) back then. You had to do or die." Jobs were growing scarce for anyone, much less a woman with physical problems still to overcome. But one year after the tornado, local need for housing remained, which Nell identified as her best chance for income.

"The mines had kept runnin', and there were people that didn't have a place to live. The town was blown away," she said. "I had enough money to buy a four-room house, and enough to buy furniture to furnish it. Me and the girls lived in two rooms, and I rented two rooms out, furnished, to people that would come to work in the mines. And the merchants were awful nice to me. They would send me renters."

The family made it through the Depression in Annapolis, and Nell never turned to government assistance that was available through New Deal programs. Lucille and Wilma graduated from Annapolis High, and by then World War II was starting to gear the national economy, especially in urban areas. The daughters married and moved to St. Louis, where other relatives lived. Nell soon followed.

She could not gain regular factory employment until 1943, but in the interim she held several jobs for low pay, including ironing in a laundry, where she stood on concrete nine hours a day, six days a week, for 13 cents an hour. Nell moved under her own power and wore high heels, but her legs and feet would hurt the rest of her life.

In 1943, with the male work force depleted because of war, Nell got the job she had wanted at Sunshine Biscuit Company, working on the line for 40 cents an hour. She brought home about $13 a week, but managed to save at least $1 from every paycheck, a practice she kept her entire working career. By the time Sunshine closed in 1958, she was making up to $40 per week, depending on the piece-work production she was part of. Faced with another job search at age 56, Nell appeared every day for three weeks at Bussmann Fuse Company. She got hired, and remained there until retirement in 1970. She never remarried.

Nell always rented dwellings in the city and had kept her house in Annapolis for retirement. She stayed in her home-town until 1985, when she moved back to St. Louis to live with Lucille. She received a pension from Sunshine Biscuit and income from the property she leased in Annapolis. When this author met Nell in June 1997, approaching her 96th birthday, she was in excellent health relative to her age and past hardships. Wilma, pointing at the 30-something male visitor, declared, "She's probably got a better heart and blood pressure than you have!"

The esteemed psychologist Dr. Carl Jung concluded humans inherit spiritual traits from ancestors as much as physical markers. For a case study in point, none could be stronger than the family of Nell (Thomas) Kelley, preceding her and following her, especially the women of that heritage.

The first known matriarch in the line of determined ones was Nell's great-grandmother, Amelia Warncke, a doctor who immigrated to America from Germany in 1842. She was pregnant on the boat coming over, yet treated sufferers of a smallpox breakout on board. By the time the boat docked in New York Harbor, Amelia's husband had died and she had given birth to twin boys, one of whom died. In 1846, Dr. Warncke was in Iron County, Missouri, where her son grew up to be a quite successful farmer and businessman. But one Fourth of July she found him dancing on a board platform at an outdoor picnic, and felt he should be home instead with his wife, Charity, and their children.

"My grandfather when he was young, he was wild, I guess," chuckled Nell. "And my great-grandmother rode up to that dance floor — she always rode a little horse and carried a horsewhip — and hitched that horse to a little tree. Granny walked right up on that dance floor to my grandfather and wrapped that horsewhip around him and said, `You git home to Charity and those children!'

"Whenever Granny did anything, it was that way."

The same moxie carried through the generations of women. Nell had a pair of aunts who lived to be 104 and 102, respectively; her mother almost reached 97 years of age. Nell became a great-great-grandmother, and, before she passed away in 1998, there were five generations of girls in the family able to know and love each other.

An obvious rock in that line is Lucille, a vibrant, attractive great-grandmother. In her seventies, Lucille still worked as a proofreader and expected to continue "until my eyes give out," she said with a laugh.

Lucille has known personal trials well beyond those caused by the Tri-State Tornado. She lost her husband, Wayne Ross, to a brain tumor, and a daughter, Joan Pritchard, to cancer at age 39. She cherished each like she did her father, Ooro, who once laughed when his little girl took scissors and lopped off her own hair. But Lucille's philosophy of survival always endured, beginning at least from the time of the storm, when she wrestled mightily against the water of an Ozark creek, hanging onto her sister for dear life.

"I've had tragedy in my life," said Lucille. "I lost my father, I lost my husband . . . But I feel that the ones who have gone wouldn't want you to dwell on it. I feel like you *shouldn't* dwell on it. Think about them of course, and remember the good times. But I don't believe you should let yourself become miserable. That doesn't accomplish anything. . . .

"You know, my daughter was a sweetheart. And when she told me she was going to die, I said, 'I want to go with you.' And she quickly bounced back at me and said, 'Mother, you can't go. You have to stay here, for the others.'

"And that's what you have to do. You have to go on for

the people that are still living."

After the Tri-State Tornado cleared the Missouri hills and crossed the Mississippi River, its enormous, violent base connected fully with the flat Illinois floodplain. Now free of the Missouri path's uneven topography, the storm hit true across its berth like the front wheel of a steam-roller and swept into Gorham, obliterating the small town.

From Gorham, a significant portion of the southwestern horizon is obscured by the Missouri bluffs across river and Grand Tower Fountain Bluff on the Illinois side a mile south. And, of course, this amorphous tornado cloaked its dagger identity, usually appearing as a black rainstorm until close enough for victims to see trees and pieces of buildings swirling hundreds of feet above ground.

Of all the communities hit along the path, Gorham may have been the one most taken by surprise.

"It was a beautiful day up until the time of the tornado," attested Clara (Mattingly) Hand, who was an 8th grader in the Gorham School. "We had just had recess and were out playing. They rang the bell and we came in. We had just taken our seats, and the teacher was in front of the room. I don't recall that she even said anything because it happened so quickly.

"Everything just got black, totally black in the classroom, and this terrible roar came outside. . ."

Seconds later the heavy building crashed down, covering Clara in the hallway as she tried to flee the first floor. She was fortunate though; the classroom door fell on her, shielding her body from the beams, concrete, bricks, and other materials falling from the second floor and roof above. Her 11-year-old sister, Lora, was also somewhere in the wreckage.

Clara's mother, Zura Mattingly, rushed to the school alongside all parents able to move upright after the storm's passing. And there she found a real nightmare amidst the screams of agony and grief. Few chidren were moving outside the mound of rubble where all others were buried, from elementary age to high school. About twenty were dead, approximately 10 percent of the district's students — an official figure that some people, including Clara Hand, thought was too low.

Consider, for example, that the four teens sitting directly

around Clara in the classroom — front and back and on each side — were killed.

Zura, panicked, searched for her two girls and found a familiar pair of shoes sticking out, motionless, from under a pile of rubble; it was Clara. Then Lora was located, and Zura praised God the girls were alive, at least, even if both were injured critically and unconscious.

At St. Mary's Hospital in East St. Louis, Clara and Lora were each treated for skull fractures. Both were blinded for a time. Lora had a ripped eyelid that doctors reattached, and glass was removed from the back of an eye socket, which restored her vision. Each girl's head was shaved because the hair was hopelessly matted with concrete grit, dirt, and cockle burrs blown by the winds.

Dozens of Gorham schoolchildren were in the hospital. Several members of the Mattingly family were too, including the young mother, Wanda, Clara's sister-in-law who tried desperately to hold her small children during the tornado. Charles Glenn Mattingly, the 3-year-old impaled in the head by a piece of wood, would recover fine, while his baby sister, 9-month-old Norma June, was one of the few miracle stories of Gorham. After being sucked away from her mother's grasp along a staircase, Norma June sustained only bruises in her flight, and was returned home by the Methodist minister, Reverend Sweckard.

Clara was the most seriously injured in her family. "I could see partially after I regained consciousness, but only just a mass of anything," said Hand. Eventually she could see with double vision, which a Murphysboro optometrist corrected with glasses.

But a more formidable ailment gripped the girl: depression. Before the tornado, Clara was a child who viewed life through the positive perspective of a happy youngster. Beyond a loving family, she had thrived in nurturing relationships with close friends and the secure, close-knit atmosphere of Gorham. The disaster changed everything, violating her young life in sinister fashion.

"There were so many things that happened, your mind was just boggled," she said.

The enormity of the losses began to weigh on Clara as soon as she came to in the hospital. She was told the four classmates who sat around her had died, and were already buried: Marie Asbury, Opal Rosenberger, Joe Bob Dunn, and Margaret Brown — the school principal's daughter whose mother was also killed. Many of the adults she had known around town — the merchants, parents, elders who were integral to her formerly solid existence — were gone, maimed, or traumatized. In the hospital, Clara heard how mass funerals were held in sheds and basements because funeral facilities no longer existed. The town's only place of worship, the Methodist Church, had been leveled across the street from the school.

The faces of her deceased friends haunted her; it seemed they had been snatched away by some fiend. When thinking of one in particular, the grief was excruciating. "I cried a lot after they told me that Opal had died, because she was my best friend," said Hand.

"And then not being able to see made it worse, because people would come to visit us, and I couldn't tell who they were. For a 14-year-old girl, I was depressed for quite a while after I left the hospital."

At home, she was confronted by the demolished condition of the community she loved. Not a building or house had been left undamaged; most were destroyed, and the recovery effort had only begun. "The top stories were all torn off the stores and the restaurants and the post office," Hand recalled. "My brother-in-law had a garage, and it was torn down . . . just so many things were torn completely away, so badly ruined that they had to rebuild."

Likewise, Clara sought to restore her broken spirit. She went back to the school site, seeking her art book for a link to Joe Bob Dunn. He was a special boy, she later recalled, who had drawn pictures of horses for her, and she wanted them back. But the art book was gone, unable to be retrieved, like him.

Memories of Opal continued to plague Clara, and she tried to reason why, how such a lively young person could be dead. "We had sang together at church and just ran around together as playmates," said Hand. "We were just real good friends. I missed her so much."

Other experiences bothered the girl. Her home was damaged, and most of her clothes and personal items had been stolen by the wind. Meanwhile, the instantaneous terror of the storm was something her mind continued to replay, stifling the youthful sense of well-being. Like many people in town, she said, "I was quite uneasy, all the time."

But positive moments did occur. One day Clara went to the Red Cross station looking for clothes, where the racks included many items retrieved from fences and trees from miles around. She found one of her own dresses that had blown away, a cotton garment with prints and a hole in front that her mother had covered by sewing on a pocket. That gave her a smile, a lighthearted look at the tornado. Delighted, she took the dress back home. Elsewhere, someone told her how the storm had stuck a sign into a cowshed on the fringe of the wrecked town, announcing "Revival Services Tonight," and that made her laugh.

Then her teacher made a real breakthrough for Clara. "Her name was Viola Schoffner," said Hand. "There were about five or six of us girls (in the 8th grade) who were left alive, and after we all got able to, she had a graduation ceremony for us on her front porch. That was all that was left of her house, it was damaged so bad . . . She gave each one of us a gift.

"That made me really, really happy, that I got to graduate from the 8th grade."

Four years later, Clara Mattingly graduated from the new Gorham High School, a building she was proud of. "It was so much better than the one we had before," she said. After one year of college in Kentucky, she married Harvey Hand from Grand Tower. She raised children, then returned to school at McKendree College to graduate and realize a dream of becoming a teacher.

"I really wanted that degree," said Hand, who taught 15 years before retiring. The discipline of education became a goal for two of her daughters; they each earned master's degrees, one at Arizona State and the other at Indiana, and the latter retired as a teacher herself.

During a 1997 interview, Clara Hand showed virtually no sign of the trauma she experienced as an adolescent. Her voice was solid and articulate in recounting the Tri-State Tornado at Gorham, from the disaster's worst elements to the humorous, and her emotion never cracked other than to chuckle or laugh. She was genuine living history about the tornado because of her openness, which she believed could benefit others. Indeed, until Clara passed away in 1999, people contacted her for information, perspective, and even comfort on the tragedy.

In 1959 in college at McKendree, Hand wrote a paper,

The Social Effects of the Disasters of Gorham, Illinois, a study encompassing the 1925 event, a tornado that followed, and two major floods. Hand's paper remains a popular read among people who know of it, and the copies continue to multiply in Illinois and Arizona, where she and her husband once lived in retirement.

Some years ago in Phoenix, Hand visited a native of Gorham, a younger sister of Joe Bob Dunn who was five when the legendary storm claimed her brother's life.

"Did you know Joe Bob?" the woman asked.

"Oh yes," replied Hand. "He sat beside me in school."

"Tell me about Joe Bob," the woman requested. "I don't remember much about him. Please, tell me all you can remember about him."

A PATRIOT

"Lefty wasn't your regular cornfield pitcher."
Melvin Williams

The research on a local legend began with a death of note in southeast Missouri: Lloyd B. Fisher of the Stoddard County community of Puxico. Folks were remembering Mr. Fisher in the multiple roles he lived: as a loving family patriarch, a war veteran, teacher, farmer, rural mail carrier, and athlete. Many people had known Lloyd "Lefty" Fisher, a baseball pitcher of exceptional talent, and the effect his role as an infantryman in World War II had on that.

It was the summer of 1989, baseball season, a proper time to imagine Lefty Fisher on the pitching mound. And, invariably, a storyteller would recall a special game from decades ago: the night Lefty matched the great Robin Roberts in hurling a shutout.

That caught a listener's attention. *Robin Roberts, the Hall of Fame pitcher? Mr. Fisher pitched a shutout against Robin Roberts?* That's right. *Where?* Sikeston, Missouri. *On a small-town field? When? How?*

According to the storyteller, Fisher met Roberts in a "barnstorming" exhibition game featuring major league stars versus local semipros. Roberts was entering his prime as a pitcher for the Philadelphia Phillies, and Lefty shut out a hitting lineup that included National League All-Stars like a batting champion and a league MVP.

The story sounded too incredible, but whether true, false, or an exaggeration, it was intriguing, and a writer's search for documentation had begun.

Facts on a 1949 barnstorming tour were elusive four decades later, and, around southeast Missouri, documentation on the year's semipro baseball was in short supply. The sport did not have centralized records, and period newspapers often provided little coverage compared to high school athletics.

A scorebook on the pitching matchup between Roberts and Fisher no longer existed, and just a few names of local players could be learned. Only a few witnesses could pinpoint the time and place it occurred, late 1949 in Sikeston, and the fact Holcomb was the team that met the major leaguers. Witnesses figured the game had to have occurred in the fall, probably October, because barnstormers toured immediately following the major league season.

A search through regional newspapers produced only one article, a small piece published at Sikeston. The barnstorming major leaguers were "Harry Walker's All-Stars." Their lineup was listed, but the report had few other details. Only two Holcomb players were mentioned, Fisher and Clyde Martin. The exact date of the game could be ascertained: Tuesday night, October 18. The story contained the number of hits for each side, and the final score, but the recall of witnesses would have to be the basis for reconstructing the game's action.

Recollections from nearly 50 years ago, however, could be problematic. Many people were convinced, for example, that Clarence Wessel of Cape Girardeau had been Holcomb's catcher that night. Wessel was one of the region's storied semipros, an outstanding receiver who played baseball until he was almost 60. Through the years, many top semipro teams in the Bootheel hired Wessel to work behind the plate. "Usually catchers were as scarce as hen's teeth," the octogenarian recalled. "Wherever somebody needed a catcher, that's where I was.

"Semipro baseball was great then," Wessel added, "but as soon as television came in, of course, the game died away. People wouldn't come out to watch us anymore."

Wessel certainly remembered Fisher. "I loved to catch Lefty," he said fondly. "He was such a wonderful guy to work with. Nothing bothered him and he had a lot of stuff on the ball: good curve, good fastball, good control. It was like sitting in a rocking chair, catching Lefty. A real pleasure."

Still, Wessel couldn't be sure he played for Holcomb against Walker's All-Stars. He did not remember any exhibition that particular fall, 1949. "Check with Kendall Sikes down in Sikeston," Wessel urged. "He had to be one of the guys who helped organize that game. He should remember something."

But Sikes had no recall, particularly of a game in which Fisher matched Roberts in a shutout. "Nope, don't remember that one at all," he said. "The best (exhibitions) we had as far as receipts were for the Negro League teams we had in here; the Kansas City Monarchs with Satchel (Paige), teams like that. We could really get the crowds for them."

Farther west in Bloomfield, the validated story of Fisher-versus-Roberts gained a few more details through Melvin "Churn" Williams, a director of the Southeast Missouri Amateur Baseball Hall of Fame. Lloyd Fisher is among the biggest names in the Hall, and Williams was a spectator at the game in Sikeston.

"It looked like two pro teams going at it," he said. "Holcomb really loaded up for that one."

Williams had other data and anecdotes on Fisher, like his no-hitter in the 1949 Missouri Semipro Tournament, and an interesting happening the first time Williams saw him pitch.

A batter foul-tipped a fastball from Lefty, and it spun off the overalls of skinny umpire Bob Wilkerson. "Bob had a pocket full of those big ol' wooden matches," Williams said wryly. "Well, those matches caught fire, and pretty quick he's throwin' off that mask and hoppin' around. He came right out of those overalls."

II

On a clear October evening in 1949, a silver bus cruised north through the sprawling flatlands of the Missouri Bootheel. The charter's roomy interior was quiet. Most of the riders, major league baseball players on a barnstorming tour, were napping, their heavy uniforms soiled from an afternoon exhibition in Arkansas.

One strapping young athlete, Robin Roberts, sat gazing out a window. The 23-year-old enjoyed the scenes of harvest in the great delta. Mechanical cotton-pickers were just starting to chew through the wide fields of white bolls clinging to brown stalks. But the cornfields really commanded his attention, the rows of stiff yellow stalks falling to the cumbersome combines. That reminded Roberts of home in central Illinois, Springfield, where the capital city limits ended as the cornfields and hog farms began.

Roberts only recently had completed his first full major league season in Philadelphia. Then he and a dozen other players met in Illinois to board the bus for the barnstorming tour, which would conclude that night in southeast Missouri. The young man was ready to go home.

Sikeston was the final stop in 20 games for Walker's All-Stars. Their travel accommodations were much improved over the early days of exhibition tours, when players often slept in barns, or "barn-stormed," but the grind of playing was just as grueling. Now in their 10th day across three states, Walker's Stars had played two games daily in different communities. The big leaguers dominated their rural opponents, of course, but 18 innings a day for the entire trip had worn them down, and injured some.

They did it for money; $1,000 apiece motivated these pros to barnstorm. Each man received $50 a game on the tour, an excellent supplement for a major league salary in 1949. Roberts, for example, had been paid $9,000 while winning 15 games that year for the Phils. The barnstorming tour made it an even $10,000 to Roberts from baseball that year, and he had a winter job lined up selling menswear.

Walker's Stars had no idea what team they would face in Sikeston. They did not know the pitcher they would face, and they did not care.

Roberts would be on the mound, and the team's player-manager and organizer was Harry "The Hat" Walker, who led the National League in hitting two years before with a .363 average. Walker was gaining experience for his future as a major league manager and coach.

The rest of the Stars lineup would intimidate a pro pitcher, much less one from the backwoods. Cincinnati power hitter Ted Kluszewski was a large, agile athlete at 6-foot-2, 225 pounds. The former football player for Indiana University played first base for the Reds, and "Big Klu" was already gaining notoriety for his biceps bulging from a sleeveless jersey. Kluszewski was bound for stardom in the big leagues, like his buddy on the barnstorming trip, Hank Sauer, who hit 31 home runs for the Cubs. Sauer was a 6-4 outfielder, and in a few years would be named the National League MVP.

Other barnstormers included Andy Seminick of the Phillies, "Handy Andy," an excellent catcher who could hit. Walker also had hired an erstwhile teammate in St. Louis, Terry Moore, the former All-Star outfielder with the Cardinals who had retired one year before. The Stars' outfield was Sauer in left, Walker in center, and Moore patrolling right. Seminick and Clyde McCullough of the Pirates swapped duties at catcher and third base, while the infield core was Bert Haas of the Giants at second base and Eddie Miller of the Phils at shortstop.

Besides Roberts, there were two other pitchers on the trip, veteran Kirby Higbe of the Giants and young Herm Wehmeier of the Reds. The pitchers normally split the games equally, or three innings apiece, and Walker helped out by taking the mound himself during easy victories. But as the bus approached Sikeston, Walker sat down next to Roberts.

"Higbe and Wehmeier both say their arms are shot," Walker told Roberts. "You pitch the first three innings or so tonight, then after we get way ahead, I'll relieve you. We'll win and then we'll go home."

"Sure thing, Skip," Roberts replied.

Walker began rousting the players from sleep. Many turned slowly in the seats, but they came awake, their chatter growing over the drone of the bus engine. Conversing animatedly and laughing, the athletes pulled on fresh socks under the long stirrup hose, tucked in thick jerseys, and re-buckled and zipped the cotton pants, which they rubbed down with open palms to smooth wrinkles. For these men who played a game like boys and got paid for it, dressing for the sport remained a perpetual energizer.

The bus rolled through Sikeston, a bustling agriculture center of 11,600 in "Swampeast" Missouri. People on the streets looked up and some waved, those expecting the big leaguers.

At VFW Memorial Stadium on the east edge of town, grids of lights burned against the evening dusk, visible for some distance across the flat farm lands. Baseball fans were still on their way, but a crowd of 1,000 already packed the grandstand as the Stars' bus rolled onto the gravel parking lot. Spectators craned their necks to see the bus door swing open and the big leaguers step out wearing uniforms embla zoned *Phillies, Reds, Cardinals, Cubs* and *Giants*.

The fans cheered loudly. Big Klu marched with his biceps bared, and Sauer had one huge hand wrapped around three bat handles. Harry the Hat grinned and waved, as did local favorite Terry Moore. The 6-1, 195-pound Roberts had a look of intensity. These visitors were national heroes of newspapers, newsreels, radio, and the new broadcast medium, television, preparing for live baseball. People were delighted.

The Stars' opponents, the Holcomb Cardinals, were the Missouri semipro champions. The Holcomb players stole glances at the big leaguers on parade, and some turned

completely to watch. But a few were not awe-struck, especially pitcher Lloyd "Lefty" Fisher and Clyde Martin, both
former minor leaguers who relished the chance to compete
with players recognized as among the best in the game.

Holcomb was a tiny Bootheel town in the delta southwest of Sikeston. The baseball team was bankrolled by
wealthy cotton planters who enticed standout players all
over the region, from Cape Girardeau south to Arkansas.
The exhibition with Walker's Stars was played at Sikeston
because of the accommodations for a large paying crowd.

The confident big leaguers warmed up quickly and
Walker signaled their readiness to play. An umpire in his
dark bulk of protective gear strode stiffly to home plate,
stooping over like Frankenstein to brush it clean. The infield
had been dragged and raked, smoothing the dirt from clods
to flake, and white chalk lines gleamed under the lights.

In the shadows along the leftfield line, Roberts began
loosening his throwing arm, pausing just a moment to watch
the opposing pitcher for Holcomb, Lefty Fisher, trot in from
rightfield. Some of the major league hitters watched too,
from the visitors dugout, but others paid no attention.

Fisher was a handsome athlete, 6-1 and 185 pounds. He
reached the pitching mound in smooth gait, then began toe-
digging the rubber with a cleated shoe. Satisfied with the
foothold, he looked in at the catcher, wound up and fired a
warm-up pitch. The fluid delivery sent the ball as a dart over
home plate, popping the airy catcher's mitt.

The stands held many fans who followed Fisher, and
they clapped and yelled encouragement. Fisher was among
the top semipros in Missouri, and he used to pitch for
Montreal in the Dodgers organization; if any local pitcher
could compete with the major leaguers, he was the one.

The game began, and Fisher did not disappoint the
locals. He gave up hits to the Stars but remained composed,
pitching around threats to keep them scoreless, and that
made the game interesting. Otherwise, it was unfolding as
expected with the Holcomb batters flailing hopelessly at
Roberts' pitches.

Holcomb's Charley Hart had batted .580 during the
semipro season and starred at the state tournament in
Jefferson City. But Roberts overwhelmed him, sending 90
mph fastballs with "action" that Hart struggled to foul off.
Releasing one pitch wild, Roberts yelled "Watch out!" barely

in time for Hart to duck it. With two strikes, Hart whiffed at a hard slider. Back in the dugout, he placed his bat in the rack as teammates asked about facing the Phillies ace. "It's like trying to hit a rifle bullet," Hart replied.

The major league hitters, meanwhile, continued having problems with Fisher. The top of their batting order came back up in the third inning, but Lefty was now compiling his mental "book" on every hitter, finding weaknesses to exploit. His fastball was topping 80 mph with lots of movement, and he mixed in off-speed pitches and curves. Walker's Stars could not get a base-runner home, and the score remained 0-0 at a time when they usually were building a comfortable lead.

In the Holcomb third, leadoff man Martin stroked a liner to the fence in left center. Roberts bore down to retire the next batter on strikes, stranding Martin, but the pitcher was slightly peeved returning to the dugout. He strode up and snatched a towel, wiping dirty sweat from his face, then gazed down the bench at his teammates. No one looked back, including Walker, who would not consider inserting himself on the mound yet. Roberts would not have allowed that anyway; ever the competitor, he wanted to put away this opponent himself, backwoods team or not.

The fans were sensing something special occurring. Semipros in southeast Missouri had a long tradition of hosting barnstorming big leaguers, including great pitchers like Dizzy Dean. But no one in the stands could recall a local team ever winning such an exhibition. They watched Fisher stymie the Stars — including Kluszewski, the cleanup hitter who struck out to start the fourth — and became more vocal in supporting Holcomb.

The crowd roared and hooted as Klu trudged back to the dugout, muttering and kicking dust. Roberts, both impressed and confounded by Fisher, motioned to a man through the dugout screen. Nodding toward Lefty, he asked, "Who the heck is this guy?"

III

Lloyd B. Fisher was born in 1920 in St. Louis, the first son and second child of Iva Lee and Benjamin Franklin Fisher. Ben Fisher was a railroad foreman, and Iva Lee was the homemaker in charge of a brood of children that would grow to five — three girls and two boys.

The Fisher children were active and talented, with a range of interests that included music, art and fashion. But the entire family, including the parents, shared a certain passion: baseball, particularly the St. Louis Cardinals. When the family moved north from the city's south side in 1933, it was no coincidence they took a flat within shouting distance of Sportsman's Park on Grand Avenue. During the 1934 World Series, the Fishers saw every game in St. Louis, with the kids standing outside the park in the Knothole Gang areas.

Ben's hobby was updating Cardinal statistics every inning, and he was prone to get angry with radio broadcasters who did not concern themselves with correct records, like Dizzy Dean in the 1940s. Iva Lee also kept a personal scorebook on the Cardinals, but she loved to attend games such as the Ladies Day events that offered her free admission. During World War II, many games had special admission for scrap metal donations, and Ben complained the house was running out of pots and pans because Iva Lee and her sister were using up the inventory to see the Cardinals.

Lloyd grew up with a dream to some day play for the Cardinals, which was not unusual. His family's love for the team aside, virtually any boy in St. Louis held the same fantasy. But Lloyd was different as an especially gifted child; baseball was definitely a part of his future.

By his teen-age years, Lloyd was a legitimate baseball prospect, one of a select few in a city teeming with quality amateur players. He could hit, catch, throw and run, and he became a dominant player in the urban area's competitive youth leagues. The boy had nicknames, including "Slats" and "Skinny," but "Lefty" stuck. His real identity was baseball, for he was an elite talent among peers.

At 16, Lefty was selected for the prestigious All-Star Game of the Junior Municipal League, or "Junior Muny." The event was held at Sportsman's Park, where Lefty took the field for the first time in front of his family beaming in the stands. It was 1936. The Cardinals were *The Gashouse Gang* with Medwick, Martin, the Dean Brothers, and more stars. St. Louis could not get enough of baseball, and young Lloyd thrived in the atmosphere.

His goal began to materialize after he graduated from Beaumont High in 1938. Pro scouts were in constant contact, led by those representing the Cardinals, and Lefty competed during the summer in the top local circuit for amateurs, the St. Louis Municipal League. Lefty was an all-around success: on the pitching mound he compiled an 11-3 mark, but he also starred as an outfielder who hit extremely well. The Cardinals offered him a contract, and he signed it at age 18.

The following spring, Lloyd Fisher was a touted prospect for Union City, Tennessee, in the Kitty League. His won-loss record was subpar, 8-12, but he pitched strong over 28 games with 121 strikeouts and a 2.96 earned-run-average. In 1940, Fisher returned to Union City with the eye of Cardinals management upon him; General Manager Branch Rickey visited the team at the start of the season, taking special interest in the lefthander from St. Louis. There were expectations surfacing elsewhere too, like a newspaper article in Louisville previewing the Kitty League, which declared "Fisher should be one of the league's outstanding southpaws."

And he was. He won the opening day game for Union City, pitched the league's first shutout the next week at Paducah, and kept on winning.

Fisher moved up to Class D ball in 1941, going to Fremont in the Ohio State League, and he had his best baseball season ever. He scarcely lost on the pitcher's mound and starred as a hitter.

"Southpaw pitcher Lloyd Fisher has been playing in the outfield for the Fremont Green Sox since the sale of Bill Ramsey, and he's clouting well over .300," noted one sports-writer. "In three consecutive games last week, he was 8 for 12 at the plate."

As a pitcher, Fisher won 18 games and established himself as a bona fide major league prospect.

One sportswriter — looking ahead to the 1942 season and noting Rickey was now the Dodgers' general manager — speculated Fisher may be acquired by the Montreal Royals of the International League in Triple-A, one step away from Brooklyn. The writer also believed Fisher was a possible candidate for a spot on the Dodgers, or "the Brooks." In St. Louis, meanwhile, Browns executive Bill DeWitt was reportedly interested in having Fisher pitch in the majors for his team the next season.

Fisher was a young man of 21, close to reaching his goal of major league baseball. Yet conflict churned within him.

His main priority was shifting from playing baseball to serving his country.

He made the decision to volunteer for the war effort before the Japanese attacked Pearl Harbor. "Lloyd Fisher, St. Louisan, who pitches minor league ball in the Ohio State League has joined the Army," reported the Post-Dispatch. "Fisher reported yesterday at Jefferson Barracks. The lefthander pitched for the Fremont club last season and won 18 games while dropping 3 contests. . . ."

At the Fisher family flat on the north side, the scrapbook on Lloyd suddenly got a new section, switching from promise in baseball to one on preparation for war: "Starting a New Chapter in Lloyd's Life," his mother wrote bravely in the headline. At Bethany Lutheran Church, the printed program made the announcement with prayer: "Next Tuesday, another of our boys is answering the call of the country, Lloyd Fisher. Our prayers follow him and all our boys. Oh, Heavenly Father, protect them, wherever they are."

Lloyd Fisher survived World War II's European theater, but not unscathed. He took part in some of the war's most intense ground-fighting, serving with valor as the Allies pushed the Nazis out of France, Belgium, Luxembourg and the Netherlands, then back into Germany, where they surrendered. For almost a year, Fisher's division fought and drove the Germans 1,400 miles, and he was wounded twice.

Now he came home to a wife and two small children. He was older, and the body was banged up a bit. Once, under heavy fire, he caught shrapnel in a leg. Then, a bomb explosion in a log bunker wrenched his back severely. Fisher was highly decorated as a soldier, but he quietly put the war medals away in a box and stashed it in a drawer. The 26-year-old's duty was behind him, and he wanted to return to baseball, the dream that remained.

But so did a multitude of others like him. The war's end had released a torrent of American workers, and the pro baseball ranks were again overrun with athletes. Jobs were at a premium, but DeWitt wanted Fisher for the Browns and signed him to a minor league contract.

Fisher got his chance to pitch and play outfield at Springfield, Illinois, but he apparently had health problems; he did not get a lot of at-bats and he pitched in only 15 games. His hitting average was a poor .208, and while he logged a 4-1 mark on the mound, his ERA was a high 4.83.

Branch Rickey was impressed enough, however, and signed Fisher to a 1947 contract for Montreal. Lefty went to spring training with the Dodgers in Florida and witnessed the furor surrounding Jackie Robinson, who would break the color barrier in baseball. But problems arose at Montreal; the war wounds must have plagued Fisher, and he was released.

Over 40 years later, his widow, Louise, had few details about the end of his career in pro baseball. "I'm not a very good one to talk about what happened," she confessed. "I can't tell you the straight of it. He went to Montreal, but he didn't stay there long."

When Fisher returned to St. Louis, he was a little downcast but certainly not confused; he still believed he could play pro baseball, but until a team called, he had a family to care for. He took jobs pitching batting practice for the Cardinals and driving a cab.

Then the rural life beckoned, especially the farm owned by Louise's family in southeast Missouri, on Crowley's Ridge near Puxico. The couple moved there and never left, raising their children and retiring. Lloyd and Louise were married 47 years when he died of lung cancer in 1989.

Two months after Lloyd's passing, this author went to the farm to meet Louise, who was joined by her son, Larry, for an afternoon interview. The Fishers were cheerful, warm hosts, and although still grieving, they discussed Lloyd's life with smiles and laughter, as though remembering a grand friend as much as a husband and father.

Louise recalled how she and Lloyd left the city for the farm in the fall of '47. The country setting was peaceful, idyllic, but hardly free of pressures. "We started in down here trying to make a livin', you know," Louise said smiling. "We bought land and everything. And we made it — barely." She laughed heartily.

Aside from farming, Lloyd took jobs as a rural mail carrier and a truck driver. Soft-spoken about himself, hardly anyone knew his baseball past, and he initially stayed away from the game. Finally one Sunday afternoon — as the local legend goes — Lefty Fisher showed up at a semipro double-header in Asherville, a tiny community near the farm.

Eyeing the pitcher's mound and watching the home team get beat in the opener, Fisher used the help of Louise's brother, Bud Madden, to convince the manager to let him pitch the second game. Stepping to the mound in work boots and winding up to throw in overalls, Lefty was untouchable.

Opposing batters were shut down, Asherville won big, and the word began spreading, although apparently not too far too soon. There was gambling on baseball in southeast Missouri, and a talent like Lefty could help tip the scales for awhile. Asherville gamblers keyed on the fact he was virtually unknown in the region, and they made a plan. "They'd tell him to show up for games wearing overalls and walking barefooted," said Larry, chuckling. "And those boys (backing the other team) would really lay the money down."

Asherville sought to keep Lefty as long as possible, but the Puxico Vets soon lured him away with better pay. In due time, the Holcomb team visited the Vets in Puxico. Holcomb expected to win with a roster boasting many of the region's best hitters, but Lefty shut them out over nine innings. Holcomb did push home a run in the 11th to win, 1-0, but the wealthy team organizers found they did not have the region's best pitcher on the payroll.

They did the next season, 1949, when Lefty Fisher joined Holcomb. With heavy bets riding on games, Lefty's pitching pay was as high as $100 and more for victories.

Odds are, however, that no one bet on Holcomb when Lefty faced Robin Roberts that October in Sikeston.

IV

The game moved past the middle innings, still scoreless despite vicious hitting displays by the big leaguers. Muscular Hank Sauer ripped a line drive rising toward left field, and Holcomb shortstop Clyde Martin leaped high to stop it. The shot tore away Martin's glove, and the ball popped out, but Sauer was held to a single. Fisher got out of the inning.

Backed by tight defense, Lefty pitched around repeated scoring threats by Walker's Stars. He showed no emotion, whether retiring a batter or giving up a hit. Occasionally he would step off the rubber to squeeze a resin bag or remove his cap to rub fingers through his sandy blond hair. The pros began to wonder how close Fisher was coming to a record for the number of "scattered" hits, meaning those he allowed without giving up a run.

Fisher had some success at the plate too, rapping a single off Roberts, but he was stranded on base when no one else reached safely for Holcomb. Roberts had already pitched nine innings of shutout ball that day, including three in Arkansas, but he kept mowing through batters, and the fans cheered for any ball Holcomb managed to put into play.

Walker still did not mention a pitching change, which Roberts would have nixed; this was his game to win or lose now, and he focused on Holcomb as though facing the Dodgers. The pitching duel moved into late innings, but neither pitcher would relent, and the score remained 0-0 after nine. Fisher had matched Roberts in the shutout!

The game went into extra innings. Fans, bouncing in their seats, were rowdy with the game's excitement on a chilly autumn night. Men got up to crowd around the infield screen, cheering for Holcomb and shaking the wire.

The big leaguers led off the 10th and Walker strode to the plate. A classy left-handed hitter, he already owned two hits off Fisher, a double and single, among the nine safeties for his team.

Fisher wound and pitched; Walker swung, pulling a long high fly into the darkness over right field. Holcomb outfielder Charley Hart followed the flight to the fence, until he was out of running room, but he had the ball in sight as it fell almost straight down. Hart reached over the fence, stretching out, but the ball landed just beyond his glove.

Hart turned around dejectedly and the crowd was quiet. The only sounds were the whoops from the Stars as Walker circled the bases for a home run. The big leaguers were finally ahead, 1-0.

Fisher retired the side, and Roberts took the mound, determined to finish Holcomb. Martin led off, batting right-handed, and slapped an outside fastball down the right field line. The ball landed fair and rolled to the corner before Terry Moore chased it down and fired it back in. Martin stood atop second base with his second double, and the grandstand roared back to life.

But Roberts was oblivious to the noise. He could tune out the crowds at Ebbets Field in Brooklyn, and he easily ignored the fans at VFW Memorial in Sikeston. He was pitching in his 13th inning of the day, and he would not be denied victory now. Rearing back on the mound and stepping hard to the plate, Roberts whipped his arm around and

grunted on pitches, sending screaming fastballs and bend-
ing curves to catcher Clyde McCullough. Holcomb batters
were missing and the catcher's mitt was popping; McCullough
was basically playing catch now with his pitcher.

Roberts claimed one strikeout, then a second, and a
final third in a row, stranding Martin on base. The game was
over, the big leaguers were grateful to win, and they lined up
to shake the hands of Fisher, Martin, and the other Holcomb
players.

V

On the final day of the 1950 National League season, the
Philadelphia Phillies defeated the Brooklyn Dodgers to clinch
the pennant. Robin Roberts was on the mound, winning his
20th game of the season and leading the Phillies to the World
Series for the first time in 35 years. They lost the fall classic
to the Yankees of manager Casey Stengel, but the fame of
Philadelphia's "Whiz Kids" proved lasting.

Roberts went on to establish his stardom in the major
leagues, winning 20 games in six consecutive seasons,
including a 28-7 mark in 1952. Always a work-horse competitor, he once tossed 346 innings and 33 complete games,
season marks any contemporary hurler would not consider
approaching. Roberts likely shortened his career through
such toil — he suffered a chronic sore arm as a veteran — but
he left the game with no regrets. He still recorded 286 major
league wins, was elected to the Baseball Hall of Fame at
Cooperstown in 1976, and moved to the Gulf Coast of Florida
to spend retirement.

Roberts never really knew the name Lloyd "Lefty" Fisher,
but he never forgot the man. Forty years after the two met in
the barnstorming game at Sikeston, Roberts responded
eagerly to a written inquiry regarding the game; he was
heartened, in fact, the event was being brought back to light.
The memory's mists of '49, the notion of major leaguers
struggling to win on a small-town diamond, had grown
special for him too.

"For us to hang on and win made a lot of sense, I guess,
because we were the big leaguers," Roberts said in a
telephone interview. "But it was such a *great* ball game. We
had some good hitters, and Mr. Fisher pitched outstanding.
He could really throw the ball well."

Roberts was also respectful of the Holcomb lineup, even

though only Fisher and Martin made hits. "Pitching against the teams we usually played (in barnstorming), those guys weren't that sharp. So we never had to reach back and get extra — except in that particular game. I did have to, especially in the 10th inning."

Roberts laughed, recalling how Harry Walker avoided the issue of making a pitching change. "In most (exhibitions) the guys would whack the other pitcher around. But in this game nobody said a word about me coming out. We hadn't scored."

For years afterward, Roberts and Walker enjoyed a joke together. Every time they met, Roberts said, "Hey Harry, I'm still waiting for you to come in and relieve me."

Today's elitist environment for major league players is largely insulated from the American public. Contemporary superstars are pampered cultural icons with multi-million dollar wealth, but in Roberts' era it was often necessary for him to both barnstorm and hold a winter job.

In the small towns now, skepticism or outright disbelief greets the old semipros who talk about playing Hall of Famers like Roberts, Dean, Spahn, or Satchel. And people are just as incredulous when former major leaguers talk about barnstorming, said Roberts. Friends and acquaintances who never saw such exhibitions cannot envision him wearing the Phillies uniform at a dusty country ballpark. They smile wider when he speaks about pitching twice a day for 10 straight days, given the major leaguers of today who are so paranoid of any injury. Then Roberts might recall the night when a semipro pitcher shut out Harry Walker's All-Stars over nine innings.

"It's funny," Roberts said, "I've been telling people about that game against Mr. Fisher, and they can't believe it. When you get to be my age, people think you might be making up stories. Now I've got a record of that game."

VI

In 1950, Lloyd Fisher still heard from an occasional baseball scout, but he had given up on the pro game. He continued to strive to better himself in other skills. Working multiple jobs, he attended Missouri Baptist College — playing basketball — which bolstered his resume as a schoolteacher. But yet another trial loomed for his family: Korea. Lloyd had remained in the Army Reserves, much against the wishes of loved ones.

"The Korean War called him back into service," said Louise, noting her husband's medals and decorations represented "two wars' worth" of campaigns. "We had a time getting started in civilian life because he was in the service so much."

Fisher was not wounded in Korea, although he was on the front lines once more as an infantryman. He returned home from war a second and final time at age 33. He resettled into family life, farming, and working for the Post Office, and he resumed playing baseball a few more years.

Over time, Lloyd Fisher became widely respected and admired for his non-athletic attributes. People were attracted to his humble but rich persona, the well-read intellect, humor, religious faith, and unwavering goodwill toward others.

Talent for sports blossomed elsewhere in the family, namely in a competitive little girl who grew into a great volleyball player. A granddaughter of Fisher's, Deanna (Miller) Hurt, graduated from Puxico High and received a scholarship from Jefferson Community College. Dee was a junior college All-American for the powerful Lady Vikes, a feared outside hitter known as "Killer Miller." She then competed for the University of Missouri, and her proud grandfather traveled to see her play at locales across the Big Eight Conference.

Eventually Fisher retired from the Post Office and was able to turn his full attention to the farm. Gardening was his favorite leisure, and he maintained three beautiful plots around the house.

"He loved the country, see," said Louise. "Before he passed away he told me, `I just thank the Lord I was able to live in the country.'"

The research into a man's life had started with what this writer had initially perceived to be his greatness: the ability to throw a baseball. Undoubtedly, when Lloyd Fisher was a boy, his dream was to pitch in the major leagues. But, as a man, he chose to serve his country and risk life itself, instead of fulfilling the fantasy to play a sport in the spotlight.

Humility was a marker of this man to the end. Just like folks around Puxico never heard Fisher brag about his baseball prowess, neither did his family ever hear of his heroics in warfare. Only after his death was the old box of medals and decorations brought out, and no one knew what they were looking at aside from the recognizable Purple Heart. The puzzle pieces of a soldier's time in battle would have to be fitted together without his help.

Larry Fisher studied war medals and decorations, and determined the oak leaf pin on his father's Purple Heart signified a double citation, for the two wounds the family knew Lloyd sustained during 1944. Then Larry realized one of the faded medals in the box was among the highest honors bestowed on an American soldier — the Bronze Star. And his father's Bronze Star had the oak leaf, representing a double citation.

What had Lloyd Fisher done in Europe to be twice-awarded the Bronze Star? What had he experienced?

It was May 1997. Time was running out on research for this book, so the first reference to be checked were military records. The proper request forms were filled out, but a recent fire at the Federal Records Center in St. Louis had destroyed the files on Lloyd B. Fisher. Notices were quickly forwarded to other archives across the country, but the process was not producing meaningful data on time.

The next avenue for information was taken: contacting survivors from the massive group of soldiers Lloyd had landed with in France, including the 331st Regiment combat team of which he was a member, and a clearer picture began to form.

After the Allies invaded the Normandy beachheads on June 6, 1944, 25 divisions landed in the following weeks, and the total number of soldiers deployed reached into hundreds of thousands. Lloyd's outfit, Company I of the 331st, hit Omaha Beach on June 26 after spending five days on a boat in the English Channel, waiting out rough weather.

On shore the peril of the battlefront was immediate, according to a decorated veteran of Company I, Vernon Bobo of Trezevant, Tennessee. "It was rough over there. . . ," Bobo recalled in a telephone interview. "The thing of it was, you were fighting just about all the time. You never rested (for over 10 months), and you always knew where the enemy was at. You never had to hunt for him.

"Just stick your head up, and he'd show ya where he was

at."

The objective of American General Dwight D. Eisenhower called for Allied forces to break through the German defenses entrenched along the Normandy coast. The 331st was part of General Omar Bradley's U.S. First Army, and on July 25 this force struck the Nazis' extreme left flank.

The Americans seized St. Lo, and in three days the First Army broke into open country, veering eastward across western France to the Seine River. To its right, General George Patton was driving his armored divisions forward. The second phase of Eisenhower's plan was in motion, to pursue the Nazis on a widening front and drive them out of France, across the Rhineland, and into the heart of Germany.

Across the rugged terrain, infantrymen fought from hedgerow to hedgerow, reclaiming the ancient farms of France one-by-one. They experienced every type of ground weapon the enemy had, including grenades, mines, machine guns, tanks, and the dreaded howitzer artillery guns, short cannons which fired bombs on high trajectories to clear tall or sheltered defenses. "That artillery is something," Second Lieutenant Lloyd Fisher wrote in a letter home:

> You never know when one is coming right
> down on you. . . . I saw one tear a man's head
> completely off his shoulders, and almost had it
> land on me. What a sight. This man had a little
> boy in Chicago that he had never seen too. A good
> Christian man. . . one of my assistant squad
> leaders.

Slowly, the Germans fell back. Paris was liberated on August 24, and Allied forces were crossing the German frontier in September. Company I advanced through Luxembourg and Belgium, then into Germany by December. But Hitler launched his great, insane counteroffensive back into France via an infamous barrier, the Ardennes Forest.

This was the Battle of the Bulge, beginning on December 16, and Company I was called back to take part. The Nazis would be repelled through horrific fighting, but Hitler would order another counterattack, and the cycle would repeat. The bloodshed continued when Company I arrived on Christmas Eve. "Oh yeah," Bobo said intensely. "It was still plenty rough, and cold." Many soldiers fought in snow up to their waists.

Robert Derickson of Hamilton, Ohio, was in the Battle of the Bulge from the start with his 329th Regiment. "We broke through (the Germans) and then was brought back, and then they really counterattacked," Derickson said by telephone. "We had to go back in and fight it all over. . . . We had five different battles."

Hitler finally withdrew his forces on January 8, 1945, after suffering heavy losses. Allied casualties were astronomical too, totaling 77,000 dead, wounded, or missing. But the Nazis were broken; the Battle of the Bulge was their last major offensive. Hitler committed suicide on April 30, and the Third Reich surrendered on May 7. The next morning, V-E Day — Victory In Europe — was celebrated across the free world.

Bobo did not know Fisher in Europe because they were in different platoons of Company I, although they were "right side-by-side, all the time," he said. Bobo added that even if he had known Fisher then, he still might not have witnessed how the latter earned two Bronze Star citations. "You just don't know that much about other individuals in a combat zone," he said, alluding to the ceaseless madness.

After the war, the two men became friends through veterans reunions. "I'm sure Lloyd was a good soldier because he was thought of highly by his men in the platoon," said Bobo. "And I know he was a fine man."

Bobo was wounded four times in Europe, and displayed courage that won him two Bronze Star citations and the medal that is a notch higher in precedence, the Silver Star. I asked him if he had any idea what Fisher must have done for the Bronze Star awards. "That's for valor," Bobo said without hesitation.

Derickson agreed in a separate interview. "It was some kind of heroic performance, something outstanding," he said. "(Fisher) had to be in the front line to earn those."

Bobo was asked what he did to earn his Silver Star. "Ahh," he said nervously, "it was knockin' out a tank that was firing on our company, and taking a terrible risk to do it."

The research trail ended with Lloyd Fisher's two younger

sisters, Janis Freebersyser of West Virginia and Maxine Gruchalla of St. Louis. The telephone discussions were now focusing on their brother's war experience; baseball seemed of no significance by comparison.

"Lloyd didn't mention the war when he first came back," said Janis, who was 13 years younger. "But over the years he began to talk about it. His throwing arm came in real handy with the grenades, because he was so accurate in hitting the German pillboxes (concrete gunner nests)."

Maxine was four years younger than the older brother she admittedly worshipped. "He was such a fine individual," she said. Growing up, she witnessed Lloyd's accomplishments, such as him becoming an Eagle Scout, and, of course, his stardom in two sports, basketball as well as baseball.

When Lloyd traded baseball for war, he wanted to be an officer in the front lines. Maxine said when he became leader of a combat platoon "over there," he cared foremost for his men, not himself. In times of danger, Lloyd led the way instead of ordering someone else to take the risk in front of him.

Maxine revealed she had a sort of secret letter Lloyd mailed from the war. He sent it to their oldest sister, Virginia or "Ginny," dating the first page October 24, 1944, Luxembourg. Lloyd wrote explicitly that Ginny was not to allow their mother or his wife, Louise, to see the letter. It stated in part:

Ginny, you'd be surprised at what you learn about men and human nature when they're facing death. As long as the American soldier has someone to lead him and tell him what to do, he's all right. But otherwise he's scared to death, and like an ostrich, puts his head in the ground and hopes.

I've seen Germans who are worse, though. Not all of them, mind you, but an awful lot of them. In France, several times we sneaked up on whole pillboxes full of them, anywhere from 20 to 50 soldiers, and no one outside on guard. And a hand grenade tossed inside, and they would all surrender. Then I've seen 6 or 7 of them attack a

whole company of GIs and scare everyone to
death.

It's a funny game. We get a lot of laughs over
what we did in certain circumstances — after it's
all over.

I've moved in on Germans at night and had
whole platoons surrender to us rather than fight
it out. I've been pinned down for hours by machine guns firing at long range, where you
couldn't see them and could just hear the bullets
cracking around you. One time I was behind a
wheat stack and could smell (bullets) burning
through the wheat, kicking the dirt up in front of
me. That's when you pray and sweat, when you
can't see them.

Lloyd continued with a passage that was startling for
what it contained: a description of the first time he was
wounded, which occurred August 8 in France, according to
military documents. He was leading the platoon through a
mine field at night, literally crawling, when he shot down an
enemy soldier 10 yards in front. A machine gun opened fire
25 yards behind the fallen German:

Most of my platoon was pinned down by the
fire, but four of us could fire back. A loud explosion behind me woke me up to that fact that they
were throwing hand grenades at us, so I took the
challenge and tossed four back at them. (Meanwhile) the other three men were firing like mad
men at their gun flashes. After what seemed like
hours, but was probably seconds, they ceased
firing.

We moved up into their trench and awaited
dawn. . . . My leg began to get stiff and I saw that I
was wounded slightly by a fragment. When it got
light enough to see, we counted seven dead
Germans around the machine gun, including one
captain. None of us were killed, although one
other man besides me was wounded.

For this leadership, Lloyd likely earned one of his Bronze
Star awards. "I don't know why I'm telling you all this," he

wrote Ginny, "except I feel I must tell someone at home, and I can't tell Mom or Louise."

In America at this time, optimism was high for Allied victory. The summertime invasions of France had the Nazis running, and citizens were expecting an end to the war. Rationing of goods like sugar and gasoline had even been suspended. But any celebrating seemed premature to Lloyd and other soldiers overseas. He wrote:

> When people talk about the war ending soon, just tell them a lot of Doughboys (Americans) are dying daily and will continue to die for a long time yet. Also, a few inches on a map are the most important part of life for those who died to take it. And anyone who is still a civilian should at least appreciate more what these boys like mine are dying for over here. . . .
>
> Don't get the idea I'm complaining, but the war isn't over yet. We're going to do the job, but it's up to people like you to be ready to accept back, into civilian life, guys who may seem to be a little wacky (ha).
>
> Write me again, Ginny, and tell everyone hello.
>
> Your little brother,
> Lloyd

One month after sending this letter, Lloyd got a field promotion to First Lieutenant. On December 11, 1944, probably in Germany, he was wounded when an explosion tossed logs atop him in a bunker. The lumbar vertebrae of his lower back were damaged permanently, which effectively ended his professional baseball career.

Maxine (Fisher) Gruchalla, today a grandmother, remains a devoted baseball fan, true to her bloodlines. She has even written poetry about her favorite Cardinal teams since the Gashouse Gang. And she appreciates what her brother, Lloyd, accomplished in the game.

But for her, baseball does not define his life.

"I know he was a patriot," she stated unequivocally. "That's what I think about him the most. A patriot. He loved this country and the people who served it, like he did."

OZAGES

> "Long before the Europeans found them, they had
> named the animals, the fishes, the trees, the
> plants, and the birds, and had named themselves,
> *Ni-U-Ko'n-Ska*, Children of the Middle Waters."
>
> *John Joseph Mathews**

Politics developing on both sides of the Atlantic in 1802 would change the course of America, and thus the world. Napoleon of France was giving up his country's long-held dream of a North American empire in "Louisiana" west of the Mississippi River. Meanwhile, in Washington, D.C., President Thomas Jefferson was expressing concern over renewed French presence at the Port of New Orleans, "through which the produce of three-eighths of our territory must pass to market."

Jefferson was as worried about national security as economics. Recognizing the dangers of French imperialism with Napoleon in power, the President had called France "our natural and habitual enemy." Jefferson began devising a plan to purchase New Orleans and the Floridas from France, but he had no idea how important his timing would become.

Napoleon, facing war with England, feared the British more than the Americans. New Orleans was highly vulnerable to conquest, which well could lead to British seizure of Louisiana, a result Napoleon wanted to avoid at all costs. He would much rather see the interior of North America fall into U.S. hands than British.

So at Paris in the spring of 1803, Napoleon shocked Jefferson's envoys by offering them the entire Louisiana region: 800,000 square miles flowering up from the Gulf of Mexico to a vast northern border west of the Mississippi. The Americans accepted, acquiring land that would become all or part of 13 states, including Missouri, for a price of $15 million.

The Louisiana Purchase instantly doubled the geographic size of the country. Now all waters flowing into the

*Mathews, John Joseph. *The Osages: Children of the Middle Waters.* University of Oklahoma Press (1961).

Mississippi, including the Missouri, the Arkansas, and the Red River from the west, originated in a U.S. state or territory.

The United States of America was a fledgling no more. Napoleon unwittingly had shoved the struggling nation onto the path of becoming a superpower.

But as a new society was thriving on the continent, another culture was unalterably changed and threatened with extinction: the American Indians. Hundreds of different tribes once had possessed lands now claimed by the United States. And the newest Americans, in their westward rush, were driving out and trampling the native peoples before them.

Some of the tribes, however, were not so easy to budge, particularly the Osage Nation dynasty based in Missouri Territory, smack in the middle of westward expansion and refusing to move.

I

The Osage warrior was a curiosity in Washington, where he was introduced to whites as Big Soldier. His given Osage name *Ah-Ke-Tah Tun-Ka*, Big Soldier was brought from Missouri Territory to meet leaders of the white man, including their president. The Louisiana Purchase was still a recent event.

Sitting before the whites, Big Soldier's "wild" but majestic appearance was riveting. Everything the Washingtonians had heard about the West, everything they had imagined, seemed vivid in this man.

The "savage" had the renowned Osage body, standing over six feet tall with well-muscled proportions. His high cheekbones were handsome, the jaw firm and square, his shoulders wide and chest robust, the hips narrow. His eyes were dark with an earnest gaze. The bronze head was shorn smooth except for a protruding shock of black hair greased and ornamented with eagle feathers; the pate was dabbed in red vermilion. His long neck was ringed in wampum and beads. Shirtless in summer, his hairless chest was tattooed in Osage clan symbols, and painted in a brilliant scene of the buffalo hunt.

People gasped at Big Soldier's ears. The lobes were slit into ribbons and pierced, hanging long under the weight of pendants and beads. Deerskin leggings that opened around bulging thigh muscles were fringed with human hair and tied off under the knees. The blue-and-cream moccasins were bison skin. The blue breechcloth was held by a leather girdle, which also secured a huge knife in skin sheath. He wore wrist bands of silver and multiple finger rings.

Most striking about Big Soldier was the collective expression of face, body and posture. The whites had heard the Osage were arrogant, but this man did not rightly fit the image. He was proud, certainly, but poised and dignified, an aura quite unexpected by many in the room.

Big Soldier was gracious, mannered, but he was not intimidated by the white men, some so powerful. When he spoke, the words were articulate, respectful, uncontemptuous — but completely honest — piercing those in the room. No one could do anything but listen.

Big Soldier recognized fate. He knew the conquering whites would succeed in driving all Indians off their lands. The Osage, his great people, were essentially finished as a superpower on the frontier, although still famed as hunters and warriors. They had fought viciously to keep their domain, but that would end in this era of the Euro-Americans, the 19th century.

The Osage once conducted extensive commerce with traders from France, England, Spain and Canada. They had been confronted aggressively by Europeans, only to become the intimidators themselves. For at least 300 years — predating the treks of De Soto and Coronado into the continent's Midwest — the Osage had ruled lands of the Lower Missouri and Upper Mississippi rivers. They repulsed tenacious raids by Indian tribes from all directions, and massacred enemies while on the offensive. But the "American," the white man from the East, would finally break the Osage and bring them to their knees.

The vast Osage Nation once stretched from the Missouri River near modern Boonville, Missouri, south 400 miles to the Arkansas River. The empire sprawled west from the Mississippi into the basin later known as Kansas and Oklahoma, encompassing rugged Ozark mountains, prairies and swamps. Generations of Osage tribesmen had taken the land's bounty, hunting buffalo on the plains and deer and bear in the forested hills and harvesting the pelts of beaver and other furbearers from the lowlands.

But the Osage lands were disappearing through treaties

with the U.S. Government. The migrating whites and tribes fleeing from the East had claimed highlands, rivers and prairies from the Osage. More treaties would steal what was left.

Big Soldier would not plead with the whites in their capital city. *Ah-Ke-Tah Tun-Ka* knew his identity; he was certain of the life he had lived and would die for. Now he challenged the whites to know the same.

"I see and admire your way of living. . ." he said. "Your warm houses, your extensive cornfields, your gardens, your cows, oxen, work horses, wagons, and a thousand machines that I know not the use of. I see that you are able to clothe yourself, even from weeds and grass.

"In short, you can do almost what you choose. You whites possess the power of subduing almost every animal you choose. You are surrounded by slaves. Everything about you is in chains. . . ." Big Soldier paused to gaze around the room. "And you are slaves yourselves. I fear if I should change my pursuit for yours, I, too, should become a slave.

"Talk to my sons," he urged calmly. "Perhaps they may be persuaded to adopt your fashions, or at least recommend them to their sons. But for myself, I was born free, was raised free, and wish to die free."

Big Soldier shifted in the mahogany chair, all eyes fixed upon him. As the Indian moved, the chair squeaked, then the room's only sounds were his beads and wampum, clicking lightly.

"I am perfectly contented with my condition," he added. "The forests and river supply all the calls of nature in plenty, and there is no lack of white people to purchase the supplies of our industry."

Big Soldier nodded graciously to his listeners. "I have spoken." He knew he had touched their hearts, but the whites replied, in so many words, how they considered their own ambitions nobly supreme. They said the land was their destiny, that God had sent them for it.

Big Soldier disagreed completely, but silently. Many wars lay ahead for his nation.

II

Researchers of Native American cultures identify two distinct groups: prehistoric Indians and historic Indians. The prehistorics, according to scientific theory, were the first people to come to North America more than 10,000 years ago, probably over a land bridge between Siberia and Alaska as the Wisconsin Glaciation Epoch was ending. The prehistorics made their way into the continental interior and became civilizations such as the Mississippians, often known as the Mound Builders of the Mississippi River Valley. Archaeological digs of prehistoric sites have revealed much about these cultures, but many important questions remain. For example, why did they disappear sometime after 1000 A.D. and before the arrival of Spanish explorers Columbus and Hernando De Soto?

The sagas of historic Indian tribes — those met by the first Europeans in America — are intense dramas of lasting importance, yet recorded history is in short supply.

The first record of the Osage was a crude map drawn in 1673 by French Jesuit priest Jacques Marquette, who noted their villages along the Missouri River. In 1684, Franquelin traveled into Missouri and found Osage villages near the mouth of the river that would be named for the tribe.

Given the mystery surrounding American Indians before Europeans, most written histories on the Osage embrace sacred oral traditions passed through generations by tribal storytellers, *Ne-Ke-A Shin-Ka*, or the Society of Little Old Men.

The essential Osage legend of origin begins with an ancestral Dhegiha Sioux tribe in the East that began moving westward. Starting from the Piedmont region of Virginia, the people entered the Ohio Valley and headed downstream, seeking to escape warfare with invading tribes like the powerful Iroquois.

Long before De Soto's 1541 march to the Mississippi River, the tribe reached the mouth of the Ohio at present-day Cairo, where it branched apart. The Down River People went a little farther south and became known as the Quapaws. Up River People moved north through the Mississippi Valley to present-day St. Louis, then west along the Missouri.

The Up River People were a dynamic group on the continent, restless and changing through the will of men and women destined for adventure, tragedy, and greatness. Ideas and ambitions continued to divide the tribe, a process of humanity repeated again and again. Factions broke off to head up the Missouri; a few hundred left first, the new tribe called Omaha, and others followed, becoming the Ponca, the Kansa, Iowa, Missouri, and the Osage.

This version of Osage origin was first published in 1886 by anthropologist James Owen Dorsey in his *Migration of Siouan Tribes*. Dorsey also noted, among supporting evidence, distinct aspects of the Dhegihan-Sioux language the Osage shared with neighboring tribes like the Missouri, Kansa, Quapaw (Arkansas), Ponca and Omaha.

But Dorsey is disputed by a prominent study, a 1959 Ph.D. dissertation at the University of Michigan by archaeologist Carl H. Chapman titled, *The Origin of the Osage Tribe.* "In all the mythological stories investigated . . . not one gave good evidence of having a specific historical basis that could be demonstrated with supporting evidence," Chapman wrote. He concluded the Osage basically developed where the whites found them in Missouri, northwest Arkansas, southeast Kansas, and northeast Oklahoma. "There was no certain historical evidence that permanent Osage villages were ever any place else," Chapman stated. Two scholars, A.P. Nasatir and Gilbert C. Din, agreed with Chapman in *The Imperial Osages*, a book they co-authored in 1983.

A half century before the Chapman study, historian Louis Houck published his research of Indian tribes in Missouri with his three-volume *History of Missouri.* Houck, a noted lawyer and businessman, endorsed Dorsey's investigation while detailing evidence to support the differences between historic Indians like the Osage and the prehistoric Mound Builders. A contemporary scholar and author, Willard H. Rollings, also followed the tribal migration according to Dorsey. Historians from within the tribe and close to it — notably Louis F. Burns in his comprehensive *A History of the Osage People* — have essentially supported the oral traditions of migration from the East.

Origin may remain a point of conflicting theory about the Osage, but written accounts since Marquette portray a clearer picture of these fascinating people and their domain.

The Osage wrapped their culture in myth. They believed their home was the center of the world, the land between earth and sky and thus closest to *Wah'Kon-Tah*, the universal life force. Indeed, the Osage roamed the geographic heart of North America, a continent once divided into territories belonging to different tribes. The Osage Nation was in the middle.

According to one Osage myth of creation, tribesmen awoke in heaven to find they were human, and *Wah'Kon-Tah* sent them to earth as People of the Sky, or *Tzi-Sho*. During the journey, the *Tzi-Sho* met deities like the god of rain and the Great Buffalo Bull, and on earth they found symbols of life: the beaver, snakes, turtles, birds, conch shells, corn and trees. Wandering earth, the People of the Sky met the People of the Land, *Hunkah*, and they merged as one tribe, Children of the Middle Waters, *Ni-U-Ko'n-Ska*. In another tradition, the first Osage man emerged from a shell and married a beaver, their union producing children that became the tribe. In another, a female beaver mated with a snake for the creation.

Osage religion was all-important. Nothing, however practical or tangent, was to supersede the omnipotent *Wah'Kon-Tah*. The universal life force had brought sky and earth together to make all things physical: the sun, wind, rocks and streams, the buffalo, beaver, and people. These were sacred creations of *Wah'Kon-Tah*, and the tribe was entrusted to guard these gifts on earth.

In their study of Nature, the Osage identified science with the spiritual. Mesmerized by the night's stars and planets, for example, they recognized Pleiades and Orion's Belt within the context of religion. Venus was identified as the harbinger of day, and the Osage called the galaxy "the heavenly path or celestial road." Scientifically they recognized the stages of the moon as measurements of time, but the sun, moon and stars were more important as symbols in their spiritualism.

"The ancient leaders created a worldview that called on the Osage to work in unison with *Wa-kon-da*," wrote Rollings. "In order for the people to enjoy a good life they appealed to *Wa-kon-da* to ask for understanding and support."

Like Christianity, which the Osage would spurn, their religious proverbs called for discipline, self-denial, and unwavering belief while in this world. True courage was morality; the Osage viewed those who did not stand for truth and justice as not human but despicable, cowardly beings. They recognized that regardless of their devotion, complete understanding of the universal life force was beyond mortals. They must only have faith of eternal life in the unknown: physical death. *That which the children of the earth do not comprehend as they travel the roads of the earth and which becomes clear to them only when they have passed on to the Great Mysteries is Wah'Kon-Tah.*

An Osage prayed morning, noon and evening. The tribe's democratic government, their hunts and warfare were forever meant to be conducted in utmost reverence to *Wah'Kon-Tah.* The Osage ancients believed that religion, with no consideration for unessential materials by comparison, would sustain the people's existence.

But while spiritual faith established the Osage empire among the Middle Waters, materialism, greed and deceit learned from others would ultimately help cause its division and downfall, a paradox evident in virtually any great civilization to ever suffer.

III

Osage society was constructed consistent with the religion of dual Nature brought together by *Wah'Kon-Tah.* The nation was divided into a pair of primary divisions or moieties: the *Tzi-Sho*, representing the sky and peace; and the *Hunkah*, representing earth and war.

Known as Sky People and Earth People, the two divisions came to encompass 24 different patrilineal clans during the height of Osage population, believed to be 8,000 to 10,000 people. Each clan consisted of a family structure headed by an ancestor patriarch. To ensure tribal unity, marriages could occur only between the two major moieties.

Osage government gave power of decision-making to the people. Chieftains came from royal bloodlines, but the final authority was the Council of Elders, which regulated every important matter, including hunting, warfare and trade. Skeptical young braves ridiculed the "Little Old Men," but their authority was unquestioned in the four government branches: legislative, executive, judicial and religious.

Years of disciplined education were required to serve on the council. Men had to be initiated into a secret society to study canons of tribal ethics and mythological codes, knowledge restricted to a select group. A man reached the council only when he had obtained seven degrees of study.

In the process of Osage government, tribal issues were presented to an assembly of warriors representing the kin clans. The order of meetings was patient, intellectual debate. Victor Tixier, a French medical student who lived and hunted with the Osage in 1840, wrote that "civilized" societies could learn from the tribe's art of discussion:

> The chiefs spoke in turn after taking their time for reflection; they paused as often and as long as they wished, sure that no voice would be raised before they had concluded their speech with "I have spoken" or its equivalent. They knew how to listen without showing impatience at the objections presented to them; later I realized that they took the trouble of pondering over them before answering them or presenting any themselves. I have never heard two speakers at the same time around the warriors' fire. A discussion between two men was never interrupted under any pretext by a third before he had been invited to speak. . . . The half-breeds do not know how to listen and discuss . . . their white blood is speaking.*

When Europeans arrived, the nation's domain contained two prominent areas of villages: the "Little Osages," and the "Big" or "Grand Osages." This had nothing to do with actual sizes of the people — most were large — but rather a legendary separation of the ancient tribe when it was surprised by a great flood. Later, another major group living southwest in the nation was called the Arkansas Band.

By the late 18th century, the Little Osages were occupying the "Great Bend" on the Missouri River from present-day Arrow Rock, Missouri, west to Malta Bend; the Big Osages lived on the upper Osage River in modern Bates and Vernon County, Missouri; and the Arkansas Band was based on the upper Verdigris River in northeast Oklahoma.

Osage villages were mobile, even ones as large as 1,000 inhabitants in 100 lodges and other dwellings. The people were ready to go on a moment's notice of war, winter weather, or hunting information.

Lodges were 20 feet high and as much as 100 feet long, depending on the clan, with pole frames covered by water-resistant rush mats and animal skins. In base villages such

---

*Tixier, Victor (ed.-McDermott; tr-Salvan). *Tixier's Travels on the Osage Prairies*. University of Oklahoma Press (1940).

as those on Great Bend or at the forks of the upper Osage, a lodge might have walls of logs and mud mortar in the French style. Inside, the floor was covered with bear skins, and a central hole served as the firepit. Wooden tripods served as chairs, and the walls were lined with comfortable beds of skins suspended on soft wood frames. At one end of the lodge was a platform that served as guest quarters. Hanging on the walls were cylindrical, hair-fringed "medicine bags" containing scalps.

Relocating occurred throughout the Osage year. In summer and fall, villages followed buffalo on the plains, where dwellings were wigwams resembling halved coconut shells. Wigwam construction was plant mats and skins covering a frame of flexible green poles with sharpened points stuck in the ground around a circle. The Osage used tepees only in western Kansas, where poles needed for wigwams were scarce.

The Osage returned to base locations along the Osage and Missouri rivers for spring planting and fall harvest. But agriculture maintenance was not a big priority. Seeds were drilled for corn, pumpkins and melons, and the fields were left alone until harvest.

The work of the village fell upon the women, who were tireless in their chores of drudgery. They cut wood, built shelter, farmed, and carried water. They could dismantle a village, then move and re-erect it in one day.

Osage women excelled as cooks. The tribe devoured a variety of meats, vegetables and fruit. One visiting trader ate dried buffalo and bear meat, fresh venison and turkey, sliced pumpkin and boiled sweet corn dried in the sun. Henry B. Schoolcraft, a noted traveler among Indians, enjoyed the following Osage breakfast: fried ham and eggs, bread, tea, lettuce, maple sugar, milk and salt on a table covered with muslin cloth. Tixier recalled a tasty turkey roast with wild strawberries for dessert. Fresh acorns fried in buffalo grease and doused in maple syrup were another favorite.

Despite an emphasis on hunting, agriculture was imperative to tribal subsistence, which was possibly a mark of a background in the eastern woodlands. Besides field crops the Osage gathered acorns, pecans, pawpaws, persimmons and strawberries, among many wild foodstuffs. All clans depended on agrarian goods to last through the winter.

A balanced diet produced from a highly diverse, fertile

homeland resulted in excellent overall health for the tribe. The Osage had tribal prophets and medicine men, but medicines from Europeans were accepted too, which probably helped them when epidemics devastated neighboring tribes.

Alcoholism, the white man's affliction so destructive to American Indians, was not a problem for the Osage in Missouri. American soldier and explorer Stephen Long wrote that among the Osage "drunkenness is rare and is much ridiculed; a drunken man is said to be bereft of his reason, and avoided." But in the mid-1800s, after the tribe was driven out of Missouri and onto the central plains, alcoholism plagued the people. One band was chastised for drinking by a Jesuit missionary, and chief had this response to such judgment from a white:

> Father, what thou sayest is true. We believe
> thy words. We have seen men buried because
> they loved and drank fire water. One thing aston-
> ishes us. . . . The whites who know books, who
> have understanding, and who have heard the
> commandments of the Great Spirit: why do they
> drink this fire-water? Why do they bring it to us,
> when they know God sees them?

Unlike many tribes, the Osage did not cast out the feeble, weak or unfortunate; they cared for widows, orphans, the sick, elderly and handicapped. When an Osage family suffered from a short food supply for any reason, others made up the difference from their own stores. In fact, any individual wealth was often dispersed among the tribe's needy.

The Osage calendar revolved around various hunts that began in late February or early March. First, bear and beaver were taken from highland forests and riverways, followed by a short break at home for spring planting of crops. The long anticipated hunt for buffalo came in May, when village groups roamed the plains until August. Back at home the Osage harvested their untended crops, then made one more hunt for buffalo and deer before the winter snows.

Spaniards are believed to have introduced horses to the Indians of America's interior during the 1600s. Prior to that, the Osage walked and ran the plains and forests in pursuit of game. Buffalo hunting on foot required the entire tribe, men, women and children, so a herd could be surrounded and kills made with hand weapons. Another method for foot hunting was to drive bison off cliffs.

Horses eventually became the commodity most valued by the Osage, for the animals spurred rapid progress for the nation. The Osage became top riders and prolific hunters, one of the first tribes to slaughter buffalo literally at will. Elite hunting parties could take 200 bison in one day, and the action was spectacular. When an Osage brave on his horse charged buffalo, the duo was risking all to run with the herd. Possessing archery skills since lost by humankind, an athletic brave riding full gallop could shoot an arrow completely through an adult bison, and he wanted to make the kill with only one shot.

The Osages' uses of firearms evolved to include hunting, but the danger of shooting each other during the buffalo chase was high. They preferred arrows in taking game of any kind, especially for furs since bullets and buckshot damaged skins. Osage bows were hickory, four-feet long, with strings made of twisted elk sinew. Arrows often were carried in a cougar skin quiver, the cat tail dangling, and the bow was packed in a deerskin sheath. The hunting arrow was a two-foot shaft with stone or metal point affixed by deer tendon. Turkey feathers controlled flight dynamics. War arrows were different, with spearheads designed to break off in the wound.

Famed for their appearance, Osages were strikingly handsome as an ethnic group with large, well-proportioned physiques. Heights of the men usually exceeded six feet, with some known to stand 6-7 and taller. White visitors described the Osage as attractive, robust, gigantic; "perfect models for sculptor," wrote Houck. Washington Irving was amazed on his visit with Osages: "They had fine Roman countenances, and broad deep chests; and, as they generally wore their blankets wrapped around their loins, so as to leave the bust and arms bare, they looked like so many noble bronze figures. The Osages are the finest looking Indians I have ever seen in the West."

Burns noted those physiques resulted from a scientific method: selective breeding. The largest, best-looking males and females might be attracted to each other anyway, but they were certainly encouraged to marry and mate. Survival of the tribe was the reason, the motive being to produce the most fearsome warriors on the continent. "Tallness was an advantage on the hunt and in warfare out on the Plains," wrote Burns, of Osage descent himself. "All Indians and Europeans who met them were in awe of these *giants*, who wore a tall roach on their heads to accentuate their height."

Osage clothing was the hides of deer, elk and buffalo cut to fit for comfort and necessity. Big Soldier's garb was indicative of the men's dress. The women were attired similarly with buckskin skirts, leggings, shirts and moccasins. The women also wore cloth garments, liked tattoos, and went topless in summer. Hairstyles distinguished maidens from wives. Unmarried women braided their long hair in two strands, and they liked to wear rolls on each side of the head. They also wove the strands together to hang down the back in one long braid decorated in rings, beads and bright ribbons.

Married women were simpler in fashion, gathering their long hair behind the head and tying it with leather or cloth. Osage children were usually naked until six or seven years old — even in winter — then they dressed like the adults. A child's hair was cut to symbolize his or her clan with specially arranged ridges, tufts and designs. At puberty, children began wearing adult hairstyles.

The Osage slit their earlobes with knives and pierced the strands, a source of great curiosity for the whites. Strings of beads and metal loops with beads or bone were hung from the ears, pulling the lobes down long.

White visitors, many of whom were searching for reasons to label Indians as savage, often noted Osage promiscuity and the indifferent or harsh treatment tribesmen gave their wives. The men did practice polygamy, securing rights to a woman's sisters at the time she was chosen for marriage.

Perhaps the Osage men might have wondered themselves about the judgmental European and American males — trappers, traders, soldiers and even clergymen, obviously married in the white world — who pursued the sensuous Osage females in the wilds to become Missouri.

IV

By the early 1700s, the French viewed themselves as friends of the fearsome Osage. But that was in Missouri, where the Osage in turn appreciated the French for nurturing the tribe's lucrative and growing fur trade with Europe. In Missouri, the dynastic Osage felt comfortable with the French, especially because the tribe controlled the major routes for trade west and southwest: the Mississippi and Missouri rivers; the east-west Continental Trail, which today roughly follows U.S. Highway 60 across southern Missouri; and the Arkansas River.

In no uncertain terms, the Osage were content as long as they could block French traders from other tribes to prevent commerce and hinder the distribution of firearms as well. They also sought to keep Spanish trade isolated in the Southwest. The Osage in Missouri had not achieved their status of commercial success by being foolish.

Farther south, along the Red River in present-day Louisiana, the French were seeking to expand their contacts without having to go through anyone. In 1714, a military and trading post, Fort St. Jean Baptiste, was established at a site known as Natchitoches. In due time, the French began to ask the area's Caddo Tribe to help them explore westward through the Red Valley.

But the Caddo were afraid. They told the French their arch enemy, the *Ozages*, was bound to be encountered along the Red, even so far from Great Bend in the Missouri.

In the blazing hot summer of 1719, the French decided it was time to ascend the Red from Natchitoches. The mission was to enhance relations with plains Indians whom the French already had met, and thus establish safe passage for trade with the Spanish at Sante Fe.

The poor Caddo had grown easily manipulated through their dependence on the Europeans for goods and protection, and they reluctantly sent braves on the expedition as guides. The French seemed careless of how far south the *Ozages* would come, and they were certainly ignorant of what the Caddos' dreaded enemy would think. The Osage rode high on the finest horses, easily ruling the river that would someday be the border between Oklahoma and Texas. They paraded many scalps taken from this valley, including those of the Caddo. But the newest leader from France, Sieur Benard de la Harpe, fashioned himself a world adventurer and scoffed at any concern, as if the Osage were mere ghosts in the Caddo mind. The Osage, he retorted, were probably many leagues north, and, besides, they were friends.

La Harpe's expedition would become his lesson.

The party set out with several Caddos and two African slaves, and by mid-August it got as far as the Kiamichi Mountains in southeast Oklahoma. But even the Frenchmen had become fearful. A rush of river breeze through the pines, a wisp of smoke, sent eyes darting for sight of the mighty ones. All were paranoid now, beset by a feeling the expedition was violating the sanctity of some god itself.

But when about two dozen Osage warriors did appear on horseback, they had set no ambush. They were just following the Caddo scouts fleeing in terror back to La Harpe.

The gigantic Osage approached with bow and arrows drawn, their faces painted in ominous black from forehead down to include the upper lip. The accompanying color meant only a "bluff" assault in the eyes of *Wah'Ton-Kah*, although the Caddos did not understand this.

In his journal account, La Harpe wrote: "Our savages wished to flee, but I assured them that if they took this action, they were lost, and there were some other ways to extricate them. We kept our countenance and the Osages appeared, on their part, to be getting ready to attack us."

La Harpe, truly a courageous man, approached the Osage with three other "well-armed" Frenchmen, whom the Osage acknowledged as friends of the nation. "But they were intending to scalp our guides. . ." La Harpe noted. "I said to them if they persisted in their demands, I would find myself forced to fight with them. This resolution made them change their attitude."

The Osage, however, were hardly backing down. They themselves had guns, but the bow and arrow was their weapon of choice in this standoff. The Europeans' muskets were cumbersome and impossibly slow to reload versus the lightning archery of the Osage, not to mention the latter's superiority in hand-to-hand combat. No, the Osage were merely bluffing, toying with the other side, gaining leverage for something else they wanted this day besides scalps, which easily could have been taken.

La Harpe confirmed the Osages allowed the expedition to proceed after receiving "presents" from him. But somehow the mission became dramatically altered from here forth. Although La Harpe did make contact with representatives of plains tribes, that occurred north of the Arkansas River, far from Sante Fe and the Spanish.

The message that La Harpe obviously accepted was the Osage "undoubtedly could prevent the implementation of any French scheme not to their liking," author W. David Baird wrote in 1972. "In other words, to get *to* the southern Plains Indians the French must first get *through* the Osages."

By tribal breeding and instinct, the Osage warrior bore the attitude to fight. He had been selected as a boy for inherent courage, as usually had his forefathers. And naturally, fighting was about business of the empire, its existence in the extraordinary heart of America. "Here were their hunting grounds," wrote Houck. "Over the high plateaux of the Ozarks and the deep valleys cut through these plateaux by water, they reigned as masters."

An Osage warrior was completely dedicated to protecting the hunting grounds and, on a closely related level, tribal trade. Everything that motivated the Osage, including religion, necessities, calendar, trade and war, was tied to the hunt. And when invaders or thieves pressed the tribe, the Osage turned to *Wah'Kon-Tah* for the blessing to eradicate. Before a war party attacked, the men fasted for days; "thus they disciplined themselves for disaster and supplicated the favor of heaven," wrote Houck.

Gifted athleticism made the Osage master horsemen and incredible distance runners; messengers could cover 100 miles a day on foot. In battle their physical size and strength overpowered opponents, and they killed without regard for age or sex. *Ne-shu-ha-du-sa,* the human scalp, was prized by the warriors and paraded reverently in the scalp dance. Black on their faces signaled trouble for enemies, but entire bodies painted in black meant disaster; they would take no prisoners then. "Black was the symbol of the merciless fire which consumed all in its path," wrote Burns.

Acts of extreme violence by the Osage included beheading victims or burning them alive, outcomes that often occurred on the buffalo plains west of Missouri and Arkansas. Here the Osage regularly battled the Pawnee or *Pa-I'n,* their historic enemy. Pawnee heads might be left on stakes for others to see. Four lodges of Kiowa Indians once were slaughtered, every man, woman and child, and their heads left in brass buckets to serve as a warning to stay out of Osage hunting grounds. In the 1790s, during the trade and war tensions under Spanish rule, any non-approved whites caught on the Missouri upstream from San Carlos — latter-day St. Charles — would be killed without question.

Calm never left the Osage on the warpath, and before the enemy was ever spotted, the warriors were bound together by common intent. They likened themselves to an army of black ants, attacking relentlessly and together. Osage emotion in battle was not trepidation, but resignation of what must be done. The warrior refused to let anxiety enter his thoughts; he was utterly fearless of death. The warrior had been specially chosen for this mindset on his first warpath as a teen, when he showed bravery and resolve or would have otherwise been banished to life as a man-squaw.

Some researchers relying heavily on Spanish documents have basically labeled the Osages as depraved cutthroats. But that reputation is largely undeserved, save for acts committed by renegade Osages operating along the Arkansas River. The tribal "atrocities" reported by Spain — which took control of Louisiana territory from France between 1763 and 1800 — must be viewed in the context of the mutual hatred between the Osage and Spanish. The core problem was the cavalier failure of Spain to respect Osage domain; these Europeans fashioned a hopeless mission to control a people they would not try to understand.

Osage violence and warfare sanctioned by tribal elders were calculated for purpose. Strangers approaching the tribe normally received the benefit of the doubt until motives could be determined. Before encroachment on their lands and even afterward, the Osage welcomed visitors to their villages. So eager to please were the Osage that they might argue over who would lodge and feed guests.

The Osage in Missouri were intelligent people committed to morals and self-restraint. Most tribes were capable of war over a single wrongful death, but the Osage often accepted gifts instead of revenge following treacherous raids and ambush by rivals. The basic, unprovoked Osage transgression against others involved lucrative horse theft, not wanton assaults and murder.

In the late 1700s, the Osage were approaching their peak of power in Missouri. Their location, resources and relations with fur traders had created a business empire unsurpassed by any Indians of the West. In 1775-1776, the Osage accounted for 42 percent of Indian trade in Upper Louisiana, producing 22,200 pounds of furs among 48,700 exported.

On the prairie-plains, wooded highlands and riverways, the Osage harvested skins the traders competed for. The Osage dealt horses captured or stolen, sold Indian slaves on the black market, and traded for firearms — a market they shut off from rival tribes south and west like the Caddo, Wichita and Pawnee.

With the best in guns, horses and men, the imperialistic Osage ranged west to the Rocky Mountains, southwest to the Texas plains, and south almost to the Gulf. At home they controlled the Missouri River east to a flourishing settlement, St. Louis, and policed the Mississippi south to Ste. Genevieve and the delta swamps. North of the Missouri, they hunted along the Grand and Chariton Rivers. Far from the base villages, they maintained satellite hunting camps. Famed as long riders, the Osage zealously guarded and extended their empire, and youthful renegades hunted and raided virtually anywhere they chose to go.

In 1793, Spain declared an ill-advised war on the Osage Nation that would bring bloody consequences for many. The Spanish, failing miserably in all of Louisiana, took a scapegoat in the Osage despite the tribe's commerce that buoyed funding for Spain's imperialistic quest. And so the Missouri region began an era of warfare that would last decades beyond the departure of the Spaniards.

The Osage harassed white settlers along the valleys of the Mississippi and Missouri. They attacked and killed emigrant Indians and independent traders found trespassing upon their Ozarks in Arkansas. As the Spanish invaded Osage territory like never before, the warriors reacted with urgent cause.

The Spanish recruited Osage enemies from east of the Mississippi, seeking those Indians willing to act as buffers between the Osage and white settlements — and to fight Spain's war. The fearful Spaniards also wanted allies west of the Mississippi in case of conflict with the British or the American menace growing strong just across the river.

The conflict was portrayed in an exquisite book published in 1961, *The Osages: Children of the Middle Waters*, by an Osage author, John Joseph Mathews. "In Louisiana,

The Spanish must now pamper the tribes of the Mississippi. . . ," Mathews wrote. "They were promising all the enemies of the (Osage), as well as many others of the Siouans and the Algonkians, arms and horses and pirogues, and stuff for clothing, as well as glittering trinkets for ornamentation and medals with the profile of Charles IV."*

The Osage responded predictably, mobilizing as many as 2,000 braves. One war party came from a village on the forks of the Osage River in present-day Bates County, the Place-of-the-Many Swans, which the French translated into Marais des Cygnes. According to the eloquent account by Mathews, this party and the clan leaders underwent more than a week of ceremonies to prepare for the fighting. Fasting, praying and dancing, they paid homage to Grandfather the Sun. Mathews gained much of his research for the book by recording oral legends passed to him by tribal elders during this century. Mathews wrote:

> The war party painted their horses, mostly with sacred symbols of their gentes (clans), and in this tribal war movement, all the gentes of both *Hunkah* and *Tzi-Sho* were represented.
>
> Early in the morning of the day the war movement was to begin, and just before Grandfather pushed back the darkness of night with his hand, two of the Little Old Men would have the two fires built of redbud and sing the ceremonial songs. At a gesture from them the warriors would rush to them to get their charcoal with which to paint their faces. They rushed to the fires, the embers dying now, and struggled with each other for the symbol of the living fire that overwhelms all things and gives no quarter; they thus captured the spirit of relentless fire in the charcoal which they would wear on their faces when they attacked the enemy.
>
> At high noon they set out to the west, despite the fact that their enemy lay to the east, downriver. But soon they would turn abruptly and strike the old trail down the river. This could

*Mathews, John Joseph. *The Osages: Children of the Middle Waters.* University of Oklahoma Press (1961).

not deceive *Wah'Kon-Tah*, but was a courtesy,
this pretending that the enemy were to the west,
the direction of war and death.*

For more than 100 miles they rode, following the river that "writhed like a snake." At its mouth to the Missouri, the warriors turned downstream for the settlements on the west bank of the Mississippi. Everywhere, the Osage faces in black met deserted countryside: no traders on the waters; no settlers in the cabins; no mercenary Indians on war path; and no Spanish in sight.

Choosing to not attack St. Louis — a fortified place which was also home of the Chouteaus, the tribe's comrade trader agents — the braves also bypassed the village of Carondelet. They rode from the Missouri Valley over to the Meramec, then headed south for Ste. Genevieve, always with the tribal verses of war in their minds and on their tongues, and casting eyes upward to Grandfather the Sun:

I go to learn if I shall go on,
To learn of the sun if I shall go on. . . .
Truly by the noon sun, I, as a man of mystery, go,
To make the Pa-I'n (enemy) to lie reddened on the
*   earth. . . .*
To make the Pa-I'n lie blackened on the earth. . . .
To make the earth brown with the bodies of the
*   foe. . . .*
To make the foe lie scattered on the earth. . . .
To make the bones of the foe to lie whitened on the
*   earth. . . .*
*To make the hair of the Pa-I'n to wave in the winds.**

"Thus it was in the autumn of 1793, when the west winds carried the war songs of the Great Osages," wrote Mathews.

According to Osage legend, the warriors killed a man at Ste. Genevieve only because he was a coward, and no one wanted his scalp. They also could not provoke Spain's soldiers to leave the fort at St. Louis, despite taunting and insulting them from a ridge nearby.

---

*Mathews, John Joseph. *The Osages: Children of the Middle Waters.* University of Oklahoma Press (1961).

There were skirmishes with Spain's Indians like the Miami, Pawnee and Potawatomi, and some Osage scalps were taken. But these Indians avoided the large parties of Osage giants, or fled. The historic enemy Pawnee, *Pa-I'n*, had long known that terrorist tactics, not direct confrontations with major parties, were the only way to thrive in fighting Osages.

The mercenary tribes' reluctance to fight except when encountering isolated Osages meant certain consequences that haunted Spanish relations with settlers. Potawatomi braves, for example, would leave villages in Illinois with great tribal ceremonies for war upon the Osage. They crossed the Mississippi at Portage Des Sioux above the Missouri mouth, but if Osages were missed or avoided, Potawatomi pride would not allow a return home without scalps. Thus their victims became white, dark-haired settlers on both sides of the river, and Spanish officials endured local outrage over such random murders.

The Shawnee and Delaware Indians also accepted Spain's offer to ally against the Osage. These two historic tribes already had members settled in the Tywappity bottoms in southeast Missouri, across from the mouth of the Ohio. The Shawnee and Delaware enjoyed an amiable relationship with Spanish government and white settlers. Louisiana Governor Baron de Carondelet officially blessed their re-settlement, authorizing French Canadian Don Louis Lorimier to establish permanent tribal villages in southeast Missouri. In the same year, Lorimier organized a river trading post, Girardot, into a settlement named Cape Girardeau. On behalf of the Spanish, Lorimier traveled up the Ohio to court more Shawnee and Delaware to immigrate.

The Osage reacted to developments in this area, although not exactly with "blackened earth" rage. They valued southeast Missouri as a hunting outpost, especially the Mingo Swamp area. Here the Mississippi Valley hills and lowlands were thick in game, especially bear, beaver and deer. But the region was also a continental crossroads that attracted a host of intruders. The Continental or Natchitoches Trail crossed the Mississippi in southeast Missouri, and the deep swamps were a haven to outcasts from both Indian and white societies. The area had always caused problems for the Osage.

More Shawnee and Delaware followed Lorimier into southeast Missouri, prompting terror tactics from the Osage, but few Indians and whites were killed. The Osage came to respect the battle intensity of the short-legged but fearless Delaware in particular, and they compromised, backing off to stay west of the St. Francois River. The Osage had larger concerns looming elsewhere, the most formidable foes the dynasty had ever known.

Thanks to Spanish recruitment, the vicious Saukee-Fox were raiding Osage lands in the north along the Missouri and other valleys — and slaughtering white settlers in the process.

Cherokee Indians, meanwhile, were escaping white encroachment upon their homelands in Georgia and the Carolinas, and they were taking special liking to "new land" west that reminded them of the Appalachian region — the Osage Ozarks of Arkansas.

Behind them, the Americans were coming.

V

The Spanish left Missouri in 1800 with their original mission of controlling the native people in tatters. For the few years leading to the Louisiana Purchase, the French tried to restore peace and order.

Missouri, however, was so different now than in pre-1770, when earnest French diplomacy influenced relative harmony among the Osage, traders, settlers, and other Indians. The change was irrevocable, for the Spaniards had opened the territory's door to killers who marauded at will. The western Potawatomies, under their raging leader Main Poc, committed wanton scalpings of whites such as a woman and her four children at St. Ferdinand. But the Potawatomi tribe was crumbling, splintered into numerous factions ranging from militant to peaceful, and it posed no real threat to the Osage.

The powerful Saukee-Fox, led by Black Hawk, were a different concern entirely. Black Hawk was a cunning warrior filled with hatred for the French, the Americans — and the Osage. And he envisioned Missouri and the plains west as home, a promised land for his nomadic tribe.

A century previous, the Saukee and Fox had actually been foes of one another in battle. Black Hawk was of Saukee blood, or Sac, and his autobiography states the original people were on the St. Lawrence River near Montreal, where the French found them. But the Iroquois drove the Saukee out and pursued them to Wisconsin, where in the late 1600s they formed a friendship with the Fox in a common village at Green Bay. The Fox had also been conquered by the Iroquois and driven from the St. Lawrence Valley.

Thus began the Saukee-Fox alliance, a force that would terrorize foes from the Great Lakes southwest to Missouri and the plains. Jesuit priests reported the Saukee were prone to kill any man they found alone, especially French, while the Fox were "a proud and arrogant people." Despite a large population, the Saukee-Fox liked to roam without maintaining permanent villages. They hunted buffalo across northern Illinois, eastern Iowa, and northern Missouri, dominating the latter regions. They shrewdly maintained connections with British traders in Canada, which served them greatly after the Americans purchased Louisiana and attempted to control all trade involving Indians.

The Saukee-Fox were warlike, experts with firearms, and masters of deceit. Their courage and physical strength were respected less than their strategy, such as attacking river villages at night by canoes. In battle, one band would paint their entire bodies white with pipe clay; the other band would paint themselves black.

The Saukee-Fox attitude toward outsiders of any race ranged from rude to ruthless. "Their names are linked inseparably from the earliest times to the present day," Zebulon Pike recorded. "Each has always been to the other what neither of them has ever been to any other Indians, or to any whites — friend." French anger for the Saukee-Fox was so intense that in the early 1700s three expeditions from Montreal chased the tribe as far as Missouri.

By the turn of the 19th century, the Saukee-Fox were rampaging through northern Missouri, terrorizing settlers and warring with other Indians. They routed the Missouri tribe, killing 200 in one battle, an exorbitant death toll, and rushed to the north shore of the Great Bend on the Missouri River. Across the water, the Little Osages nervously prepared for war, but the fight was one-sided against a Saukee-Fox force as strong as 1,000 warriors. Soon the Osage fled their ancient grounds, never to live again on the Missouri and Grand Rivers.

Black Hawk's personal badge of pride was his claim of

going on the war path at age 15 to kill his first foe, an Osage, probably around 1780 in present-day St. Charles or Lincoln County, Missouri:

> A leading chief of the (Mascouten) nation came to our village for recruits to go to war against the Osages, our common enemy. I volunteered to go, as my father had joined him; and was proud to have an opportunity to prove to him that I was not an unworthy son, and that I had courage and bravery. It was not long before we met the enemy, when a battle ensued. Standing by my father's side, I saw him kill his antagonist, and tear the scalp from his head. Fired with valor and ambition, I rushed furiously upon another, smote him to the earth with my tomahawk — run my lance through his body — took off his scalp, and returned in triumph to my father! He said nothing, but looked pleased. . . .

When the United States purchased Louisiana, the Saukee-Fox had undisputed possession of northern Missouri from the Grand east to the Mississippi. And they did not hesitate to begin attacking Osage villages to the south.

Osage legend recalls it rained on the final day of May in 1804, at the mouth of the Osage River. A Frenchman floated downstream to the Missouri, hauling Osage furs from the Place-of-the-Many-Swans. But he also bore a written message from the Chouteaus for delivery to Osages there, a piece of paper that inflamed their souls like fire. The tribe's friends, the French or "Heavy Eyebrows," were leaving. This land was now "owned" by the "Long Knives" or "Hairy Ones," the Americans and their nation, the United States.

Stunned, Osages gathered around a fire crackling under a canopy of great oaks allowing only drips of rainfall. Two leaders dominated the discussion, Makes-Tracks-Far-Away and Arrow-Going-Home. The former stood up, enraged, and threw the paper into the flames. Instantly the black ashes fluttered up atop the heat and were snatched away by the breeze, carried west. Makes-Tracks-Far-Away wanted this to be a sign; his heart was desperate to believe the Long Knives would never come, and the French would really stay.

The next morning, June 1, daylight came and the rain was gone. But heavy, gray-tinged clouds moving overhead revealed scant patches of blue. A party of strangers appeared from the east, coming upstream along the south side of the Missouri with a keelboat, canoes, and pack horses led along a riverside path. Captain Meriwether Lewis and Lieutenant William Clark camped their men at the mouth of the Osage, where they remained for two days. The Lewis and Clark Expedition was headed west on behalf of the Americans.

The Osage population of the time was upwards of 8,000 people, with thousands of warriors and many more women and boys capable of fighting. Their business trade remained lucrative, their domain vast. The U.S. President respected their stature. "The truth is," observed Jefferson, "they are the great nation South of the Missouri, their possession extending from thence to the Red River."

But success had wrought the ominous by-products: internal dissension, disrespect for *Wah'Kon-Tah*, erosion of values. The imperialistic Osage, while numerous, were scattered over great distances and communication was difficult. Factions emerged within bands or with new ones, and young upstarts strove to usurp authority from the tribal elders. The influence of wealth, prestige, and selfish ambition was helping dismantle Osage society.

To the chagrin of chiefs in the north, Arkansas had a certain appeal of climate and freedom that drew tribesmen south. Osage renegades flocked to the area. The Americans were as concerned as tribal elders, given reports such as those from Pike, the explorer and soldier. "The village on the Arkansas serves as a place of refuge for all the young, daring, and discontented with ammunition," he wrote. "They are at liberty to make war without restraint."

The Arkansas Band was led by ambitious young warriors tired and impatient with old doctrines. Contact with Europeans had already flushed traditions from the tribe: braves ignored the bow and arrow in favor of guns and trapped the sacred beaver for skins; squaws traded for blankets and cloth rather than practice the tedious manufacture of buffalo robes; and sustenance from the land was being replaced by dependence on materialistic trade.

But the immediate threats to Osage stability were external. Jefferson's evolving Indian relocation policy — to put all non-conforming Indians west of the Mississippi — was driving waves of tribes into Osage territory. Besides the heavily armed Saukee-Fox and Potawatomi, Miami and Ottawa raided from the north and east. In the south, the Cherokee, Choctaw, Chickasaw, Kickapoo, Delaware and Shawnee continued to push boldly onto Osage lands.

The U.S. Government was effectively setting up tribes to perform genocide on one another, and American immigrants were invading too, coming farther and farther up the river valleys of the Missouri, Gasconade, Osage, Arkansas and Red. The Americans girdled trees or chopped them down, and laid down their geometric farm fields, creating musket-shot ranges around their cabins and villages. Many were prone to shoot, on-sight, any Indians that approached, youth or adult. A prevailing white attitude viewed Indians as vermin to exterminate.

The Little Osages and Big Osages grudgingly avoided the Mississippi Valley, and withdrew west along their namesake river while trying to hold onto their Ozarks.

VI

In October of 1805, Osage chieftains met with representatives from several enemy tribes in St. Louis for a "peace conference" arranged by the Americans. Already the Osage were labeled "bad Indians" by America for refusing to share their domain with any tribes being driven west; the meeting was primarily to tighten control on them. A treaty agreement was signed among those present, but notably absent was Main Poc, the vengeful Potawatomi leader. His absence forewarned tragedy two months later, when Main Poc led his braves across the Mississippi at Portage Des Sioux and into Missouri.

The renegades found an easy target in an Osage River camp south of the Missouri Valley. Osage warriors were gone on the winter hunt, leaving more than 100 women and children undefended. Main Poc's party swooped in at mid-morning, killing and scalping 34 women and children, and hauling away twice as many prisoners. Safely back in Illinois, Main Poc delivered most of the captives to the Saukee-Fox. The same sort of depravation had occurred in the spring of 1799 under Spanish rule, when Kickapoo Indians discovered an Osage hunting camp was highly vulnerable with most of the braves away. The Kickapoos charged in to kill 46 people, mostly women and children.

Now Osage chiefs and braves went to St. Louis, but with faces smeared in the mud of mourning, not the black charcoal of war. They had no choice but to avoid retaliation. Now cut off from French, Canadian and British traders, the Osage faced trade sanctions by the Jefferson Administration for any attacks, however justified. "In obedience to the injunctions of their great father, they forebode to revenge the blow!" Pike declared.

Instead, the Osage pleaded their plight before Louisiana Governor James Wilkinson, and the Americans began negotiations with the raiders. Later, 46 of the captives were returned to the Place-of-the-Many-Swans for an emotional reunion with loved ones. Main Poc held the rest of the prisoners before finally releasing them in 1807.

But the campaign to force Osage submission to U.S. demands was only beginning, and the Cherokee were proving particularly adept at carrying out the mission. Cherokee invaders committed some of the worst atrocities ever recorded against the Osage, including a notorious massacre of women, children, and elderly.

In the 1770s Osage scouts began spotting Chickasaw along the Arkansas and Red Rivers. The Osage attacked, but the rugged Chickasaw were hardly intimidated. Armed by British and American traders, and with villages east of the Mississippi safe from Osage retaliation, the confident Chickasaws continued crossing over to hunt. They traveled in large groups that wiped out small parties of Osage they found moving or encamped.

But a powerful Osage nemesis followed the Chickasaw: Cherokee were sighted along the lower Arkansas in 1786. Cherokee lands in the mountains of Georgia and the Carolinas were being overrun by whites and depleted of game, and they sought a new home on the frontier. The Osage Ozarks seemed like a familiar paradise for the Cherokee, which may well be fact, according to modern geologists. Recent findings suggest the Arkansas mountains are actually a western loop of the Appalachians cut off hundreds of millions of years ago by the Mississippi Delta drainage.

Ten Cherokee families moved to the Saint Francois River region in 1796, and the Osage responded. When parties of the tribes met, results were deadly. But following their fights in the 1800s, the Osage had to accept gifts "to cover the dead" and appease the Americans. The Cherokee, meanwhile, were unwavering on avenging their fallen with more blood, and relatively free to do so.

Cherokee population in the region boomed, infuriating the Osage, and conflict between these tribes escalated into the perpetual cycle of revenge. Their undeclared war of hate would last decades, and the Americans were behind it all without firing a shot.

The Jefferson Administration exerted pressure on the Osage in various ways, urging the nation to give up territory either north or south to create space for eastern tribes. That request ignored, the Americans covertly set up trade embargoes that shut off or stymied Osage business. Critical players in the tactic were the Chouteaus, the founding family of Saint Louis, according to research by author Willard H. Rollings in *The Osage: An Ethnohistorical Study of Hegemony on the Prairie-Plains*.

Pierre Chouteau and his sons, Auguste Pierre and Paul Liguest, were Osage Indian agents for the United States and supposed friends of the tribe. But the Chouteaus worked backroom influence to close fur trading with Indians along the lower Arkansas, St. Francois and White rivers.

"By depriving (the Arkansas Osage) of the necessities and comforts which commerce brings them, they will be forced to return (north)," Pierre Chouteau wrote to Wilkinson in July 1805. The Chouteaus wanted all Osage back in central Missouri to enhance their lucrative business in St. Louis. To help accomplish the agenda, the Chouteaus manipulated cronies within the tribe.

The Arkansas Osage, meanwhile, were defiant. Led by a dynamic chief, Clermont II, and Cashesegra, they refused to return north despite the trade ban. Instead, they vowed to cultivate more crops and hunt more game for food. And they would continue to fight enemies in the region, if needed.

"We want no war," Cashesegra said in 1806. "The Chickasaws, Choctaws, Cherokees, Delawares and Arkansas (Quapaws) are all at war with us. We don't want to be at war with them. We want to hunt and kill our game in peace."

With Louisiana Territory open for American settlement, non-Indians poured through Osage land, killing game and sometimes stealing horses. Osages countered by harassing outsiders, stealing horses and livestock, robbing and killing.

The Osage suffered the same abuses in turn, but were usually judged the aggressors by American authorities.

In the spring of 1808, new Louisiana Governor Meriwether Lewis halted all business with the tribe and ordered traders and non-Osage hunters back to St. Louis. Tension was high as traders left the villages with badly needed guns, powder, ammunition and hunting supplies. A chief loyal to the Chouteaus, Pawhuska, led followers in escorting traders back to safety, and Lewis urged other tribes to attack any Osage not with Pawhuska. The governor sent troops and mounted dragoons to patrol Osage domain.

There was a prime motive to pressure the Osage that particular year. In late summer, Pawhuska's band had signed a treaty with the Americans. Supposedly a boundary was to be established between the Osage and United States, but when Captain William Clark drew up the line, the tribe had given up all land east of the Osage River villages, more than 50,000 square miles.

The Osage Nation was outraged since most of its leaders had not negotiated in the treaty. Their objection was based on tribal law mandating that consensus of the people must be reached in major decisions. Pawhuska and a few minor chiefs hardly qualified, but the Osage argument was over-ruled, if not ignored. Tribal leaders ultimately signed the treaty, including the besieged Arkansas Band, whose imminent survival depended on arms from the Americans.

The 1808 treaty created Fort Osage near present day Sibley, and the Americans touted the structure as a haven for northern Osages. But Fort Osage only attracted enemies; the Saukee-Fox and Iowas, among others, repeatedly attacked there, killing and looting without consequence from the United States. Instead of protecting the Osage, the Americans left them open to assaults. Within three years, by 1811, Big and Little Osages abandoned the fort.

Osage loyalty to America in the War of 1812 was unrewarded, tested, and insulted. The Saukee-Fox and other northern tribes sided with the British, yet the United States settled a group of moderate Saukee on the Missouri River near the mouth of the Osage. The Osages loathed living so close to a bitter enemy, but could do nothing.

The war's end in victory for the United States solidified American control over the country, and every Indian tribe was doomed. "After the war, Native Americans had to deal with the government strictly on American terms," wrote Rollings.

Pressure tightened on the Osage as the population dwindled dramatically because of fighting, invasions, and depleted game. British and Canadian traders were banished from the country for good, and Missouri swelled with tribes migrating from the East. The Cherokee, in particular, kept massing, reaching a watershed point for the Osage in 1817: for the first time, the Cherokee matched the Osage in population inside the territory, each tribe with about 6,000.

Still more enemies of the Osage were strong, growing, and aggressive. An estimated 1,200 Shawnee, 600 Delaware, 2,000 Piankashaw, 60 Peoria, plus thousands more Indians like Kickapoos were now hunting on Osage land. The Osage were friendly to none, save for what remained of the Missouri Indians, a Dhegiha-Sioux tribe the nation adopted.

Life for the Arkansas Osage was isolated and hostile. They lived at war. On the hunt and in their villages, the band contended with Chickasaw, Choctaw and Quapaw raiders. Compounding difficulties, the United States was adamant they return north to consolidate the Osage Nation. But the Arkansas Band's biggest problem was the Cherokee. Because of a critical cession in 1816 known as Lovely's Purchase, they were confronted directly by Cherokee power.

William Lovely, American agent for the Cherokee, called a meeting supposedly to talk peace with the Osage. But when Lovely and Cherokee leaders reached the meeting site, agent Pierre Chouteau was an intriguing no-show for the Osage. The results were disastrous.

Somehow, the Osage gave away three million acres of prime buffalo prairies, which Lovely — and Washington — wanted for the Cherokee. Clermont II protested, insisting he consented only to a parcel of land to be granted, and that was for whites, certainly not the hated Cherokee.

For two years, the federal government delayed approving Lovely's Purchase, but Cherokees poured into the region and assumed possession of lands they would fight for. In 1817, Cherokee leaders planned a major offensive against the Osage Nation, and the build-up in arms and manpower began. War parties arrived regularly from the East, and for months the Cherokee waited to strike. In October, the Osage men were on the plains, hunting buffalo. Osage villages through the Arkansas and Verdigris Valleys — women, children, the elderly and sick — stood naked to attack. Thus came the incident to be known as the Massacre of Claremore Mound, a few miles northeast of present-day Tulsa.

American officials had marked the Osage villages of northeast Oklahoma as barriers to the contested plains. A Cherokee force of 500 led a mass of warrior-accomplices like Chickasaws, Choctaws, and "several whites." Riding unchecked through the Arkansas Valley into Oklahoma, the party swung north along the Verdigris and stopped just short of Claremore village. Every Osage warrior was gone.

A messenger entered the village to request leaders meet with about a dozen Cherokee nearby. An elderly Osage man was the only one who could answer the call, and he went out to meet the visitors. The Cherokee then understood no opposition existed in the village, and the old man was brutally decapitated. The huge force rode in and destroyed everything in sight, slaughtering 38 women, children, and elders. More than 100 were taken prisoner. Everything of value that could be carried was stolen, and the rest was torched, including food stores for winter. The Cherokee returned downstream to their villages for celebrations featuring scalp dances. Americans lauded this great "victory" over the terrible Osage and watched as the captives were sent to Cherokee villages in the East as payment for providing braves.

This infamous Cherokee depravation on the Osage was fully in compliance with Washington's plan for the frontier. Not only was the massacre condoned, but, incredibly, it favored the Cherokee in the Lovely dispute. The Cherokee were recognized as victors, and they claimed right to the contested Osage land. Secretary of War John C. Calhoun instructed Governor Clark in a communique: "You will, as far as practicable, and consistent with justice, make the arrangements favorable to the Cherokee," Calhoun mandated. "The President (James Monroe) is anxious to hold out every inducement to the Cherokees, and the other Southern nations of Indians, to emigrate to the West of the Mississippi."

Osage leaders were summoned to St. Louis, where the 1818 Treaty approved the Lovely Purchase. The Osage lost their land to the Cherokee, who then reneged on a promise to return the 100 prisoners. Clermont II refused to participate in the signing, continuing to protest, and he called for Osage retaliation against the Cherokee despite the Americans. Fort Smith was erected on the south bank of the Arkansas River to separate the two tribes, but Osage vengeance would not be satisfied for decades.

Thomas Nuttall visited both rivals in 1819, and chronicled explosive tension. "It appeared, from what I could learn," wrote Nuttall, "that the Osages, purposely deceived . . . at the instigation of the (Chouteaus), had hatched up a treaty without the actual authority of the chiefs, so that in the present state of things a war betwixt the Cherokees and the Osages is almost inevitable."

Nuttall observed the Osage were completely surrounded by enemies. This great nation appeared to be at the threshold of war that likely would mean annihilation.

The Americans now cared little about either the Cherokee or Osage, since their agenda had been met with the Lovely Purchase. Plans were already under way in Washington for removal of the entire Cherokee Nation to Indian Territory, which later resulted in the horrible, forced march from the Appalachians to Oklahoma — the Trail of Tears.

The Osage-Cherokee conflict continued into 1820, and Clermont II's son, Skitok, joined the fray with gusto. Known as "Mad Buffalo," he robbed and killed three Cherokee hunters on the Poteau River south of the Arkansas. Cherokees screamed of injustice, demanding Skitok be turned over, but they continued to overlook the Claremore massacre and keep prisoners. The Osage refused to surrender Skitok until an exchange for the captives was made.

Talk of all-out war was prevalent, and at one point the Osage received word the Cherokee had declared it. Both sides postured, at times mobilizing hundreds of warriors, but there were no major casualties again until the fall of 1821, when 250 Cherokees followed the Osage onto the prairies. The Cherokee were accompanied by some Delaware, Creek, Choctaw, Shawnee and whites, according to Rollings.

Since the massacre four years before, all Osages traveled on hunts. But they separated into groups on the plains and, once again, the Cherokee found a camp of Osage elderly, women and children. After wiping out a dozen guards, Cherokee raiders killed 29 women and children, and they took 90 prisoners and a large cache of meat. This time

Osage warriors managed to cut off some of the enemy and drive them off the plains, but there apparently was a price for that — back in the Cherokee camp, an Osage woman and two children were murdered and fed to hogs.

The United States arranged peace talks at Fort Smith. The two Indian powers agreed to halt hostilities, and the Cherokee pledged to return to the fort in a month with Osage prisoners. But when the Osage made their return trip to the fort, they were attacked by a Choctaw party riding from the Red River. Then the Cherokee disappointed the Osage by having few prisoners to give back. Incredibly, the peace held as the southern Osage stayed patiently with diplomacy.

The tribe, however, was weak from fragmentation. Osage leadership was broken down, splintered, miles apart in every way. The northern bands still wanted to fight, even though diplomacy with the Cherokee was the only solution. The Osage obviously could not defeat this foe by force.

Hunters continued to invade Osage land. Missouri, the principal domain of the Osage, was granted statehood in 1821. Areas of the new state along the Mississippi and Missouri rivers were crowded with Americans. Many were now pushing into the Ozarks, and other Indians kept coming from the East. The Osage clung to the precious few valleys they still had, but intruders kept appearing.

More clashes were inevitable. In November 1822, a Big Osage party found Cherokees hunting in the North Canadian Valley west of Fort Smith. A prominent young Cherokee, Red Hawk, was killed, infuriating his chieftain uncle, Thomas Graves, who had led the 1821 massacre of Osages. Graves demanded blood revenge for Red Hawk.

The Osage had other concerns, however, and continued their assaults on trespassing hunters that resulted in the deaths of whites. Trouble once again revolved around young Skitok, who led an attack on nine whites and 12 mixed-blood Quapaws in the Blue Valley. Skins and dozens of horses were stolen and four whites were killed, including an army officer.

The raid again raised the ire of the Americans. Officials at Fort Smith demanded Skitok. Clermont II faced grave decisions, caught between his people, his family, and the United States. He returned many of the stolen skins and 21 horses, but he would not give up his son.

The political standoff dragged on, and the United States

determined Fort Smith was too far from the Osage for proper intimidation and control. Five companies of soldiers under Major Matthew Arbuckle moved farther up the Arkansas River and erected a new military post at the mouth of the Neosho, later named Fort Gibson.

On June 7, 1824, a massive display of 4,000 Osage approached the fort and camped four miles away. Soldiers cowered behind the stockade walls. The Osage knew they could crush Arbuckle and his men in any battle, but the war was already over. The Americans were truly unstoppable. The next morning, Clermont II, accompanied by 400 warriors, made a solemn ride to Fort Gibson. Skitok and five other young warriors were surrendered.

The Americans seemed to be appeased. They were not quick to levy harsh sentences on the prisoners, and a meeting was called with Osage leaders. Political committees were appointed with delegates from both nations, and the Saint Louis Treaty was agreed on in 1825.

But the Americans dictated the terms. Osage control of their land was over. They were instructed to completely remove themselves from Missouri, the land between Sky and Earth, and go to a reservation in Kansas.

For more than a decade, Clermont II stubbornly refused to abandon Osage villages on the Verdigris in Oklahoma. He did not want to go to the reservation, per orders of the Americans. Skitok remained in prison for a time, then was released.

Thousands of Osage lives likely were spared, but these survivors felt spiritual death at the hands of the Americans. Their freedom as Children of the Middle Waters had vanished with the Saint Louis Treaty.

VII

In 1840 a medical student in Paris, Victor Tixier, made a journey to America; accompanying him was James Trudeau, a school friend who had suggested the trip. Their destination in America was a classic among the French — the Mississippi River Valley.

Trudeau, 22, was born in America, and had already traveled along the Mississippi. His grandfather, Zenon Trudeau, was a commandant of St. Louis under Spanish rule, and the family retained friends throughout the valley.

With his experience and connections on the storied river, Trudeau knew adventure lay ahead for the young travelers.

Tixier, 24, left France for a diversion from lingering illness as much as excitement. A talented young man who loved art, Tixier wrote a journal and sketched pictures while traveling. He was not impressed by the nine-week voyage across the Atlantic and into the Gulf of Mexico, but the sights of America inspired him. Beginning with a dawn entrance to the mouth of the Mississippi, Tixier recorded vivid descriptions of the river in the mid-19th century. Captivated by the wild world about, Tixier extended his tour of America from a planned three months to nine. And he would contribute to history.

As Tixier moved into the interior, he worked harder at writing, resulting in a book published first in France and later in America: *Tixier's Travels On the Osage Prairies*. And despite containing the century's ignorant view of American Indians as "savages," Tixier's journal will endure as an important, revealing account of the Osage lifestyle in frontier America.*

From New Orleans, Tixier and Trudeau figured to take steamboats up the Mississippi to the Illinois, enter the Great Lakes at Chicago, then go down to New York on the Hudson. But along the way they hoped to meet Indians. And on board the steamer *General Pratte*, Tixier met a passenger who changed their direction: Major Paul Liguest Chouteau, son of Pierre Chouteau, the former Osage agent.

"The Major is one of those men whose faces show natural kindness," wrote Tixier. "For a long time he lived the life of the Osage on the prairie. . . . The Major persuaded us to visit the nation with whom he had lived; he promised to recommend us to the chiefs."

When Chouteau mentioned the possibility of the Frenchmen hunting buffalo with the Osage, "I accepted the Major's suggestion immediately," wrote Tixier. "It allowed me to realize my greatest desire. I was going to live among the redskins in the manner of the redskins!"*

The trip up the Mississippi was eventful. Approaching Natchez in May of 1840, the *General Pratte* survived one of

---

*Tixier, Victor (ed.-McDermott; tr-Salvan). *Tixier's Travels on the Osage Prairies.* University of Oklahoma Press (1940).

the worst tornadoes in recorded history. The huge storm's swath actually enveloped the river shore-to-shore, rushing northeast to Natchez to level the town and kill at least 317. Boats taking direct hits were destroyed, and many others were swamped and sunk. Tixier was witnessing nature's awful power in the American Midwest, the "Tornado Alley" of the world. He recorded damage to one large steamer, and the sinking of another.*

A few days later, below Cairo, Illinois, the captain of the *General Pratte* challenged the *Ohio Belle* to a steamboat race. Tixier estimated the Mississippi's downstream current to be 5 mph in bringing the flow's tremendous resistance, yet the steamers fired their engines to reach an upstream speed of 12 mph. The passengers were excited, but cognizant of the danger. Tixier wrote:

> These races between ships are the most frequent causes of those terrible accidents which happen on the rivers of America. The Americans have little regard for human life, and they always go ahead without worrying whether their boats may blow up. The *Ohio Belle* was obviously gaining on us. Our Captain was urging the stokers and shouted 'Fire up!' while striking the funnels. However, we soon saw the mouth of the Ohio and docked in front of Cairo, a great city to be. Our honor was saved; we had arrived before our rival, which continued toward Louisville without stopping.*

During the 19th century, Cairo received mixed reviews from visitors, the majority being negative. Tixier obviously bucked the trend. "The planning of Cairo is gigantic," he wrote. "Admirably situated, this city will receive the products from the north and the west by way of the Mississippi; and those from the east by the Ohio River."

Above Cairo, the steamer ran aground in shallow water, but to everyone's relief it was freed quickly. "The ladies had been very much afraid, and not without reason," Tixier observed, "for the boiler often blows up in such circumstances." Beyond Cape Girardeau, Tixier noticed the bottomlands in Missouri had narrowed with steeper ridges and "rounded" hills. The cliffs, he stated, had spawned a regional industry in gunshot factories.

The *General Pratte* arrived in St. Louis on May 12, and Tixier realized how French influence had faded in the great valley. An old house was "shielded on one side by a wall with loopholes, which protected it 25 years ago from the attacks of the Osage," Tixier wrote. "At that time people went to New Orleans on sailboats. It was a six months trip that one never undertook without writing his will." With the advent of steamers, he noted, the trip of 1,221 miles had been cut to five or six days.*

Tixier also found the Osage Indians — whose fame was still lingering in Paris because of yesteryear visits by tribal figures — had been driven out of Missouri. The old Indian removal policy had been made into federal law, the Indian Removal Act of 1830. Tixier met an Osage in St. Louis, an aging, well-known chieftain named Big Soldier.

Decades before, Big Soldier had addressed the President of the United States; then, while touring with five other Osage leaders in France, General Lafayette had presented him a medal. Now elderly but still statuesque, Big Soldier sat on a breezy veranda beside the Mississippi, smoking a penny calumet and telling stories through a young interpreter, Edward Chouteau. Big Soldier still held affinity for Paris, and Tixier was charmed, writing, "He had been astonished by what he had seen in our country, and remembered with particular pleasure that he had married three times there. . ."

Big Soldier told Tixier "that our visit would greatly please the Osage, who were very devoted to our compatriots, and that all the warriors in the nation would. . . receive us in their lodges during the hunting season."*

On May 15, Tixier and his friends — which apparently included Alexander Gu'erin of Bordeaux and an unknown he called "Foureau" — loaded weapons and harness in a trunk and boarded the *Mail,* a steamer westbound up the Missouri. Three days later they arrived at Lexington, 311 miles upriver from St. Louis, took a room, and sat down to a dinner that gained an average review from Tixier: roast salt pork, "poorly baked dough which doubtless are called 'biscuits,'" cornbread, water, and plenty of tea.

---

*Tixier, Victor (ed.-McDermott; tr-Salvan). *Tixier's Travels on the Osage Prairies.* University of Oklahoma Press (1940).

Next morning at dawn, the party started a bumpy wagon ride to Independence. For lunch on the trail they shot plentiful game that included doves, rabbits, quail and prairie hens. The Chouteaus had provided the travelers with letters of introduction to area farmers and the Osage, and their first contact was a family 12 miles from Independence.

"Like all the western settlers, our host came from the eastern states," Tixier stated. "He was born in Ohio, which he had left 12 years before. He invited us to spend a few days on his farm to hunt deer and wild turkeys. It was a tempting offer, but the Osage were soon going to leave for bison hunting, and we departed very early."*

At a hotel in Independence, the innkeeper was skeptical of the Frenchmen's motive for traveling. "It was impossible for me to make him realize that we just wanted to visit the Osage to complete our education and for the pleasure of it," Tixier recorded. "He was sure that we were hiding our real purposes. In this country where everybody is speculating, people see speculation everywhere."*

The party found obtaining horses was difficult, since the traders of the Sante Fe Trail had left. Finally they found and bought five "good" horses in Independence, and one pony from the Shawnee Indians. The Frenchmen headed for the prairie on May 20. Soon they were in southeast Kansas, living among the Osage and hunting buffalo.

Tall prairie grasses stretched to the horizon, undulating gently in the June breezes. In a wide, dry creekbed, 30 elite braves, the pride of the Osage Nation, mounted bareback on 30 hunting horses. The skills of both men and horses were elite, earning them the supreme rank of buffalo killers.

The snorting steeds were charged, pawing intently; those of reputation wore eagle feathers on forehead and tail, honor badges from past hunts. The braves' bare chests were painted in colorful hunting scenes; bows and bobcat skin quivers with arrows were draped around their shoulders. Each wore a large knife sheathed in his girdle. Squaws stood in the creekbed with pack horses, ready to retrieve the meat. At the rear of the hunting line, hundreds of people were making camp along a small river, anticipating the feast.

On the prairie 800 yards distant, under bright sunshine, the enormous buffalo herd was a black band above shimmering grasstops. The braves on their horses burst from the cover of the creekbed, and bison on the fringe of the herd broke and ran. The Osage riders whooped as their horses broke into full gallop.

On a low hill, young Tixier watched the drama unfold.

The fleeing buffaloes sent a dust cloud rising fast over the plain. The animals had amazing speed, despite their thick bodies and short legs, but the horses closed in quickly to cruise dangerously with the herd.

The intense riders drove the horses on into the rumbling, dusty fury of stampede, adrenaline fueling the senses of men and animals. Braves and their horses sorted the quarry, ignoring calves and bulls. Fat cows were preferred, and the hunters quickly focused on specific targets and gave chase.

"The race is a merciless one. . ." Tixier described. "But it is often only after a long race that the hunter is close enough to his victim to kill it."*

One buffalo was desperate to get off the plain, where its pursuers gained swiftly, and jumped into a ravine. But the warriors were relentless, whipping their horses into making daring leaps down into the depression. The bison was overtaken in loose rock, and before it could turn with tail upraised and charge in defense, a brave shot a pistol bullet in its neck while another aimed bow and arrow. Tixier wrote:

> The hour of death has come. An arrow shot by
> a skillful hand penetrates the bull's chest behind
> the last rib, sinks completely into its body and
> often pierces the skin on the other side. If the
> arrow has not completely disappeared into its
> chest, the savage drives it in with his foot. Rarely
> is a second arrow needed. An arrow kills more
> efficiently than a bullet.*

The herd moved into the distance, away from the killing field, and resumed grazing. The earth thunder ceased, the turf smelled freshly turned, and dust hung suspended in a slowly thinning haze. Hunters were scattered about the plain where fallen bison lay, coughing up blood, fatally wounded. At an animal's death, a brave dismounted and

---

*Tixier, Victor (ed.-McDermott; tr-Salvan). *Tixier's Travels on the Osage Prairies*. University of Oklahoma Press (1940).

rolled the carcass over. He tied his horse to a bison horn and withdrew the knife. Tixier described the butchering process in the field:

> He first cuts off the tail and the tongue, which belong by right to the one who has killed the beast. The tail is the trophy of the conqueror. The skin is split under the belly by a long cut; the hunter drinks the milk, if the beast is a cow, then cuts off the udders and skin. The Osage then choose their meat. At first, casting aside the shoulders and the legs, they lift in one piece the flat muscles of the chest and the stomach, break the (desired short-ribs) and put the loins aside. . . . *

Squaws and pack horses arrived at the kills; a few braves took two animals. All told, 19 bison were down. The news spread quickly back to camp, where the Osage rejoiced and begin erecting spits over fires.

Several braves loaded meat onto pack horses and then headed away on their galloping hunters to find more buffaloes. Those without an attending squaw arranged the meat for transport on their horses. A rack of short-ribs was placed on the mount's back; the breastbone with ribs was stacked in two pieces, and bundles of loins and intestine were tied in skin straps and hung. Thick-haired skin was placed as a cover for the improvised saddle.*

The braves rode into camp, their prancing chargers aware and proud. Massive racks of meat were moved in, huge bloody cuts on big bones, and children chased the parade, squealing in delight.

Spits were loaded, quickly filling the air with the aroma of fresh meat roasting over fire. Short-ribs, large cage ribs, loins and humps hung dripping and sizzling, and squaws hurried about the wigwams, preparing for the meal.

In the summer of 1840, Tixier was fortunate to witness the Osage on the buffalo hunt, and he appreciated what he was seeing. In a few short decades, the Osage buffalo hunts on the prairie-plains had disappeared forever.

The Osage did not believe "the white man can be happy," Tixier surmised. "On the other hand, a great many whites do not understand the happiness of the redskins."

Who can judge? Careless, forgetful, they sleep
among dangers; but their senses, when it is
necessary, warn them in time. Their skill, their
tricks, make them triumphant. Their tastes are
such as to suit their nature; their needs are
limited. In times of abundance they show a brutal
avidity, but when food is lacking they are satisfied
with roots and never complain. In times of peace,
they are exceedingly lazy; in war they are indefatigable. They will travel a hundred miles without
eating, without stopping; happy, they are quiet;
unhappy, they show greatness.*

VIII

In 1879 a Ponca chieftain, Standing Bear, reportedly sued
the federal government for his freedom to leave the reservation on which he had been placed. During the trial, an issue
in question was whether the American Indians were human
or not. Standing Bear sat in disbelief, tears flooding his
cheeks.

"Look! He cries!" declared his lawyer. "Only humans
cry!"

By then the Osage were gone from Kansas, driven away
again. Finally, though, they had a permanent home in
Oklahoma, one the Long Knives could never take from them.

The settlers kept coming to Kansas to measure the land in
acres, to plow it, to fence it. And, in springtime, when the
mules yanked the steel blades through the earth and the dirt
turned up in orderly ridges along straight furrows, the
arrowheads rose to the surface too, like schools of fish,
glimmering under Grandfather the Sun. For many planting
seasons, the arrowheads were so plentiful the farmers
usually ignored them. There was always work to be done on
their little, fenced-in plots.

But a farmer might stop once to pick up an arrow point
and roll it over in study, touching a fingertip to the flint's
sharp point, razor edges, and chipped scales. He might be

*Tixier, Victor (ed.-McDermott; tr-Salvan). *Tixier's Travels on the Osage
Prairies.* University of Oklahoma Press (1940).

awed by the beautiful symmetry, the artistry, and his mind might expand enough in the moment to appreciate the ones who left the marker behind. He might imagine the thundering bison and the braves in pursuit, clamping their legs around charging horses while pulling up bows and arrows. But then the farmer might just as easily perish the thought, so as to justify his own existence here and the belief that was meant to last.

"Savages," he would dismiss, tossing the arrowhead aside.

BELMONT

"I can't spare this man. He fights."
Abraham Lincoln

Seven months into the Civil War, a battle was brewing along the Mississippi River in southeast Missouri. This would be the first clash between North and South along the strategic waterway, and an obscure but fight-ambitious Union officer was initiating it: Ulysses S. Grant, a brigadier general headquartered at Cairo, Illinois.

The battle would be staged at a steamboat landing known as Belmont, Missouri's easternmost point. Confederate forces held Belmont, which was directly across the river from Columbus, Kentucky, where the South had constructed a major fort atop limestone bluffs rising above the delta plain.

In November 1861, Columbus was a bustling town of westward expansion, a key terminus on the Mobile & Ohio Railroad. Two months earlier, citizens had cheered as Rebels led by Gen. Leonidas Polk occupied the area. The Confederates fortified the bluffs with 140 heavy cannon pointing strategically across the Mississippi. Some were the world's largest guns, capable of firing 128-pound shot. The Rebels also lined the river with torpedoes and mined incoming roads. Finally, a gigantic chain with 20-pound links was stretched across the Mississippi atop rafts to Belmont landing, designed to block Union boat traffic.

The Confederates touted Columbus as an impregnable "Gibraltar of the West," the most fortified point in North America with at least 10,000 soldiers occupying the site at any given time.

Twenty miles upstream at Cairo, Grant was hardly intimidated. In fact, he repeatedly asked his superiors for permission to attack Columbus-Belmont. Finally, in November, Grant got his chance of sorts when he was ordered to conduct a non-offensive "demonstration" above Columbus to discourage the Confederates from sending more troops into Missouri through Belmont.

Grant, however, would make a final decision on what action to take. The young officer already was on his miraculous rise from a public unknown to becoming the war's most powerful general and, ultimately, President of the United States. Such a destiny usually involves climbing a ladder of significant individual events, risks and experiences. The Battle of Belmont became one of those steps for Grant.

After heading downriver from Cairo for Columbus with 3,100 men on three steamboats, intelligence scouts told Grant that more Rebels were moving into Missouri via Belmont. This information, coupled with his troops' readiness to fight, spurred him to change the mission. He now would attack the Rebel camp at Belmont, in full view of the enemy guns 700 yards across the river at Columbus.

In a definitive book on the general's campaign from Missouri to Vicksburg, *Grant Moves South*, author Bruce Catton noted the man "comes down in history as a stolid, stay-put sort of character, but actually he was nothing of the sort. He had the soldier's impulse to strike rather than to receive a blow. . . ."

Grant proving himself a fighter, however, was not history's memorable theme from Belmont. What endures is the fact he should not have survived. Among all the bloody fields he would see, from Shiloh east to the Wilderness campaign, none put Grant's life in more peril than did Belmont, his first battle of the Civil War.

I

One hundred and thirty years after the Battle of Belmont, a group of Missourians organized a historical re-enactment on the original battlefield in Mississippi County. In late September 1991, local historian and event publicist Kevin Pritchett gave a tour of the site, consisting of about three square miles of private farmland along the Mississippi. The big river still cut narrow and swift past Belmont Landing, and the view was easy across to the Kentucky bluffs and Columbus-Belmont State Park.

The former village at Belmont — two or three houses during the war — was a soybean field. Most of the timber had been cleared earlier in this century, and the swamps were drained by a network of dredge ditches and transformed into some of the richest farmland in the world. But much about the dirt roads and remaining virgin woods had not changed since the battle long ago. Locals still knew where to find cannon balls buried in the dark earth.

The Battle of Belmont is barely mentioned in most war

histories. The State of Missouri, in remembrance, has erected but a small placard stand on the riverbank. Casualty statistics reveal no largess in the numbers compared to the carnage of Civil War battles to come, although the American deaths at Belmont were more than twice the number killed during the modern Desert Storm operation. Records of Belmont vary somewhat, but about 10,000 men probably fought there. A general consensus is the South sustained 642 casualties including 105 killed; the North, 607 casualties with 120 killed.

Historians debate whether a clear victor emerged. They do agree the momentous battles of 1862-65 reduced Belmont to a minor event. But this was more than a skirmish, and the legend is large because of Grant.

The fighting lasted all day as two jittery, inexperienced armies clashed in an environment of terror similar to the Wilderness in Virginia, reputed to be the war's harshest battlefield. Enter the Belmont grounds today in the Mississippi River Delta and see a jungle virtually impassable without a machete. Moss drapes the tops of massive oaks and grapevines hang like heavy cables over a dense undergrowth of scrub trees and bushes. Even without leaf cover in winter, visibility in the thicket is restricted to only a few feet.

Pritchett walked the river road that curls north around the area and rises only a few feet above the onrushing Mississippi. Pritchett peered into the towering, dark woods that blacked out the bright afternoon sun, and spoke of the battle. "This was a violent, deadly, face-to-face struggle," he said. "This was the Civil War, and right here is where a lot of those guys got their first taste of it."

Men and boys died here, shooting at point blank range, stabbing each other with bayonets, and hacking flesh with Bowie knives. At one point the Federals had to retreat, and Pritchett wondered aloud how anyone in a panic could escape. "They were yelling, screaming, running through here in those old wool uniforms and carrying knapsacks, guns and powder. They were being chased and fired on the whole way."

And, of course, Pritchett talked about Grant, who became the battle's headliner not on name alone, but by personal feats of the day. Grant cheated death time after time, beginning early when his first horse was shot from under him. Pritchett noted the obvious "implications for history" had the bullet killed Grant instead. "Lee may have actually won the war," he said.

Grant mounted another horse, but at least three more times fate spared him being gunned down by an enemy that never would have known the significance. Instead the Rebels came to rue the name of Grant, whose armies tore across their South, and they regretted the day he got away in southeast Missouri.

"That's when you have to believe in destiny for a certain individual," said Pritchett. "It's mind-boggling to think the war's top general and future president should have died right here. Think about what would have happened to the war! Without Grant, the North might not have taken Fort Donelson, Shiloh, or Vicksburg. That was Grant's southern campaign, his design, and it broke the Confederacy.

"As close as Grant came to dying here, it just wasn't meant to be."

When you visit the Belmont battle site, the mind's eye conjures the fight. You imagine opposing waves of young men charging and colliding with flashing bayonets amidst the acrid smoke of muskets and cannons. And at Belmont, standing on the flat plain where the battle swarmed about, you look east across river and consider the *cannon*, those huge guns that were on the Kentucky bluffs.

Grant and his men experienced the guns' fury. After they made an impressive maneuver to hold the Columbus guns silent while they routed the Belmont camp, the general lost control of his rookie troops who thought they had victory in hand. Rebels had fled to the riverbank, so the Federal greenhorns began ransacking the camp. Then, however, they got blasted from the bluffs as Confederate gunners fired shots that rained down in weights of 32 pounds, 64 and 128. Most balls exploded on impact, and with Rebel reinforcements headed across the Mississippi in boats, the Yankees skedaddled in sudden retreat.

On an autumn weekend in 1991, thousands of Civil War re-enactors and spectators gathered at Belmont to mark the 130th anniversary of the battle. The event included artillery firings on both sides of the river. A cluster of small cannons boomed off Belmont Landing, trading blank powder charges with Rebel guns on the bluffs at Columbus. The shock waves reverberated back and forth over the water between Missouri and Kentucky. People whooped and cheered at the racket, watching fire spurt from the cannon barrels.

One personable re-enactor wore Confederate gray and talked in a Tennessee twang, discussing his original Civil War cannon with some onlookers. The beautiful artillery piece had an iron barrel and spindly wheels, and looked like a lawn ornament from a plantation of the Old South — which it essentially was. According to the owner, the model was one of only nine turned out for the war by a Nashville foundry, Ellis & Sons. It was a compact and mobile weapon for wealthy landowners who felt compelled to own such defense.

The piece shot a 6-pound, 6-ounce cannon ball propelled by about 1.5 pounds of powder. Known then as a "6-pound iron," the gun no longer used that size shot. The re-enactor had the inner barrel fitted with a steel sleeve to prevent the iron from blowing apart. But its power and accuracy remained intact.

"To kind of give ya an idea. . . " he said, nodding toward river traffic passing swiftly down the Mississippi, "we could hit one of those barges, no sweat. We could take out that pilot house rot now, probably first shot.

"We shoot nickel balls in competitions these days, and from 300 or 400 yards, this gun is just three or four inches off (target)."

He said the gun's accuracy range was a mile and a half. "It'll blow a hole through an oak tree just like it wudn't even there. I mean it's awesome." The re-enactor looked back across the river to the Kentucky shoreline, at the ridge tops with the old fort's earthen breastworks, and the park buildings.

"I'd say outa two shots, we could go 'n put one right up'ere in the middle of that pavilion," he wagered of the 6-pounder. "Awful easy."

The re-enactor was asked to consider the Battle of Belmont and the ground he stood on, with cannon balls like 64-pounders and 128-pounders whistling in from the bluffs.

"Oh yeah, wicked," he shuddered. "Just wicked."

II

About an hour after daylight on November 7, 1861, Grant and his 3,100 men attacked upward of 10,000 Rebels at Columbus-Belmont after moving south by steamers during the night. The flotilla hit the Missouri shore at Hunter's

Point, about two miles north of Belmont camp and a half-mile farther from the guns at Columbus.

The three transports were escorted by a pair of crude gunboats, the *Tyler* and *Lexington* , both former steamers hastily converted to arms by the Union Army at Cincinnati. Ironclads were still under development, and the *Tyler* and *Lexington* wore five-inch-thick oak armor. They were strange looking, awkward craft with steampipes exposed dangerously. But they were formidable threats with their smoothbore cannon firing 32- and 64-pounders.

Grant's force knew their deployment was seen at the fort, where sentinels sounded the alarm and the bluffs began to resound with thundering cannon blasts. But the Federals had landed just above accuracy range for the Rebel guns, and their gunboats steamed forward to return fire.

The Yankees hurried over the gangplanks onto a sandy gray shore. The ground was low and marshy leading into an open cornfield. Grant had five regiments of infantry, including four from Illinois: the 13th, 22nd, 27th and 31st. The 7th Iowa and two Illinois cavalry companies known as Dollin's and Delano's were also deployed. The Yankees toted four field guns.

Grant ordered most of the troops to form columns in the cornfield, then led some down the shoreline to post against surprise attack. He placed others in a dry slough to protect the transports, working in concert with the gunboats.

It was 8 a.m. on a chilly day. A hazy sky whitened the sun as Grant returned to the field to find his troops frolicking like schoolboys with the teacher away. A Rebel shell had landed in mud without exploding, and the men had dug it up to remark and joke on its size. Grant rode up, ended the foolishness and started the men marching in columns toward Belmont on a dirt road through woods. They would attack from the land side, seeking to flank the Rebels at the west and pin them against the river.

From the bluffs at Columbus, Confederate Gen. Polk monitored the situation. He knew a separate Union force was marching from Paducah toward Columbus, and, convinced Grant's raid was a diversion for a larger attack, Polk refrained from sending too many troops across river. The 13th Arkansas occupied Belmont, along with a cavalry unit from Mississippi. Polk ordered help from four more Tennessee regiments: the 12th, 13th, 21st and 22nd.

A Rebel soldier later recalled the Columbus troops were rallied by an aroused Brig. Gen. Benjamin Franklin Cheatham, who alleged the Yankees were "murdering the sick men in their tents" at Belmont. "Instantly the rage of our men was such they could hardly be restrained," wrote the soldier. "Many of them swore to swim the river if necessary to reach the enemy, and would give no quarter."

The boilers in two Rebel transports soon had "steam up," and the reinforcements landed at Belmont by 9 a.m. to give both sides a relatively equal force on the Missouri side. Led by Gen. Gideon J. Pillow, the Rebels came out to meet the Yankees. A mile and a half north of Belmont, skirmishers opened fire in timber.

On the bluffs, Confederate gunners had to cease their fire for risk of hitting their comrades.

In Columbus hundreds of citizens stared anxiously at the Missouri shoreline. Their view showed little but the usual long, dense tree line. Then "the quick flash and distant boom of the artillery told that the work of death was being done," recounted the town newspaper, *The Daily Confederate News*. "Suddenly from the deep wood . . . the roaring volley of musketry. Never before had our ears listened to sounds like that."

Grant's favorite bay horse was shot from under him, but he leaped on another and the Yankees kept advancing. He later recalled in *Personal Memoirs* the fighting was "growing fiercer and fiercer, for about four hours, the enemy being forced back gradually until he was driven into his camp." Shielded in a treeline, the inspired Federals picked off easy targets in the clearing, and a cloud of smoke thickened over the ground. Then they charged again, breaking the Rebels' left flank and pushing it toward river.

The battle was now visible to Columbus citizens. "The war was drawing nearer to the riverbank," stated the newspaper. "They come, they come! Into the open field they pour, pursuers and pursued. Who runs? Who flies? Alas it is the Southerner (who) flees — the Northerner pursues."

The Rebels scattered, bound for cover behind the tall, dished riverbank, and the jubilant Yankees yanked down the camp's Confederate flag.

Polk had already lowered his spy glass. He ordered Cheatham to take more reinforcements to Missouri and land upstream from the camp to cut the federals off from their transports.

Union troops, foolishly ignoring the enemy power immediately across river, thought they had won. Grant wrote, "The moment the camp was reached our men laid down their arms and commenced rummaging the tents to pick up trophies. Some of the higher officers were little better than the privates." Men ran wildly about, laughing, grabbing souvenirs, singing. A regimental band struck up tunes like "Yankee Doodle Dandy," "The Star Spangled Banner" and "Dixie." Grant could not restore order, as many officers paused to give passionate oratories of victory for the Union cause.

The afternoon was now past 1 p.m., and Polk and Cheatham were aboard two oncoming steamers that Grant described as "black — or gray — with soldiers from boiler-deck to roof." Grant ordered the camp set on fire to gain his troops' attention. Across river, Confederate gunners responded by blasting the clearing. The Yankees panicked amidst violent explosions. They saw the formerly beaten Rebels under Gen. Pillow re-emerging from the riverbank, only farther upstream.

Some Union officers wanted to surrender. "We are surrounded and lost," one cried.

"No," Grant refused. "We have whipped them once. We can whip them again." He turned to his sobered troops, now back in formation. "We cut our way in, and we'll cut our way out!" Grant yelled.

The Yankees charged back north, bound for their transports along the way they had come, the interior road through woods. Skirmishers and cavalry provided cover for the retreat. Pillow's men tried to stop them only to be driven back over the riverbank. But Cheatham had landed with reinforcements that ripped into the fleeing Federals' flank, inflicting heavy casualties.

As the Yankees fled, musket balls spattered through dry leaves overhead, adding spring to their steps. To gain speed they stripped themselves of coats, knapsacks, cartridge belts and other bulk. The Confederate soldier who wrote of the battle recalled the fighting "soon became a rout, and a running fight to their boats, some three miles. The Confederates pressed them hard . . . and did sad execution on the running men."

III

A standard biographical sketch of Ulysses S. Grant published in 1968 began by stating he "was a puzzling figure in American public life. He was a failure in his early ventures into both business and military life." The encyclopedia goes on to note Grant's mediocrity as a student at West Point, graduating in the middle of his class of 1843; his reluctant but courageous duty in the Mexican War for a national cause he despised; his post-war experience as an officer marred by drinking, disagreements with a superior, and the resignation of his captaincy in 1854; and Grant's years in St. Louis — home of his wife, Julia Dent Grant — as a failure in businesses such as farming and real estate.

This view of Grant has been played in countless books, articles and films. The narrative basically goes that at the start of the Civil War, Grant was an impoverished do-nothing nearing middle age, perhaps an alcoholic, who had been reduced to working as a store clerk for his father's business in Galena, Illinois. Even during the war, as Grant's bold leadership in the West was attracting the attention of Lincoln, his adversaries in the Army brass sought to discredit him with the familiar allegations.

Fortunately for the Union, Lincoln was more convinced of Grant's worthiness of high rank. Responding once to the naysayers, Lincoln said that if Grant was indeed drinking whiskey on duty, then he wanted to know the brand, so he could send it to certain Union commanders who were afraid to fight.

In summer 1861, one year after Grant had moved his family to Galena for work, he returned to Missouri as a Union colonel in command of the 21st Illinois regiment of volunteers. A few important points can be ascertained about Grant in this period:

He was a devoted husband and father, very much in love with his wife and four children. The eldest son, Frederick Dent Grant, would often travel at his father's side as a boy attache during the war, even suffering a leg wound during the siege of Vicksburg.

Grant had admirers in high places, such as Illinois Governor Richard Yates, who appointed him a colonel, and U.S. Representative Elihu B. Washburne of Galena, who would continue to support Grant's ascent through the ranks. Neither Yates nor Washburne had known Grant before the spring, when he rushed to help organize Illinois volunteer regiments after the outbreak of war.

And Grant was utterly devoted to his country, the Union, which was the only reason he fought so hard in the Mexican War. Grant was a Democrat in Galena, but he once said, "There are but two parties now, traitors and patriots, and I want hereafter to be ranked with the latter." As for the Union cause, his perception was that of the Republican Lincoln, whose primary objective was to preserve the nation by stamping out rebellion. Like the President, Grant focused strictly on winning the war.

But Grant also believed Union victory would doom slavery, a result he apparently would welcome, although he was no abolitionist. A former slave owner himself, Grant believed slavery was the covert reason the United States attacked Mexico in 1846, the motive being to establish new slave states in the West. And, of course, he was convinced the South seceded following the 1860 election not over states' rights but rather to preserve the slave labor so vital to its cotton economy.

On the issue of slavery versus abolition, Grant witnessed a profound study in Missouri. The 24th state was established in 1821 under the Congressional Missouri Compromise, symbolizing the divisive cloud that eventually separated the country. In the years following, abolitionist groups, including the Mormons, tried to reform pro-slavery Missouri, only to be driven out under threat of annihilation.

The deadly politics of slavery continued to fester nationally, exploding in Kansas in 1854 when a federal bill granted that territory and Nebraska the option of being admitted as free or slave states. Proslavery forces in Missouri cared little about Nebraska, but their already bloody rivalry with Kansas abolitionists ignited border warfare years before the South seceded.

The Missouri-Kansas border area spawned some of America's most dreaded guerrillas in the violence over slavery. Opposing leaders were epitomized by abolition fanatic Jim Lane in Kansas and pro-South William Quantrill of Missouri. As these vigilantes carried out personal, gruesome crusades across the countryside — often in retaliation to each other — untold innocents on both sides were victimized. Homesteaders and even entire towns learned to turn chameleon when the raiders came, voicing the politics that satisfied their intimidating visitors of the moment. Citizens or communities known to have taken a side, or those merely accused of it, lived in fear of the brutal consequences they often suffered.

In April of 1861, President Lincoln asked each state to furnish 75,000 volunteers for the Union. Missouri had not seceded and would remain "neutral," but newly elected Governor Claibourne "Claib" Jackson defied the President, declaring his state would not supply a single soldier to battle "her sister states of the South." Jackson appealed to Missourians to "rise" and "drive out" any Union invaders, and he mobilized the state militia, fanning anti-federal hysteria. But Congressman Frank Blair Jr. in St. Louis, hoping to meet Lincoln's quota, began organizing the antislavery Germans into volunteer regiments called the Unionist Home Guard.

The federal arsenal at Liberty near Kansas City was seized by a pro-South mob, spurring a controversial event in St. Louis. Union Capt. Nathaniel Lyon realized if his St. Louis arsenal fell to rebels, so did the state. Lyon, a fervent abolitionist and veteran of the Kansas border war, had little tolerance for anyone opposing his views.

A fortified state militia gathered in St. Louis at a base named Camp Jackson, and on May 8 a boat docking at the levee was discovered to be transporting arms sent by Confederacy President Jefferson Davis. Lyon responded the morning of May 10, leading four regiments of Dutch volunteers on a march across the city to Camp Jackson. A crowd of citizens formed in step behind, including Army Colonel William Tecumsah Sherman and an Illinois mustering officer, Ulysses S. Grant, who was visiting the city.

The camp surrendered to Lyon without bloodshed. One thousand militia men were disarmed and taken prisoner for a march back to the arsenal. Then trouble began.

Mobs lined the streets, shouting "Damn the Dutch" and "Hurray for Jeff Davis." Stones were hurled at the Federals, and a confrontation with a drunken man escalated into him shooting an officer. Gunfire continued until the arsenal was reached, scaring off Sherman and others. Twenty-eight people were dead, including a baby, two women, three prisoners, and two Union men.

Enraged protestors filled the streets through the night.

In front of the famed Planter's House, Mexican War hero and former Governor Sterling Price ranted against "military despotism." The next day Price was in Jefferson City, stoking the fear of Governor Jackson and the legislature. Germans were rumored to be headed upriver from St. Louis to take the capital, and Jackson hastily commissioned Price as Major General of Militia to defend Jefferson City.

In a Planter's House meeting one month later, Lyon personally threatened the lives of Jackson and Price "rather than to concede to the State of Missouri." Lyon, now a brigadier general, also threatened to see "every man, woman, and child in the state dead and buried." Lyon demanded his adversaries leave St. Louis within the hour and declared: "This means war."

Jackson, Price, and secretary Thomas Snead returned to Jefferson City on a locomotive they drove, stopping along the way to cut telegraph wires and burn bridges. They arrived at 2 a.m., June 12, with no doubt Lyon would now invade the capital. Three days later Lyon and his troops arrived by steamboat on the Missouri River, only to find the capitol building abandoned.

Jackson had fled by river with a rebel legislature, and Lyon pursued them upstream to Boonville, where a small battle took place. But Jackson and his loyalists escaped again, this time by horseback into the Missouri interior where steamers could not give chase.

Later, U.S. Grant would accuse Jackson's state government of having taken "refuge with the enemy."

The Missouri atmosphere of paranoia, division and distrust greeted Colonel Grant on his arrival at Hannibal in early July of 1861 with his 21st Illinois regiment of volunteers. He felt anxious, fearful of entering "the field of battle" in Missouri, a state he knew had high potential of becoming a major war zone. But Grant was bound to duty, and his Missouri experience would galvanize the tactics, organizational skills, courage and resolve that later would make him a supreme commander of mass armies.

Over the next few weeks, Grant and his 1,000 troops moved across northeast Missouri. Camped near the Salt River in late July, the regiment was ordered to pursue Militia Colonel Thomas Harris. On the march, Grant was disheartened to find houses, farms and roads deserted for miles. As the regiment approached a hilltop that could reveal either the Harris camp or soldiers ready to fire, Grant admittedly was terrified. But the camp was abandoned, Harris having fled with his men a few hours before.

"My heart resumed its place," Grant wrote in *Memoirs*. "It occurred to me at once that Harris had been as much afraid of me as I had been of him. . . . From that event to the close of the war, I never experienced trepidation upon confronting an enemy. . . ."

Heading back to camp, Grant discovered citizens had returned to their houses and farms, ready to greet the Federals. Travelers were not afraid to meet them on the road. Grant surmised that after his regiment had passed earlier, the people returned home and were surprised to find their property undisturbed: "They had evidently been led to believe that the National troops carried death and devastation with them wherever they went."

Grant was assigned next to Mexico, Missouri, where he learned of abuses committed against locals by Union troops. He immediately posted notice no soldier was to enter a home or property without invitation from the owner, and the order was obeyed. The citizens of Mexico reciprocated with courtesy and hospitality, but all parties remained leery of each other.

A collection of correspondence, from *The Papers of Ulysses S. Grant*, provides a fascinating perspective from his military career, including his time in Missouri. In a letter to his father dated August 3, 1861, Grant gave this view on the wartime attitude in the Mexico area:

> I find here . . . a different state of feeling from what I expected existed in any part of the South. The majority of this part of the state are Secessionists, as we would term them, but deplore the present state of affairs. They would make almost any sacrifice to have the Union restored, but regard it as dissolved and nothing is left for them but to choose between two evils. Many too seem to be entirely ignorant of the object of present hostilities. You can't convince them but what the ultimate object is to extinguish, by force, slavery. . . .

Grant also mailed a letter home to Julia, informing her he was a leading candidate for promotion to brigadier general. His regiment was breaking camp at Mexico:

> I am glad to get away from here. The people have been remarkably polite if they are seceshers, but the weather is intolerably warm and dry and as there is neither wells nor springs in this country we have drank the whole place dry. People here will be glad to get clear of us notwithstanding their apparent hospitality. They are great fools in this section of country and will never rest until they bring upon themselves all the horrors of war in its worst form. The people are inclined to carry on a guerilla warfare that must eventuate in retaliation and when it does commence it will be hard to control. I hope from the bottom of my heart I may be mistaken but since the defeat of our troops at Manassas (Virginia) things look more gloomy here.

Within days, Grant learned he was promoted to brigadier general in charge of the important District of Southeast Missouri, which included southern Illinois and the confluence of the Mississippi River with the Ohio at Cairo. He was first sent to the Union post at Ironton 70 miles below St. Louis, the southern terminus of the St. Louis, Iron Mountain and Southern Railroad.

On August 10, he mailed a letter to his wife, noting his recent visit to former business partner Harry Boggs in St. Louis, who was also a relative of Julia's. Grant wrote that Boggs "cursed and went on like a Madman. Told me that I would never be welcome in his house; that the people of Illinois were a poor miserable set of Black Republicans, Abolition paupers that had to invade their state to get something to eat."

That same day in southwest Missouri, Brigadier General Lyon was killed in the Battle of Wilson's Creek below Springfield, which would stand as the deadliest clash in Missouri. The Union sustained 1,317 killed, wounded or missing, and the Confederates had 1,222. Militia General Price gained some revenge in the death of Lyon, not to mention a resounding defeat of Union forces.

Price then embarked on a campaign through west and central Missouri, but the Federals continued to hold key cities, railroads and ports, and the state's chaotic, dual personality would not cure itself.

Grant, meanwhile, took an immediate liking to Ironton, a friendly, picturesque community nestled among Ozarks peaks. The area was "one of the most delightful places I have ever been in," he wrote Julia. Here Missouri's stifling heat was offset by shaded, breezy valleys cut with cold-water springs and rivers. Grant's stay at Ironton would be brief, but he apparently developed a vision there for taking the Union on a southern campaign through the valleys of the Mississippi, Cumberland and Tennessee rivers. Later, those valleys would become domains of Grant, and apparently he first pondered the possibilities at Ironton. According to a friend in the community, Colonel John Emerson, Grant studied beside a spring branch he drank from. Watching the water flow and marking maps in red pencil, Grant identified the Mississippi, Cumberland and Tennessee as keys to the conflict. Whichever side came to control those waterways, he believed, would win.

Moreover, Grant must have believed he could be important in accomplishing that objective for the North. As an educated, seasoned soldier, the 39-year-old fully recognized the sluggish, apprehensive nature of the initial army leadership that so flustered Lincoln. This was war, and time to get on with the business of fighting, as far as Grant was concerned.

IV

Grant arrived at Cairo as district commander on September 4, and his "quiet" nature and "plain" appearance were evident. The short man wore a common, black hat of felt pulled down over his brow, hiding the blue eyes and bearded face that usually were expressionless anyway. His dark civilian clothes were not the blue uniform of sword, sash, feather, gold buttons, and one star on each shoulder that a typical officer of his rank paraded in proudly.

Catton wrote, "It would be pleasant to be able to record that someone recognized a historic moment when Grant entered Cairo, but nobody did. . . ."

Alone, without entourage, Grant found Union headquarters in a converted bank building crammed with noisy people. The officer in charge, Illinois Colonel Richard Oglesby, sat busy at a table. Grant introduced himself, but Oglesby missed the significance and his attention returned to others in the room. Grant lingered silently a little longer before writing his order of assuming command on a piece of paper and slipping it to Oglesby.

"U.S. Grant was at last in command of troops on the Mississippi, looking south," wrote Catton.

That same day, Confederate regiments under Pillow ended a march through western Kentucky at Columbus. The town, obviously "secesher" in sentiment, celebrated because the Rebels were the first to violate Kentucky's neutrality instead of the dreaded Yankees. Across river at Belmont, a small group of Federals had removed their cannon and returned north.

A Union plan to occupy Columbus was foiled, thanks in part to General Polk of Memphis, who recognized the urgency to gain the strategic bluffs and sent Pillow ahead to do it. But the Union had bungled matters for itself the previous week and missed the opportunity. Confusion over the seniority between brigadier generals Grant and Benjamin M. Prentiss was the culprit.

The Commander of the West in St. Louis, General John C. Fremont, was preoccupied with Price's force of 10,000 in west-central Missouri and the officer most responsible for a communications mix-up. In August, Prentiss arrived at Ironton to relieve Grant of district command because superiors erroneously believed the former was the ranking officer. But the commission as general for both men was stamped May 18, and Grant's former captaincy rank made him the senior by law.

The final weeks of August were a tangle of confusion before Grant finally was renamed the District Commander of Southeast Missouri by Fremont. Unfortunately, Prentiss was not informed of the development as Grant hastily established temporary headquarters at Cape Girardeau. Grant's mission was to initiate Fremont's plan to sweep the Missouri Bootheel clean of Rebels and guerrillas, secure Belmont, and take the bluffs at Columbus.

The operation was under way by September 1, when Grant had a late-night confrontation with Prentiss on the cobblestone streets of Cape Girardeau.

Prentiss had marched troops from Ironton to nearby

Jackson, where Grant had intended him to halt. But Prentiss had come on to Cape Girardeau after ordering his regiments to follow the next morning. When Grant instead commanded Prentiss to keep his troops at Jackson and await further orders, the latter failed to understand or accept that he no longer was the ranking officer. Prentiss balked, and the disagreement rose into his offering to resign, which Grant refused.

The next day, Prentiss placed himself under arrest and left for St. Louis, presumably to resolve the matter according to his thinking, and the Fremont plan came to an abrupt halt. Troops already at Belmont were withdrawn, and Grant was fortunate to make a peaceful takeover of Paducah in time to stop the Confederate advance at Columbus.

Later, in *Memoirs*, Grant acknowledged the "great mistake" by Prentiss, but he downplayed any consequences, praising the latter as "a brave and very earnest soldier." Courageous soldier indeed, for it was Prentiss and his men from Illinois and Iowa who would save Grant's force from slaughter at the horrific Battle of Shiloh on April 6-7, 1862. There, on the first day of fighting, Prentiss was the only commander to hold his line long enough to stave off the South. Prentiss dug in at the infamous center hilltop called Hornet's Nest — named for Rebels charging repeatedly like "maddened demons" — before he finally surrendered at 5:30 p.m. with 2,200 surviving troops. Some 25,000 other Federals, including Grant and Sherman, had fled to the Tennessee River bottoms and were ripe to be conquered. But the Confederates stopped their advance after the exhaustive fight with Prentiss, and 25,000 Union reinforcements arrived overnight for a crushing counterattack to victory.

The remaining weeks of September passed, followed by October, with "nothing important" happening in the Southeast Missouri District, according to Grant. In northwest Missouri, at Lexington on the Missouri River, the Union suffered another embarrassing defeat by Price, and Fremont was ridiculed by the Northern press. Fremont was growing indecisive in his command and seemingly indifferent toward the critical Mississippi.

Even if Grant could not attack the enemy, his daily schedule was consumed with vital tasks from dawn until midnight and beyond. The Cairo garrison was woefully understocked and lacking in resources such as transportation, cavalry equipment and artillery. There was not even a large map of Kentucky to work with, and Grant was deluged with raw recruits and volunteers who required training.

Other issues demanded his attention, such as packet boats illegally supplying the Confederates with needs, which Grant had to police. The problem was enormous in scope on the Mississippi, but Grant worked to combat it.

Slave owners from Missouri and Kentucky badgered Grant over their runaways, and he could not convince them his command was no sanctuary for the escapees. Sometimes runaways did come to the Federals at Cairo, and Grant would neither aid nor apprehend them, only send them on their way. He was determined to keep the slave issue off his agenda, at least in this period of the war, but it was difficult to ignore. His father even goaded him about it, referring to editorials in the Northern press calling for a war on slavery. Grant's reply, preserved in *The Papers of Ulysses S. Grant*, was terse in tone for him:

> My inclination is to whip the rebellion into submission, preserving all constitutional rights. If it cannot be whipped in any other way than through a war against slavery, let it come to that legitimately. If it is necessary that slavery should fall that the Republic may continue its existence, let slavery go. But that portion of the press that advocates the beginning of such a war now, are as great enemies to their country as if they were open and avowed secessionists.

Another problem was government contracts, which in southern Illinois were rife with corruption, causing Grant to often pay inflated prices for inferior products and services. His father was a bother for influence peddling, regularly recommending people to Grant for a job, an appointment or special favor, but the general denied every request. Jesse Root Grant, a businessman, once wrote his son for help in securing a contract for supplying harness to the army. "I cannot take an active part in securing contracts. . . ," Grant answered. "(It) is necessary both to my efficiency and the public good and my own reputation that I should keep clear of Government contracts."

Through it all, Grant remained focused on warfare, formulating plans and rewriting them as conditions changed. He deployed picket guards in the vast swamps to seek out their Rebel counterparts, resulting in skirmishes. He utilized the gunboats for reconnaissance trips, often going along himself to keep an eyewitness perspective on enemy locations and activities. He knew the Confederates continued to bolster Columbus with more defensive works, heavy guns, troops, and steamers for transport.

Grant understood that a direct attack on the Kentucky fort had become impossible without a mass infusion of reinforcements for Cairo, which was not going to happen. Still, he was nearly obsessed with making some sort of offensive; more and more, his attention focused on Belmont.

And he always kept an eye peeled for M. Jeff Thompson, the rebel renegade roaming southeast Missouri.

The flamboyant Thompson hailed from the same area of northwest Missouri that spawned other notorious guerrillas. But he was not as grimly determined to wreak bloodshed and havoc as were the likes of Quantrill, "Bloody" Bill Anderson or a pair of young gunslingers and future outlaws, Jesse James and Cole Younger.

As a former mayor of St. Joseph, Thompson's initial brush with history was his ceremonial placement of the first bag of mail on a Pony Express racer. An avowed secessionist, Thompson held a romantic view of the 1776 revolution, and, after Lincoln's election, he attempted to organize a battalion of militia in St. Joseph. Then came the fall of Camp Jackson at St. Louis, and Thompson rushed to Jefferson City to offer his services to Claib Jackson. Thompson, however, found the governor unimpressive and inattentive, and he startled the politician by declaring Jackson was "cowardly and lacking common sense." Thompson stalked off on a search for comrades who would be more appreciative of his talents.

He ended up in southeast Missouri, alone, with 75 cents in a pocket of his makeshift clothes. He rode atop a long-toothed horse wearing a rope bridle. But he wore a long feather in his hat, and the spirit within was indefatigable, the charisma intact. Thompson wooed hundreds of local males, then thousands, many of whom were barefoot. His effective sales pitch was a racist call to rise against rule by the Dutch — the region had a flourishing German population — or seeing one's self lowered to equality with those inferior "niggers."

Thompson had found a home in the Bootheel, quickly becoming the local legend known as the "Swamp Fox." His merry outlaw persona mesmerized folks, an example being his curious relationship with the town of Charleston. He once robbed the Charleston bank of $56,000, only to be welcomed back to town, again and again, for safe harbor in hiding out or receiving supplies.

The spotlight certainly fell on Thompson after Fremont became obsessed with militia, guerrillas, and state sentiment as a whole. On August 30, Fremont decreed martial law on Missouri that included a death sentence for rebel guerrillas and a startling emancipation proclamation for every slave whose owner was not loyal to the Union. Fremont had intended to quiet Missouri, but the effect was quite the opposite, igniting a furor that spread throughout the states. Lincoln seethed, and in two months he would remove Fremont as western commander. Thompson responded immediately from the swamps with a proclamation of his own, declaring that for every rebel executed through Fremont's order, he would personally "HANG, DRAW and QUARTER a minion of said Abraham Lincoln."

The concerned Union brass in St. Louis saw Thompson and his men as phantoms darting in and out of the Bootheel's vast timbered swamps and low sandy ridges. Thompson was especially fond of the foreboding Mingo Swamp tucked between Crowley's Ridge and the Ozark escarpment. He seemed immune to capture or confrontation, and some Federals were almost loath to try; he had masterfully conned them into thinking his ill-equipped force of about 3,000 might be 10 times larger and heavily armed.

Grant, however, wanted Thompson's hide.

V

In late October, Fremont personally led a march of 25,000 troops from Jefferson City, chasing his nemesis Price in western Missouri. Meanwhile, Grant's men at Cairo were clamoring for action. "They were growing impatient at lying idle so long," he recalled, "almost in hearing of the guns of the enemy they had volunteered to fight against."

Then information reached St. Louis that the Rebels were sending reinforcements through Belmont into Missouri, probably along the road leading to Charleston 12 miles away. On November 1, Grant got his long-awaited orders, although they were not exactly what he had in mind. He was told to have "your whole command ready to march at an hour's notice, until further orders," and "take particular care" in arming his troops. But the instructions called only for an appearance of threat, a "demonstration" on both sides of the river above Columbus in hopes of dissuading the Confederates from sending out troops.

The Swamp Fox figured prominently in the next dispatch to Grant from St. Louis. Thompson, it said, was poised in the edge of the Ozarks near Greenville with 3,000 men bent on striking the Union. Cairo was told to send troops from Cape Girardeau and Bird's Point to help repel the guerillas — a Yankee force was also headed south from Ironton — and drive them into Arkansas.

Grant instructed Oglesby to march from Bird's Point west toward Sikeston with Illinois volunteer regiments and cavalry. Grant's orders made no secret he wanted Thompson not merely chased, but eliminated: "The object of the expedition is to destroy this force and the manner of doing it is left largely to your discretion."

On November 4, however, the operation expanded considerably as Grant was ordered by superiors to stage a demonstration directly against Columbus; a separate force under Brigadier General Charles F. Smith would march south from Paducah.

Grant, hearing that Rebels were headed west from Columbus to join Price, strengthened in his resolve. Grant forwarded new orders to Oglesby, telling him to turn south for New Madrid and be ready to assist at Belmont, if needed. (The expedition to deliver the message was led by Col. W.H.L Wallace, who later would write *Ben Hur*.) Then Grant gathered all available soldiers — 3,114 total — at Cairo and prepared steamers, gunboats and artillery for a trip down the Mississippi to Columbus-Belmont.

The flotilla took off the night of November 6, moved to within 10 miles of the target, and landed at 2 a.m. to await daylight. Wallace sent Grant word that Confederate forces were crossing into Missouri at Belmont to cut off Oglesby. According to Grant, his mind changed at this point. Now convinced the leadership at Columbus needed a fight to temper their boldness, and seeing his own troops "elated" over the prospect of battle, Grant decided to "push down the river, land on the Missouri side, capture Belmont, break up the camp and return."

The Battle of Belmont was coming to a climax. Hazy sunlight was fading, and the Mississippi seemed topped in glass at Hunter's Point north of Belmont. From the woods came the retreating Yankees, rushing across the cornfield to the landing and their transports.

Grant emerged on horseback and hurriedly tended to matters. First he saw that wounded from a farmhouse hospital were moved on board the boats. Then he rode down the shoreline road to discover the two sets of guards he had placed were gone. He raced back to find them already on the boats, and he pondered returning them to their posts.

But there was no time for that now; the Rebels were coming.

As the main body of Yankees cleared the woods, Grant rode back through the cornfield to rally any stragglers himself. The dry stalks reached over his head and the blades intertwined across the rows, blocking his vision in any direction.

A few moments later, as the front of 6,000 Rebels pursuing north reached the cornfield, General Polk looked askance to see the last Yankee in the Union rear. The lone rider appeared on horseback in a corn row, a dark figure in a dirty soldier's overcoat and hat, headed south and oblivious to the enemy mass less than 50 yards away. An easy target.

"There is a Yankee," Polk pointed out to his men. "You may try your marksmanship on him if you wish."

Incredibly, no one accepted Polk's offer to shoot.

The rider, U.S. Grant, was startled to look up and see the Confederates. Ducking down, he jerked the reins toward river, starting the horse in a walk that quickly accelerated into a run.

Grant came out on the river road still hundreds of yards below the transports, which were pulling away. By now enemy muskets were blasting from the trees, killing a boat pilot, and Grant had to cut directly into the fire. Union soldiers cowering on the decks watched the race unfold, figuring Grant would die.

With no solid footing on the sandy shore 20 feet below,

Grant had to keep his horse up on the road, exposed to the whirring bullets. He rushed onward, planning to go crashing over the riverbank at the only boat waiting on him. Then his steed made a remarkable maneuver.

"My horse seemed to take in the situation," he recalled. "My horse put his fore feet over the bank and without hesitation or urging, and with his hind feet well under him, slid down the bank and trotted aboard the boat . . . over a single gang plank. I dismounted and went at once to the upper deck."

The transports were on low water, and enemy fire from higher ground level riddled the upper decks and smoke-stacks. Grant, exhausted from battle, tried to stretch out on a sofa in the captain's room. But the adrenaline still boiled inside, and he could not rest with the noise. He got up, and suddenly a musket ball crashed through a window pane and struck the head of the sofa where he had just reclined.

The danger was over, ending Grant's day in Missouri. Under cover from gunboats, the transports moved safely upriver, stopping only to pick up the 27th Illinois, which became detached during the retreat and had to march farther north to escape.

Catton wrote that "the trip back to Cairo was pretty solemn, and once the excitement of getting away died down the men were rather subdued." The officers gathered in a cabin for dinner, exchanging animated conversation about the battle — except for Grant, who barely spoke. "We thought he was hard-hearted, cold and indifferent," recalled a captain who was present, "but it was only the difference between a real soldier and amateur soldiers."

Interesting stories circulated about events that followed. Grant returned to Columbus on a truce boat to discuss burial for the Union dead and negotiate a prisoners exchange. He and the Rebel commander Cheatham had an amiable conversation, sharing their common interests such as Mexican War experience and horses. Cheatham joked the war could be best settled "by a grand international horse race on the Missouri shore." Another tale was Grant returned again on a boat to get roaring drunk with Cheatham, although the steamer captain vehemently denied this version in a newspaper letter, contending it was a different Union officer and Grant was not on board.

Under another truce flag, Colonel N.B. Buford of the

27th Illinois offered a toast before Polk and his staff, saluting, "To George Washington, the father of his country." The smiling general raised his glass. "And the first Rebel," he added.

Yet tragedy loomed heavy in the battle's aftermath. Half the town of Columbus was turned into hospitals for the wounded, and the place was besieged by relatives and friends of Confederate soldiers. Grant wrote, "I learned later, after I moved farther south, that Belmont had caused more mourning than almost any other battle up to that time."

Burial detail fell on the Columbus troops, who laid down the dead of both the South and North. The Confederate soldier who wrote of the fight, William G. Stevenson, recalled the task:

> We dug trenches six feet deep and four feet wide, and laid the bodies in side by side, the members of each company together, the priest saying over them his prayers; the hole closed by three volleys of musketry. The federal dead were also gathered, and buried in like manner, except the religious service and military salute.
>
> Our company buried their dead just before sunset; and when the funeral dirge died away, and the volleys fired over their graves, many a rugged man, whose heart was steeled by years of hardship and crime, shed tears like a child and for those bound to him by such ties as makes all soldiers brothers. One of the worst men in the company excused this seeming weakness to a companion thus: "Tim, I haven't cried this twenty years; but they were all good boys, and my countrymen."
>
> The next day when the roll was called, and they answered not, we thought of their ghastly faces as we laid them in the trench, and hearts beat quick.

On November 9, "a sad accident added to the gloom," wrote Stevenson. The Rebels celebrated what they felt was a convincing victory with a ceremonial firing of the gigantic Lady Polk cannon, one of two 128-pounders at the fort made by the Whitworth foundry in Memphis. The Lady still held a ball and powder packed during the battle, and the gunner warned the crowd of the potential danger. "But they heeded not and pressed close around. The general stood near, why should not others?" stated Stevenson, who stood 30 feet from the cannon:

> The next moment occurred the most terrific explosion I had ever heard. As the dust and smoke cleared away, we saw the shattered remains of nine men; two more died subsequently from wounds received here. Both the percussion shell and gun had burst. General Polk narrowly escaped; his cloak was swept from him and cut in two as with a sword.

VI

Grant was harshly criticized in the North for his raid on Belmont, but he defended the move as necessary to discourage Rebel movements into Missouri. Plus, he stated in *Memoirs*, "The National troops acquired a confidence in themselves at Belmont that did not desert them through the war."

Three months later, February 1862, Grant combined land and water forces for two victories in Tennessee. After taking Fort Henry on the Tennessee River, Grant's force captured strategic Fort Donelson and 15,000 Confederates on the Cumberland. Donelson was the first major defeat for the South and won fame for U.S. "Unconditional Surrender" Grant. Adoring fans sent him whiskey and cigars.

The Union conquests flanked Columbus to the east, effectively surrounding the Confederates there and forcing them to withdraw south. National troops occupied Columbus in March, and a few weeks later Grant won the bloodbath at Shiloh. The Confederacy's downfall had begun.

Columbus, once considered for a new national capital after the Louisiana Purchase, never returned to glory following the Civil War. Paying a price for loyalty to the rebellion, the town saw new roads and rail lines routed elsewhere, isolating it against the river in remote western Kentucky. A series of disastrous floods destroyed the original town site in the bottoms, and in 1927 the Red Cross relocated 40 buildings and homes onto the bluffs. Many citizens had moved on.

Today Columbus is a sleepy community of 300, but the restored fort is a main attraction in the region. Each year thousands visit the picturesque bluffs to see original earthworks and artifacts, including links of the giant chain and an iron chunk of the destroyed Lady Polk cannon. A companion Whitworth that fired 128-pound shot, the Columbiad, was dumped into the river when the Confederates abandoned the fort.

The chain still lies across the river bottom, having never stopped a Union vessel, buried and enduring as a symbol for dashed Rebel dreams to control the Mississippi and win the war.

THE SOCIAL GAME

"There were schools where we went to play, and we were called everything but our names. We were ready for it."

Fred Johnson

No kid ever went far around Dixon, a town of about 1,000 in central Missouri. But it was even easier to find John Brown; just drive down the main drag, Highway 28, to the corner of 4th Street, and there he would be, outside his house, shooting a basketball. Some days he would be out there 10, 11 hours around that goal, dribbling left and right, going up to shoot with either hand, learning the jumper, even the hook.

There was no harm done. The boy was 14 years old. He made decent grades in school and did virtually everything asked of him by teachers and his mother. He stayed out of trouble, did not hang out with the wrong kids, and was courteous and respectful toward others. No one could say anything bad about this kid, even if all they could identify him with was basketball. It was just that instead of being inside, talking on the telephone or watching some new TV show like *Gilligan's Island*; instead of being downtown along a street, pining for a 16-year-old to pick him up in a car to ride around; John Brown preferred to practice basketball.

"I was just out there shooting around, play, play, play," he recalled 30-some years later. "I just liked it, ya know? It was something you can do by yourself. You don't need another person."

At that time, 1965, most people in Dixon appreciated John Brown's dedication to basketball, even if it was just a game. He would go on into high school and help the team do what it practically always did, win 20 games in a season. Perhaps Dixon would even win a regional title along the way, given the work ethic of a kid like him, even if the team would lose early in the state tournament, which is what it always did. Heck, if the kid worked hard enough, he might even get a basketball scholarship for college and miss the draft, if the war was still going on then.

But no one could see anything more for John Brown in basketball; no one, except for Millard Hauck, the man closest to a father figure the teen had.

Millard Hauck was a self-made man, as successful an entrepreneur as any around Dixon. He was the local Chevrolet dealer, among his business interests that included oil sales and building construction. But for the kids he was also the most hands-on sports booster around town. Mr. Hauck started baseball leagues, coached teams, and spent money from his pocket on facilities and equipment. But he was especially drawn to John Brown and his close friends.

Hauck had a son in the group, Paul, who was two years younger than anyone, but talented enough to stick with them in basketball. "Millard started a lot of kids off in the third, fourth, fifth grade with basketball," said Brown. "He asked me to start playing in about the fourth grade, and it was the same nucleus of guys. We didn't have (friends) coming into the town or moving away. It was me, Randall Irvin, and the Hauck cousins, three of them: Fred, Henry, and Paul."

Soon, Millard Hauck sought competition for the boys away from Dixon. One Saturday morning, he loaded them and his wife in a station wagon, drove south toward Fort Leonard Wood, and took a right on Route 66, bound for Springfield. "We had our first game at the Boy's Club in Springfield," said Brown. "We got beat like 42 to 2 or something. We went back a week later and it was 42 to 6.

"But we just kept going back, and finally, after about a year, we started winning."

The next part of the story mystifies Brown yet today. Somehow, Millard Hauck could see potential for basketball in these boys, and greatness in at least one, and he began working them at the game like high schoolers. Millard held practices for them almost daily, year-round, emphasizing dribbling, passing, shooting. He demanded they dedicate themselves to winning, and the boys responded, even so young.

"And it just so happened guys got big later on," continued Brown. "A couple of the Haucks got to be 6-4, I (grew) to 6-7. But in those days when we were starting out, in the fourth grade, *you can't tell that.*"

Millard Hauck evidently could. And one day in Dixon, driving past the house at Highway 28 and 4th Street, he saw

John Brown outside practicing basketball, as usual. The Chevrolet pulled over and stopped, and Hauck got out. He walked over to the kid who stood 5-foot-8 and said, "John, someday you'll play pro basketball and sign for at least 100 thousand dollars."

Brown is still amazed when considering the incident. "I don't know how Millard was really able to say that," he said. "I guess he saw my mom was tall and had big hands, and he saw that I really liked to play. And he made me a wager that if I didn't make it, he'd provide me a college scholarship or something. He was just that sure. But it gave me insight to working a little harder . . . and, *it happened* for me, ya know?"

II

As American soldiers fought in Europe and the Pacific during World War II, including a significant proportion of blacks, a different sort of battle ignited in earnest at home: civil rights. Blacks began open, mass protests against the oppression that had dogged their race in America since so-called emancipation.

Among the issues rooted in white racism and segregation sanctioned by "separate but equal" laws, blacks were enraged their young men could be drafted for service while factories booming with the war effort could deny them fair employment opportunity. Northern cities were torn apart over skin color, and the term "race riot" became familiar across the nation.

But conflict over social equality was long part of life in the Mississippi River Delta, cotton country. In Bootheel Missouri, black farm laborers continued their long-held practice of gaining safe haven in forming their own "sharecropper" communities, with or without support from the government and private outside sources.

During this period, a forceful black man moved his family into New Madrid County from Memphis. A graduate of Tuskegee Institute, Travis B. Howard believed the philosophy of Booker T. Washington, who contended that when blacks could come to acquire land and businesses, they would be afforded the same respect and privileges of whites.

Howard worked toward that end in Bootheel Missouri, intending to purchase farm land for disenfranchised blacks in the area. But Howard could not secure the financial support he needed from local institutions, according to black historian and civic leader Alex Cooper of Hayti. Cooper has concluded that Howard went into Arkansas for funding, where he secured it.

About 110 acres were purchased along U.S. Highway 61 south of the town of New Madrid. In the initial years, Howard and his family were the principal occupants, according to Cooper, who believes there were likely other blacks with homes on the land. The place became known as "Howardville."

Besides farming, Howard was a teacher at area black schools, and in 1954 he joined African-Americans in celebrating the U.S. Supreme Court decision outlawing segregation in America, *Brown versus the Topeka Board of Education.* But any rejoicing was quickly subdued, put in check. Blacks realized that in the Delta region of southeast Missouri — basically all or most of six counties, Stoddard, Scott, Mississippi, New Madrid, Pemiscot and Dunklin — many whites in control would do everything possible to undermine or ignore the law abolishing segregation, an order from the highest court in the land notwithstanding.

Cooper states that following *Brown versus Topeka* there was a concerted local effort to dissuade, if not prevent, black schools and communities from integrating their students into white schools. In his historical manuscript on the period, Cooper wrote:

> It was during the late 1950s and the early 1960s that many of the school districts in the Bootheel region began to define strategies and make plans as to how to circumvent the 1954 decision of the Supreme Court that abolished the separate schools systems. . . .

> The prevailing attitude in the Delta Counties ranged from passive resistance to delaying tactics to outright refusal of some federal funds, rather than to comply with the law. The most commonly employed tactic was that of delaying implementation of the decision of the court. This was done by constructing and/or equipping all-black schools, increasing the salaries of faculty, and, in effect, overwhelming the black community. . . .

Howard and other black educators in New Madrid

County apparently grew tired of local feet-dragging on integration. They decided to accept a payoff from whites and go their own way in educating their children. "A new high school was constructed in New Madrid County in the all-black town of Howardville," wrote Cooper. "It is the clearest example of a delaying tactic employed by a (white) school district."

The new school for grades 7 through 12 opened for the term year 1957-58, consolidating area black schools. Students were drawn from settlements outside Howardville, including Catron and the North Lilbourn Project, which continued to maintain elementary schools. Howard was entering his senior years in age, but he became the school's omnipresent, omnipotent administrator. He assumed the roles of superintendent and principal, all in one impact personality.

The students could not have hoped for a better mentor.

"Travis B. Howard was a strong-willed man," said Lennies McFerren, a son of sharecroppers and a 1966 graduate of Howardville High. "He was a man who seemed to be a giant to us at that particular time. He was strong-built, a tall man that really, really cared about his students. I can still remember so many of the things that he said to us — and the things that he did — to show us which path to take."

Howardville High graduate Robert Pledger remembers the reminders Mr. Howard drilled. "It was always, 'Hey, young people. You need to get an education'," Pledger mimicked in a deep voice, laughing.

"We'd have an assembly in the gym, and he didn't need a microphone," recalled Anne Conner, the city clerk at Howardville. "You could hear him all over in there."

"You could hear him all over *Howardville*," said McFerren, who became a high school administrator and one of the most successful basketball coaches in Missouri preps history. "He called everybody by their last name: 'Mac-Ferren!' I can still hear him calling me, from one end of that big hall to the other. . ." McFerren obviously relished the memory.

"He had us intimidated just for the sake of his stature. Just to look at the man, you knew that you were not going to cross him," McFerren continued. "But he really was a caring man. He really cared about that school and that community."

In late 1964, the federal "Great Society" legislation

began allocating funds for housing at areas like Howardville, and the community experienced significant growth, according to Cooper, who is a retired director of the Delmo Housing Corporation. "With the school being built out there and the availability of funds through the Farmers Home Administration to build houses, that gave rise to the real building in the community," he said.

Howard, working with FHA officials like Cooper's brother, Roy Cooper, soon found a *town* covering the farm he once developed, including land he donated for the cause.

"Whatever needed to be done, he was going to do it. That's the type person he was," said McFerren. "He spent a lot of his money that people didn't really know where it was coming from. Up until I became a grown man in education myself, I didn't realize it either, because he wasn't out there trying to toot his own horn. It was just that if something needed to be done for the school or community, he saw to it."

"There hasn't been anybody I've known that I could say was a better person than Travis B. Howard," asserted McFerren. "And his legacy lives on in the town named for him, and that's the way it should be."

The students of Howardville High sat through many civics lessons from Mr. Howard. He preferred assembly speeches, wherein the basic elements of living he addressed were discipline, hard work, fortitude, fairness, truth and responsibility, which pretty much ruled out a life of laziness, shortcuts, negativism, deceit, hypocrisy, and projecting blame. And Mr. Howard was adept at making any students in the audience squirm who knew his words meant them.

"I used to get on the front row, man," said Pledger, who became a minister. "I'd get right down there where I was lookin' up at him. And *laugh* — that man could keep me laughin'. I mean, he was tellin' the truth, but it was the way he'd say it that got me."

Speakers were solicited to visit the school, successful blacks for Howardville schoolchildren to meet and emulate. Like Mr. Howard's son, Elston Howard, an All-Star catcher for the New York Yankees who appeared in nine World Series classics.

Mr. Howard believed sports were important to the community, a wholesome, common passion that could involve virtually everyone from youth to elderly. He believed winning athletics could instill pride in Howardville among all and gain recognition for the school and community. Thus he hired William C. Jackson to coach the Howardville Hawks boys basketball team, the only sports program the high school could fund.

Jackson was one of the region's most successful coaches of any race, having logged a 151-49 record in nine seasons coaching basketball at black schools like Catron. A native of West Virginia and a World War II veteran, Jackson had starred in football and baseball at Lane College in Jackson, Tennessee. Jackson's expertise and the athletic talent at Howardville produced an immediate juggernaut, with the Hawks winning 22 and losing three in their first season.

"Without a doubt, you could say it was a sort of dynasty," said McFerren, who, beside himself, had brothers and relatives who starred for the Hawks under Jackson. "But when you say *dynasty*, you have to define that by including state championships. You only become a dynasty when you win championships."

McFerren should know. As a coach at Charleston High beginning in the 1977-78 season, he won seven Missouri Class 3A titles among nine final four appearances in 16 years. Today, he coaches and is a principal at New Madrid County High School, near Howardville on Highway 61.

"At Howardville when I played, we had those dynasty-type seasons up until the state playoffs," said McFerren. "Everybody knew Howardville because of that basketball team."

Fred Johnson remembers the Howardville Hawks. Johnson was a freshman black student when the Oran School District integrated in 1965-66 in Scott County, and he quickly starred on the varsity basketball team. With the Bootheel's cotton legacy unique to Missouri, integration was instantly turning many of the region's small schools into basketball powerhouses to contend for state titles, sooner or later. But Howardville, said Johnson, "was already there."

"Howardville had super, super teams," he said. "They didn't stop playing ball the entire year, and they would be in top shape. They could run, shoot, and they would not be intimidated." Johnson laughed, recalling the rugged Coach Jackson stalking the sidelines. "Heck, I know those players wouldn't be intimidated, if they could play for Coach Jackson. *He* was intimidating. Aww man, was he ever!"

Both Oran and Howardville won Class M Regional championships in '66. They met in the first round of the state tournament at Houck Fieldhouse in Cape Girardeau. Oran was talented too, and extremely well-coached by Gene Bess, still young in a career that has become known among basketball coaches across American, preps to pros.

"We had lost to Howardville the first game of that season," said Johnson. "But pretty soon we went on a 29-game winning streak, and we felt like we were ready for 'em in Cape. Then we come out and those cheerleaders they had were doin' that Train cheer, and those people they had were in the stands rockin'!"

The game was a slugfest, with Bess matching his controlled offense and man-to-man defense against Jackson's free-wheeling offense and fullcourt zone press. Howardville had the edge when the game came down to a key play involving the freshman forward, Johnson, and the senior Hawks guard he admired so much, McFerren.

"Lennies controlled that team on the floor," said Johnson. "That man used to come flying down the court and throw blind passes — and there was always somebody on the other end."

In the final minutes, Johnson recalled, McFerren drove for a layup and Johnson stepped in front to draw a charging foul. "That was his fifth foul," said Johnson, "and that's when we figured we had a chance." From there, Oran came back to win in overtime.

McFerren, despite his immense success as a coach, rues the chances missed as a player. "My teams at Howardville never made it (to a final four), and that was our failure right there," he said.

By the time McFerren graduated, the social order of America was changing rapidly, and Howardville High and the community were not immune. The all-black school was fast becoming an oddity, even in the Bootheel, where the white, vestige attitude favoring segregation was bowing to the reality of law, if not for what was right. The region's most stubborn white districts were giving way to integration. But Howardville, so independently proud by then, forged ahead with its school.

McFerren said as the '60s progressed, it became increasingly difficult for the Hawks to compete in basketball. "Really — and I don't want this to sound like sour grapes —

but we had a tough road to hoe on the court as an all-black school," said McFerren, citing problems such as lack of practice equipment.

"But the real challenge was in games. Being one of the only all-black schools left anywhere, many people looked down their nose at us. I know that was going on because when you have (game) officials at that time who looked at our coach differently than they looked at other coaches, then you have a problem right there."

Whether handicaps were real or imagined, no one in the Hawks program took time to sulk, especially around the driven leader. "Coach Jackson was a man who really stood his ground," said McFerren. "He really knew where he was going, and he knew what it took to win."

Jackson knew time was running out on Howardville High, which would soon have to follow the law itself and integrate with whites. And what Jackson wanted, just once before that happened, was for the Hawks to prove an all-black school could win a state championship in basketball.

"You know that was the goal," said McFerren.

III

In research on renowned Basketball Towns of Missouri, the road inevitably leads to Bradleyville, a "don't blink" sort of junction in the Ozarks near Branson. And typically the search begins with a tip from someone in a larger community or city, for a small-town hoops legend is not statewide until recognized in the metro areas.

In 1993, longtime Springfield sportswriter Marty Eddlemon discussed Missouri's rural phenomenons of the game, teams like Puxico, of course, but also Versailles of 1947 and the dominant New Haven squads of the late '50s. "I think the magic is really when the little schools beat the big schools," said Eddlemon, smiling. "I imagine that's the part of it in Indiana too."

Eddlemon was a Hannibal High grad in 1944, when little Bismarck defeated Lebanon, 40-38, to win the state championship for one class that included all schools of any size. "Red Regan was the Bismarck star, and he was the sensation of the state," said Eddlemon. "He was a two-handed shooter that was double-teamed in the final and passed off, but he still scored a lot."

The one-class tournament in Missouri ended for good in

1949, and many people regretted its passing. But a Christmas tournament in Springfield would continue to pit small schools against the large, and become synonymous for prep basketball in southwest Missouri: "The Greenwood Blue and Gold Tournament, to me, is probably the best tournament in the state of Missouri because you've got the little schools coming in to beat the big ones," said Eddlemon. "And I think that's the real charm of the game for years, going back to Bismarck winning the whole shea-bang and Versailles scaring St. Louis Beaumont to death.

"The Blue and Gold gives you the chance to see the Bradleyvilles come in and beat the (Springfield) Parkviews, and that's the only tournament left like that."

Bradleyville High in the '60s maintained an enrollment of around 75 students total, grades nine through 12.

A year later, this author was at St. Louis University, talking with Billikens basketball coach Charlie Spoonhour, who started his career at rural prep schools across southern Missouri. When the topic became small-school powerhouses, his pink, moon face gave a look like, *You don't know about Bradleyville?* Then he proceeded to give me a quick lesson in trademark Spoonese. "I was at Salem in the late '60s, and we came close to Bradleyville once. We were in the tournament at Springfield, the Blue and Gold, or whatever they call that thing," he said. "We were tied with 'em at the end of three quarters."

Spoonhour recalled it felt pretty good to be competing with one of the state's hottest teams of any size. Then, he said, "Some guy from Bradleyville leans over the rail there at SMS Arena — it had to be a Combs, 'cause that family supplied most of the players on that team — and he said, 'Lon and David, if you guys don't get busy, we're not goin' huntin' tonight!'"

Spoonhour, being from northeast Arkansas himself, understood a boy's passion for raccoon hunting by moonlight; at Bradleyville, that was how several players celebrated victories, by going right out to run the hills with their trusty dogs. He knew Bradleyville would be motivated in the fourth.

"And they beat us by 10," Spoon added. "They had the Combses, and Maggard, and Pellham. Bradleyville was good."

Spoonhour was right about the Combs clan. The next

step for information on the story was logical enough — call the first Combs found listed from Bradleyville, which was Joe, in a high school handbook.

Bingo. Joe Combs, I found, had graduated in 1966 from Bradleyville High, where he started on the basketball team. Later, he taught and coached at the school. Personable and helpful over the phone, Joe noted the Combs boys on any given year's team were usually cousins linked by a grandfather, John Riley Combs. "My grandfather had 15 children," he explained. "Five were boys, and they raised families around here."

From Springfield, the way to Bradleyville began by heading south on U.S. Highway 65 with the flow of out-of-state cars, trucks toting boats, and tour buses enroute to Branson. I broke away from the pack at Ozark — the town booming in the exploding growth of the Springfield-Branson corridor — and took Missouri Route 14 east to Sparta. At this point, I was cresting the Ozark Plateau, from which a high finger extended south with an ancient path atop it that someone surfaced this century and called a "highway," Route 125.

Now I was on the road to Bradleyville, and the smell of cut timber — the fresh sawdust of sawmills — hit immediately on 125. There were a few tiny towns along the way such as Chadwick, and a few deserted places that constitute little more than a sign, like Oldfield; but mostly the blacktop was through elevated wilderness, dipping and ascending atop the ridge like a roller coaster on its highest track. Sycamores and oaks crowded the narrow road, their summer foliage often shading it across, and visibility ahead averaged less than 100 feet to the next curve. But when the trees broke along the east shoulder, the view was spectacular to distant ridgelines on the other side of riffled valleys below. In virtually every open pasture atop the plateau, there were broken trees, killed by high winds or lightning strikes.

It was a beautiful first Saturday in June, 1997, and scant few cars passed in the opposite direction during the 20-some miles to Bradleyville. Turtles were everywhere on the road, black snakes writhed into grass at the shoulder, and a big dark buzzard rose reluctantly from road-kill to hover overhead until the intruder drove by. The road descended into Swan Creek Valley, site of the erstwhile town Garrison and a vacant general store made of cut brownstone blocks with a rusting Coca-Cola sign still out front. The remaining miles of 125 to Bradleyville followed a narrow valley branching off Swan.

Just north of Bradleyville sat an old barn with a basketball backboard nailed to a side. But the rim was missing, and the earth below, surely beaten bare at one time by countless footsteps and pivots, was grown-over in weeds. And that scene captured the dormant state of the game in this Basketball Town of lore, where the school once brought home state championship trophies while graduating young men to succeed in the world at-large. In the 1990s, the team was losing.

"The kids (with talent) today are the ones who smoke cigarettes, drink beer, and burn tires in the middle of the road," said Leon Combs, Bradleyville Class of 1953. "These are the same type of guys that 30 years ago were playing ball *at night after games*. What's missing is the winning attitude and leadership."

Town population in 1997 was listed at 92. The community itself had aged well beside Beaver Creek, and was perhaps more beautiful than ever before. The homes were not large, but well-kept with colorful flower gardens and those white plastic chairs and tables on clean patios. The grass around town was mowed in most spots, park-like, even to the banks of the sparkling stream. Highway 76 intersected with 125 at the business section comprised of several small but tidy stores with customers on Saturday, including BJ's Pizza and Recreation, Billy Jack's Package, Combs Grocery and Feed, Jim's One-Stop, and Combs Dry Goods — adorned by a Red Wing Shoes sign. A barber shop was the only storefront that appeared to be vacant.

East of town, a picturesque ranch sprawled from Highway 76, and three Bradleyville alumni greeted me at the hilltop office. They were all basketball players and brothers, so naturally the name was Combs: Leon, Jerry and Joe, in that order of age. Leon, a graduate of the University of Missouri School of Journalism who went on to obvious success in sales and business, had returned home in recent years and purchased the ranch, among other interests. Jerry lived and worked locally, and Joe was a schoolteacher who coached the basketball team as late as 1995.

The articulate, witty Leon was working on a book about Bradleyville Eagles Basketball, and he quickly disclaimed any part of the winning '60s. During his four seasons on the varsity in the early '50s, Bradleyville was winless in two and won but one game in each of the others. "One year we lost to Branson in the sub-regional, 64 to 6, and I know they had their third string in most of the game," Leon recalled.

"I think I was a freshman, only about 5-foot tall, and it seemed like I looked up and saw the bottom of tennis shoes the whole time." Leon did score two of the six points, and he must have been hustling. "I got a writeup in the Springfield paper that went something like, 'Leon Combs played like he didn't know his team was 60 points behind,'" he mused.

When Jerry approached high school at the decade's end, fortunes on the court began to change. His class of boys had learned solid fundamentals of basketball in 8th grade under Coach Ralph Jewell Snowden. In high school they had fiery coach Jim Shannahan for two years, and Bradleyville competed hard against other teams. But, Jerry recounted, the Eagles fell in a Class S Regional final to Nixa on the latter's home court, losing by two free throws in the final seconds, and Shannahan lost his Irish temper. "The ref made a bad call, and (Shannahan) told him to step outside so he could 'stomp every damn tooth out,'" Jerry chuckled. "And he was waitin' for him." The referee took an alternate route out of the building, and Shannahan moved on to another job.

In summer 1961, a pair of brothers came to Bradleyville High: Omar Gibson, who assumed duties as district superintendent, and Ray Gibson, who became the basketball coach. Both instilled discipline and grace that extended top to bottom in the school system, according to the Combs brothers, and Coach Gibson made a few adjustments in the basketball team. He increased conditioning, worked to eliminate turnovers as part of his controlled game plan, and insisted on sportsmanship. He also inherited a championship team in the making.

Four seniors returned to start: Jerry, 6-foot-3 at center; forwards Roy Combs and Bill Roberts, both over 6-foot; and guard Leon Boyd. Then there was the freshman who would dominate: 6-3 shooting guard Darrell Paul. The sixth man was a scoring threat off the bench, Eddie Hunsaker.

All the boys came from relatively poor families used to hard work in the timber. Combs cousins Jerry and Roy, for example, got out of bed in the dark each morning and headed for cut-over timber acreage, starting work by daylight to salvage what wood was left to sell for charcoal processing. They cut and stacked three cords on a 16-foot flatbed truck, parked the rig at a kiln on Highway 125, then caught a school bus. After school they came back to unload the wood and collect $21. The money was split three ways between each boy and expenses for the truck.

Leon Boyd was an incredible coon-hunter in the fact he ran with his old dog wherever it went. Even the heartiest hunters would huff and puff up and down the hills at night, content to catch their dogs at the tree to shine a light up. Not Boyd. "I never saw nothin' like it," said Jerry. "From the first step that dog made barking on a trail that may go 10 miles, Leon was right there shining a light on it. And he was there at the end too, shinin' that light as soon as that dog was on the tree."

Most of the lasting memories of Darrell Paul involve basketball, on the court and off. According to research by a cousin, Leon Combs, Paul's parents gave him a ball at about age 6, and the little boy would hardly put it down. By the time he was in junior high, Paul made spending money at carnivals shooting free throws, hitting 25 straight at the old-time booths paying double-or-nothing. "That was nothing for him," said Leon. "He could hit 150 in a row."

Paul would die of leukemia at age 27, a tragedy that contributed to his larger-than-life status around Bradleyville. But he became revered because he was one of the greatest shooters ever to play schoolboy basketball in Missouri.

Leon scrolled-up on the computer screen, continuing with his book notes: Ray Gibson said Paul was the best open shooter he ever saw; Paul was deadly from 25-30 feet in the 8th grade, and had extremely quick hands in going up with the shot; Paul set a scoring record at the Blue and Gold Tournament that lasted 30 years, although he played before the 3-point shot was sanctioned.

Gibson recalled that before one game in 1962, Jerry Combs told him, "I drove by Darrell's house last night and he was still shootin', so we'll be on tonight."

Paul was said to have grown during his freshman year, *three inches*, from 6-3 to 6-6. At the same time, fortunes grew for Bradleyville basketball. The Eagles claimed third place in the Blue and Gold, defeating big-school Joplin Parkwood for the trophy. They won tournament titles at Forsyth and Ava, then entered the postseason by rolling to the Class S

Regional crown at Crane. Bradleyville won its first two state tournaments games at Springfield, then headed to the final four in Columbia.

At this point, recalled Jerry, the team lost some of its nerve. The boys dreaded going to compete so far away from their fans, a following that by now included people from other towns and counties. "We figured nobody would come to Columbia," said Jerry, "and we get up there and it's like Old Home Week in the stands. I bet there wasn't a soul left in Douglas County or Taney County."

Despite the support, the Eagles were still rattled as their semifinal against Alma began with a morning tip-off. The Bradleyville boys felt lost on the airy court in cavernous Brewer Fieldhouse, despite their experience at the SMS Arena. They especially had trouble getting their bearings to shoot. The goals seemed suspended in midair, lacking familiar backdrops like walls and a roof, and the morning sun cast a bright glare through the windows. Even the marksman Paul could not find his range. Struggling to score, the team took a timeout, and Paul shook his head at Gibson. "Coach," he said, "there's somethin' wrong with them baskets."

Still, the boys summoned the resolve to win the semifinal and move into the championship game, where they defeated North Harrison, 59-49, to claim the Class S title. Tiny Bradleyville was the hottest sports topic in southwest Missouri, and the story took an interesting twist when Ray Gibson announced he was leaving Bradleyville.

After one year of high school coaching and one state championship, Gibson headed to the College of the Ozarks to begin a career in higher education.

Young Argil Ellison graduated from Arkansas Technical College in 1962. As a physical education major aspiring to teach and coach basketball, Ellison inquired about a job opening at Bradleyville, Missouri. He went to an interview, and was offered the position as athletic director and basketball coach.

The young man signed the contract with Bradleyville High, and passed it back to Principal Noel Short and District Superintendent Omar Gibson. Then Ellison became fully informed about the situation he was entering. "By the way . . ." he was told, "your team won the state championship last year."

Ellison recalled his mouth dropped. "And there I was," he said, chuckling.

Problem was, the team Ellison inherited was hardly the one that won the Class S title the year before. Four key seniors had graduated: Jerry Combs, Roy Combs, Boyd and Roberts, the bedrock of Bradleyville's run to the championship. Thus, Ellison's new team, the 1962-63 Eagles, won 17 games while losing 11. The record would have been decent for many programs, but Bradleyville had become a basketball town expecting more, so the local grade on Ellison's first campaign at the Eagles helm was deemed only average. Some fans thought the young coach was in over his head.

Ellison soon proved himself, however. Bradleyville went 25-5 in 1964, 29-3 in '65, then 28-2 in '66, the senior season for Joe Combs. "Argil Ellison was just a great coach," Joe said. "Probably, he's the best coach that ever was at Bradleyville. He had total control. You didn't question anything he said, and you'd do anything for him. You actually enjoyed doing anything for him."

Yet, after Ellison's fourth year at Bradleyville — including three seasons averaging 27 wins and three losses each — people still grumbled. The problem was he failed to lead the Eagles to another state title. "I went through four years there and went through some pretty troubling times," he said. "Then we won the state championship, so. . ."

Things worked out, and in record fashion. Early in the 1966-67 season, the Eagles lost to Sparta to drop their record to 3-1. They got back on track with a victory in the next game, then rolled into the Christmas break on a winning streak, feeling good about their chance to win the Greenwood Blue and Gold Tournament in Springfield. Bradleyville won its first two games there, advancing to the semifinals against Springfield Parkview, the number-one ranked team in a newspaper poll of coaches in southwest Missouri.

Bradleyville was led by a new wave of Combs descendants: three juniors, 6-5 postman David Combs, gritty point guard Lonnie Combs, and forward Duane Meggard. David remembers a headline that appeared in a Springfield student newspaper the morning of the Parkview game: "Hicks From the Sticks Will Meet Their Match Tonight." David said he and Lonnie Combs read the newspaper together. "I told

Lonnie, 'Parkview may be pretty good, but they still have to play us.'"

Parkwood ended up wishing otherwise. Bradleyville stunned the mighty Vikings, winning the semifinal, and the Eagles went on to claim the Blue and Gold championship over Houston. Southwest Missouri was smitten with the small-town hoops phenomenon, especially an adoring media. "Springfield fans loved it," said Joe Combs. "Those who really appreciated basketball just kind of reveled in how the whole thing about Bradleyville happened."

The Eagles did not lose the rest of the season, winning the 1967 Class S Championship by defeating previously undefeated Archie in the final, 60-47. Most of the starters returned the next season, and the team kept rolling, winning the Blue and Gold again, a monumental feat. "We won that tournament two years in a row, and that was probably my greatest accomplishment as far as personal achievement goes," Ellison said. "It probably meant more than winning the (Class S) state championship. There was no weeding-out of teams at the Blue and Gold."

Bradleyville was also accomplishing something at the time that meant more to fans in the state at-large: a record winning streak. The Eagles had not lost since the start of the previous season in that early defeat to Sparta. The streak hit 40 wins, then 50, and by the time Bradleyville reached the 1968 final four, the Eagles had won an unprecedented 62 straight games. They defeated Glasgow in the semifinals and returned to the state championship game.

Bradleyville's opponent for the 1968 Class S title would be the Howardville Hawks, a relatively unknown team from an all-black school in Bootheel Missouri. David Combs confirmed the Eagles knew little about Howardville, but no one was really concerned. Bradleyville expected to enter a game and immediately dictate terms, to control the game. The philosophy had been working a long time over a huge winning streak. The Eagles expected their dominance to continue against Howardville.

"We went into the game probably a little overconfident," Combs said. "And before we realized what was going on, they were stickin' right with us."

For a long time in his life, including the beginning of his coaching career, Charlie Spoonhour followed a boyhood idol, Tommy Hewgley. Spoonhour was a freshman in high school at Rogers, Arkansas when Hewgley was a senior starring in football and baseball. Later, Hewgley was coaching high school basketball at Exeter in southwest Missouri when he helped land Spoonhour the coaching job at Rocky Comfort High School.

In 1962-63, both had ingredients for great teams at their respective schools. "We were supposed to have the best team in southwest Missourah at Rocky Comfort," Spoonhour recalled, "but on Halloween our kids went out throwin' hedge apples from the back of a bob truck and had an accident. Some of 'em were banged up.

"Anyway, Tommy's team developed and was better 'n ours anyway. Exeter went 35-and-0 (and won Class S), and Tommy was offered the job at Bloomfield, over in the Bootheel."

Hewgley accepted, and Spoonhour followed, taking his buddy's offer to be the assistant coach at Bloomfield. The result was an outstanding program in a basketball-crazed, resourceful town. Hewgley and Spoonhour did not produce a state championship in four years at Bloomfield, but they delivered two final four appearances in Class M, the greatest achievements ever for the school in basketball. The community's great hoops fans would be eternally grateful.

Moreover, beyond basketball in that era, Bloomfield was promoting social progress in the Bootheel. Bloomfield High was taking the initiative among area schools to start embracing all-black teams as equals on the basketball court. Bloomfield High scheduled games with schools like Howardville, Hayti Central, and O'Bannon of New Madrid, and extended invitations to its prestigious holiday tournament.

Hewgley and Spoonhour were meeting and competing against the coaches and athletes emerging from segregation's darkness. And the former southwest Missouri boys got educated a bit. They were now in a rural area remarkable for a high population of African-Americans, and if any laboratory could be found to study equality among races, the Bootheel's basketball courts offered proof.

"The Bootheel had better athletes than southwest Missouri," Spoonhour said. "And you ran into some well-coached basketball teams. You were in hard games all the time."

Howardville, in particular, was a hard game for anybody

in southeast Missouri. "Howardville was coached by William C. Jackson," recited Spoon, "and they were durn good. Howardville was up-tempo. They had good players, and when you have good players, you oughta take advantage."

Hewgley and Spoonhour sought the competition of Howardville, and the Hawks were invited to the Christmas tournament. "Bloomfield brought Howardville to the invitational," Jackson said by telephone from Charleston, West Virginia, where he lives in retirement. "We had some battles at Bloomfield. They always invited Howardville to the invitational."

Howardville also threatened Bloomfield's regional reign in Class M, according to Spoonhour. He said the Hawks nearly short-circuited Bloomfield's run to the final four in 1965. Howardville moved out of Class M for the 1966-67 season, landing in Class S with schools under 200 enrollment. "We didn't cry much over that," Spoonhour recalled. "I thought that was a good deal," he laughed.

Howardville fell short of the Missouri S Tournament in '67, but Jackson and his players had a final chance before the school closed after one more year. In 1967-68, Howardville High's last year of existence, the players continued the mission to bring state recognition not only to themselves, but for their race. And they succeeded.

IV

When Howardville won a Class S Regional title and qualified for the 1968 state tournament, few people outside southeast Missouri took notice. The Hawks' record was 16-7, but their losses included three to Matthews, a Bootheel school featuring black stars that would go on to win the Class M championship, the region's first state title since Puxico's back-to-back crowns in '51 and '52.

In the opening round of the Class S Tournament, Howardville defeated Couch, then eliminated St. George of Hermann in the quarterfinals. Finally reaching the final four in Columbia, the Hawks destroyed Lathrop in the semis, 65-43. The *Kansas City Star* reported, "Lathrop was never in the game. The Mules could not handle Howardville's pressing defense. . ."

Missouri media and fans had discovered Howardville, especially a trio of flashy stars in 6-7 big men Reuben Marsh and Lewis Little, and 5-5 Nathaniel Thomas, a crowd-pleasing point guard who would hide along the sidelines before taking off on a fastbreak.

And the Howardville *cheerleaders* were instant sensations at Brewer Fieldhouse, igniting the crowd of 5,000-plus with spirit theretofore unseen at state final fours. The Howardville cheerleaders were accomplished dancers and acrobats with a signature act in "The Train," their grand entrance into a gym or arena moving in a "choo-choo" line that won fans instantly. "Everybody loved the Howardville cheerleaders," said Lennies McFerren. "They were probably more exciting than the basketball team for some people. They put on a show, and people came from miles around to see 'em come in with that train thing."

Saturday night, March 2, Brewer was packed as the Howardville cheerleaders got everybody rocking with The Train. The Class S championship game preceded the M final, and the announcement of the starting lineups for Bradleyville-Howardville kept the crowd's charge going; but no one could know how great a thrill the game would become.

The contest began like any other with two teams trying to execute a plan to win. Howardville, with the twin 6-7 guys in Marsh and Little, tried size and speed against Bradleyville, which countered with Ellison's controlled but opportunistic offense. Both teams were highly conditioned and able to exert defensive pressure over the full court, but Ellison preferred a "matchup zone" that countered the opponent's offense.

But once the game got under way, neither team got to follow a particular plan; neither could come to dictate terms; neither could gain the upper hand. The result was a classic game. Bradleyville might have had a chance or two to pull away, but Howardville would respond and stay close.

On the court, Bradleyville's outstanding 6-5 postman, David Combs, battled inside the lane with Marsh and Little. He saw his guards, Lonnie Combs and Garlin Pellham, having to work the utmost to move the ball and get an open shot against the Hawks backcourt that swarmed on defense. "With us being over-confident and them coming out to play well, that gave them momentum to stay in the game," Combs said.

"And then we were kind of rattled that game. . . . No one played exceptionally well on our team that game. But that's not taking anything away from Howardville. They were a lot better than we gave them credit for, and a lot bigger than we thought they were."

The Hawks' determination electrified the crowd. "Howardville fought back from the brink of defeat so many times that the overflow crowd . . . was in hysterics," wrote Fritz Kriesler in *The Star*.

Howardville led by one point after one quarter, Bradleyville was up by two at halftime, and Howardville tied the game to end the third quarter, 43-43. With two minutes left in regulation, defending state champion Bradleyville clung to a three-point lead, which evaporated. Howardville came back to tie the score, 57-57, then stalled with the ball for much of the final minute, looking for a shot. At 15 seconds, ballhandler William Gray saw one and drove for the basket, darting to a lay-in that gave the Hawks a 2-point lead with 15 seconds to tick.

Brewer was in pandemonium as Bradleyville headed back upcourt on offense. The Eagles 63-game win streak was in jeopardy as well as the state championship. Time waned before David Combs delivered in the clutch, nailing a 10-foot jumper with four seconds to go. Regulation ended tied, 59-59, and the title match went into overtime.

The fans got no relief in the first overtime, which saw both teams blow chances to win before ending again in a tie, 63-63. At the buzzer, a Howardville cheerleader slumped to the floor along the sideline, seemingly passed out.

By the end of the second overtime, both Marsh and Little had fouled out for Howardville, and Bradleyville had a bid to end matters, taking possession of the ball in the final seconds with a 2-point lead. But Gray struck again, making a steal and dashing to a layup with six seconds left, deadlocking the score again at 69-all. Along the sidelines, more Howardville cheerleaders were keeling over.

Decades later, Ellison, a retired school administrator in Bowling Green, paused to remember the Howardville cheer-leaders. "They got to either hyperventilating or getting too hot or whatever," he smiled. "I mean they were just passing out. Heck, we had to stop the game because of the Howardville cheerleaders. Here they were, falling out. . ."

At the end of the third overtime, more cheerleaders went to the floor, for the score remained tied, 73-73. A state title game was headed into a record fourth overtime.

Howardville won the tip to start it, and controlled the ball for 90 seconds before Gray missed a jumper. Back downcourt came Bradleyville, and David Combs rammed in a basket at 1:22 left. The Eagles were up, 75-73, giving David 31 points and a new tournament scoring record. Howardville had two chances to tie, but Thomas turned the ball over once, and Combs blocked his driving layup on the Hawks' final gasp. Maggard added a free throw for the Eagles, and Bradleyville had repeated as Class S champions.

The Howardville Hawks had fallen short of their goal for a state championship in basketball, but they had made their statement for equality on the state stage of high school basketball.

The game, at least, is unforgettable for those who witnessed it. "Bradleyville and Howardville was the best," Spoonhour said.

"It was one of the greatest thrills of my life, seeing and winning a game like that for the state championship," Ellison said. "Both clubs at various times thought they had it won."

The theatrics did not end after four overtimes. Spoonhour said the Howardville cheerleaders "were all stretched out" on the sidelines. "They were just beached over there," he said, laughing. "And then they announced Howardville had won the pep club award, and those cheerleaders came to life! They just sprang up!

"Then they danced around the floor and the place went crazy."

V

The Bradleyville dominance ended quickly after the second consecutive state championship in 1968. The Combs boys, Pellham, and Maggard graduated; Argil Ellison left to become coach at Bowling Green High in northeast Missouri; and the Eagles lost their first game the next season, halting the winning streak at 64 games, still a record.

But as fast as Bradleyville's renown deflated, another small-school phenomenon developed in central Missouri: Dixon in 1969, led by John Brown, a 6-7 athlete who could shoot, pass, and handle the ball. The other starters were hotshot guard Randall Irvin and the Hauck cousins, Henry and Fred at the forwards, and Paul at point guard.

"It was just a rare team, very unselfish," said Lynn

Whitten, then the assistant coach under head coach Bob Ogle. "John averaged 30-plus points a game, Randall averaged 21 or 22, and I think the rest of the starters averaged double figures."

Dixon's scoring attracted the media and fans, making headlines such as a record 172-36 win over Stoutland. The Bulldogs averaged more than 100 points a game in the regular season, and remained undefeated as they entered the Class M final four at Brewer Fieldhouse in Columbia. After Dixon bumped off undefeated Hermann in the semifinals, the opponent for the state championship was a relatively unknown — but undefeated — team from southeast Missouri, Oran.

Media and fans were handing Dixon the trophy before the game started, but the familiar storyline of the powerhouse crushing the underdog did not play out. The drama was instead David-versus-Goliath, with Oran as the former making a bid to topple mighty Dixon.

"Dixon was huge (physically)," said Fred Johnson, the Oran scoring star, who at 6-2 was the tallest of any team starters. "But we were not intimidated. It became just a true battle. They had us down 10 points in the second half, and we just kept clawing away."

The game also continued a different theme that was obvious to 6,000 people in attendance, if not openly discussed: the all-white team, Dixon, versus one with four black starters, Oran. And like Bradleyville-Howardville the year before in Class S, the Dixon-Oran Class M final was a classic, although it will always be remembered for an unfortunate, strange ending.

With 12 seconds left in the fourth quarter, Dixon led, 75-73, but Johnson went to the free throw line with two shots. Today, Oran supporters and Johnson recall a deafening noise from Dixon fans and cheerleaders as he took the first free throw and sank it. Conversely, Dixon supporters remember Johnson took more than 10 seconds to shoot, which violated a time-limit rule for a free throw. The rule, rarely enforced, was so obscure many athletes, fans and media had never heard of it.

As Johnson took the ball for his second free throw — which could have tied the score with 12 seconds to play — he first hesitated, which is about the last point in the story where 6,000 can generally agree. What happened next will always be debated among witnesses.

Before Johnson could shoot, referee Gene Barth blew his whistle, took the ball away from Johnson, and called a 10-second violation, awarding possession to Dixon. The Bulldogs won, 76-74, after Irvin added a free throw, to claim the state championship and complete a 36-0 season. Oran finished 35-1.

With the game over, the second-guessing began. *Star* sportswriter Fritz Kreisler wrote from Columbia that "Dixon and Oran, two fantastic teams . . . battled through 31 minutes and 48 seconds of dead-even basketball . . . only to have the Missouri Class M high school championship decided by an official."

Former Oran coach Gene Bess said Johnson held the ball too long before shooting the first free throw, but he contended the player was allowed only seven or eight seconds on the second attempt. "The referee made two bad calls," said Bess. "He should've made it on the first (free throw), if he was going to call it. Not the second one."

In Dixon, Whitten disagreed, estimating Johnson took 12 to 13 seconds on the second attempt.

In St. Louis, Spoonhour said, "Fred probably went a little more than 10 (seconds). . . . But it was a terrible thing."

Regardless, all parties today prefer to accentuate the positives. Bess expressed regret the game is remembered most for controversy, "because it was just a great bunch of young athletes that played their hearts out.

"There was great emphasis on that game," said Bess. "It was two small towns with a lot of pride at stake, and I don't think it was played that well by either team. But it just went to the wire with tremendous competitive spirit."

"And," he added wryly, "those were two pretty good high school teams going at it."

The competitiveness, the success, carried over for many participants in the game. Notably, John Brown fulfilled his prophesy from Millard Hauck, becoming a two-time college All-America for the Missouri Tigers, and a number-one draft pick by the Atlanta Hawks. Per Millard's prediction, Brown's first contract was for six figures, and his NBA career spanned seven years. Later, he owned a real estate business in Rolla. "Millard passed away years ago," said Brown. "It was suddenly with a heart attack, and he was only in about his mid-50s. He really was an amazing man. You just have to give this guy a lot of credit."

Bess became one of basketball's most respected coaches for his junior college dynasty at Three Rivers Community College in Poplar Bluff. The Raiders under Bess appeared frequently in the juco men's final four, winning two national titles at the competitive NJCAA Tournament in Hutchinson, Kansas.

The referee who made the notorious call, the late Gene Barth, went on to a distinguished officiating career in NCAA sports and the NFL.

Fred Johnson excelled in coaching, winning state titles in girls basketball at Scott County Central and leading the Sikeston boys team to the Class 4A final four. In 1997, he confirmed he was haunted by the rare 10-second violation that was called on him as a prep player.

"I've lived with that since 1969," said Johnson, who recalled he first thought Barth was taking the ball to quiet the crowd, which was a common procedure. "When I found out it was because he said I held it 10 seconds. . ." Johnson paused. "That particular night became the longest one of my life. I felt I'd let the team down, and the community too. It took a while for me to understand I didn't.

"It was not a failure by me, it was just a part of growin' up," said Johnson, then he chuckled. "You give me that ball nowadays, I'd shoot that sucker so fast the ref's hands wouldn't get down."

Johnson was grateful to basketball because it gave order in life for a youth he admitted "had a mean streak." Bess was a demanding mentor whom Johnson did not understand as a teen, but did later, as an adult. "The man was teachin' lessons we had to have to succeed in life. Basketball was just the start of it," he said.

In small communities of the time, the game was an escape for boys who initially faced bleak prospects. At Bradleyville, timber country, David Combs worked all night in a charcoal kiln, making it easy for him to enjoy the remaining waking hours before school — which he spent practicing basketball. In the Bootheel delta, Johnson and other blacks were taking the same perspective on drudgery versus play, even if basketball meant hard work too.

In the delta, Johnson grew up in small houses set amidst the huge cotton fields around Oran. He was raised by his grandparents, field hands, natives of Mississippi who labored in a job that neither Fred nor his uncle of the same age, John Johnson, wanted for themselves. "I had to go to the fields and pick cotton, chop cotton," said Johnson. "Me and John knew basketball was our chance to get *out* of those fields."

When Fred, John, and a handful of other black teens integrated Oran High in August 1965, the school was ready for them. "We did not encounter racism in the school," said Johnson. "We had too strong an administration and too good of teachers for that to happen."

But a minority white faction in the community opposed integration and blacks, said Johnson. Black youths were often ignored or scowled-at on Oran streets, and one restaurant refused to allow them to enter, he said. But basketball changed some people, at least.

"They would come watch us play the game," noted Johnson. "Before, they'd see us around town and weren't friendly. Then all of a sudden, they started identifying us: *Hey, that's ol' Fred!*. They started getting closer to you, speakin' to you. God yes, basketball tore that barrier down."

For Johnson and many others, high school basketball was the game of competition on the court, and a preparation for what happens off it. Basketball was, and remains, the social game in the small town, hardly perfect in virtue, but perpetually teaching values to adults as well as the children who play.

In the Bootheel and elsewhere during the '60s, basketball was a social laboratory and a lightning rod. Johnson recalled both his grandparents and Bess helped prepare him for the racism the game would bring.

"Coach Bess told us to go in a gym and play and don't show any emotions," said Johnson. "Just play to win and keep your minds focused, and everything would come out all right. Because those same people that were callin' you those names during the game were going to come shake your hand at the end. And they did.

"Coach Bess said they were just tryin' to get in your head, and true enough, that's the way it was."

SOURCES

Tornado

Books, Publications
A Pictorial History of Jackson, Missouri. The Cash-Book Journal, Jackson (1993).

Annapolis Centennial 1871-1971. Annapolis Centennial Committee (1971).

Felknor, Peter S. *The Tri-State Tornado: The Story of America's Greatest Tornado Disaster.* Iowa State Univ. Press, Ames (1992).

Flora, Snowden D. *Tornados of the United States,* Revised Edition. University of Oklahoma Press, Norman (1954).

Video
Towers Productions. *Wrath of God: Tornado Alley.* A&E Television Networks, New York (1996).

Maps
Annapolis, Mo. City of Annapolis (1996).

Missouri Route Map: Designated Routes and Numbers. Missouri State Highway Commission (1922).

Road Atlas 1995. Rand McNally & Company, United States.

United States Department of the Interior Geological Survey: Missouri East & Illinois West. United States Department of the Army Corps of Engineers (1927).

Newspapers
Cash-Book Journal, Jackson
   Current Local, Van Buren
   Ellington Press
   Farmington News
   Fredericktown News
   Greenville Sun
   Perry County Republican, Perryville
   Perry County Sun, Perryville
   Southeast Missourian, Cape Girardeau
   St. Louis Globe-Democrat
   St. Louis Post-Dispatch
   St. Louis Star
   Wayne County Journal-Banner, Piedmont

Interviews
Gerald Angel
Ann Blechle
Clara Brown
Luellen Cook
Edward Fellows
Cecil Hackworth
Clara Hand
Bernice Jones
Nell Kelley
Lucille Ross
Edmund Weber
Barney Winkler

Contributors, Acknowledgments
Wilma Persky
Department of Geo-Science, Southeast Missouri State University
   Thomas Grazulis
   Anthony Hackworth
   John Holbrook
   Darlene Langley

Jeff Martin
Billie Mills
Perry County Historical Society
Peggy Platner
Frank Nickell
Perry Statler
Angie Sutton
Art Winkler

A Patriot

Books, Publications
Blum, John M.; McFeely, William S.; Morgan, Edmund S.; Schlesinger, Arthur M., Jr.; Stampp, Kenneth M.; & Woodward, C. Vann. *The National Experience: A History of the United States,* Sixth Edition. Harcourt Brace Jovanovich, San Diego, New York, Chicago, Atlanta, Washington, D.C., London, Sydney, & Toronto (1985).

Phillies Publicity Office. *Phillies 1987 Media Guide.* Philadelphia Phillies National League Baseball Club (1987).

Reichler, Joseph L. (editor). *The Baseball Encyclopedia: The Complete and Official Record of Major League Baseball,* Sixth Edition. MacMillan Publishing Co., New York (1985).

Schlossberg, Dan. *The Baseball Catalog.* Jonathan David Publishers, Inc., Middle Village, N.Y. (1980).

Southeast Missouri Amateur Baseball Hall of Fame. *Hall of Fame Banquet.*

Board of Directors, Sikeston (1988).

St. Louis Cardinals Public Relations. *St. Louis Cardinals 1987 Media Guide.* St. Louis Cardinals National League Baseball Club (1987).

Newspapers, Magazines
Daily American Republic, Poplar Bluff
Jefferson City Tribune
Louisville Courier-Journal, Kentucky
Puxico Press
Sikeston Standard
Sports Illustrated, New York
St. Louis Post-Dispatch

Interviews
Bob Andrews
Vernon Bobo
Louis Chaney
Larry Fisher
Louise Fisher
Janis Freebersyser
Maxine Gruchalla
Charley Hart
Robin Roberts
Clarence Wessel
Melvin Williams

Collections
Louise Fisher: family sports articles, scrapbook, military documents, military medals and decorations.
Maxine Gruchalla: letter from Lloyd B. Fisher, Oct. 24, 1944, Luxembourg.

Contributors, Acknowledgments
DeWayne Beckemeier
Classic Cards Company
Marion Cooper

Robert Derickson
Gene Fisher
Kendall Sikes
Topps Chewing Gum, Inc.

Ozages

Books, Manuscripts
Baird, W. David. *The Osage People.* Indian Tribal Series, Phoenix (1972).

Bradbury, John. *Travels in the Interior of America.* Sherwood, Neely & Jones, London (1817).

Burns, Louis F. *A History of the Osage People.* Ciga Press, Fallbrook, Calif. (1989).

Chapman, Carl H. *A Preliminary Survey of Missouri Archaeology.* Garland Publishing Inc., New York (1974).

Chapman, Carl H. *The Origin of the Osage Indian Tribe: An Ethnographical, Historical and Archaeological Study.* Doctoral dissertation, University of Michigan, 1959. Garland Publishing Inc., New York (1974).

Din, Gilbert C., & Nasatir, A. P. *The Imperial Osages: Spanish-Indian Diplomacy in the Mississippi Valley.* University of Oklahoma Press, Norman (1983).

Edmunds, R. David. *The Potawatomis: Keepers of the Fire.* University of Oklahoma Press, Norman (1978).

Hall, James, & McKenney, Thomas L. *History of the Indian Tribes of North America,* Volume II & III. Lithograph prints by J.T. Bowen. D. Rice and A. N. Hart, Philadelphia (1854).

Houck, Louis. *History of Missouri,* Volumes I, II, & III. R.R. Donnelly & Son, Chicago (1908).

Houck, Louis. *The Spanish Regime in Missouri.* R.R. Donnelly & Son, Chicago, (1909).

Jackson, Donald (editor). *Black Hawk: An Autobiography.* University of Illinois Press, Urbana (1955).

Mathews, John Joseph. *The Osages: Children of the Middle Waters.* The Civilization of the American Indian Series. University of Oklahoma Press, Norman (1961).

Mathews, John Joseph. *Wah' Kon-Tah: The Osage and the White Man's Road.* The Civilization of the American Indian Series. University of Oklahoma Press, Norman (1932).

Rollings, Willard H. *The Osage: An Ethnohistorical Study of Hegemony on' the Prairie-Plains.* University of Missouri Press, Columbia & London (1992).

Schoolcraft, Henry B. *Travels in the Central Portions of the Mississippi Valley.* Collins & Hannay, New York (1825).

Tixier, Victor; McDermott, John Francis (editor); Salvan, Albert J. (translator from French). *Tixier's Travels*

on the Osage Prairies.
University of Oklahoma
Press, Norman (1940).

Woodward, Grace Steele.
The Cherokees. University of
Oklahoma Press, Norman
(1963)

Contributors,
Acknowledgments

William Allen
Charles Brown
Pat Diaz
Robert Forister
Steven Gregg
John Holbrook
Wes Johnson
Mercantile Library, St.
Louis

Belmont

Books, Manuscripts

Blum, John M.; McFeely,
William S.; Morgan, Edmund
S.; Schlesinger, Arthur M.,
Jr.; Stampp, Kenneth M.; &
Woodward, C. Vann. *The
National Experience: A
History of the United States,*
Sixth Edition. Harcourt
Brace Jovanovich, San
Diego, New York, Chicago,
Atlanta, Washington, D.C.,
London, Sydney, & Toronto
(1985).

Burns, Ken; Burns, Ric;
& Ward, Geoffrey C. *The Civil
War: An Illustrated History.*
Alfred A. Knopf, New York
(1990).

Catton, Bruce. *Grant
Moves South.* Little, Brown
and Company, Boston and
Toronto (1960).

Cramer, Jesse Grant
(editor). *Letters of Ulysses S.
Grant 1857-78.* Printed by
G.P. Putnam's Sons, The
Knickerbocker Press, New
York and London (1912).

Grant, Ulysses S.
*Personal Memoirs of U.S.
Grant.* Literary Classics of
the United States, Inc., New
York (1990).

Grant, *Ulysses S., III.
Ulysses S. Grant: Warrior
and Statesman.* William
Morrow & Company, Inc.,
New York (1969).

Kennedy, Frances H.
(editor). *The Civil War
Battlefield Guide.* The
Conservation Fund, printed
by Houghton Mifflin
Company, Boston (1990).

McFeely, William S.
Grant: A Biography. Norton
Publishing, New York (1981).

*Merit Students
Encyclopedia,* Volume 8.
Crowell-Collier Educational
Corporation (1967, 1967).

Monaghan, Jay. *Civil War
on the Western Border, 1854-
1865.* University of Nebraska
Press, Lincoln and London
(1955).

Muscovalley, John M.
(editor). *The Battle of
Belmont, Mo.: A Brief History.*
Including: A passage from
*Thirteen Months in the Rebel
Army,* By an Impressed New
Yorker, William G. Stevenson
(1862); and the *Daily
Confederate News,* Nov. 11,
1862. Compilation printed

by The Advance-Yeoman, Wickliffe, Ky. (1974).

Official Atlas of the Civil War. United States War Department. T. Yoseloff, New York (1958).

Collections
Simon, John Y. (editor). *The Papers of Ulysses S. Grant.* Volume 2 and 3. The Ulysses S. Grant Association, Carbondale, Ill.

Video
The Battle of Columbus-Belmont. Columbus-Belmont State Park Museum, Columbus, Ky.

Articles, Publications
Davis, Stephen. *Jeff Thompson's Unsuccessful Quest for a Confederate Generalship.* Missouri Historical Review, Volume 85, No. 1. State Historical Society of Missouri, Columbia (1990).

Johnson, Timothy D. *Benjamin Franklin Cheatham at Belmont.* Missouri Historical Review, Volume 81, No. 2. State Historical Society of Missouri, Columbia (1987).

Pillars, John (editor). *Eighth Illinois Times,* Volume 1, No. 1. Carl Hell, Cairo, Ill. (1991).

Interviews
Confederate Re-Enactor (requested anonymity)
Kevin Pritchett

Contributors, Acknowledgments
David Barton
Kim Little
Lyn McDaniel
Frank Nickell
Frank Williams
Sue Ann Wood

The Social Game

Books, Manuscript
Chaney, Matt. *My Name Is Mister Ryan: The Greatness in People Series, Part One.* Four Walls Publishing, Poplar Bluff (1994).

Cooper, Alex. *Contributions of Blacks in the Bootheel Since 1960.* Hayti, Missouri (1960s).

Stewart, Norm, with John Dewey. *Stormin' Back: Missouri Basketball Coach Norm Stewart's Battles On and Off the Court.* Sagamore Publishing Inc., Champaign, Ill. (1991)

Show-Me Showdown: Missouri High School Basketball Championship 1996. Missouri State High School Activities Association (1996).

Newspapers
Dixon Pilot
Kansas City Star
St. Louis Post-Dispatch

Collections
Paul Hauck: scrapbook with newspapers articles, photographs, and

documents related to Dixon High School Basketball, 1967-69.

James Leon Combs: research for his book, *Bradleyville Basketball: The Hicks From The Sticks.*

Interviews

Gene Bess
John Brown
David Combs
Jerry Combs
Joe Combs
James Leon Combs
Alex Cooper
Marty Eddlemon
Argil Ellison
Paul Hauck
Al Jackson
William Jackson
Fred Johnson
Lennies McFerren
Robert Pledger
Charlie Spoonhour
Lynn Whitten

Contributors, Acknowledgments

Ray Brassieur
Anne Connor
Carroll Cookson
Ron Hopson
Howardville Multipurpose Center

In Appreciation

The author is grateful to the following individuals and organizations that provided varied assistance and considerations in helping make this book possible:

Jerry Beaver
Sally Buck
Randy Clanahan
CMSU Department of Graphics
CMSU Educational Development Center
First Midwest Bank of Southeast Missouri
Katie Hanson
Kelli Lutz
Marty Mishow
Victor and Sheila Ortega
Jeri Reese
Steve Shock

W9-BAH-234

Chuck Tomasi
Kreg Steppe

Wordpress forums

Sams **Teach Yourself**

WordPress

in **10 Minutes**

800 East 96th Street, Indianapolis, Indiana 46240

Sams Teach Yourself WordPress in 10 Minutes

Copyright © 2010 by Pearson Education, Inc.

ISBN-13: 978-0-672-33120-6

ISBN-10: 0-672-33120-9

Library of Congress Cataloging-in-Publication Data

Tomasi, Chuck.

   Sams teach yourself WordPress in 10 minutes / Chuck Tomasi and Kreg Steppe.

         p. cm.

   Includes index.

   ISBN 978-0-672-33120-6

   1. WordPress (Electronic resource) 2. Blogs—Computer programs. 3. Web sites—Design—Computer programs. I. Steppe, Kreg. II. Title.

   TK5105.8885.W66T65 2010

   006.7'8—dc22

                                        2010005881

Printed in the United States of America

Second Printing April 2010

Trademarks

All terms mentioned in this book that are known to be trademarks or service marks have been appropriately capitalized. Pearson Education, Inc. cannot attest to the accuracy of this information. Use of a term in this book should not be regarded as affecting the validity of any trademark or service mark.

Warning and Disclaimer

Every effort has been made to make this book as complete and as accurate as possible, but no warranty or fitness is implied. The information provided is on an "as is" basis. The author and the publisher shall have neither liability nor responsibility to any person or entity with respect to any loss or damages arising from the information contained in this book.

Bulk Sales

Pearson offers excellent discounts on this book when ordered in quantity for bulk purchases or special sales. For more information, please contact

>   **U.S. Corporate and Government Sales**
>   **1-800-382-3419**
>   corpsales@pearsontechgroup.com

For sales outside of the U.S., please contact

>   **International Sales**
>   international@pearsoned.com

Associate Publisher
Greg Wiegand

Acquisitions Editors
Laura Norman

Rick Kughen

Development Editor
Wordsmithery, LLC

Managing Editor
Patrick Kanouse

Project Editor
Seth Kerney

Copy Editor
Chuck Hutchinson

Proofreader
Water Crest Publishing

Indexer
Ken Johnson

Technical Editor
Yvonne Johnson

Publishing Coordinator
Cindy Teeters

Book Designer
Anne Jones

Compositor
Mark Shirar

Contents at a Glance

Introduction 1

1 Introducing WordPress 5

2 Completing Your Profile 15

3 Creating Posts and Pages 27

4 Configuring Your Blog Settings 55

5 Managing Comments 75

6 Personalizing the Appearance of Your Blog 93

7 Using RSS and Data Migration Tools 113

8 Setting Up Hosting 131

9 Installing WordPress 139

10 Using Themes on Your Own Site 153

11 Customizing Your Site with Plug-ins 169

12 Blogging on the Go 187

13 WordPress Support 205

Index 213

Contents

Introduction   **1**

1 Introducing WordPress   **5**
Understanding What WordPress Is 5
Getting Started with WordPress.com 9
Migrating From Another Blog 13
Summary 13

2 Completing Your Profile   **15**
Finding Your Profile 15
Profile Options 16
Completing Your About Page 25
Summary 26

3 Creating Posts and Pages   **27**
Creating Posts 27
Editing Existing Posts 36
Creating Pages 39
Summary 54

4 Configuring Your Blog Settings   **55**
General 55
Writing 58
Reading 62
Discussion 65
Media 70
Privacy 71
Delete Blog 72
OpenID...73
Domains 73
Summary 74

5 **Managing Comments** **75**

Understanding Comments 75

Allowing or Denying Comments 77

Managing Comments 82

Best Practices 90

Summary 91

6 **Personalizing the Appearance of Your Blog** **93**

Themes 93

Widgets 100

Making Additional Changes 103

Summary 111

7 **Using RSS and Data Migration Tools** **113**

Syndicate Your Blog with RSS 113

Other Useful Tools 118

Backing Up Your Data 123

Migrating Your Blog 124

Importing from Another Blog 128

Summary 130

8 **Setting Up Hosting** **131**

Why Host Your Own Blog? 131

Understanding Your Responsibilities....................132

Setting Up Your Domain Name...........................133

Setting Up Your Web Hosting Account....................136

Finding Support 137

Summary 137

9 **Installing WordPress** **139**

Using Automated Script Services 139

Installing WordPress Manually 140

Uploading Your Files 143

Creating the Database 146

Running the Install Script 147

Summary 151

10 Using Themes on Your Own Site   153

Changing the Look and Function of Your Site 153

Searching for and Installing a Theme 157

Widgets 166

Summary 168

11 Customizing Your Site with Plug-ins   169

What Are Plug-ins? 169

Using the Plug-ins Dashboard 170

Finding Plug-ins 172

Installing a Plug-in 177

Upgrading Plug-ins 181

Removing a Plug-in 183

Popular Plug-ins 184

Summary 186

12 Blogging on the Go   187

Setting Up Your Blog for Remote Access 187

Posting from Other Websites 189

Using Mobile Applications 192

Using Email to Post 196

Using ScribeFire 200

Summary 204

13 WordPress Support   205

Looking for Help 205

Free Support 205

Paid Support 209

Other Learning Resources 210

Summary 211

Index   213

About the Authors

 **Chuck Tomasi** is an IT manager for Plexus Corp., a contract electronics company headquartered in Neenah, Wisconsin. He has almost 30 years of IT experience and is also a devoted husband and proud father of two. Chuck is an accomplished writer and public speaker on New Media. His first book, *Podcasting for Dummies* (co-written with Tee Morris and Evo Terra), was ranked #1 by Neilsen BookScan in its category. He is a regular contributing writer to the Friends In Tech and Tech Talk for Families blogs. Chuck is a pioneer in podcasting who began working with the media in 2004 when it was still in its infancy. He is the co-host of the light-hearted weekly tech/science podcast Technorama, which was a finalist in two categories at the 2007 Parsec Awards for podcasting excellence. He also produces and hosts the Gmail Podcast, a collection of short audio tips. As a speaker, Chuck has led training sessions on podcasting for the National Park Service, spoken at the New Media Expo on how to build listener loyalty, presented a session at the National HDI (Help Desk Instutite) conference on effective customer communications, and done numerous presentations for his local HDI chapter. Chuck is also the founder, host, and regular presenter for Fox Cities Managers, a local group of professionals dedicated to leadership excellence in northeast Wisconsin.

Find out more about Chuck at http://www.chucktomasi.com.

Kreg Steppe has 20 years of experience as an IT professional. Kreg is a husband and father of one. He has several interests in creative writing, photography, audio production, and web application development. Currently working as a web developer, he has 10 years experience with web technologies including HTML, JavaScript, PHP, MySQL, Apache, and IIS. His work leads him to create rich and robust solutions including writing a custom intranet, extranet, and workflow applications. He is also a podcasting early adopter. In late 2004, as podcasting started to get recognition, Kreg became involved with several podcasts, emerging as a consummate assistant to budding podcasters. In early 2005 Kreg joined Chuck Tomasi and launched Technorama, a podcast with a lighthearted look at all things tech and sci-fi. Working on Technorama, and as a member of Friends In Tech podcasting group, Kreg has had several years of audio production experience including creative writing, coordination logistics, and editing. Most recently, Kreg spoke at Create South 2009 regarding "Sharing Your Photography and Social Media" as an amateur photographer and with an interest in social networking (http://www.kregsteppe.com).

Dedications

I dedicate this book to my wife, Donna, who has provided the encouragement, time, and support to allow me to realize my goals. To my daughters Julie and Liisa—the light of my life. To my parents, who provided a solid foundation of values and inspire me to keep reaching higher. I love you all very much. —Chuck Tomasi

I dedicate this book to my family, who are all a source of encouragement and motivation. To my wife Kim, who has constantly pushed my boundaries and shown me I can do things that I didn't think possible before. To my son Harrison, who is an endless inspiration. To my parents, who also have shown that hard work and character pay off in the long run. I thank and love you all. —Kreg Steppe

Acknowledgments

From Chuck, special thanks to Tee Morris for ushering me in to the world of writing. Thanks to Kreg Steppe, who convinced me to stop spending my time writing my own blog software and start using WordPress.

From both of us, our eternal gratitude to Laura, Charlotte, Rick, and everyone behind the scenes at Pearson who helped shape raw knowledge into useful, educational information.

We Want to Hear from You!

As the reader of this book, *you* are our most important critic and commentator. We value your opinion and want to know what we're doing right, what we could do better, what areas you'd like to see us publish in, and any other words of wisdom you're willing to pass our way.

You can email or write me directly to let me know what you did or didn't like about this book—as well as what we can do to make our books stronger.

Please note that I cannot help you with technical problems related to the topic of this book, and that due to the high volume of mail I receive, I might not be able to reply to every message.

When you write, please be sure to include this book's title and author as well as your name and phone or email address. I will carefully review your comments and share them with the author and editors who worked on the book.

Email: consumer@samspublishing.com

Mail: Greg Wiegand
          Associate Publisher
          Sams Publishing
          800 East 96th Street
          Indianapolis, IN 46240 USA

Reader Services

Visit our website and register this book at informit.com/register for convenient access to any updates, downloads, or errata that might be available for this book.

Introduction

Blogging has been booming for years, and it shows no sign of slowing down. It is an easy and organized way to deliver news, tutorials, and podcasts; it's even an easy way to share personal thoughts and stories. It was the social network before other social networks existed. Like blogging, WordPress has grown over the years to a mature platform that is accessible to everyone, including you. Starting your own blog can be a fun and rewarding experience, but getting there might take a little work. Navigating your way through installation, profile accounts, themes, and plug-ins will be easier after you complete the lessons in this book. You will have all the knowledge you need to start your own blog right away.

About This Book

As part of the *Sams Teach Yourself in 10 Minutes* guides, this book shows you all the caveats of setting up a blog with WordPress either as a hosted blog or on your personal website. All the topics are separated into easy-to-handle lessons that you can complete in 10 minutes or less. The lessons cover the following tasks and topics:

- ▶ Creating a blog at WordPress.com or installing your blog on another server

- ▶ Configuring and customizing your blog

- ▶ Writing blog posts and pages

- ▶ Mapping your way around the WordPress Dashboard

- ▶ Adding media to your posts

- ▶ Installing themes and plug-ins

- ▶ Customizing widgets

- ▶ Drawing attention to your blog

- ▶ Making your WordPress blog search engine-friendly

- ▶ Blogging on the go

Who This Book Is For

Sams Teach Yourself WordPress in 10 Minutes is for individuals who want to create and operate a personal weblog or website for an organization using WordPress. WordPress is one of the most popular blogging systems, but uninitiated users might need help getting started with it. There are a lot of options and choices to be made within the software. Do you want to host a personal blog or a blog for a business? Maybe you want to show off your photography, or maybe you want to use WordPress to start a podcasting site. WordPress can do all these things, and it includes something for everyone. The advice in this book can make your foray into blogging with WordPress more satisfying.

Each lesson focuses on a particular subject such as installation or managing comments. You can skip around from lesson to lesson or follow through the entire book from beginning to end.

What You Need to Use This Book

To use this book, you first need a can-do attitude and the curiosity to learn something new. You probably already have the tools you need to start using WordPress: an Internet connection, a computer, and a web browser. If you have those, you are ready to go.

You might also need a credit card or some other payment type to purchase your own domain, and you might need to subscribe to hosting services if you want to host your own WordPress site. You can learn more about these things in Lesson 8, "Setting Up Hosting."

Conventions Used in This Book

Whenever you need to watch for something in particular or are directed to click on something, those items will appear as **bolded** text, such as "Click on the orange **Download** button." There are also some special sidebars that call out Tips, Notes, and Cautions.

TIP: Tips are nuggets of information that are good to know as you proceed. Tips might also offer shortcuts for getting things done.

NOTE: Notes are extra information that might give you a deeper understanding of a topic and help you expand your knowledge.

CAUTION: Cautions are warnings that alert you to possible consequences or an outcome of using a particular task or feature.

Screen Captures

The screen captures in this book were taken using the Firefox web browser. If you use a different web browser, your screens might look slightly different.

Also keep in mind that the WordPress developers are constantly at work, and new releases and updates are frequently available. Often new features are added or pages are slightly redesigned. These updates mean that the screen captures in this book might differ a little from what you see when using WordPress. Just remember: Don't panic. Even though things change regularly over time, the basic principles and functionality are the same.

LESSON 1

Introducing WordPress

In this lesson, you learn the basics of WordPress, different ways you can run WordPress, and ways to create your account on WordPress.com.

Understanding What WordPress Is

WordPress is a powerful blog (short for web log) publishing system and content management system that is simple to set up and use. You can set up and manage your entire blog from any web browser. You don't need to be a web programmer or have a degree in information technology to start using it. All you need to know is how to log in, type your content, and click a button so the world can read your masterpiece.

So why should you use WordPress for your blog or—as many people have done—as the framework for your entire website? The answer is simple: It is easy to use, expandable, and affordable, and it offers a great community of support. Consider the following personal example.

Recently, our local chapter of a national organization recognized it was time to update its website. The content was fairly static. We would update it once or twice a month to announce the next meeting. Furthermore, our webmaster was the only one who could make changes to the content, and he was available for limited hours each week. Taking a cue from another chapter in our region, we looked at WordPress. It allows for more dynamic content, allowing any of the chapter board members to contribute and manage the content. Dynamic content leads to frequent readers, and having frequent readers (it is hoped) leads to more chapter members. WordPress worked for our neighbor, and it worked for us. Within a couple of months of our conversion to WordPress, our website was a thriving community with comments and conversations. As we had hoped, memberships also rose. The website was no longer an afterthought; it was at the core of how we communicated with our members.

Options for Using WordPress

WordPress comes in three basic modes: WordPress.com, WordPress.org, and WordPress MU (multiuser). Each one is described in this section so that you can decide which is right for you.

WordPress.com is what's known as a "hosted" solution, meaning a lot of the heavy lifting of installing and configuring the software has been taken care of for you. The benefits of this solution are that it is free and it doesn't take long to start using. You don't need to worry about paying for hosting, running a web server, or downloading software updates. You just create an account, name your blog, and start creating content. The drawback is that WordPress.com is not always as flexible as some people like. For example, you cannot install themes and plug-ins, run ads, or edit the database. To start using WordPress.com, visit its site at http://wordpress.com.

> NOTE: Although WordPress.com is a free service, it is financially supported by optional paid upgrades, VIP services, and Google AdSense advertising.

The second way to use WordPress is to download and install the software yourself from WordPress.org. This task requires a little more technical savvy (and money). The advantage is that you have more control over the appearance and functionality of the way your site is run. The additional flexibility, though, creates additional complexity. Don't worry; installing your own WordPress is not all that daunting, and you can read more about it in Lesson 10, "Installing WordPress." With this option, you need to pay for web hosting, so you can shop around for the service that best fits your needs. You need to ensure your hosting provider has PHP version 4.3 or greater (the programming language WordPress is built on) and MySQL version 4.1.2 or greater (the database behind WordPress).

The final way to run WordPress is to use WordPress MU (multiuser). It is the same software that runs WordPress.com, but it's meant for large organizations such as schools, networks, or companies that want to run dozens of blogs under one central administration. The use of WordPress MU is beyond the scope of this book. If you want more information on WordPress MU, you can find it at http://mu.wordpress.org.

WordPress Features

There are several reasons to consider WordPress instead of other blogging software sites or packages.

WordPress is extensible, meaning you can start with a basic setup and add on many plug-ins to extend the functionality of your software (see Table 1.1). The capabilities of plug-ins range from taking a simple poll to distributing audio and video files with your regular content. The official repository of WordPress plug-ins is available at http://wordpress.org/extend/plugins/.

One nice feature about WordPress is that you can always start simple with WordPress.com. Then, if you decide you want to extend your features beyond what WordPress.com can offer, you can migrate it later to your own website using the software downloaded from WordPress.org. If you think you might one day migrate from WordPress.com to your own website, there are some factors you should take in to account. We talk about them in Lesson 8, "Using RSS and Data Migration Tools."

Table 1.1   WordPress.org and WordPress.com Feature Comparison

Feature	WordPress.org	WordPress.com
Cost	Free	Free
Requires hosting	Yes	No
Requires download	Yes	No
Requires setup/installation	Yes	No
Ability to install your own templates	Yes	No
Ability to use sidebar widgets	Yes	Yes
RSS	Yes	Yes
Ability to install plug-ins	Yes	No
Ability to set up multiple blogs with one account	No	Yes
Customizable style sheets	Yes	$15/year

PLAIN ENGLISH: **RSS**

RSS stands for Really Simple Syndication. It is a method that computers use to exchange information. For the purposes of WordPress, RSS allows people to "subscribe" to your blog, much like they subscribe to a magazine. Rather than people coming to your site to check for new content, an application periodically checks all subscribed sites (also known as "feeds") for new content and presents it much like email. RSS functionality is being incorporated in many popular applications such as Microsoft Outlook and Internet Explorer. It is available in specialized applications, called RSS readers, such as Mozilla Thunderbird. There are even RSS readers available as web applications—such as Google Reader—and several for your iPhone.

WordPress has a large community of fiercely loyal followers that provide an excellent support network. If you have questions, you are likely to find the answers at http://wordpress.org/support or http://codex.wordpress.org. If you cannot find answers to your questions in this book, the Codex website is an excellent resource.

The History of WordPress

Although WordPress was one of three leaders in both rate of adoption and brand strength as measured in the 2009 Open Source Content Management System Market Share Report, it had its humble beginnings just a few short years ago. In early 2003, a young man by the name of Matt Mullenweg found that his favorite publishing software (called b2) was without a lead developer. He decided to take up the task to enhance and rebrand b2 as WordPress. He was soon joined by Mike Little and the original b2 developer, Michael Valdrighi. A few months later, the first release of WordPress was made available. In August 2006, the software had more than 1 million downloads. In 2007, that number reached 3 million.

> **Have a Strategy**
>
> Before you start using WordPress, it pays to have a vision, or a plan, of what you want your blog to be. Is this something for friends and family to keep up with, or is it a publication for an organization you belong to? Do you have a theme or brand to adhere to, or are you allowed to experiment? Do you have a name for your blog? All these issues should be considered before you dive in.

Getting Started with WordPress.com

Here's an example of how easy it is to start using WordPress. Let's assume you have been tasked with creating a website for your local chapter martial arts club.

To start with WordPress.com, follow these steps:

1. Go to the main WordPress.com site at http://wordpress.com.

2. Click the **Sign Up Now** button.

3. Create a user name and password, and fill in the email address. Be sure to review the terms of service and check the box that states you have read and agree to them. Click Next. See Figure 1.1.

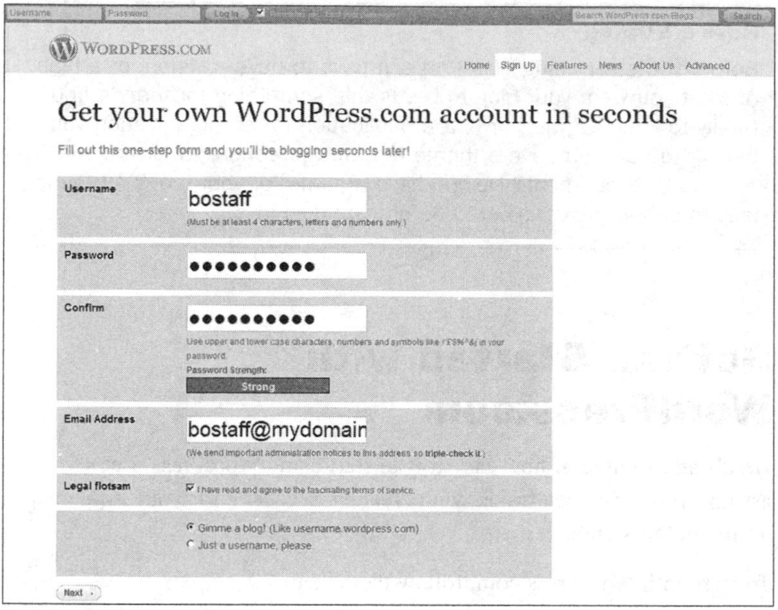

FIGURE 1.1 The Sign Up screen on WordPress.com.

4. Name your blog. The blog domain is the web address where people will find your blog. By default, it is the same name as your user name. Change the blog domain if you want to use a web address different than your user name. The Blog Title is the name of your blog. You can change this at any time in the blog settings. Select the language your blog uses and choose your privacy option. Finally, click **Sign Up**. See Figure 1.2. For our example, I used the blog domain bostaff.wordpress.com, the title "Fox Cities Martial Arts," left the language as English, and chose to make the blog visible to search engines.

CAUTION: **Choosing Your Blog Domain**

Choose your blog domain carefully. Once it is set, it cannot be changed.

FIGURE 1.2 Choose your blog address and title.

5. Update your profile. Enter your first name, last name, and little text about yourself. When you are done, click **Save Profile**. See Figure 1.3.

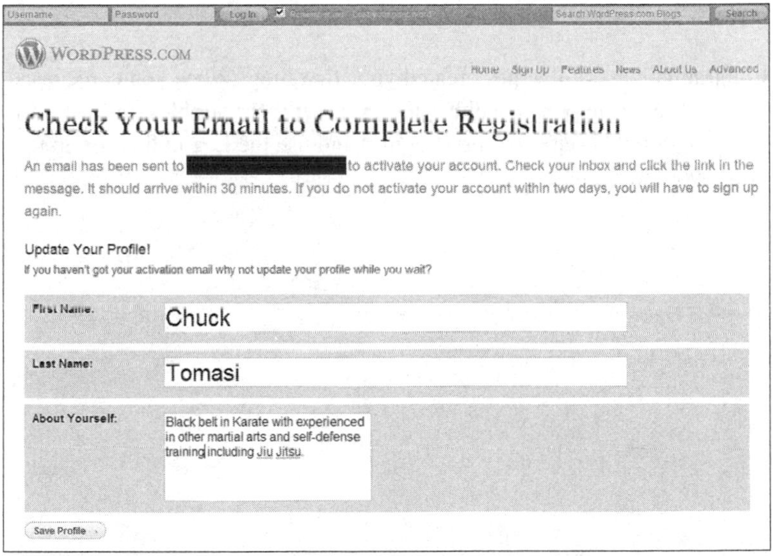

FIGURE 1.3 Include a little more information in your profile.

6. Check your email. When you get the confirmation message from WordPress.com, click the link to activate your blog. The link takes you to a page that says Your Account Is Now Active. See Figure 1.4. Click the link on the page to view your site or log in. Until you receive the email and click on the link, you cannot publish any content to your blog.

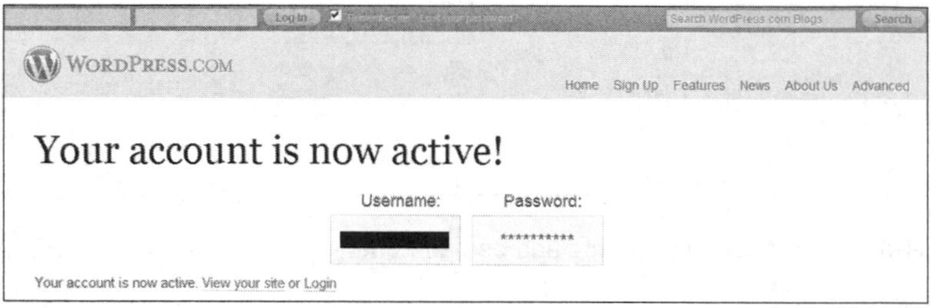

FIGURE 1.4 After your account is active, you can log in and start creating content.

7. Click View Your Site.

Congratulations, you've just created your first blog! When you come back to WordPress.com, you can either log in directly at your blog address—for example, http://bostaff.wordpress.com—and use the Log in link, or go to http://wordpress.com.

Migrating From Another Blog

If you already have a blog with another popular site or software, WordPress makes it possible to migrate your content. Currently, you can import from any of the following blogs:

- ▶ Blogger
- ▶ LiveJournal
- ▶ Movable Type or TypePad
- ▶ WordPress
- ▶ Yahoo! 360

See Lesson 8 for more information on migrating your blog to WordPress.com.

Summary

In this lesson, you learned what WordPress is and how it can be used. You also learned how quickly and easily you can log in to WordPress.com and create your own account.

Completing Your Profile

In this lesson, you learn the value of setting up your profile, where to locate your personal profile, how to set the various options, and what each option does.

Finding Your Profile

> NOTE: **Profile Differences Between WordPress.com and WordPress.org**
>
> The profile options mentioned in this lesson apply to WordPress.com. Where necessary, exceptions for WordPress.org users are noted.

Let's begin by finding your profile. If you are not already logged in to WordPress.com, start by taking one of the following steps:

- Go to http://wordpress.com, log in, and click the **Dashboard** link under the name of your blog.

- Go to http://yoursite.wordpress.com, click the **Log in** link, and enter your login ID and password. If your browser remembers you from a previous session, click the **Site Admin** link.

After you are logged in, look at the side menu on the left and scroll down if necessary to locate the section labeled Users. As you move your cursor over the Users label, a downward-pointing triangle will appear. Click the triangle to expand the menu options. In that list, click **Your Profile**. Your screen should now look similar to the one shown in Figure 2.1.

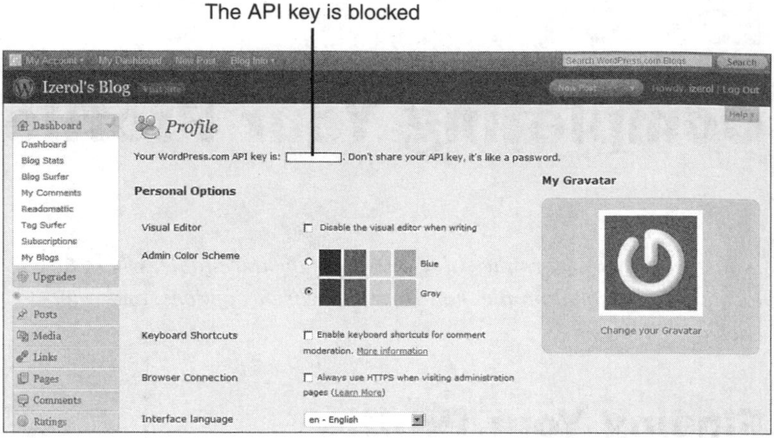

The API key is blocked

FIGURE 2.1 Taking the time to set the various options in your profile gives your blog a more polished look.

Profile Options

Your user profile contains several options to help manage and personalize your blog including personal preferences, contact information, and how you would like to be represented online. The information in your user profile applies to all the blogs you own on WordPress.com. Most of the information in your user profile is not displayed publicly.

Your Personal API Key

The first item displayed at the top of the profile screen is your Personal API key. This key is your personal identifier to the WordPress.com system. It allows the system to identify you if you choose to use services and enhancements the system has to offer, even if you host your blog elsewhere. It is generated automatically when you create your WordPress.com account. Treat the API key like a password and do not share it. The most popular use of the API key is with the WordPress antispam service Akismet. You can find more details about Akismet in Lesson 5, "Managing Comments."

PLAIN ENGLISH: **API**

API stands for Application Programming Interface. It is a method by which programmers allow other programmers to access to his software so that a program that they write can enhance or extend the functionality of the original program.

Personal Options

The Personal Options section of the user profile defines the basics of how you interact with WordPress. Options include the color scheme for the administrative interface, the image you present to the world, and even what language you use.

Visual Editor

The Visual Editor setting allows you to turn on or off the enhanced functionality of the editor when you are composing content such as a blog posting or page. I recommend leaving this box unchecked so that you can see the text you create much as it will be displayed when the reader reads it. The Visual Editor operates much like most common word processors do with WYSIWYG ("wizzy-wig," which stands for What You See Is What You Get) functionality. For example, when you click the icon for a bulleted list, you see a list of bullets in the editor window. If you uncheck Visual Editor, the icons change to Hypertext Markup Language (HTML) tags, and you aren't able to edit your text unless you understand HTML, which is beyond the scope of this book. If you do know HTML, you can still see it and manipulate it even with the Visual Editor enabled.

Admin Color Scheme

The Admin Color Scheme option gives you a choice of using blue or gray highlights and borders in your WordPress admin screens. This is a personal preference. Choose whichever you feel most comfortable with.

Keyboard Shortcuts

Keyboard Shortcuts were introduced in 2008 to help you rapidly manage comments using your keyboard instead of several mouse clicks. By default, Keyboard Shortcuts is turned off, so if your blog gets a lot of comments or you manage them en masse, you might want to consider

turning it on. To turn on Keyboard Shortcuts, check the box next to
Enable Keyboard Shortcuts for Comment Moderation. Read more
about comments and moderating them in Lesson 5.

Missing Options?

This book is based on WordPress version 2.9. WordPress.com users
are automatically upgraded to the latest version of software.
WordPress.org users need to upgrade themselves. If you do not see
some of the options mentioned in this book, you should upgrade
your WordPress software to the latest version.

Browser Connection

To enable an encrypted connection between your browser and the server
when you manage your blog or its settings, which is recommended, check
the **Always Use HTTPS When Visiting Administration Pages** box. By
default, this option is disabled (unchecked). Although enabling this option
is not mandatory, it is a good idea, particularly when you reset user passwords. Without the feature enabled, all information is passed between
your computer and the WordPress.com server in "clear format," meaning
anyone with moderate technical skills could listen to your conversation. If
you enable this feature, all traffic between your browser and the server is
encrypted, so anyone listening gets a garbled message.

Interface Language

WordPress.com supports a wide variety of languages. When you select a
language, all the settings, application labels, and other features of
WordPress.com are translated. Changing the Interface Language setting
does not modify the language in which the content is presented, so if your
posts are written in English, changing the interface language to French
will not translate your postings.

Primary Blog

As mentioned in Lesson 1, "Introducing WordPress," WordPress.com
allows you to operate multiple blogs from the same account. The Primary
Blog setting in your profile lets you specify one blog as your primary

blog, which is the default blog displayed when you look at stats and other information in the Global Dashboard.

Proofreading

The Proofreading section allows you to enable and disable certain types of grammatical checks the Visual Editor performs when you click the **ABC Check** button. Depending on what options you choose in your profile, the proofreading feature will catch or ignore these. For example, checking the Clichés option instructs the proofreader to underline phrases such as "Have a nice day."

The same button can also check for spelling errors and make style suggestions. For example, say you enable the proofreading feature and later type the sentence **I got all the way threw the test without a mistake.** Clicking the ABC Check button runs the proofreader and identifies the word *threw* as a possible mistake and allows you to correct it. When you click the underlined word, the proofreader makes the suggestion "Did you mean...through?" If you find the grammar checker catching phrases you use repeatedly, you can add them to the list of phrases just under the series of check boxes in the Proofreading option. For example, the proofreader often underlines the word *Technorama*, the title of one of the blogs I operate. Typing the word in the Ignored Phrases text field tells the proofreader not to underline the word, but to ignore it.

Name

The following sections describe how to set or change your name and the way it is displayed to others (see Figure 2.2).

Username

The Username is the name that you use for logging in to the system. It cannot be changed after it is set—not even by a user with Administrator rights.

First Name, Last Name

The First Name and Last Name fields are used, of course, for your first name and last name (surname).

Nickname

Your nickname can be different from your login name. It is the name that people will know you by. For example, I signed up with the account "ctomasi," but I want everyone to know me as "chucktomasi" on this blog. I can use the nickname to differentiate it from my login name. This capability is helpful because the login name cannot be changed.

Display Name Publicly As

The value selected from the Display Name Publicly As list is how the system displays your name when you make a post. You can choose from your login name, nickname, first name only, last name only, or both in either order (see Figure 2.2). Changing this setting later updates any previous postings you have made. The system stores your real name with the posting and displays the value you select from the list.

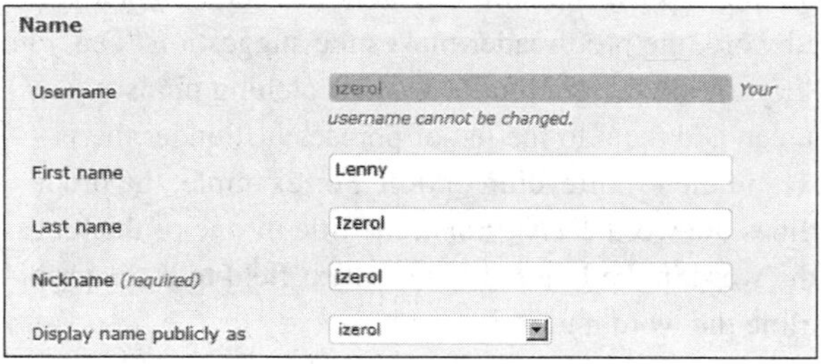

Name

Username	izerol	Your
	username cannot be changed.	
First name	Lenny	
Last name	Izerol	
Nickname (required)	izerol	
Display name publicly as	izerol ▾	

FIGURE 2.2   How the name part of the profile might be filled out.

Contact Info

You use the Contact Info section to provide information regarding how other users can contact you. The only required field is E-mail, which is how WordPress contacts you when you have new comments or user registrations. WordPress automatically uses the email address you entered when you registered. If you try to change your email address here, WordPress puts your original email address back and sends a message to the new address you entered with a link that takes you to the settings where can make the actual change. The correct place to change your email address is in General Settings (explained in Lesson 4, "Configuring Your Blog Settings").

Optionally, you can provide your website, AOL Instant Messenger (AIM), Yahoo IM, and Jabber/Google Talk IDs for those who might want to reach you through one of those online services (see Figure 2.3).

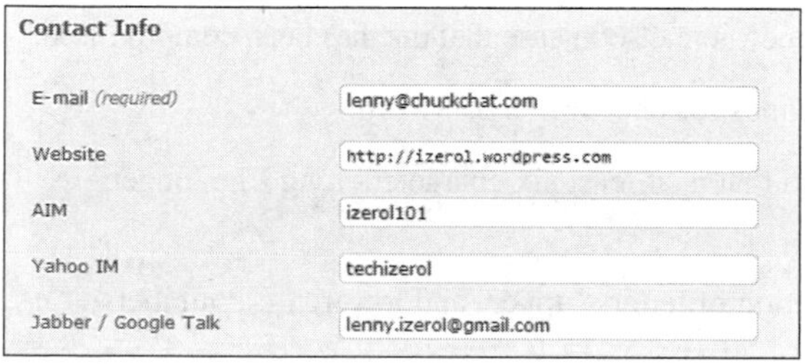

Contact Info

E-mail *(required)*	lenny@chuckchat.com
Website	http://izerol.wordpress.com
AIM	izerol101
Yahoo IM	techizerol
Jabber / Google Talk	lenny.izerol@gmail.com

FIGURE 2.3 Provide additional contact information to let others know how to reach you.

About Yourself

If you want to let your readers know a little bit more about you, fill in the About Yourself section. Although you aren't required to complete the fields in this section, sharing a bit of yourself with your readers is not a bad idea.

Biographical Info

The text area labeled Biographical Info is a place for you to give a brief overview of yourself. The information you include here can be a simple one-line entry such as "Personality on the Technorama podcast," or it can be something a little more detailed. I recommend entering really in-depth personal information in the About page, which is explained in the "Completing Your About Page" section.

New Password

At some point, you might need to change your password. If you host your own blog, you probably want to change your password right after you set up the blog with a default Administrator account and random password. Change your password in the section at the bottom of your profile.

Choosing a new password can be tricky. The goal is to use something meaningful that you are likely to remember, yet challenging enough so someone else won't be likely to guess it. Optimally, you don't want to use a password that has been used somewhere else in case that one has been compromised.

Here are a few guidelines for choosing a password:

▶ Use a password that is at least six characters long (the longer, the better).

▶ Use a combination of letters (upper- and lowercase), numbers, and symbols.

▶ Try to stay away from dictionary words.

▶ Use mnemonics (memory devices) to help you remember passwords.

▶ Change your password regularly. This procedure is a nuisance, but it's less painful than losing valuable data. Some people on the Internet seem to have nothing better to do than try to break into accounts on popular sites like WordPress.com.

WordPress offers a "strength indicator" just under the password field. As you type your password, WordPress tells you how good your password is on a rating from very weak to strong.

Examples of poor passwords are

▶ *wordpress*—All lowercase—too obvious.

▶ *1234abcd*—Although this example uses a combination of letters and numbers, it is fairly easy for a computer to calculate this combination.

▶ *Bunny*—Too short and uses a word from the dictionary.

Examples of strong passwords are

- *My1stBl0g!*— A decent length (10 characters); uses uppercase, lowercase, numbers, and symbols. Uses a mnemonic for "my first blog" to help you remember.

- *Ra!s!ns+Ch0c0late*—Although these look like dictionary words, symbols and numbers replace some letters, which makes it more difficult for a computer to crack but easy for a human to remember.

- *2Maps&2Chart$*—Uppercase, lowercase, numbers, symbols, and good length. Sometimes you only need to look around the room to find a good password.

Your Gravatar

Gravatar is a concatenation of "global recognized" avatar. An avatar is a photo or other graphic that represents you. Avatars are usually 80 × 80 pixels in size. Normally, as you navigate around the Web, you need to upload an avatar to each site. A gravatar allows you to use one avatar across multiple sites, chat rooms, forums, and so on. You might see one in a WordPress site if the theme has been designed to display them.

There are several ways to set your WordPress gravatar. These include

- Uploading an existing image from your computer.

- Using your webcam to take a snapshot of yourself. You need a machine with a functioning webcam and Adobe FlashPlayer installed to take this approach.

- Using a link to an existing online image.

- Using your previous WordPress.com avatar (if you had one).

- Going to http://en.gravatar.com set your avatar there and having WordPress.com reference it.

This example uses an image from the local computer. The following steps walk you through one way of setting your gravatar:

1. Click on the image that looks like a sideways **G** in the upper right on your profile page (or the **Change Your Gravatar** link just below it). A window displays in front of the other text on your browser window (see Figure 2.4).

2. Click the link **Upload a New Image from Your Computer** to instruct WordPress to use an image on your computer as your gravatar.

3. Click the **Browse** button and look around for an image that suits you. When you have located an image, select it, click **Open**, and click the **Next** button.

4. The image file is sent to the server, and the gravatar image is displayed on the screen. A square on top of your image indicates the actual part of the image that is displayed (as shown in the two preview windows on the right).

5. Resize the box on top of your image by dragging the handlebars to change the size of the image area. You also can drag the square to a different area on your image.

6. After you have selected the appropriate area and your preview windows look the way you want, click the **Crop and Finish!** button.

7. Provide a rating for your image by clicking on the appropriate letter. Descriptions of the ratings are provided. Depending on the rating, your image may not be displayed on all sites that use gravatars.

8. Click the **X** in the upper right of the window to close the Gravatar window.

Your gravatar is associated with your email address; in this case, it's associated with the email address you provided for your WordPress.com account. If your gravatar does not appear right away, you might need to refresh your screen or click **Your Profile** (on the left).

Behind the scenes, you just interacted with the gravatar.com website to set your image across multiple websites.

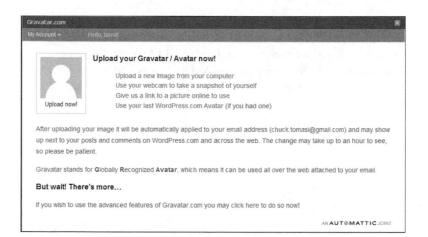

FIGURE 2.4   The screen for uploading your gravatar.

Remember to Save Your Changes

You must click the **Update Profile** button at the bottom of the page if you changed any options (excluding your gravatar). If you make changes and do not click Update Profile, your changes are lost.

Completing Your About Page

Another way to tell your readers more about yourself is to set up a page with more detailed information than what is in your profile. WordPress presents a tip with a link at the top of the Dashboard like the one shown in Figure 2.5. If the tip is not available, use the side menu on the left, click the Pages section, then click About from the list of pages. You can find more information about creating and editing posts and pages in Lesson 3, "Creating Posts and Pages."

⌂ *Dashboard*

WordPress tip: <u>Update your about page</u> so your readers can learn a bit about you.

FIGURE 2.5   WordPress offers some useful tips on the Dashboard, such as this one about updating your About page.

Summary

In this lesson, you learned to set up your profile. You also learned that setting preferences for your profile makes navigating and using WordPress.com more enjoyable and effective for you and your blog's readers.

LESSON 3

Creating Posts and Pages

In this lesson, you learn how to create and manage posts and pages. This lesson introduces you to the basics of content creation and then more advanced topics such as including images, audio, and video to enrich your readers' experience.

Creating Posts

Posts are the lifeblood of any blog. They are the reason people come back to a blog or subscribe to an RSS feed. If a blog doesn't have an influx of new content, most people have no desire to visit. As a result, creating and maintaining posts are some of the most common activities you will perform on your site. Posts don't need to be fancy or laborious to create. The less time you spend thinking about how to operate the tool, the more time you can spend creating content. WordPress has provided several easy ways to create new posts.

The easiest way to create a new post is to click the **New Post** button in the upper-right corner of the administrative screen. You can always create a new post from the side menu under Posts, Add New. See Figure 3.1.

> NOTE: **The New Post Button**
> The New Post button is context sensitive, so it may not always appear as New Post.

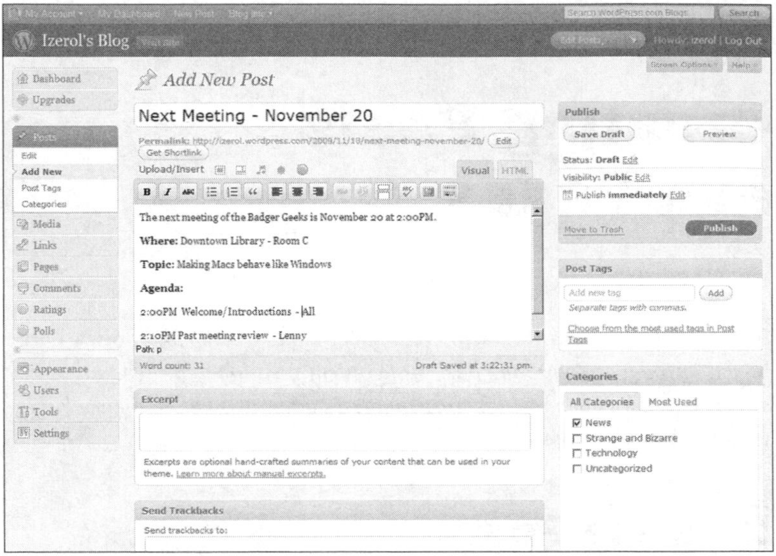

FIGURE 3.1   Adding a new post.

The first field at the top of the Add New Post page is the post title. This is the "headline" of your post. A good title is the key to a good post. It should grab the attention of your readers and draw them in. Often, it is the only part of your post some people will see, such as an RSS index listing.

After you finish entering your title and tab (or move your cursor) to the next field, a URL appears just below the title with the label Permalink. For now, this is the link to your post.

There are also two buttons below the title:

▶ **Edit**—This button allows you to modify the suffix of the URL. By default, WordPress creates the URL based on the date and the title words. Although you cannot change the date, you can change the part with the title words if you choose, as long as it remains unique. WordPress removes symbols such as $, &, and @ from the title to avoid confusion with special symbols used by web addresses. Use the **Edit** button next to the permalink to modify the URL. For example, add the word "percent" where WordPress removed the "%" symbol.

▶ **Short Link**—This button provides a quick way to take your long URL and collapse it down to something easier to reference in a short messaging system like a mobile text message or Twitter. For example, your default permalink is http://your-name.worpress.com/2009/11/27/funniest-bumper-stickers, and the short link is http://wp.me/pGy8H-k.

At a minimum, all you need for a basic post is a title and text in the message body. Then click **Publish** and you've created a post! Of course, there are many options to add more pizzazz to your posts. The following sections describe how to format and enhance your posts.

The Visual Editor

Just below the title is the body of the post. This is the place where you enter the text (and other items) of your post. This area operates much like a standard word processor offering indentation, bullet lists, bold, italic, centering, and other formatting options. More advanced content items are covered later in this lesson. You can find out what each icon does by passing your cursor over it.

Consider, for example, that you want to write a quick review of *Sams Teach Yourself WordPress in 10 Minutes.*

In the title area, enter **Book Review: Sams Teach Yourself WordPress** in **10 Minutes**.

In the message body, begin typing some pertinent information, such as the following:

```
Author: Chuck Tomasi and Kreg Steppe
Pages: 208
ISBN: 0672331209
Comments: Two thumbs up. "STY WordPress in 10 min" covers the
necessary information to get me up and running on WordPress.com
quickly and easily without a lot of extra "fluff" to get in the
way. The authors know their topic and stay on track. The informa-
tion is presented in a clear and logical order. I am new to
WordPress and I don't know a lot about online services and social
media, I had no trouble getting started with WordPress. I will
continue to use this as a reference should I need to host my own
blog (and customize it) in the future.
```

That's not too bad, but a little plain. Let's take a look at the Visual Editor toolbar and see how it might help us enhance our post. Some of the icons are covered later in this lesson to demonstrate how to include more than text in your post.

▶ When you highlight the word *Author* and click the **B** icon on the toolbar, the word turns bold. By repeating this procedure for the words *Pages*, *ISBN*, and *Comments*, you can enhance the look of your post by making the headers stand out.

▶ You might also highlight the title of the book and click the **I** icon to make the title italic. Don't go overboard with formatting, though.

▶ You can use the button that has the ABC with a line through to create "strikeout" text. Bloggers commonly use strikeout as a reminder to come back and update posts as new facts related to the topic emerge. By highlighting some text and clicking the strikeout icon, you leave the text in the post, but readers can see that it is obsolete.

▶ The icon to the right of strikeout lets you create a bulleted list. To create a new bulleted list, start with your cursor at the beginning of a new line and click the bullet list icon. A bullet appears, and you can begin typing your first list item. At the end of the first item, press **Enter** and a second bullet appears. Continue this process until you complete your list. When you are done, press **Enter** on a blank bullet (typically your last one), and your list is terminated. To create a bulleted list from existing text, highlight the lines where you want a bullet and click the bullet list icon.

▶ Numbered lists operate just like bullet lists. The icon for numbered lists is next to the bullet lists and has a 123 with lines next to it.

- The next three icons let you change the alignment of your text. For existing text, place the cursor on the line you want to align and click one of the icons to set it right-justified, centered, or left-justified. For new text, click the appropriate alignment icon first and then start typing. When you want to switch, choose a different icon and begin typing additional text.

- If you have a very long post, you might decide to use the More icon. This icon looks like a small white rectangle over a larger white rectangle with a dotted line between them. To use the More icon, place your cursor at a spot two or three lines into your post. For this example, place it right after ". . . get in the way." Now click the **More** icon, and you see a dividing line appear in your text. When readers view your post in their web browser, they will see the first couple of lines and then a link labeled Read the Rest of This Entry>>. If readers click the link, they are taken to a page with the entire post. This feature provides a good way for you to get lots of posts in a small space but still have the ability to be verbose.

- The button with the ABC and the check mark lets you spell check your posting. If WordPress finds an error, it underlines the error in red. Click the underlined word and several options are presented to allow you to correct or ignore the word.

- The second icon from the right toggles full-screen mode. If you prefer to temporarily clear your screen of everything that is not part of your post, you can click this icon to focus on your writing. Clicking it again goes back to the default view.

- The rightmost icon is known as the Show/Hide the Kitchen Sink button, which displays or hides an entire second row of icons. This button lets you change the font size, style, and color, as well as insert symbols, change your indent level, undo changes, and redo changes.

Be choosy about using enhancements in your post. Using too many can detract from the message you are trying to convey.

TIP: **Use Keyboard Shortcuts to Speed Up Your Work**

As you move your cursor over the icons on the Visual Editor toolbar, make a note of the text that appears when you hover over each one for a second or two. WordPress lets you know what keyboard shortcuts you can use to accomplish the same task without using your mouse. For example, hovering over the Bold icon displays (Ctrl+B). This means you can press B while holding down the Ctrl key, represented as Ctrl+B (Windows) (or ⌘-B for the Mac). Different browsers use different keys to access the shortcuts. You might have to hold down Alt+Shift instead of Ctrl. Rather than moving to the icon, clicking **B**, then typing text, and clicking the icon again, you can press Ctrl+B (to turn on bold), type your text, and press Ctrl+B again (to turn off bold). The more your hands stay on the keyboard, the faster you will become.

WYSIWYG Editing Versus HTML

To the right of the Visual Editor toolbar are two tabs labeled Visual and HTML:

▶ **Visual**—This is the default option when you're creating posts. It allows you to create your post in a WYSIWYG (what you see is what you get) format common to most word processors today.

▶ **HTML**—Clicking this tab switches to show what is going on behind the scenes. It reveals the actual HTML codes necessary to display your text in a browser the way you intend (see Figure 3.2). Although you probably won't use the HTML window to enter the text of your posts (unless you are skilled with HTML), you might use the window to embed HTML code that you get from a third party.

FIGURE 3.2 The HTML tab lets you view see HTML code and insert HTML code from a third party.

Using Excerpts, Trackbacks, and Discussion Options

Following the post message body on the screen is a text area labeled Excerpt. This optional bit of text gives a summary about your post. It is optional because it can be used to replace the full content in your RSS feed if you use the option to display summaries in Settings, Reading. And, depending on the WordPress theme used, you can use it where summaries are preferred to full content. These places include

▶ Search results

▶ Tag archives

▶ Category archives

▶ Monthly archives

▶ Author archives

The next section below Excerpt is Send Trackbacks. Trackbacks are a way to notify other blogs that you have linked to them, which is useful for getting not only your readers but also readers from another blog involved in the conversation. Trackbacks work like this:

▶ Person A writes something on her blog.

▶ Person B wants to comment on Person A's blog, but wants her own readers to see what she had to say, and be able to comment on her own blog.

▶ Person B posts on her own blog and sends a trackback to Person A's blog.

▶ Person A's blog receives the trackback and displays it as a comment to the original post. This comment contains a link to Person B's post.

If you link to other WordPress blogs, the trackback function is automatic, and you can leave it blank. For non-WordPress blogs, enter the URL of the other blog's post in the space provided.

Finally, in the main column are the Discussion options. They allow you to enable or disable comments and trackbacks on a post-by-post basis (overriding the settings in the global discussion options in Settings, Discussion).

Publish Options

The options in the Publish section on the right allow you to manage when and how your post is released to your readers.

▶ **Save Draft (button)**—The Save Draft button allows you to save your work as you continue writing. Few things are more frustrating than writing for a long time and then losing your work. Saving as a draft simply keeps a recent backup of your article on WordPress. Your content is saved but not yet published.

▶ **Preview (button)**—If you want to see how your post will look before it is made public, click the **Preview** button. A preview is useful when you have embedded images, additional formatting, or something else besides simple text and you want to verify the layout appears as you would expect.

▶ **Status (field)**—The Status defaults to Draft to indicate the post is under construction. You can click the **Edit** link next to the word *Draft* and change it to *Pending Review* if you want to have an editor review it before it is posted.

► **Visibility (field)**—The Visibility option allows you to change who can see your post. By default, it is set to Public, but by clicking the **Edit** link, you get several options, including password protected and private. Another handy feature under Visibility is the check box labeled Stick This Post to the Front Page. Some people like to use this option for announcements or other information they want to make available all the time. For example, if our local radio-controlled airplane club is having a monthly meeting in three weeks, I want that meeting announcement to stay on the front page even if there are a dozen more postings between the time I post the announcement and the meeting. Of course, I will have to remember to edit the article and uncheck that option at some point in the future.

► **Publish (field)**—You also can change the time the article is published. This capability is useful for dated material. For example, our local radio-controlled airplane club just got a pre-release of a new model to write a review. As part of the agreement, the review must be posted on the first of next month to coincide with the product release. When I click the **Edit** link next to Publish: Immediately, a date and time appear. I can set the date to the first of next month, determine what time it will show up, and click **OK**. After reviewing and setting all my options, I can click the **Publish** button.

► **Publish (button)**—The simplest action in this section is the Publish button. When you click it, your content is online for the world to read.

Post Tags

Post tags provide a way to group similar post topics together in an informal way. When you create a post, you can add optional tags that work much like keywords. Posts with the same tags can be automatically linked together. Some WordPress themes display the tags to quickly access posts with the same tags. For example, my personal blog has a posting on it about my martial arts training. If I include tags such as *karate*, *training*,

exercise, and *bo staff*, they are easily searchable among other
WordPress.com blogs using the Dashboard, Tag Surfer feature. From an
information organization standpoint, you should start getting in the habit
of putting a few tags in each post. Post tags are managed from the side
menu under Posts, Post Tags.

Categories

Categories are another way to organize your information. They are more
structured than post tags in that they can be hierarchical (one category can
have one or more subcategories). When you create your blog, have a good
idea of what types of information you will be sharing and create categories around the major groupings. For example, in my personal blog, I
write about personal and professional topics. I further break down the personal topics into family, exercise, personal development, and hobbies. I
have created my categories around these major groupings. When I create a
post, I know it generally fits at least one of these categories. Before I publish the post, I can check the appropriate category (or categories). Now if
someone comes to my blog and wants to see what I've written regarding
my personal development program, he can click a category link (typically
displayed on the front page of my blog under a Categories heading) and
see those posts grouped together. Try not to go overboard on categories.
Again, some forethought is recommended here.

> NOTE: **Using Tag Surfer**
>
> If you select the **Dashboard**, **Tag Surfer** option from the side menu,
> any tags you put in that list are automatically available to your post
> categories.

Editing Existing Posts

Whether you've spotted a typo, need to make an update to a meeting
agenda, or take something offline for legal reasons, you are going to need
to make changes to your posts at some point. Editing existing posts is
done by going to **Posts**, **Edit** in the side menu (see Figure 3.3).

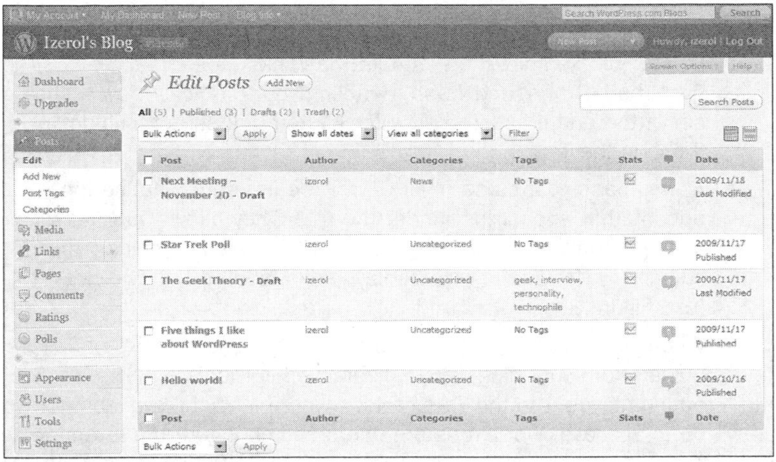

FIGURE 3.3   A typical list of posts.

The Edit Posts list lets you see a number of properties about each post, including the author, any categories or tags applied, a quick link to statistics regarding your post, how many comments were made about it, and the date when it was last modified or published.

List Basics

WordPress displays the index of posts, pages, comments, links, and media files in a list. Most lists in WordPress have the same basic functionality. Following is an overview of basic list operations:

▶ The column titles are available at the top and bottom of the list of articles for convenience when you're managing a long list of articles.

▶ Clicking **Screen Options** displays check boxes corresponding to the list column titles. Checking or unchecking turns on or off any of the columns in the listing after you click the **Apply** button.

▶ The Screen Options also allow you to control how many items are displayed in the list.

▶ Most lists have Add New near the top of the screen so that you can quickly add a new entry.

▶ Many lists have links that enable you to quickly view grouped items. For example, the Posts list has links labeled All, Published, Drafts, and Trash, enabling you to quickly view a subset of the entire list. The view for All items does not include those in the Trash.

▶ As you pass your cursor over any of the list items, notice the options that appear just under the title. They allow you to easily manage items. For example, on the Edit Posts list, placing the cursor anywhere on a row displays links labeled Edit, Quick Edit (see Figure 3.4), Trash, and View (or Preview for a draft).

▶ When you use the Trash link on a post, page, comment, or upload from your blog, it is not removed immediately. The Trash option moves it to the Trash folder, where it is still available for up to 30 days. WordPress.org users can configure the retention period by modifying their wp-config.php file. When you trash an item, an Undo link appears at the top of the list, allowing you to recall your trashed item immediately in case of an accident. Posts, pages, comments, and media each have their own Trash folder. To see items in the Trash folder, click the **Trash** link at the top of the list. Items in the Trash folder can be restored easily by placing your cursor over the item you want to restore and clicking the **Restore** link. Inversely, you can remove the file permanently by clicking the **Delete Permanently** link. The Links list uses a standard Delete link. After a link is deleted, it is permanently and immediately removed from the system. Previous versions of WordPress had a simple Delete feature that immediately removed items from the system.

▶ On the left of each list is a series of check boxes. Whether you are managing posts, users, or other list items, use these check boxes to select one or more items to perform a "bulk action" on them. Check the check box on the top or bottom title row to select all list items currently displayed. An example is approving comments en masse. You can either select all the comments one at a time or use the topmost (or bottommost) check box to check them all and then use the Bulk Actions drop-down list and click the **Apply** button to approve them all at once.

Other list options vary depending on specific functions to that list, such as filtering posts by categories. Don't be afraid to experiment with the list links.

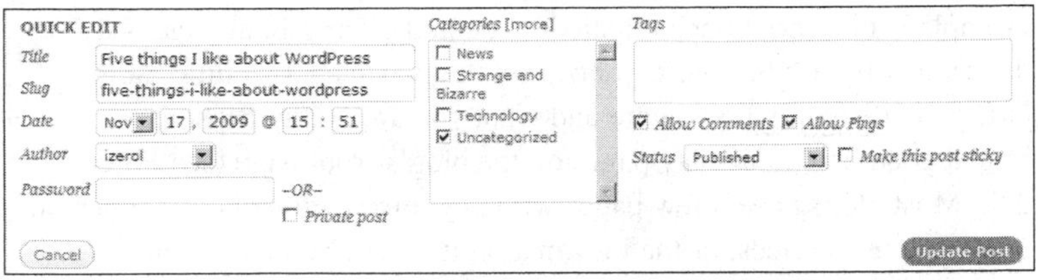

FIGURE 3.4 Quick Edit allows you to edit nearly all post attributes from the edit list.

Other tools, specific to the Edit Posts listing, can be used to filter and modify the way your posts are displayed in the list. If you are extremely prolific and have hundreds of posts to sort through, you can try to find your material by using the filters just above the list column headings. They let you filter by certain dates and/or categories. Alternatively, you can use the search box to search for text in any of your posts.

You can also make edits on multiple posts by checking each entry and then use the Bulk Edit menu to select **Edit** and click **Apply**. A set of options appears at the top of the list similar to those found in the Quick Edit option. Using these options allows you to set categories, tags, the author, and other attributes on multiple posts at once.

Two additional icons appear at the top right of the Edit list to change the view from List view to Excerpt view. List view provides you with a concise list displaying just the article title. When you change to Excerpt view, you get a preview of posts just below the title. Some people find this feature useful, whereas others think it makes the list too long. You can choose which option you prefer. A sample of the Edit list is shown in Figure 3.3.

Creating Pages

Pages contain static content that is quickly accessible from nearly anywhere on the blog, as opposed to a more dynamic influx of regular posts. As with posts, you can insert images, links, or any other type of information that the Visual Editor supports to create your page. One good example is the About page (created by default). The About page is a description of you or your organization. It gives readers a little more background about who you are and what you are doing. Most themes have a good way to display pages on the blog's front page (see Figure 3.5). Most blogs have a few pages with key information about the person, organization, services, or the information it offers. You can arrange your pages hierarchically with a parent page having multiple pages under it. For example, your About page may also have pages with more detail on your work history or hobbies.

FIGURE 3.5   This theme displays pages as tabs across the top.

Creating Basic Pages

Creating a page is similar to creating a post. There are some differences that I will point out as we walk through the process. To create a new page:

1. Click **Pages** from the side menu.

2. Click **Add New** from the Pages section.

3. Give your page a title. Keep your page title short (one or two words). Many themes display page titles horizontally. Short titles work much better in this situation.

4. Add the content. Page editing uses the same Visual Editor as the post editor, so all the same formatting tips described in the "Creating Posts" section also apply to pages.

5. Set the attributes. Unlike posts with tags and categories, pages have an Attributes section on the right. Defining the parent page allows you to arrange your pages hierarchically. For example, you may have a sporting goods products page that has "sub-pages" for hunting, fishing, tennis, and so on. All these pages would have the same parent page. The main page is the parent by default. The attributes section also has an option that allows you to define how your pages are ordered. If you leave all pages at 0, they are sorted alphabetically by title.

6. Set the comments and trackback options. Again, like posts, pages can allow comments and trackbacks (references) if the appropriate check boxes under the page body are checked.

7. Publish your post. The same options to publish your page (date, time, visibility, and so on) are also available.

Editing Pages

Managing pages is similar to managing posts. Begin by selecting the **Pages** section in the side menu. A list of pages is presented (see Figure 3.6). Refer to the "List Basics" sidebar earlier in this lesson for the funda mentals of managing WordPress lists.

You can edit any page by clicking on the page name or using the **Edit** link that appears just below the title when your mouse cursor passes over the row containing the page information.

When the editor appears, change the title, content, or other options to suit your needs. You can find more information on the editor's features in the "Visual Editor" section earlier in this lesson. When you are done making changes, click **Update**.

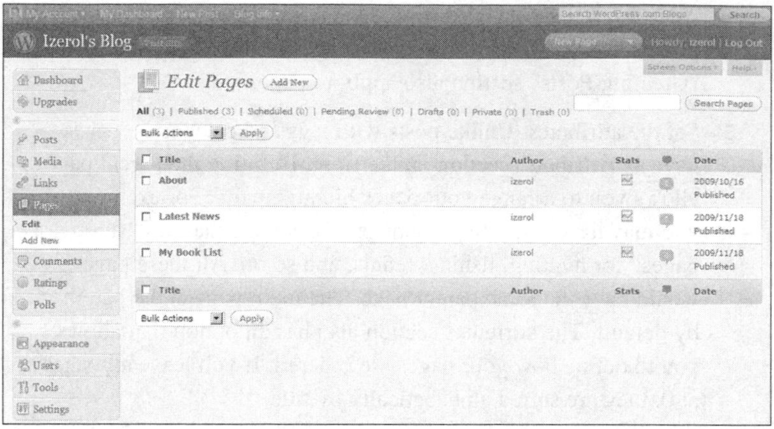

FIGURE 3.6   A typical page listing.

Creating More Advanced Content

Creating basic text is nice, but WordPress is capable of so much more. What's more, web users these days expect references, images, and even audio and video from your site. WordPress has a way to accomplish all this without requiring you to know any web programming language.

Adding Hyperlinks

Hyperlinks are references on a web page that, when clicked, take you to another location on the same page or to a different page altogether. Hyperlinks can either be text or an image. To place a hyperlink in your post or page (aka article), you first need to know the location of the other page. Follow these steps to add a text hyperlink:

1. Edit your article.

2. Open a second browser window or tab.

3. Go to the page you want to link to.

4. Select the text in the address bar. Be sure to get the entire address. Placing your cursor in the address bar usually highlights everything by default. However, if you don't have everything

selected, you can press Ctrl+A (Windows)/⌘-A (Mac) to select all text.

5. Right-click your mouse and select **Copy** or press Ctrl+C (Windows)/⌘-C (Mac).

6. Close the second browser window or tab.

7. In the Visual Editor, use your cursor to select the text you want to use as your link.

8. Click the icon that looks like two links of a chain.

9. The Insert/Edit Link window displays with several fields (see Figure 3.7). Fill in the fields as follows:

   ▶ **Link URL**—This is the address you copied from the address bar in the other window. Type or paste the complete web address by pressing Ctrl+V (Windows)/⌘-V (Mac).

   ▶ **Target**—This identifies where the new page will be displayed.

   ▶ **Title**—The text in the title is what pops up when you move your cursor over the link. Many times it is the same as the text of the link, but can be different. For example, the text might contain "Chuck Tomasi" and the title contains "Chuck's home page."

   ▶ **Class**—The class identifies the style in which the link is displayed. The values in this field refer to the cascading style sheet (CSS) values. CSS is beyond the scope of this book. It's OK to leave the class with the default value "—Not Set—".

10. Click **Insert**.

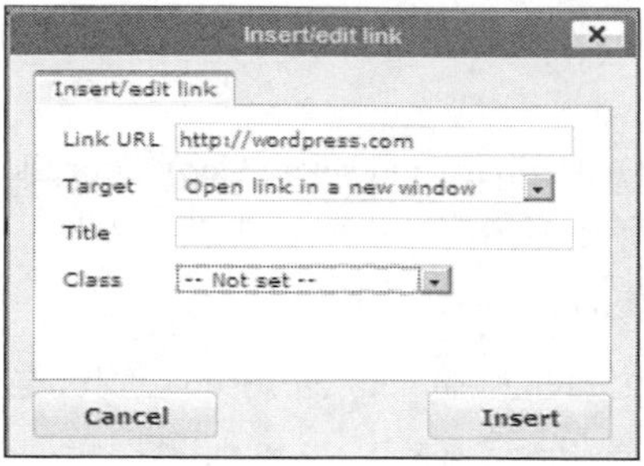

FIGURE 3.7   You only need to know the URL to create a hyperlink.

> TIP: **Check All Your Links**
>
> Be sure to verify your links connect with the pages you intend by testing them. If you need to correct your link, place your cursor anywhere on the linked text and click the **Link** icon.

Adding Images

Adding images to your article communicates much more information than text alone. Inserting images into your article is available four ways:

1. From your computer

2. From a URL (another website)

3. From the gallery (available after images are uploaded)

4. From the media library

Begin any of these methods by placing your cursor in the body of your text where you want to insert the image and then click the **Add an Image** icon (see Figure 3.8). The Add an Image window opens (see Figure 3.9).

Adding an Image From Your Computer

To add an image from your computer, follow these steps:

1. Select the left option (**From Computer**) at the top of the Add an Image window. You can upload JPEG, GIF, or PNG image files by clicking the **Select Files** button.

2. Use your computer's browse feature to select the file(s) you want to upload.

3. Click **Open** (Windows) or **Select** (Mac). Your file is uploaded, and a thumbnail of your image is displayed with various properties.

4. Click the **Insert Into Post** button. Use the scroll bar on the Add an Image window to look further down if you don't see the button displayed.

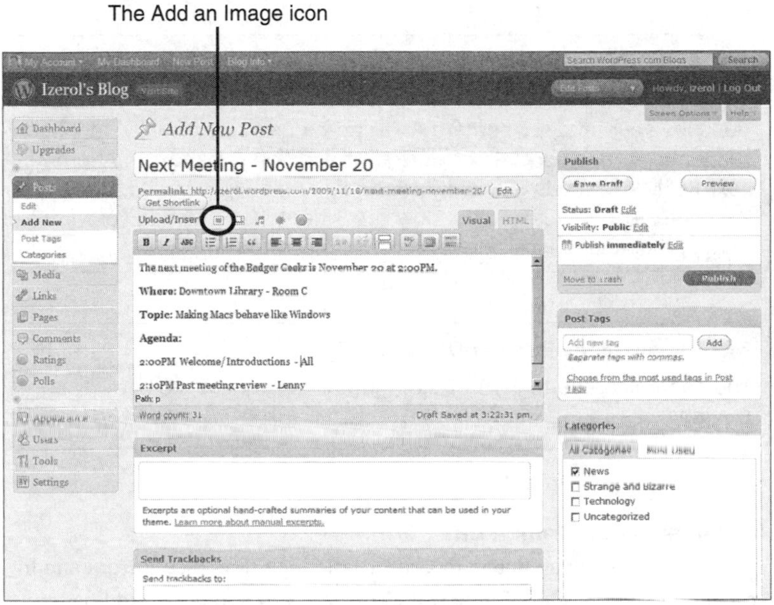

The Add an Image icon

FIGURE 3.8 Use the Add an Image icon to include photos, icons, and other graphics.

Your image is then inserted into your post. If you need to modify any of the image properties, such as alignment, size, caption, and so on, click your image and two icons appear in the upper-left corner of your image. Click the icon that looks like a mountain and sky to edit your image; click the red circle with a slash through it to delete your image.

FIGURE 3.9   Images can be added to your article several ways.

TIP: **Add Alternate Text for Accessibility**

When you add images, consider using the Alternate Text field to describe your image. Alternate text can be used for visually impaired readers who use special software that scans for the text in Alternate Text fields and reads it audibly. When you upload an image, the Alternate Text field is listed below the Title. When you edit your image, the field is listed under the Advanced Settings tab.

NOTE: **How Many Images Can I Use?**

You can upload up to 3GB of files before requiring a storage upgrade.

Adding an Image From a URL

Another way to add an image to your article is to reference it from another location (someone else's site) or add it by using the URL. Adding an image by using a URL saves you disk space and ensures changes to an image at the source are reflected on your site. The downside is that your site is generating traffic on the other server instead of your own server, which is sometimes frowned upon. Another disadvantage is the lack of control you have on the image you are using. If someone on the other site deletes the file, you will find yourself with a missing image. Before you use this option, be sure you have permission to include images through the URL. To add an image from a URL, do the following:

1. Determine the URL to the image you want to use by going to that page and right-clicking on the image.

2. Copy the URL. Depending on your browser:

   ▶ Firefox: Choose Copy Image Location.

   ▶ Internet Explorer: Choose Properties and copy the text from the Address (URL) field.

   ▶ Safari: Choose Copy Image Address.

3. Click the **Add an Image** icon from the toolbar.

4. In the Add an Image window (see Figure 3.10), click the **From URL** tab.

5. Copy the the Image URL by placing your cursor in the Image URL field and typing Ctr+V (Windows), ⌘-V (Mac), or right-click and choose Paste.

6. Add descriptive text to the Alternate Text field.

7. Enter a caption (optional).

8. Specify how you want the image aligned (optional).

9. If you want the image to link to another site or page when the reader clicks on the image, enter the URL in the Link Image To field (this field is blank by default).

10. Click the **Insert Into Post** button at the bottom.

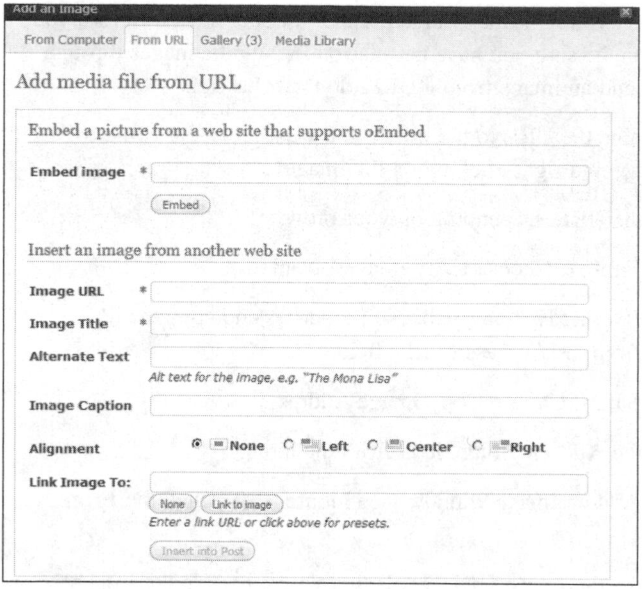

FIGURE 3.10 Referencing media from another site.

Your image is now part of your article. To edit the image properties, click the image and then click the icon that looks like a mountain and sky that appears in the upper-left corner.

When the Add an Image window appears, notice that there is a second way to insert an image by using a URL (refer to Figure 3.10). The option at the top uses a protocol known as *oEmbed*. Without getting too technical, oEmbed is a new technology to address some problems discovered with referencing media from another site with a direct URL. The advantage of oEmbed is that it provides additional information about the media being requested so that the software (WordPress in this case) can be smarter about how it is embedded. The capability to embed an image is supported by many popular media sites such as YouTube, Flickr, and Hulu; more are being added all the time. For more information about oEmbed, visit www.oembed.com.

Adding an Image from the Gallery

Your gallery is a collection of images attached to a post or page. It is a subset of the media library (a collection of all images and media files uploaded to your blog). When you add another image to the same article, a fourth option labeled Gallery appears on the top of the Add an Image window (see Figure 3.11). This option enables you to view the images attached to that article and insert them as a collection in the post.

For example, let's say I have several images from my summer vacation. Rather than inserting the images individually to the post or page, I can create a gallery using the following steps:

1. Click the **Add an Image** icon.

2. Click the From Computer tab to upload the images the same as you would to insert the images in to a post.

3. Instead of clicking **Insert into Post**, click **Save All Changes**.

4. Click the **Insert Gallery** button to add all four images at once.

Changing the settings of your gallery is similar to images. Click on the gallery after it is added to your post or page and use the upper-left icon to change where the image thumbnails link to, the order of the images, and how many columns to display. Click **Update Gallery Settings** to save your changes. You can find additional information about the Gallery at http://en.support.wordpress.com/images/gallery/.

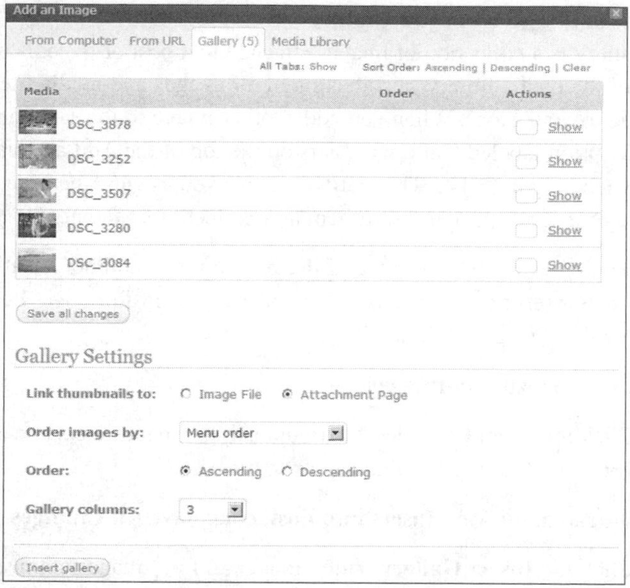

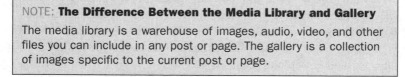

FIGURE 3.11 The Gallery tab lets you insert a collection of images.

NOTE: **The Difference Between the Media Library and Gallery**

The media library is a warehouse of images, audio, video, and other files you can include in any post or page. The gallery is a collection of images specific to the current post or page.

Adding an Image From The Media Library

The final way to add an image to your article is from your media library. After you load images into your media library, you can easily add images to an article:

1. Click the cursor where you want to insert the graphic in your text.

2. Click the **Add an Image** icon from the toolbar.

3. When the Add an Image window appears, click **Media Library** at the top.

4. Locate the image you want to include using the Search or Filter options.

5. After you locate the image, click the **Show** link on the right side.

6. Enter the title, alternate text, and other fields to format the image the way you like.

7. Click the **Insert Into Post** button at the bottom

Your image is then included as part of your article. The benefit of using images from your library is they can be used multiple times from one copy. This capability can save you time if you use a logo in multiple places. Updating your logo in the library updates it everywhere automatically. Also, you control what is in your media library, unlike referencing an image from another site.

NOTE: **Image Links**

By default, images uploaded from your system and those from the media library link to a full-size image of the one displayed in your article. That is, when readers click the image in your post or page, they go to a full-size version of your image. To change this, edit the properties and set the Link URL field to the address you want to link to.

Adding Audio

Adding audio to your blog can turn your readers into listeners. There is something more intimate about hearing someone's voice than reading her words. Some bloggers have combined blogging with audio production to create a new media form called *podcasting*. Podcasting is beyond the scope of this book, but you can learn more about it in *Podcasting For Dummies*, Second Edition, by Tee Morris, Chuck Tomasi, and Evo Terra.

There are three ways you can include audio in your blog. The first is to upload an MP3 file somewhere on the Internet and insert a "short code" to use the built-in audio player in WordPress to play the file. (Creating and uploading the MP3 file are beyond the scope of this book.) If you have a file you want to reference and know the URL, you can do the following:

1. Edit your article.

2. Switch the Visual Editor to HTML mode by clicking the **HTML** link above the text edit box.

3. Enter the short code in the format: [audio http://mydomain.com/audio/myfile.mp3], replacing the URL with your appropriate address.

4. Save your article.

Your article then has a simple embedded audio player that visitors to your site can click and hear.

The second way to include audio in an article is to buy the space upgrade from WordPress (available under Dashboard, Upgrades) to enable upload-ing of audio files to your media library. From the Visual Editor, you can also use the **Add Audio** icon (shaped like musical notes). Audio files sup-ported are WAV, MP3, MP4, M4A, and OGG. After you purchase the upgrade, the process of uploading and managing audio files is similar to managing images.

The final way you can add audio to a post is to create a link that refer-ences your file elsewhere on the Internet. This requires your readers to download the file and play it on their machine.

CAUTION: **Be Aware of Copyrights**

Whenever you're dealing with audio and video, be sure you under-stand and respect copyright laws associated with the material you are using. When in doubt, do not use other people's work.

Adding Video

High-speed Internet access is becoming more common every day. People are turning to the Internet for video to satisfy their entertainment and educational desires.

The first way you can embed a video from another site is to use the same method as linking an image from a URL. As with images, you need to know the URL of the video you are linking to. Most YouTube videos display the URL on the right side of the screen when you play it, so adding them is simply a matter of copying and pasting the URL from one window to another.

1. Open your article for editing.

2. Click the **Add Video** icon (shaped like a frame of a movie reel, to the right of the Add Image icon).

3. Click the **From URL** tab on the Add Video screen.

4. Enter the video URL—for example,
   `http://www.youtube.com/watch?v=sC0l06_223I`.

5. Click **Insert into Post**.

The second way you can include video is to purchase the VideoPress upgrade from WordPress (available under Dashboard, Upgrades) to upload and host your own video files in the media library. Uploading files can be done either from Media, Add New, or using the Add Video icon above the Visual Editor when you edit your article. Uploading or selecting the video from the media library follows the same steps you use with images. After you upload or select from the media library, the screen to define the attributes is a bit different (see Figure 3.12), allowing you to set a title, description, and rating. The selection also shows a short code you can use to embed the video, or you can click the **Insert into Post** button to include the video.

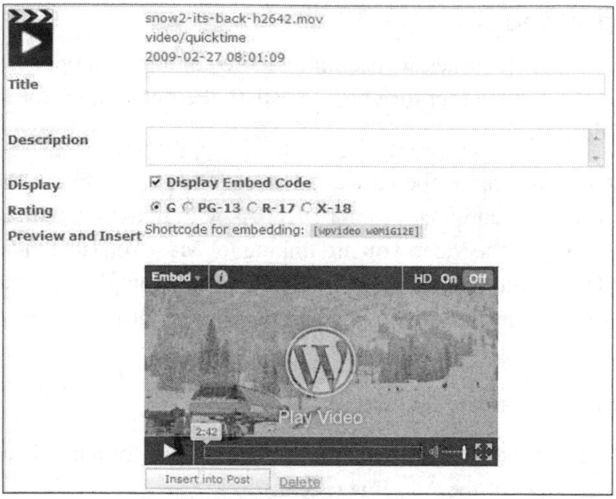

FIGURE 3.12 Setting the options on an embedded video.

The advantage to putting your video on a site like YouTube is that it is free. The disadvantages are that videos are limited to 10 minutes or less, and if you ever want to produce content as part of a business, YouTube does not offer some of the controls and statistics you may need. To address those needs, you might want to consider the VideoPress upgrade.

Summary

Adding new content is a common activity for bloggers. WordPress makes it easy to access the buttons and links to create posts and pages. The less time you spend focusing on how to use the tool, the more time you can spend on creating the content. Finally, your content can be enhanced by using some formatting, images, audio, and video to provide richer content and attract more visitors to your site.

Configuring Your Blog Settings

In this lesson, you learn the various options to configure the global settings on your blog to determine how people and other systems use it.

Before you start creating content, it pays to ensure you have your blog configured to best meet your needs and those of your visitors. The information you entered when you set up your account was a good start, but there is more. Many of the default settings work fine, but in some cases customizing settings can help you and your readers use the system more effectively. The system settings control how the system behaves for everyone who uses it—from the way the time and date are displayed to the way you are notified when a comment is made.

The Settings section on the side menu is your key to configuring your system and the way people interact with it. The system settings are subdivided into General, Writing, Reading, Discussion, Media, Privacy, Delete Blog, OpenID, and Domains. Each of these subpanels is described in greater detail in this lesson.

General

The General subpanel contains many of the settings related to the blog and some of the general interface properties (see Figure 4.1). The nine settings in the General subpanel are described in the following sections.

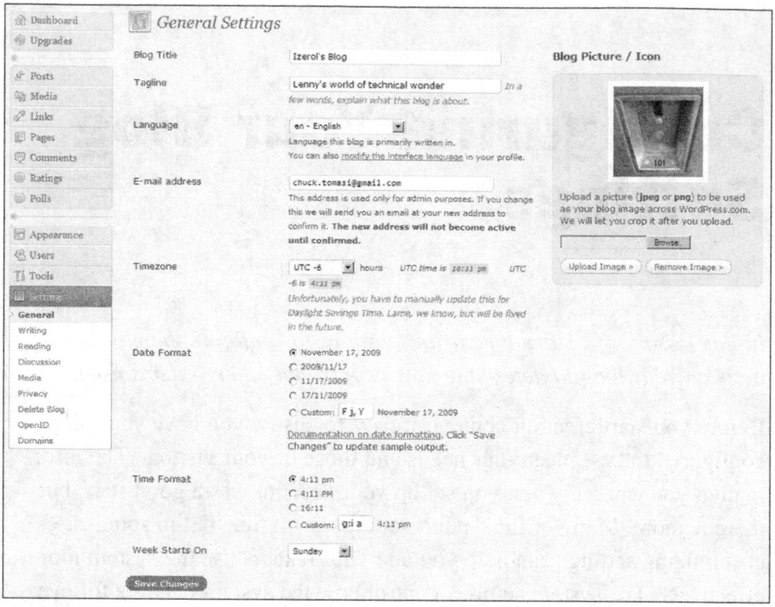

FIGURE 4.1   The General Settings screen.

Blog Title

The Blog Title setting shows the title of your blog as it appears to others who are searching for or subscribing to it. Examples include "Valley Fair Orchestra," "Dean's Car Blog," and "Gmail Podcast."

Tagline

The tagline is a short one-line description that lets people know what your blog is about. For example, one of my blogs is about Gmail and has the tagline "A collection of short hints, tips, and tricks to help you get more from your Gmail Account."

Language

In the Language field, select the language the blog is written in. The default language is English. Note that this is different from the interface language readers may have set in their profiles.

E-mail Address

The email address listed in the General Settings subpanel is for administrative purposes only and is not visible to your visitors. For example, it is the email address to which notifications are sent when new comments need to be approved. When you change the email address, a verification message is sent to the new address to confirm it for security reasons. The new email address is not active until the verification is complete.

Timezone

The Timezone setting controls the display of times on the blog (such as when posts were made). The Timezone setting shows the current coordinated universal time, or UTC. You can change the Timezone setting to the offset of your timezone to UTC. Unfortunately, you have to manually adjust for daylight saving time. If you do not know the correct offset, you can use the UTC and sample current time to determine the proper value.

Date Format

The Date Format setting lets you choose how to display dates in your blog. Alternatively, you can create your own custom format using the WordPress defined date codes. Documentation on the date codes is available just below the custom date format option.

Time Format

The Time Format field allows you to choose how the time is displayed in your blog. You can choose 12-hour, 24-hour, or another variation with the custom setting.

Week Starts On

WordPress recognizes that not everyone considers Sunday the first day of the week, so it offers the Week Starts On option, which allows you to start your calendar on any day of the week. Typically, this is Sunday or Monday, but you can use any value if your situation requires it.

Blog Picture/Icon

The Blog Picture/Icon area shows the icon or the blavatar (short for blog avatar) of your blog. When people see references to your blog on WordPress.com, they see this image. To upload a new image, follow these steps:

1. Click the **Browse** button.

2. Select a JPG or PNG format image file from your system and click **OK**.

3. Click **Upload Image**.

4. Crop the image by resizing the dotted line cutout template and clicking **Crop Image**.

5. Click **Back to Blog Options**.

CAUTION: **Make Sure to Save**

If you have changed any of the General settings, be sure to click **Save Changes** at the bottom of the screen to ensure your changes take effect.

Writing

The settings in the Writing subpanel apply to everyone who has permission to create content (posts and pages) on your system. These settings define how the authoring process actually works. See Figure 4.2 for the settings in the Writing subpanel.

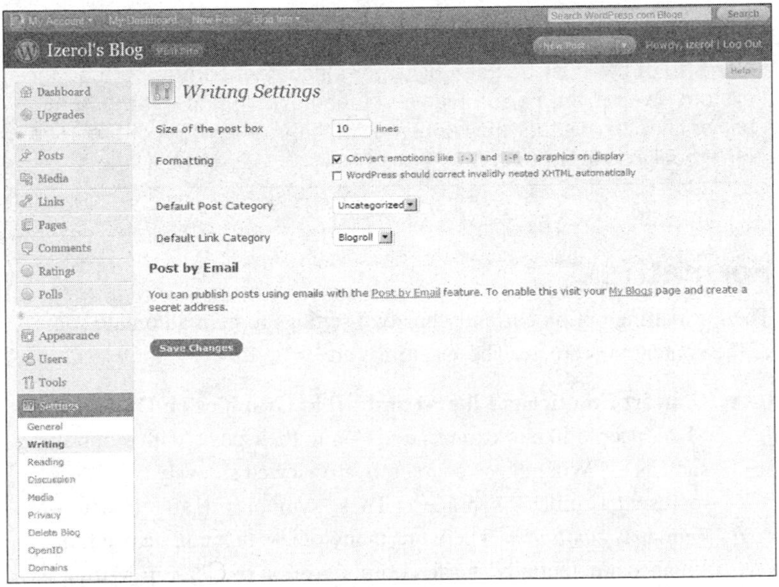

FIGURE 4.2 The Writing Settings screen.

Size of the Post Box

When you create a new post or page, a text box with tool icons is used to compose your content. This is known as the Visual Editor. To control the number of rows the Visual Editor text area displays, you can change the Size of the Post Box setting on this screen. You are not limited to only the number of lines of text specified with this setting; instead, after you've exceeded the number of lines of text the text box can accommodate, a scroll bar appears on the side of the text box. If you use a Netbook (small form-factor laptop) with limited vertical resolution, you might want to set this value lower so the text box fits on the screen. If you have a higher-resolution screen, you may choose to increase this value so you can get a better idea of what your completed work looks like.

CAUTION: **Be Aware of Coauthors' Limitations**

The Size of the Post Box setting is for all content contributors on the system. Even if you have a high-resolution screen and set the number of lines to 40, that may not work well if one of your editors uses a Netbook to create posts.

Formatting

The Formatting option currently has two settings to help automate some of the content you create. These settings are

▶ **Convert Emoticons Like :-) and :-P to Graphics on Display—** Many people like to express emotion in their posts with symbols such as :-). When these characters are viewed sideways, they represent a smile or happiness. These symbols are affectionately known as *emoticons*. There are many others that can be used to enhance a potentially sterile communication or clear up writing that might be interpreted incorrectly. When you enable this option in WordPress, the software automatically recognizes key symbol sequences and replaces them with an appropriate small graphics (turning the smile the right side up, for example), making it easier for the readers.

▶ **WordPress Should Correct Invalidly Nested XHTML Automatically—**This option is useful for people who create their posts and pages using the HTML tab on the Visual Editor instead of using the graphical interface. For example, rather than change a font size with the icon from the Visual Editor toolbar, they use XHTML code. If you use the graphical interface of the Visual Editor or are really good at writing XHTML, you can leave this option turned off. You might consider turning it on if you are a casual XHTML writer who could use some assistance to avoid some possible aesthetic, and potentially catastrophic, issues with your system.

PLAIN ENGLISH: **XHTML**

XHTML stands for Extensible Hypertext Markup Language. This is the language web pages are written in and how WordPress ultimately presents content to your browser. It is possible to use WordPress to create XHTML directly, or flip between graphical and XHTML modes in the Visual Editor. In some cases, you may find it necessary to insert XHTML code directly in to your content.

Default Post Category

When you create a new post, you have the option of selecting one or more categories. The Default Post Category setting allows you to have one category automatically selected. By default, it is set to Uncategorized. More information on categories is presented later in this lesson.

Default Link Category

Links, typically displayed on a blog's (front page) sidebar, can be categorized like posts. When you create a new link, the Default Link Category setting determines the default category, possibly saving you a mouse click. The default value is Blogroll.

Post by Email

It is possible to set up WordPress to allow content to be published simply by emailing it to a "secret" address. To set up Post by Email, refer to the section "Email Posting with WordPress.com" in Lesson 12.

NOTE: **Post by Email Formatting**

To use Post by Email, you need to use a mail client that supports rich text formatting or HTML content. Most desktop clients today have this capability.

When you use Post by Email, WordPress retains as much formatting as possible. Single images are placed inline with your text. For more information and details about formatting, visit http://en.support.wordpress.com/post-by-email/.

CAUTION: **Make Sure to Save**

If you have changed any of the Writing settings, be sure to click **Save Changes** at the bottom of the screen to ensure your changes take effect.

Reading

The Reading options control how your posts and pages are presented to readers who receive your content via a web page and through an RSS feed. See Figure 4.3.

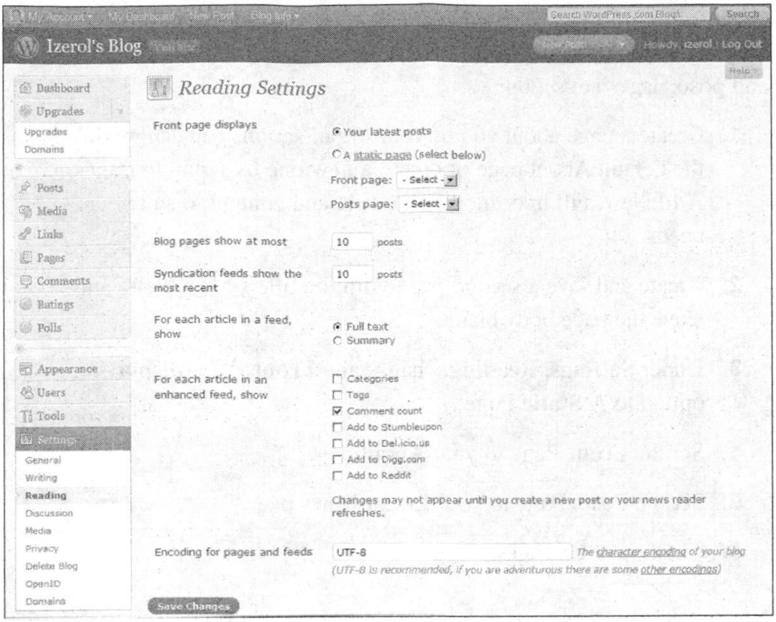

FIGURE 4.3 The Reading Settings screen controls how posts are displayed on your web page and RSS feed.

Front Page Displays

The Front Page Displays setting determines what is displayed on the front page when people first visit your blog. By default, they see your latest posts. This is the default setting because most readers like to see the latest information when they come to visit.

Alternatively, you can configure WordPress to show a static page on the front screen. Selecting A Static Page option and defining a specific page gives your site a more commercial feel with information about you or your organization on the front page. The second option, Posts Page, lets you configure how people find your posts if you are using a static front page. Refer to Lesson 3, "Creating Posts and Pages," for information on creating and maintaining pages. Here is an example of how the front page and posts pages are set up:

1. Create a page about you or your organization. You can modify the default About page or create a new one by going to **Pages**, **Add New**. Fill in or modify the title and content to suit your needs.

2. Create and save a second page with the title **Latest News** and leave the page body blank.

3. Under **Settings**, **Reading**, change the **Front Page Displays** option to **A Static Page**.

4. Set the **Front Page** to your About page.

5. Set the **Posts Page** to your Latest News page.

6. Click **Save Changes**.

Now when you view your site, your About information is displayed on the front, and a link to the Latest News containing all your posts is listed with the other pages.

CAUTION: **Using the Front Page Option**

If you set the Front Page option to one of your available pages and leave the Posts Page option as -Select-, readers might not be able to find your posts unless you have the Archives widget available. Refer to Lesson 6, "Personalizing the Appearance of Your Blog," for more information about widgets.

Blog Pages Show at Most

As people are reading through your posts from your blog page or archives, you have the option to display as many or as few posts as you like. The default for the Blog Pages Show at Most option is 10. Depending on the average length of your posts, you might want to make this number higher if you have lots of short postings, or lower if your posts are more lengthy.

Syndication Feeds Show the Most Recent

Using the Syndication Feeds Show the Most Recent setting, similar to the preceding setting, you can control how many posts are available in your RSS feed. The more posts you send, the more people have to download and potentially catch up on reading.

For Each Article in a Feed, Show

For your RSS feed, you can send out a summary (the first 55 words) or the full text of your article by changing the For Each Article in a Feed, Show setting. Summaries are useful if readers have limited bandwidth. However, they force the readers to click something for the full content if they find your information useful. Some bloggers prefer to send the full text so the readers have the entire post at their fingertips.

For Each Article in an Enhanced Feed, Show

You can choose to enhance your feed by including categories, tags, comment count, and some social web links. You do so by altering the For Each Article in an Enhanced Feed, Show setting. These are all option fields, and they may generate interest if your readers want to inform others or interact with you a little easier.

Encoding for Pages and Feeds

Encoding lets you change the character encoding you write your blog in. There are many options to choose from. Unless you are certain you need to change the Encoding for Pages and Feeds setting, leave it at the default value (UTF-8).

Discussion

One of the advantages of blogging over traditional media (magazines, newspapers, and so on) is the ability to interact and provide instant feedback to what you read and see. On the Discussion subpanel (see Figure 4.4) of the Settings, you can configure how people and other blogs interact with you.

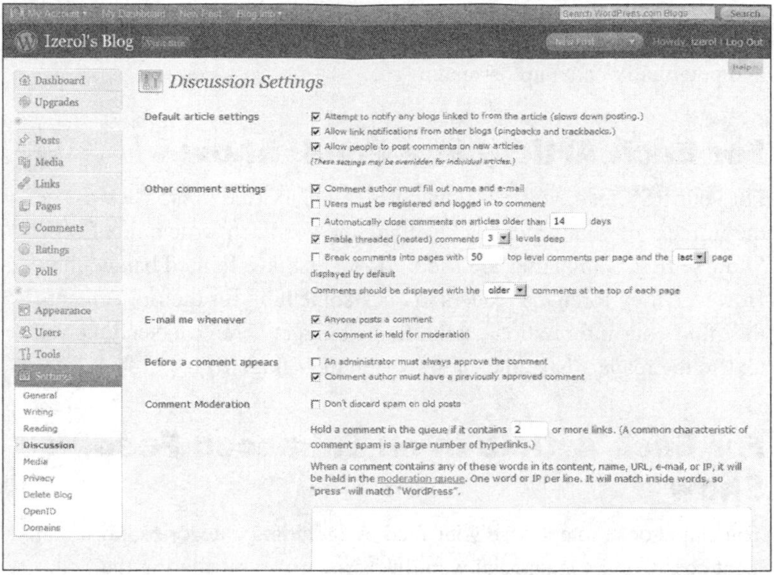

FIGURE 4.4   Part of the Discussion Settings options that determine how comments, notifications, and avatars are handled.

Default Article Settings

The three settings in Default Article Settings determine the default settings for new posts and pages. They can be overwritten individually per article. The first two options deal with communicating between blogs when one blog references another. Notification between sites is a great way to see who is talking about you and, in turn, letting other bloggers know you are talking about them.

Other Comment Settings

The Other Comment Settings section controls how visitors create comments and how comments are displayed. The settings include

► **Comment Author Must Fill Out Name and E-mail**—This setting determines if people leaving comments are required to leave their names and valid email addresses (the option is checked) or can leave anonymous comments (the option is unchecked).

► **Users Must Be Registered and Logged In to Comment**—You can limit your comments to only registered WordPress.com users by checking this option. If you leave it unchecked, any visitor is allowed to make a comment.

► **Automatically Close Comments on Articles Older Than __ Days**—This setting allows you limit the number of days you are willing to accept comments on an article after it is published. After the number of days has elapsed, comments are no longer accepted. This feature is useful to mitigate spam attacks. It is common for spammers to continue to attack an old post after they discover it.

► **Enable Threaded (Nested) Comments __ Levels Deep**—Turn on this option to allow visitors to reply to other comments inline/nested. When turned on, it can allow for better discussions and responses. Standard convention uses a maximum of three levels deep; anything higher and the theme layouts may not work as expected.

► **Break Comments into Pages with __ Comments per Page and the __ Last Page Displayed by Default**—If your posts/pages get a lot of comments, you may want to split the comments into pages. You can choose how many top-level comments to show for each page. You can also choose which page to show by default when a visitor first views the comments.

► **Comments Should Be Displayed with the __ Comments at the Top of Each Page**—This setting allows you to display your comments oldest to newest or put the newest at the top.

E-mail Me Whenever

The E-mail Me Whenever section contains two options. The first, Anyone Posts a Comment, notifies the author when comments are made to a post. If you check the second, A Comment Is Held for Moderation, an email is sent to the address you set in the General settings. If you leave this option unchecked, you can moderate your comments from the Dashboard or Comments.

Before a Comment Appears

The Before a Comment Appears settings control how comments appear on the blog. When checked, the first option requires all comments to be approved by an administrator. The second option allows people who have made previously approved comments to bypass any further approvals.

Comment Moderation

The Comment Moderation setting allows you to further refine moderated comments. You can opt to discard spam on old posts; hold comments if they contain a large number of links (a common spam characteristic); or identify key words, phrases, or addresses that might appear in a spam comment. This option does not mark the comment as spam, only that it needs to be moderated.

Comment Blacklist

Similar to the preceding option, the Comment Blacklist setting allows you to identify spam comments by key words, phrases, or addresses that appear in the contents.

Comment Reply via Email

The Comment Reply via Email option allows you to reply to comments right from the notification email. You need to enable Email Me Whenever: Anyone Posts a Comment to be able to reply to comments via email.

Subscribe to Comments

The label Subscribe to Comments has one option that reads Don't Allow Visitors to Subscribe to the Comments Made on This Blog. When this option is unchecked, readers are provided a checkbox option at the bottom of the comment section marked Notify Me of Follow-up Comments via Email. If the reader checks this option, she is sent an email message whenever someone else makes a comment on the same blog item. The person commenting does not have to have a WordPress.com login to leave comments or receive notifications. The email address the reader provides is used to send the notifications. If Subscribe to Comments is checked, the option to receive follow-up notifications is not presented.

Avatars

Avatars are the icons that represent people in the virtual world. This section defines how you wish to display avatars on your blog.

▶ **Avatar Display**—This setting determines if avatars are displayed next to comments.

▶ **Maximum Rating**—When people create their avatars, they give ratings to them similar to movie ratings. This option allows you to filter avatars beyond a certain rating.

▶ **Default Avatar**—For users without a defined avatar, you can choose to display a default (static) avatar or a custom one generated based on their email address.

CAUTION: **Make Sure to Save**

If you have changed any of the Discussion settings, be sure to click **Save Changes** at the bottom of the screen to ensure your changes take effect.

Media

The Media settings allow you to override the default WordPress settings for image sizes in your blog (see Figure 4.5). This capability gives you some flexibility on the size of images to work better with your theme. All image sizes are specified in pixels and keep the dimension proportions (so they won't look squashed) to the maximum height or width. For example, specifying 300×300 won't force a 1600×1200 image to be square; it is converted to 300×225.

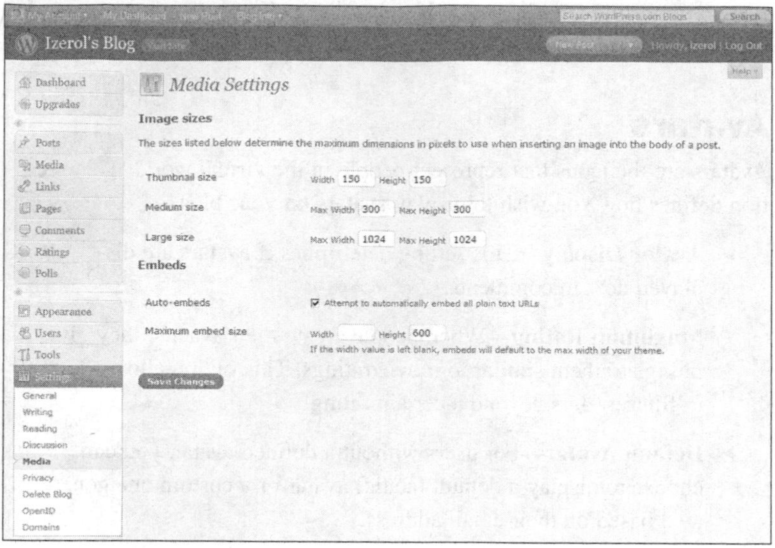

FIGURE 4.5 The Media Settings screen lets you control how embedded content is displayed.

Image Sizes

The following three settings indicate the maximum image size in pixels when you insert an image into a page or post.

▶ **Thumbnail Size**—This option specifies the size of the thumbnail images that are displayed as a preview of your images. Images are cropped and resized to fit the dimensions you set.

▶ **Medium Size**—This option sets the maximum size for an inline image in your post or gallery.

▶ **Large Size**—This option sets the maximum size of an image in your gallery, typically on its own page, free from the constraints your theme may impose.

Embeds

The following two Embed options enable you to control how embedded content (typically video) is displayed on your blog:

▶ **Auto-Embeds**—If this option is checked, WordPress attempts to convert plain URLs to embedded content. This makes it quite simple to place YouTube videos on your site, for example.

▶ **Maximum Embed Size**—This option lets you specify the maximum height and width of your embedded content. This capability helps keep the site clean when you have a theme with a narrow column for your posts and you try to embed a wide video. If you leave the width column blank, embedded content defaults to the width specified by your theme.

Privacy

Privacy settings control who can find and read your blog. They are accessed from the Privacy subpanel under Settings (see Figure 4.6). These settings are different from the privacy settings on individual posts discussed in Lesson 3. The three options for entire blog privacy are

▶ **I Would Like My Blog to Be Visible to Everyone, Including Search Engines (Like Google, Sphere, Technorati) and Archivers**—This is the default option. It indicates that your blog is open to the public.

▶ **I Would Like to Block Search Engines, but Allow Normal Visitors**—This option allows human visitors but prevents search engines from finding and indexing your information.

▶ **I Would Like My Blog to Be Visible Only to Users I Choose**—
Using this option, you can add and remove up to 35 users who
have access to your blog. Users must have registered
WordPress.com accounts. Upgrades are available if you require
more than 35 private users on your blog.

> NOTE: **Privacy Is Not Absolute**
> WordPress.com employees can read any blog regardless of privacy
> settings.

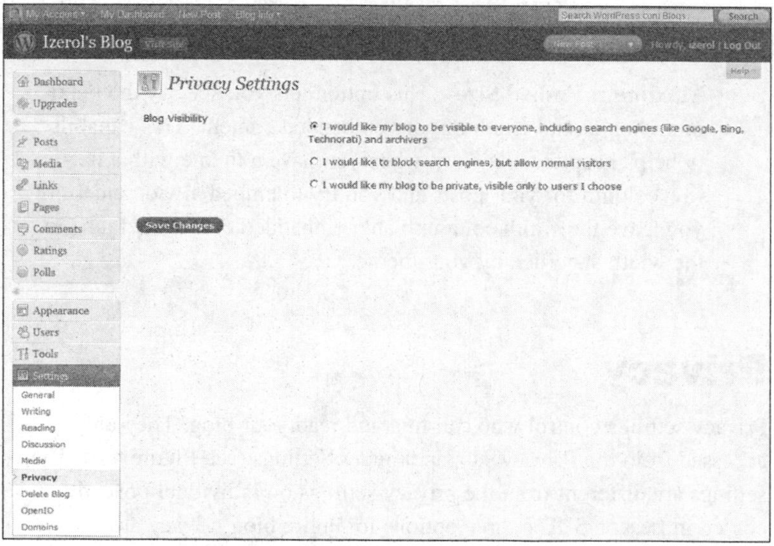

FIGURE 4.6   The Privacy Settings screen.

Delete Blog

The Delete Blog option lets you delete your blog from WordPress.com.
Blog deletion requires confirmation. When you delete a blog, it is gone
forever. There may be a time when you no longer maintain your blog or

have so many that one becomes obsolete, and this is your option to remove it. Even after you delete a blog, that WordPress domain name can no longer be used.

OpenID

OpenID is an open standard that allows you to sign in to sites using your WordPress.com account. Your OpenID is your blog URL (for example, http://myblog.wordpress.com). You can maintain the list of blogs that you trust and can use your OpenID as a login by adding it to the list in the OpenID section under Settings.

CAUTION: **OpenID Is Specific to a Site, Not a Person**

Anyone with an administrator account on your blog has access to your OpenID. Granted, you should already trust your administrators.

Other sites that use OpenID can be found at www.myopenid.com/directory.

Domains

The Settings, Domains page is identical to the Upgrades, Domains page. On this page you can make changes to any mapped domain you own. You can map your WordPress.com domain (for example, example.wordpress.com) to any domain you own (such as example.com) so users think they are going to your domain and end up at your blog. If you ever plan to host your own WordPress blog at some point in the future, you should consider paying for the domain mapping service.

Summary

The general settings control the global behaviors of your blog. How people and other blogs interact with your system is up to you to control.

LESSON 5
Managing Comments

In this lesson, you learn what comments are, whether to allow them, and if you allow them, some best practices for managing your feedback.

Understanding Comments

One of the most exciting aspects of blogging is receiving comments. Comments are a way for your readers to interact with you, the author. They give your readers a way to provide feedback to you. Comments also allow readers to interact with each other.

When you first publish an article (a post or a page), it might have a 0 Comments or Leave a Comment link at the top or bottom of the post (depending on your theme). See Figure 5.1.

Five things I like about WordPress
November 17, 2000 by izarol

The five things I like most about WordPress are:

» It is free
» It is quick to setup
» It is very easy to learn
» It supports RSS
» It's my way to publish to the world

How about you? What do you like? Leave a comment.

Posted in Uncategorized | Edit | Leave a Comment »

Leave a comment

FIGURE 5.1   WordPress makes it easy for readers to leave comments for you.

To leave a comment, the reader simply clicks the Leave a Comment link. The page of multiple posts is replaced with a page displaying the entire content of the specific post about which the reader is commenting. Text input boxes for the reader to leave a comment are at the bottom of the page. If you have comments enabled, one of two different options is displayed.

If readers are not already logged in to WordPress (which most won't be), several fields appear requesting the following information (see Figure 5.2):

- ▶ **Name (required)**—This is the reader's name. Readers can use real names, nicknames, or handles to identify themselves.

- ▶ **Email (required)**—Readers need to identify themselves to WordPress in the event that they need to be notified later. Email addresses are not displayed publicly.

- ▶ **Website (optional)**—If readers have websites and want to enter the addresses, their names are displayed as hyperlinks so anyone clicking on their name is directed to their site.

- ▶ **Comment text area**—This is the place where readers leave their feedback to you, the author.

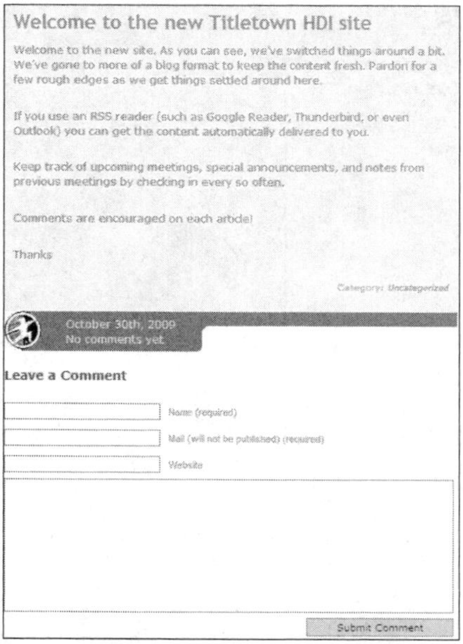

FIGURE 5.2 Readers need to leave their name and email if they are not already logged in.

Some blogs may have a Notify Me of Follow Up Comments via Email check box. This option allows readers to be notified when responses are made to their comments. This feature allows them to follow the discussion more easily without having to return to the article periodically.

After readers complete the information and click the **Submit Comment** button, the comment is recorded.

For cases in which a reader is already logged in to WordPress (that is, they operate their own blog on WordPress.com), they are not prompted for name, email, or website and can leave the comments by filling in the comments text area and clicking the **Submit Comment** button.

> NOTE: **Finding Other Blogs**
>
> You can find other blogs on WordPress.com by entering text in the search box in the upper right. You can also log in to WordPress.com and click either the Freshly Pressed or Tags tab just below the WordPress.com logo.

Allowing or Denying Comments

You decide whether you want to allow or deny comments on an article. When you allow comments, it shows that you are open to feedback and encourages discussion. Discussions build author-to-reader and reader-to-reader relationships that build loyalty. Most sites, even some of the really big news sites, enable their readers to leave comments.

There is nothing wrong with denying the use of comments in your blog, but you must recognize that denying comments sends a much different message to your readers. Human beings are social creatures and like interaction; that is why social media sites are growing so fast. Blogging is just one form of social media. By choosing to disallow comments, your readers are likely to perceive you as closed off and aloof. This is generally a bad thing on the Internet today. Whether you receive one comment a year or 1,000 a day, WordPress makes it easy to manage your comment traffic.

Reviewing the Discussion Settings

We covered many of the settings that control the default behavior for comments in Lesson 4, "Configuring Your Blog Settings." You can find the settings for comments on the side menu under Settings, Discussion. These settings control whether your readers can leave comments, how long comments are available for an article, how much information readers need to provide when leaving comments, and so on. You should review all these settings as you develop a comment management strategy.

The three check boxes at the top of the Discussion Settings screen (see Figure 5.3) are of particular interest because they can be overridden by settings on each article. The first two deal with interaction between WordPress blogs, and the last one is between your reader and your blog. The first three settings are as follows:

▶ **Attempt to Notify Any Blogs Linked To from the Article**—Notice this setting says "attempt." It does not ensure that you will be successful when you reference other blog addresses in your post. Your success depends on how their settings are configured.

▶ **Allow Link Notifications from Other Blogs (Pingbacks and Trackbacks)**—This setting controls whether your blog accepts pingbacks and trackbacks from other blogs. It is the other half of the equation to the first setting.

▶ **Allow People to Post Comments on New Articles**—Use this check box to establish whether you allow readers to make comments. If this setting is checked, the check box at the bottom of the New Page or New Post page is also checked. If it is unchecked, the default on those pages is off also. Depending on the theme, readers may still see a prompt to leave a comment even if this setting has been disabled.

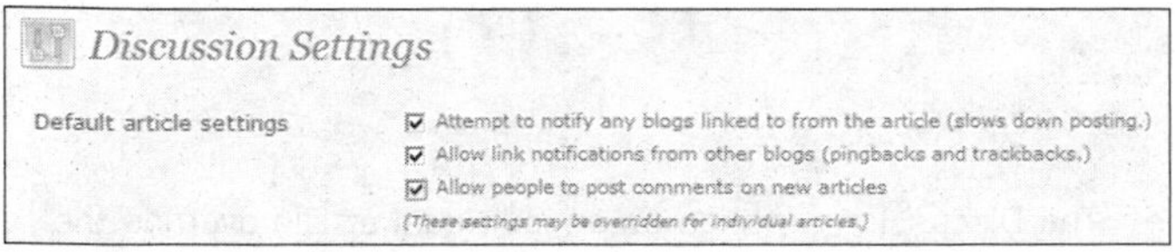

FIGURE 5.3 The first three Discussion Settings control the default for an individual article but can be overridden by settings on each individual page or post.

PLAIN ENGLISH: **Pingbacks and Trackbacks**

Pingbacks and trackbacks are electronic "tips of the hat" to let others know you mentioned them. They are a way for blogs to communicate with each other. For example, if I leave a link in one of my articles to an article in Kreg's WordPress blog and configure my blog to send notifications, he gets an email with a link to my reference as long as his blog is set up to receive these notifications. It's not a bad idea to know what people are saying about you. It is best practice to leave these incoming notices turned on.

There are differences between trackbacks and pingbacks. For more information, visit http://codex.wordpress.org/Introduction_to_Blogging and review "Managing Comments" within the "Things Bloggers Need to Know" section.

Changing the Setting for Individual Articles

As you create or edit an article, look near the bottom of the screen for a section labeled Discussion (see Figure 5.4). You might have to scroll to find it. If you do not see it, check your Screen Options to ensure it has not been turned off.

FIGURE 5.4   The Discussion Settings on an individual article override the global Discussion Settings.

The first setting allows or disallows readers to leave comments. Just because someone can leave a comment does not mean the comment is automatically displayed to the public. Refer to "Managing Comments" in this lesson for more information.

The second setting allows or disallows other blogs to notify you of a reference to your article. These blogs may still create a link from their site to yours, but you won't be notified if this setting is not turned on.

Dealing with Comment Spam

All this communication between people and blogs sounds wonderful. It is easy for people to leave comments, and because the process is so easy and open, some people try to exploit it by sending you unwanted comments known as spam. For the first couple of years of WordPress's life, spam was not a major issue. As WordPress grew, so did the target.

To be fair, you are not likely to get too many comments (good or bad) when you first get set up. Unless you are a national TV or radio personality, or you are in a band with 100,000 fans, your site will not be of much interest to comment spammers right away. Comment spammers often target high-profile sites or sites that have been around for some time. When you are just starting out, the spammers won't know you exist. As your blog is linked to, and mentioned by, others, your profile will grow.

Typically, comment spammers find an old post, perhaps a year or two old and start adding their unwanted comments there. One way to limit this practice is to turn off the ability for readers to make comments after a certain amount of time. Refer to the section about Discussion Settings in Lesson 4 or more information on this feature.

WordPress deals with comment spam with a software extension (or plug-in) called Akismet. Like email spam filters, Akismet uses a complex formula of words and phrases to identify legitimate and unwanted comments. If a spam message passes through Akismet's filter, you can identify the comment as spam (see "Managing Comments" in this lesson), and Akismet will learn from its error to capture similar messages in the future. The learning process is not limited to only your input. Akismet's database of comment spam is a collection of all WordPress blogs, which increases the power of the software. This feature is enabled automatically and is not configurable if you are using WordPress.com. However, WordPress.org administrators need to configure it manually. Refer to Lesson 11, "Customizing Your Site with Plug-ins," for more information about plug-ins and Akismet. Whether you are using WordPress.com or hosting your own site using the software from WordPress.org, you can quickly see how effective Akismet is by viewing the information at the bottom of the Right Now Dashboard widget (see Figure 5.5). Akismet does not delete any comment spam in the event that it gets a false positive. Click the **Comments** link in the Akismet information to see a list of comments that Akismet suspects are spam. From this list, you can review the comments and determine whether they are valid spam or should be approved and visible to the public. See "Using the Comments List" in this lesson for more information.

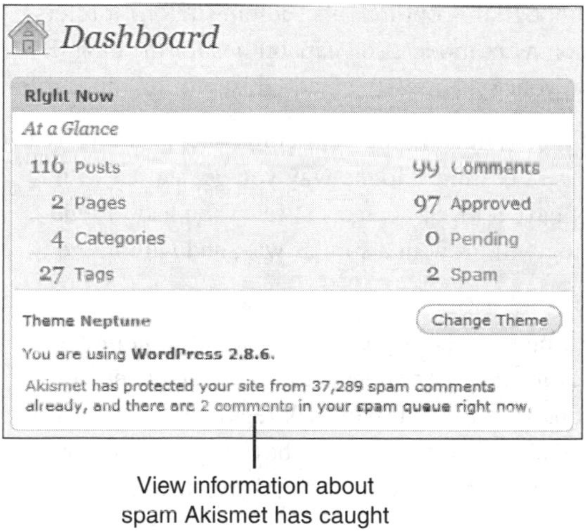

View information about
spam Akismet has caught

FIGURE 5.5   Akismet's stats are available from the Right Now Dashboard widget.

Don't let comment spam deter you from blogging. By using a few good practices, such as using Akismet and limiting the time an article is available for comment, you can minimize the impact of spam.

Managing Comments

Managing comments allows you to control whether you review and approve each comment before it is made available to the public. For the new blogger, this is not a big time investment. If you allow all comments to be available to the public immediately, you could subject yourself to possible legal consequences if one of your readers makes a comment about another person or organization and the target of the comment feels he has been portrayed inaccurately. The legal ramifications of allowing and disallowing comments are beyond the scope of this book. The best way to protect yourself against being a part of a legal dispute is for you to moderate comments (using your best judgment).

You can enable comment moderation from Settings, Discussion. Check the Before a Comment appears: An Administrator Must Always Approve the Comment option. Although this option says "administrator," it refers to any person who has comment moderation capabilities for the blog. By default, this is anyone on your system with an administrator or editor role.

When you first start your blog, moderating your comments is not likely to take much time. The process is similar to the way you got started with email. You likely did not have a lot of contacts at first. You had to send mail to get mail. Your blog will grow in a similar way, and with it, the comments will grow.

If you are lucky and your blog starts to get a lot of activity, you might find yourself with a lot of incoming comments to review and approve. One option in this situation is to ask for help. Ask regular commenters if they are willing to help moderate. If you already have regular contributors, ask them if they would like to be editors to assist with comment management.

There are several ways to access comments and manage them from the Administrative Dashboard. They include

▶ The shortcut button at the top right. Using the drop-down arrow, select Comments (see Figure 5.6).

▶ The Recent Comments widget on the Administrative Dashboard.

▶ The Comments subpanel on the side menu.

FIGURE 5.6   Accessing comments from the shortcuts menu in the upper right.

TIP: **Quickly Spot Outstanding Comment Approvals**

A number listed on the comments subpanel indicates the number of comments pending approval. No number indicates all comments have been approved.

The Recent Comments Dashboard Widget

One way to manage the incoming comments is to use the Recent Comments widget on the Administrative Dashboard (see Figure 5.7). If the widget is not displayed, check the Screen Options in the upper right to ensure it has not been unchecked (turned off) at some point.

FIGURE 5.7 The Recent Comments Dashboard widget makes it easy to quickly approve, trash, edit, reply to, or mark as spam incoming comments.

By default, this widget shows the five most recent comments to your system. New comments awaiting moderation are highlighted in yellow. As you pass your cursor over each comment, several options appear just below the text of the comment. They include

- ▶ **Approve (or Unapprove)**—If a new comment is awaiting approval, click the **Approve** link to have it show up in your blog. If the comment has already been approved, the link reads Unapprove. Clicking **Unapprove** removes the comment from your blog but does not delete it from your system.

- ▶ **Reply**—Using the **Reply** link is a convenient way to respond to comments without ever leaving the Dashboard.

- ▶ **Edit**—Use the Edit link to bring up the editor; change the name, email address, or URL; fix typos in a comment; or change the status or the date the comment was posted. Click the **Update Comment** button to apply your changes.

▶ **Spam**—If you encounter an unwanted comment and believe it to be spam, click **Spam** and it is removed immediately.

▶ **Trash**—Clicking the **Trash** link moves a comment to the comment Trash folder. Refer to the "List Basics" sidebar in Lesson 3, "Creating Posts and Pages," for more information on managing your trash.

Additionally, clicking the **View All** button takes you to the Comments List to see and manage more comments. This button performs the same action as the Comments subpanel on the side menu or choosing **Comments** from the shortcuts menu.

Using the Comments List

The comments list gives you access to multiple comments at one time (see Figure 5.8). The function and layout are similar to that of other lists discussed in earlier lessons.

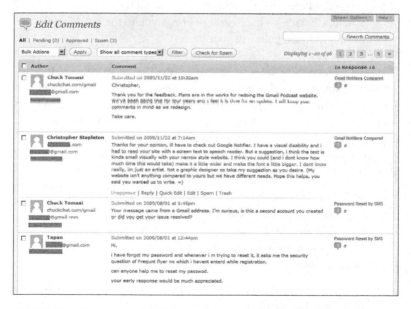

FIGURE 5.8　The comments list displays many features to help manage comments.

Currently, three columns display for comments—Author, Comment, and In Response To. The Screen Options drop-down in the top right of the screen enables you to control the display of two of the following two columns:

▶ **Author**—This setting displays who wrote the comment, her email address, website (if entered), and the Internet address from which she entered this information. Clicking the web address brings you to that page. Clicking the email address composes an email using whatever client you have set up on your computer (Outlook, Outlook Express, Mac Mail, and so on). Clicking the IP address filters the comment list to comments made from the same IP address as the one listed.

▶ **In Response To**—This column displays the title of the article the comment is related to, the number of comments made on the same article, and a hash sign (#). Clicking the article title brings you to the editor. Clicking on the number of comments brings you to a filtered list of comments that are all related to the same article. Clicking on the hash sign brings you to the article as it is displayed to the public in your blog.

The only column that cannot be disabled is the Comment column. It displays the date the comment was submitted and the text of the comment. The date is a link to the blog article as it is displayed to the public in your blog. As you move your cursor over each row of the comment listing, several options appear just below the comment text. These options enable you to modify an individual comment quickly. The following options are displayed:

▶ **Approve (or Unapprove)**—If a new comment is awaiting approval, click the **Approve** link to have it show up in your blog. If it has already been approved, the link reads Unapprove. Clicking **Unapprove** removes the comment from your blog but does not delete it from your system.

▶ **Spam**—If you encounter an unwanted comment and believe it to be spam, click **Spam** and it is removed immediately.

▶ **Trash**—The Trash link moves a comment to the Trash folder. Refer to the "List Basics" sidebar in Lesson 3 for more information on managing your trash items.

▶ **Trash**—The Trash link moves a comment to the Trash folder. Refer to the "List Basics" sidebar in Lesson 3 for more information on managing your trash items.

▶ **Edit**—The **Edit** link brings you to the comment editor (see Figure 5.9). The comment editor lets you update the various fields associated with the comment including the commenter's name, comment text, and so on. Click the **Update Comment** button to apply your changes.

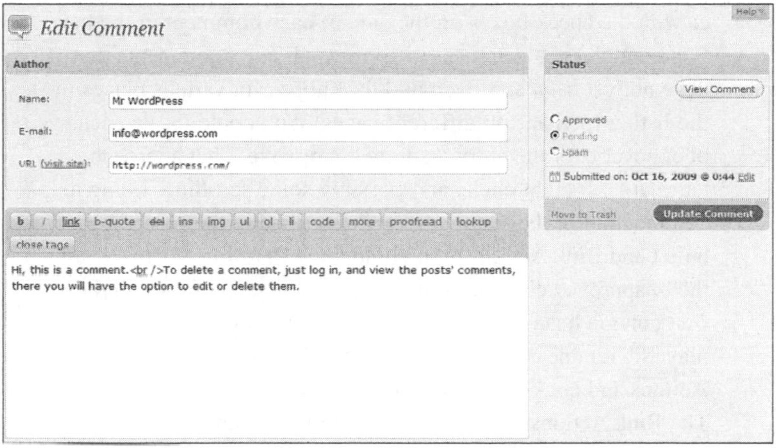

FIGURE 5.9 The comment editor lets you change any comment attribute.

▶ **Quick Edit**—The Quick Edit link is similar to the Edit link with the exception that you do not go to a separate screen to make the edits. The name, email, URL, and comment text are available to edit directly in the list. Click the **Update Comment** button to apply your changes or use **Cancel** to abort.

▶ **Reply**—Clicking the **Reply** link is a convenient way to respond to comments without leaving the comment list.

Above the comment listing are several additional options to help you find comments (see Figure 5.10). They include

- ▶ **A search box**—The search box provides you with a simple method to find words or phrases in your comments. Simply enter the text you want to locate in the text box and click **Search Comments**. Your results are displayed in the comment listing.

- ▶ **All, Pending, Approved, Spam, and Trash**—The links just below the title Edit Comments provide a quick way to filter your comments based on the current status. With a single click, you can locate all comments classified as Pending (unapproved), Approved, Spam, Trash, or All (approved and unapproved) comments.

- ▶ **Bulk Actions**—The Bulk Actions drop-down list is used together with the check boxes on the side of each comment in the list. For example, say you want to approve all eight comments that have not yet been approved and they appear in various places in the listing (perhaps on different pages). You could locate each one, hover over the entry, and click **Approve**. That approach takes at least eight clicks and possibly some scrolling. Using a combination of the status features described in the preceding bullet and Bulk Actions, you could click **Pending** to display all the unapproved comments and then click the check box in the first column header. This approach selects all the entries displayed with one click. Finally, choose **Approve** from the Bulk Actions and click the **Apply** button. That's a total of four clicks. The Bulk Actions list also appears at the bottom of the comment listing (see Figure 5.10). The list contains the following options:

  - ▶ **Unapprove**—Unapprove all selected comments. This changes the status of the selected comments to Pending and removes them from the public view.

  - ▶ **Approve**—Approve all selected comments.

  - ▶ **Mark as Spam**—Identify all selected comments as Spam and remove them from the system.

  - ▶ **Move to Trash**—Move all selected comments to the Trash folder.

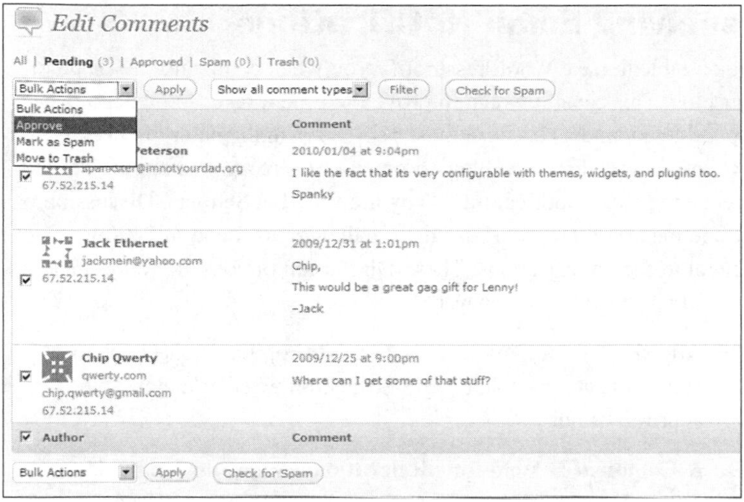

FIGURE 5.10 Using bulk actions can save you time when managing multiple comments.

▶ **Comment Type Filter**—Displayed next to the Bulk Actions list with a default value of Show All Comment Types, this filter lets you display all types of comments, normal comments from readers, or pingbacks/trackbacks from other systems. After you select the type of comment to display, click the **Filter** button.

▶ **Check for Spam button**—This button runs all your comments through the spam filter (Akismet) again. This capability is useful if the service has learned a new spam technique and you have comments that are pending approval. This option also appears at the bottom of the comment listing.

▶ **Page index**—The page index appears on the right side just below the search box when you have more than 20 comments in your listing. You can use the page numbers to go directly to the displayed number or use the forward and backward arrows to advance one page in either direction. This option also appears at the bottom of the page listing.

Receiving Email Notifications

It is possible to have WordPress notify you when comments are made to your blog. This capability can improve the time it takes to moderate and respond to comments because most people are in the habit of checking their email more than their blog comments. There are two options related to receiving email notifications. They are found in Settings, Discussion on the side menu. Both options use the email address found in Settings, General to send notifications. These Discussion options are found under the heading Email Me Whenever:

▶ **Anyone Posts a Comment**—When this option is checked, all comments generate an email notification whether they require approval or not.

▶ **A Comment Is Held for Moderation**—When this option is checked, an email is generated any time a comment requires approval. Note that this may not generate an email for all comments if the comment author has previously submitted comments that have been approved and the Comment Author Must Have Previously Approved Comment option is enabled.

Best Practices

There are several guidelines for managing your comments effectively. These are by no means required rules; they are simply ideas that bloggers have found to work well.

1. Check your comments regularly. If you are using email notifications, you will be notified moments after a comment has been made (depending on the way your Discussion Settings are configured). If you are not using email notifications, make it a practice to check your comments at least twice as often as you post. If you post once a week, check for comments twice a week. If you post daily, check multiple times a day. In reality, you are likely to get comments half as often as you post, but checking more frequently gives better customer service to your readers.

2. Respond to all (nonspam) comments. Treat each comment as an invitation to a conversation. Someone has a question or feedback for you. Respond to them as you would in person. Remember that the conversation is public.

3. Use an email alias. If possible, set your General Settings email with an email alias. An email alias points to your proper address without revealing your usual address. When mail is sent to the alias, it is redirected to your mailbox. This allows you to filter incoming comment notifications and act on them based on the alias address. It also allows you to change the alias without modifying your WordPress configuration should you decide to use a distribution list or transfer responsibility of comment management to another person. Suggestions of email aliases include comments@yourdomain.com, wordpress@yourdomain.com, or feedback@yourdomain.com. Check with your mail service provider or administrator to see if you can set up an email alias for your name.

> **NOTE: What Kinds of Comments Will I Get?**
>
> If you write a post in which you express a strong opinion or evoke an emotional response, you should expect to get some strong comments. If you write something technically incorrect, your readers are likely to correct you. If you ask a probing question, you are likely to get answers.

Summary

Comments are the primary means by which your readers and other bloggers interact with you. After you have configured your comments the way you like, management of new comments is relatively easy with the exception of an occasional spam comment.

LESSON 6

Personalizing the Appearance of Your Blog

In this lesson, you learn how to give your site a whole new look and feel without a lot of work or technical skill.

Themes

Themes are what give a WordPress blog its personality. WordPress provides the theme functionality to allow you to easily change the look of your site without being a professional web developer. You have probably seen dozens of WordPress blogs and not realized it (including msnbc.com) because many of the blogs use a different theme than the default that's supplied with every WordPress blog (see Figure 6.1). A theme is a set of files that define font sizes, margins, screen layout, and more. Your postings, pages, links, and other settings remain the same, but the way they are presented changes. Some refer to this as "skinning" your site, but WordPress refers to it as themes.

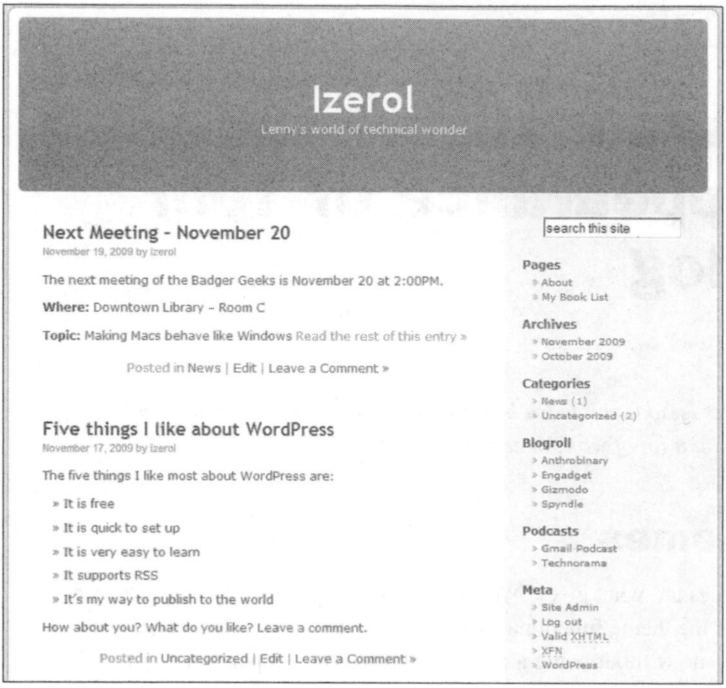

FIGURE 6.1   While functional, the default theme "Kubrick" is a bit plain.

You can change a few things, such as your blog title and tagline, without getting involved with themes, but they have minimal impact on the overall personality of your site.

Themes are very easy to set up and at the same time allow you to customize nearly every aspect of WordPress. This is one area where WordPress.com and WordPress.org differ. Although the basic functionality is the same, the features vary. With WordPress.com, you can choose from dozens of themes. WordPress.org has thousands to choose from. WordPress.com allows you to do custom CSS (cascading stylesheets) with an optional upgrade fee. WordPress.org allows you to customize your CSS for no additional charge. Refer to Lesson 10, "Using Themes on Your Own Site," for more information on customizing themes on your own blog.

Branding

Your blog reflects part of who you are, or rather whom you would like to represent online. For the sake of this lesson, I assume you are setting up a blog for your own purposes. With that assumption, selecting a theme is purely a matter of personal choice.

If you are setting up a blog for an organization or website that already has a defined brand (color scheme, logo, and so on), you should consider hosting your own blog and enlisting the help of a web developer or read one of many books on the PHP programming or cascading style sheets (CSS) to fine-tune your blog. PHP programming and CSS are beyond the scope of this book.

Finding and Applying a New Theme

To start locating and applying a new theme, log in and click on **Appearance** on the side menu. The Manage Themes page appears, as shown in Figure 6.2.

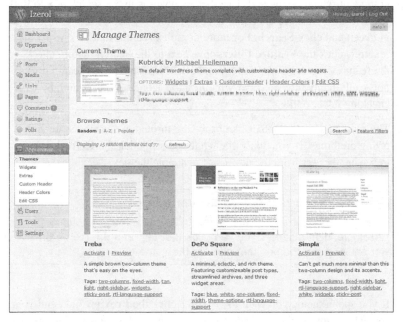

FIGURE 6.2 The Manage Themes page is your key to refacing your blog.

Your current theme is listed at the top of the page. There are several options available to your theme. They are covered in the "Making Additional Changes" section later in this lesson. Further down the page are 15 random themes. There are currently more than 70 different themes you can choose from. Each theme includes a thumbnail image so you get an idea of what it looks like.

NOTE: **Limited Theme Choices**

With WordPress.com, it is not possible to use themes other than the standard themes provided. However, additional themes are available to you if you host your own blog using the software available from WordPress.org. Additional information is available in Lesson 11.

Using the theme browser just under your current theme, you can find themes alphabetically, see the most popular themes, or search for a theme based on keywords (tags) or features. Each theme has one or more tags to help identify and organize it. Use these keywords in the search box to find specific attributes. For example, if you are looking for a green theme, type in **green** and click **Search**. For more complex searches based on specific features, click the **Feature Filters** link next to the Search button, check the features you are interested in, and click **Search**. If your search does not result in any hits, consider widening the scope of your search by checking fewer options.

The random search is rather like browsing through a clothing store and trying on things. If you don't like what you see, click the **Refresh** button to see another set from the dozens of available themes.

TIP: **Use Theme Tags to Find Similar Themes**

The tags for each theme are links. If you see a feature you like (for example, right sidebar), you can click that tag, and the theme browser shows more themes that contain the same tag.

If you spot a theme you want to "try on," click the **Preview** link, and your content is displayed in the window that pops up (see Figure 6.3). This preview has no impact on what the current visitors to your blog are seeing.

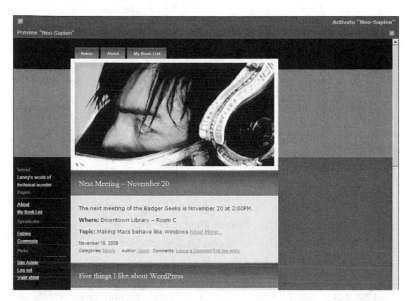

FIGURE 6.3 The Preview link lets you see what your content looks like if you apply the theme.

If you like the theme and want to apply it to your site, click **Activate "name"** in the upper right of the preview window. If you want to keep shopping, click **X** in the upper left to close the window. Your theme represents you, so have some fun with it.

CAUTION: **Don't Change Too Often**

You can change your theme any time you like by going to the **Appearance** menu option, locating a new theme, and applying it. However, you should realize your readers may get confused if you change your theme frequently. Changing your theme changes the location of links and icons. Try to settle on a theme and make only minor changes afterward.

Links allow you to create a collection of other websites you want to share. By placing websites in your link library, you can easily present them on your front page with the Links widget. Refer to Lesson 7 for more information on

Widgets. You do not need any knowledge of HTML to display links. All you need is a title and the URL of the other site. In turn, you can request others add your blog to their links.

Adding a New Link

To create a new link, click the **Add New** subpanel under Links on the side menu. Clicking this option displays several fields to identify your new link (see Figure 5.9). At a minimum, fill in the first two fields. Following are the link-related fields:

- ▶ **Name**—This is the name as it is displayed on your web page. It should be an accurate representation of what you are linking to—for example, the name of another blog.

- ▶ **Web Address**—This is the complete web address (including http://) of the site you are linking to.

- ▶ **Description (optional)**—You can add a description here so you can provide additional information when someone hovers their mouse cursor over the link.

- ▶ **Category (optional)**—From this field, you can select a category (or create an additional category) to organize your links.

- ▶ **Target (optional)**—If you choose, you can identify how the link is displayed with one of the following targets:

    - ▶ **_blank** causes a new browser window to appear with the linked page when the link is clicked.

    - ▶ **_top** presents the new linked page in the top frame of the current page. If your site is designed with frames, selecting this option removes existing frames.

    - ▶ **_none** is the default behavior if you choose no target; it places the content in the current window.

    This is purely a personal preference if you want new content to go in a new browser window (allowing readers to still maintain a page with your content), minimize the number of open windows (or tabs) readers have, or let them choose how they want their browser to behave.

- ▶ **Link Relationship (optional)**—The link relationship is based on a protocol called XFN, which stands for XHTML Friends Network. It allows you to identify the type of relationship you have with the people or sites you are linking to. To learn more about XFN, visit http://gmpg.org/xfn. The different types of link relationships are as follows:

- ▶ **Identity**—This check box identifies the link as one of your websites.

- ▶ **Friendship**—Select the option that most accurately represents your association with the other person or site.

- ▶ **Physical**—If you have physically met the other person (or people) face-to-face, check the Physical check box.

- ▶ **Professional**—Check this check box if the other person is a professional acquaintance (coworker or colleague).

- ▶ **Geographical**—This option identifies your geographic location in relation to the other person. Co-resident signifies you live with the other person. Neighbor is in a similar geographic region (city, town, or village). None indicates you either don't know or don't care.

- ▶ **Family**—If the other person is related to you, choose the option that best represents your relationship in the Family section.

- ▶ **Romantic**—You also have the option to select one or more options if you are romantically involved with the other person.

▶ **Advanced (optional)**—The Advanced section allows you to set additional options. The image address lets you link to another site's image and display it along with the link. There are two things you need to know to use this feature. First, know whether your current theme supports images in the links. Second, know the direct URL to the image you are going to use (for example, http://mydomain.com/images/logo.jpg). The RSS address allows you to specify the RSS feed alongside the site's link. Again, not all themes support this feature. Notes is a place for you to capture any additional thoughts you have about the link you have collected. There may come a point in the future when you don't recall adding the information, and these notes may be your only clue where it came from and why it was added. Finally, rating allows you to rate your links from 0 (worst) to 10 (best). Some themes sort the links by ranking.

▶ **Keep this link private**—This check box on the right keeps the public from viewing the link. Only site administrators can see private links.

Be sure to click **Add Link** to save your settings.

Widgets

A widget is a tool or content that displays some type of information on the sidebars of your blog. Although themes give you control of how things are displayed on your blog, widgets enable you to control what is displayed.

Widgets make it easy to add, move, or remove content from the left or right sidebars of your blog provided you are using a widget-ready theme.

> **TIP: Use Widget-Ready Themes**
>
> When selecting a theme, look for themes that are widget ready (use the tag "widgets"). Customizations to non-widget-ready themes require HTML, CSS, and PHP programming knowledge.

You can find the Widgets page in the Appearance menu under the subpanel labeled Widgets (see Figure 6.4) or from the Widgets option on the Manage Themes page.

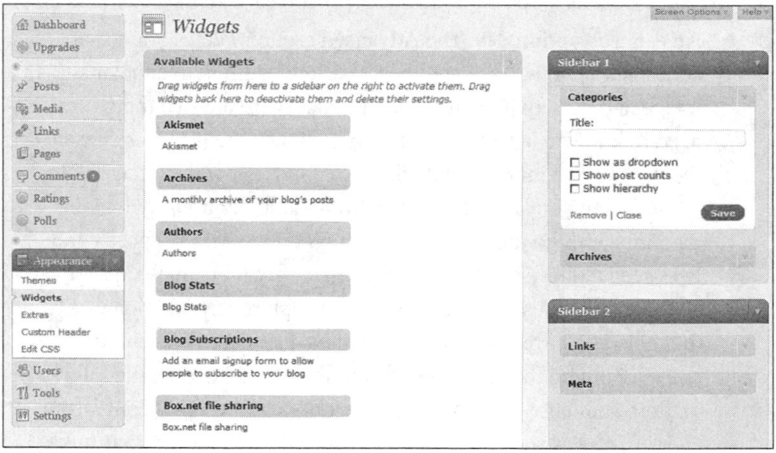

FIGURE 6.4   The Widgets page.

Each widget has a unique function. There are dozens of widgets and new ones being developed all the time. A few of the commonly used widgets you may want to familiarize yourself with are as follows:

- ▶ **Archives**—The archives widget shows a historical collection of your blog posts listed by month. After you have been blogging for a year or two, you might consider the Display as Drop Down option to save space in your sidebar.

- ▶ **Calendar**—The calendar widget displays a monthly calendar of your post activity with clickable links displaying all posts for that date. It does not let you set up a calendar of events. It is used only to display your post activity.

- ▶ **Categories**—The categories widget alphabetically lists the categories of your blogs, which makes it easier for your readers to find your content.

- ▶ **Links**—The links widget displays the entries you have made from the Links subpanel. The links widget is a good way to recommend other sites to your readers.

- ▶ **Meta**—The meta widget contains links to log in and log out, site admin, RSS feeds, and WordPress.com. If you have multiple contributors to your blog, adding the meta widget provides them with an easy way to log in.

CAUTION: Where's the Login Link?

If you do not use the Meta widget anywhere, no Login link is presented to administer your blog. Adding /wp-admin to the end of your blog address accomplishes the same thing—for example, http://mysite.wordpress.com/wp-admin

---

- ▶ **Pages**—The pages widget adds a list of your blog's pages to your sidebar. This widget might not be necessary if your theme includes a navigation bar.

- ▶ **Search**—The search widget provides a way for readers to do a simple text search of your content. Despite all the tags and categories, some readers find it easier to search for content.

▶ **Text**—The text widget allows you to add arbitrary text or HTML to your sidebar. You can have multiple text widgets with different content in each.

More details about widgets are available at
http://en.support.wordpress.com/topic/widgets-sidebars/.

Adding Widgets

The Widgets page displays two major sections in the center and a number of sidebar boxes on the right, which vary according to your theme. The Active Widgets are available for your use. To add a widget to your blog, drag one from the Active Widget section to the appropriate sidebar section on the right. If the sidebar shows only a dark gray title bar, use the triangle to open it. This feature allows you to place widgets in that box.

If you do not place anything in a sidebar box, the theme uses whatever widgets are defined in the theme.

Most widgets have options associated with them, such as allowing you to change the title or display lists as drop-down lists. When you drag a widget to the sidebar, a triangle appears on the right of the widget title bar. Click the triangle to view and set the options. Click **Save** when you are done making changes to your widget options.

There is no Save or Update button on the Widget page. When you are done configuring the widgets, you can immediately see their effect by viewing your site.

Removing Widgets

To remove a widget from your sidebar, drag it to either the Active Widgets or Inactive Widgets section of the screen. Both sections have the same effect in terms of removing the widget. However, if you've made any changes to the widget, such as URLs or other text, those changes are lost if you put it in Active Widgets, whereas your changes are preserved when you put the widget in Inactive Widgets.

Making Additional Changes

In addition to using themes and widgets, there are some additional ways you can customize your blog's look and feel.

Extras

The Extras page (see Figure 6.5) is available from Appearance, Extras or the Extras option from the Manage Themes page.

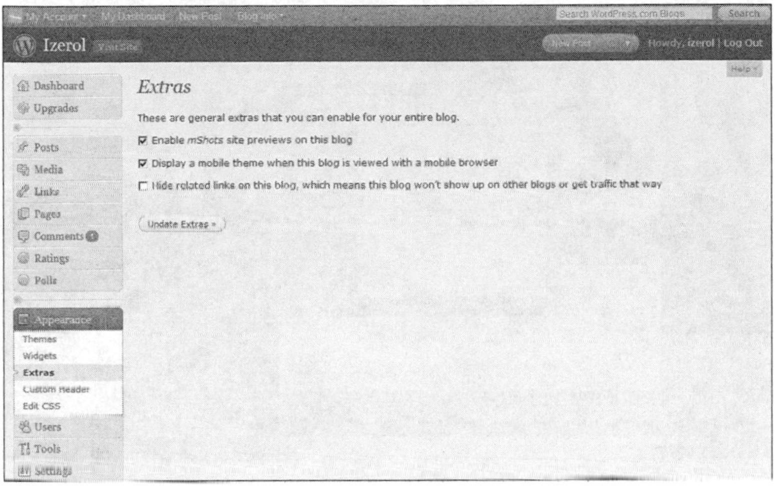

FIGURE 6.5 The options on the Extras page.

The Extras page has three options available that you can enable for your entire blog.

mShots—Preview Links

mShots allows a blog reader to get a preview of the sites you link to without leaving your site. To turn on this feature, check the **Enable mShots Site Previews on This Blog** option on the Extras page. When the reader moves his mouse over a link to another site, a window pops up with a preview of that site (see Figure 6.6). The preview for some sites appears instantaneously, but some sites take a few seconds to generate a preview.

NOTE: **Disabling mShots**

Your readers can disable mShots for all WordPress.com sites by clicking **Turn Site Previews Off** in the bottom-right corner of the preview window. However, re-enabling mShots is a bit trickier. To re-enable mShots, your readers need to remove the cookie "nopreview" for the domain ".wordpress.com." Consult your browser's documentation for detailed information on managing cookies.

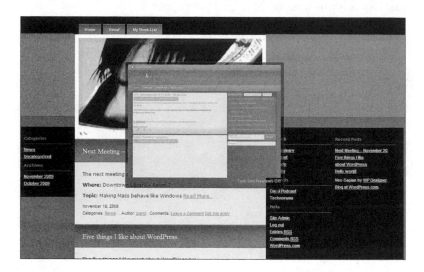

FIGURE 6.6   mShots show a preview of sites you link to.

Mobile Browsers

The Extras page also has an option to assist readers with mobile browsers. When you check the **Display a Mobile Theme When This Blog Is Viewed with a mobile browser** setting, you enable one of two mobile themes specially designed for readers using the browser on their mobile devices (see Figure 6.7). The themes are designed to load quickly. The first is designed specifically for the iPhone, iPod Touch, and Android phones. This theme takes advantage of some of the browsing capability of the platform, giving readers access to the following:

▶ Posts, pages, and archives

▶ Commenting and post loading using AJAX (for faster interaction)

▶ Scaled header images if a custom image is used

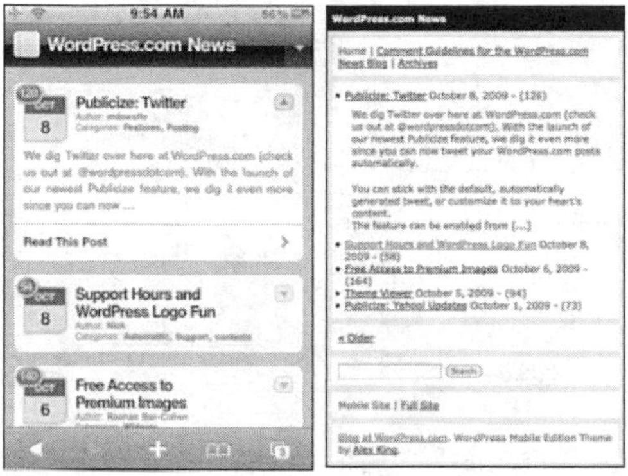

FIGURE 6.7   Two theme options available to mobile browsers.

When readers view your site with the mobile theme, the layout does not appear as with a desktop browser. iPhone, iPod Touch, and Android users can switch to your normal theme by turning off the mobile site option at the bottom of the page.

Other mobile browsers get a less fancy theme but still get quick load times. These browsers have a Full Site link at the bottom of the page. The effectiveness of this link is browser dependent.

Possibly Related Posts

WordPress.com came out with a feature called "lateral navigation" that scans the content of your post and then displays other posts from other blogs that may be related (see Figure 6.8).

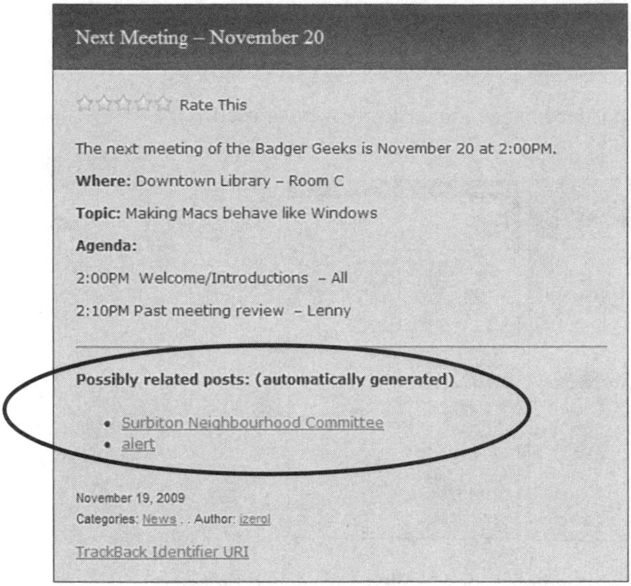

FIGURE 6.8   Possibly Related Posts can point your readers to similar material.

Some blog administrators find this feature annoying, stating that it takes readers away from their blog. The feature is controlled by the Hide Related Links on This Blog option in Appearance, Extras. If you remove related links from your blog, WordPress removes you from other blogs also—which can impact traffic to your site.

If you have made any changes to the Extras page, click **Update Extras** to save your changes.

Custom Header Image

Some of the WordPress.com themes look terrific. However, you might think that the header image does not match your personal tastes. Fortunately, some of the themes, including the default (Kubrick), enable you to upload your own header image.

To find out which themes support custom headers, follow these steps:

1. Go to **Appearance, Themes**.

2. In the Browse Themes section, click the **Feature Filter** link.

3. Check the **Custom Header** option.

4. Click **Apply Filters**.

The first 15 themes that support custom headers are displayed. Activate the theme you would like to use.

To change the header image, follow these steps:

1. Go to **Appearance, Custom Header** or the **Custom Header** link at the top of the Manage Themes page to see the Header Image page (see Figure 6.9).

2. Click the **Browse** button (or **Choose File** button on a Mac) to locate an image file on your computer.

3. After you locate an image, click **Open** (or **Choose** on a Mac).

4. Click **Upload**.

5. When your image is finished uploading, it is displayed with a highlighted rectangle.

6. Drag and resize the rectangle to crop the image the way you like. The rectangle stays the same proportions to the original image to ensure it is not stretched when it is displayed at the top of your blog.

7. Click **Crop Header**.

8. View your blog front page.

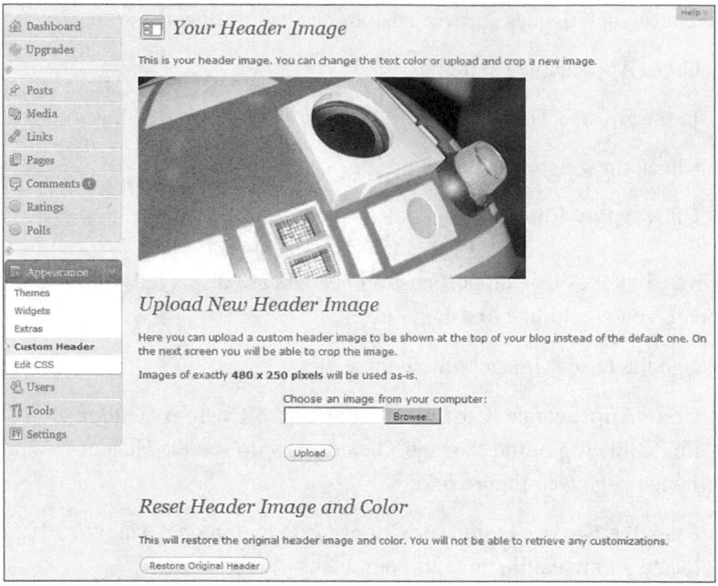

FIGURE 6.9   It is possible to upload a new header image with many themes.

You can restore the original header image at any time from the Header Image page by clicking the **Restore Original Header** button.

Edit CSS

The Edit CSS option allows you to fine-tune the appearance of your site by creating your own cascading style sheet (CSS) or augmenting the current theme's CSS. To get to the CSS Stylesheet Editor page (see Figure 6.10), go to **Appearance, Edit CSS** in the side menu.

FIGURE 6.10 The CSS Stylesheet Editor allows you to fine-tune your site appearance.

> **NOTE: CSS Customizations Require Upgrade**
>
> CSS customizations are a paid upgrade to WordPress.com users. You can modify the style sheet and preview the effect your changes have, but you cannot apply them to your site without the upgrade. Go to **Dashboard**, **Upgrades** for details and current pricing.

By default, a placeholder message appears in the main text box. This message is entirely comments (denoted by starting with **/*** and ending with ***/**). Please review these comments before proceeding.

To enter your modifications, remove the existing text and enter your CSS.

> **PLAIN ENGLISH: Cascading Style Sheets**
>
> Cascading style sheets provide a set of style templates that define colors, fonts, image sizes, backgrounds, and more. They free the software author from thinking about the layout details. CSS also enable themes to allow third parties to customize the look and feel of the software package.

Just below the editing window are two options affecting how your changes are applied to your blog's theme:

- ▶ **Add This to the (Current) Theme's CSS Stylesheet**—This option augments your changes to the theme's existing style sheet. There are specific ways to override styles that you need to be aware of. Click the **View Original Stylesheet** link to display the theme's current settings.

- ▶ **Start from Scratch and Just Use This**—Choose this option if you want to build the entire style sheet. You still need to comply with the theme's HTML structure. You can refer to the original style sheet to ensure you include all rules/styles. If you miss something, your blog may not appear as you expected.

The Limit Width option modifies the default image size for full-size images, videos, and other media when it is inserted in your blog. Use this option if you have modified the main content area using custom CSS. It does not change the width of existing images and videos, nor does it change the width of your blog.

After you complete your changes, you can see what effect the changes have by using the **Preview** button. If you have not purchased the Custom CSS upgrade, you will not be able to save your changes. Otherwise, use the **Save Stylesheet** button to apply the changes to your site.

If you find something that was once working is suddenly behaving unexpectedly, you can use the CSS Revisions section at the bottom of the Edit CSS page to review and reverse changes that you have made. Each time you click the **Save Stylesheet** button, an entry in the revision history is made.

Here are some suggestions to make your learning CSS curve a bit easier if you are just getting started:

1. **Read.** There are lots of good books and websites that can guide you through cascading style sheets. Online resources include

   ▶ W3 Schools CSS material: www.w3schools.com/css/

   ▶ Web Design Group guide to CSS: www.htmlhelp.com/reference/css

   ▶ Editing WordPress CSS: en.support.wordpress.com/editing-css

   ▶ CSS 2.1 Specification: www.w3.org/TR/CSS21

2. **Start with small changes.** Begin your changes with a simple color modification or font family change and understand what impact your changes have.

3. **Use a validation service.** Free websites like http://jigsaw.w3.org/css-validator are set up to ensure you avoid errors by checking for proper CSS syntax and semantics.

4. **Use the Firebug add-on or Web Developer Toolbar (Firefox users).** Firefox has add-ons that allow you to see and modify CSS on a live page. If you use another browser, use your browser's **View, Source** option to understand where specific styles are applied.

Summary

Using themes and widgets, you can quickly give your blog an entirely new look and feel without in-depth web development knowledge. With the optional upgrade to customize the style sheet, you can further refine your blog's appearance. The personality of your blog is limited only by your imagination.

LESSON 7

Using RSS and Data Migration Tools

In this lesson, you learn what RSS is, the value of having an RSS feed, and how to set one up. You also learn how to back up and migrate your data to another blog.

Syndicate Your Blog with RSS

RSS stands for Really Simple Syndication. It is a method by which readers can subscribe to your blog by means of an RSS file, often called an RSS feed.

When your readers subscribe to RSS, they don't have to visit your website periodically to check for new content. Instead, programs such as Mozilla Thunderbird, Google Reader, NetNewsWire, Microsoft Outlook, and Internet Explorer download the RSS files from all sites readers subscribe to at regular intervals. The postings are then displayed much like email to make it easy for the readers to quickly glance over the headlines and open postings that are of interest.

RSS feeds are available from most blog and news sites. They are typically indicated by an orange icon (see Figure 7.1) or the words *RSS* or *Subscribe*.

FIGURE 7.1   The RSS icon is a quick way to indicate people can subscribe to a site.

> TIP: **Add an RSS Feed**
>
> If your blog does not currently have an RSS feed available, consider adding one to increase readership. With RSS functionality becoming more popular in applications, a large number of people on the Internet use RSS readers almost exclusively for content delivery (see Figure 7.2).

FIGURE 7.2   RSS applications like Google Reader deliver websites directly to you.

Setting Up an RSS Feed

You can set up RSS feeds for posts or comments. The most common feed is the one containing your most recent posts. To create an RSS feed, follow these steps:

1. Select **Appearance**, **Widgets**.

2. Add the RSS Links widget to your sidebar by dragging it from Active (or Inactive) widgets to the sidebar.

3. Click the downward-facing triangle on the right side of the RSS widget (see Figure 7.3).

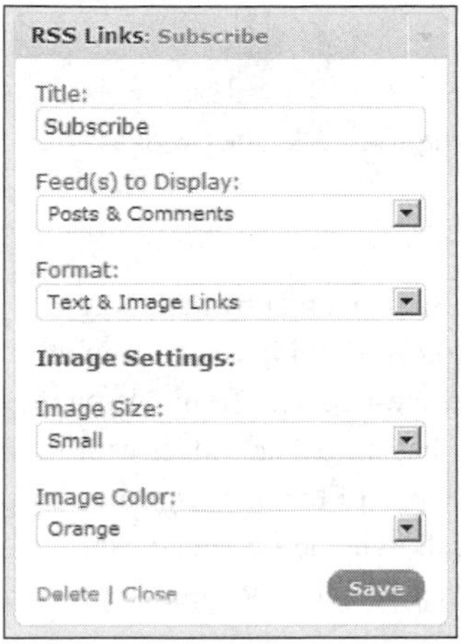

FIGURE 7.3 Use the RSS Links widget to allow your readers to subscribe to your blog.

4. Provide a title for your sidebar widget. Many people simply put "Subscribe".

5. Indicate which feeds to display. You can choose to have either a feed for your posts, a feed for your comments feed, or one of each.

6. Select how your feed links will be displayed with the Format option. You can choose to display an RSS icon (image), text, or both. If you choose to display an image, two additional options appear that let you set the image size (small, medium, or large) and the image color.

7. Click the **Save** button to save your changes and then **Close** to close the widget.

Now when readers want to subscribe to a feed on your site, they right-click on the orange icon, copy the link location, and paste it into their RSS reader. From then on, they will automatically know when you have posted something to your site.

Your link shows up on your page similar to the one shown in Figure 7.4.

FIGURE 7.4   Sample RSS links and icons using the RSS Links widget.

Adding Other RSS Feeds

You can also add feeds to other sites using the same widget by including their RSS feed. Having a feed from another blog is useful if you have multiple blogs that are related and want to show the latest content from one on the other. For example, I have a personal blog that has a sidebar widget with links from my various podcasts. When I update one of the podcasts, the content on my personal blog is updated automatically via the RSS feed (see Figure 7.5). To obtain the RSS feed from another site, follow these steps:

1. Visit another website or blog and look for the orange icon, *Subscribe*, or *RSS*.

2. Right-click and choose the option to copy the link location.

3. Paste the link location into your RSS feed URL space in the RSS widget.

4. Click the **Save** button and then the **Close** link.

FIGURE 7.5   The RSS widget allows you to show content from another feed on your site.

Using a Redirected Feed

An RSS feed is a convenience for your readers. However, you might want to better understand how many people are subscribed to your feed and what posts are generating traffic. You can do that by using a redirected feed.

Using a redirected feed might sound like something the "big guys" use to track statistics and drive traffic, but it's also useful for occasional bloggers to just find out the health of their feed.

A common way to do this is to create one feed that you make public and keep your real feed private. The public feed sends subscribers through a service that gathers statistical information about their habits. One popular service is called FeedBurner. It offers basic stats free and extended services for a fee. To get set up with FeedBurner, do the following:

1. Go to the FeedBurner site (http://feedburner.google.com).

2. Create an account or log in with your Google account if you already have one.

3. Enter your blog or RSS feed URL in the box under the label Burn a Feed Right This Instant (see Figure 7.6).

4. Click **Next**.

5. Edit the Feed Title and Feed Address if necessary. In most cases, the default values work fine.

6. Click **Next**.

7. The critical part is done. FeedBurner displays the URL of the feed you can publish to the public. Use this as the URL in your RSS widget described earlier. If you want to collect additional feed stats, click **Next** one more time and check the options you like; otherwise, click **Skip Directly to Feed Management**.

8. Click **Next**.

Log in to FeedBurner and check your stats, growth, and readers' behaviors at any time.

Enter your blog address or RSS URL

FIGURE 7.6 FeedBurner makes it easy to collect subscriber statistics.

TIP: **Set Up a Redirected Feed Right Away**

If you are considering gathering statistics about your blog, it is strongly recommended that you establish and publish the redirected feed right away. If you make your default WordPress feed and then decide to gather stats with a redirected feed later, all your readers will have to unsubscribe from the original feed and resubscribe to the new feed, which can cause you to lose some of your audience.

Other Useful Tools

Several other useful tools in WordPress don't seem to fit anywhere else in the side menu, so they are placed under Tools, Tools.

Turbo: Gears Status

Gears is a way to speed up your blog experience. Normally, your web browser has to download everything from your blog to your local computer each time you perform an operation like editing a post. Turbo mode uses a Google technology known as Gears to download certain pieces of the system to your local machine so it doesn't have to be downloaded each time—making your blog tasks faster.

> CAUTION: **Gears Support for Mac OS X**
>
> At this time, Gears is not compatible with Mac OS X higher than 10.5 (Leopard).

Gears currently supports Firefox version 1.5 and higher, Internet Explorer version 6 and higher, and Safari 3.1.1 and higher. To use Turbo mode, follow these steps:

1. From the side menu in WordPress, select **Tools, Tools**.

2. In the Turbo section, click **Install Now**.

3. If get a Gears Security Window, check the setting labeled **I Trust This Site. Allow It to Use Gears** and click **Allow**.

4. Click Install Gears from the Google site (see Figure 7.7). The download link recognizes and defaults to your current computer system (Windows, Mac, and so on).

5. Review the terms of service and click **Agree and Download**.

6. Run the installer that gets downloaded and restart your browser if instructed to do so.

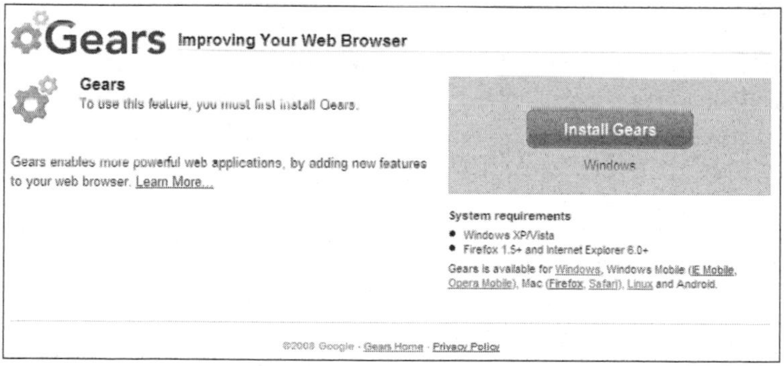

FIGURE 7.7 You need to download Google Gears and allow it access to use Turbo mode.

Downloading the necessary components may take a minute or two. When the process is complete, you are using Turbo mode.

> NOTE: **Results Will Vary**
>
> If you have a high-speed Internet connection, you may not see a marked improvement in performance.

Press This

Press This is a small web application that streamlines the process of posting articles as you are browsing around the Web. As you are browsing the Internet and come across text, images, or video you want to reference, you can use Press This to quickly make a post in your blog.

You can find Press This under Tools, Tools in the side menu. To start using Press This, follow these steps:

1. Either drag the **Press This** link to your browser's link bar or add it as a favorite.

2. Find a story you like and then click the Press This link (or favorite).

3. The Press This window appears with the title and link in the article body already filled in (see Figure 7.8). Add your additional text, images, categories, tags, and other standard post material.

4. Click **Publish**.

Your post has been published. Press This offers you the options to view your post, edit your post, or close the window. When you are done, your main browser window is still where you left it. Press This can be a real time saver.

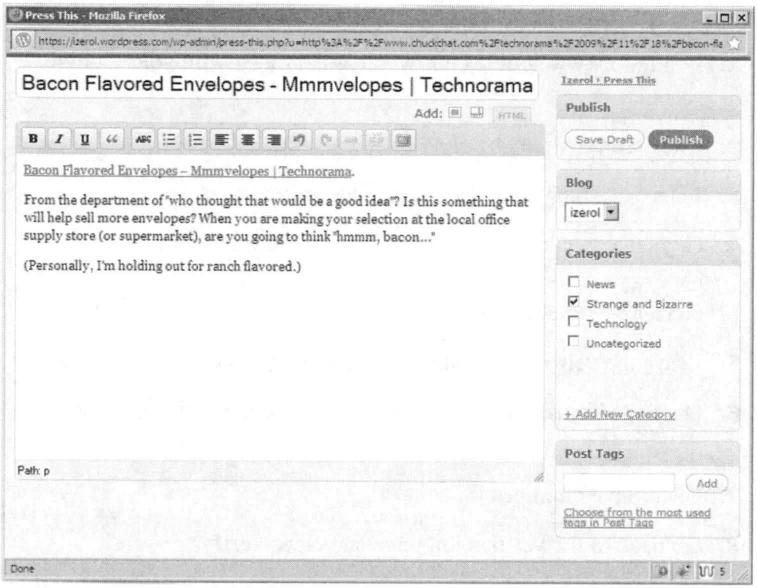

FIGURE 7.8   Grab bits of the Internet and post it back to your blog with Press This.

Webmaster Tools Verification

Google, Bing, and Yahoo! offer tools that provide you with detailed information and statistics about how your readers access and index your website. They can provide you with additional information to the standard WordPress statistics. Using the webmaster tools is completely optional. You can verify your site with one or all if you like with no impact to your site's performance or your readers' experience.

Before you can use these tools, you need to sign up for an account with the service of your choice and verify your blog. Use the instructions from the appropriate following section to verify your blog with one or more of the services.

Google Webmaster Tools

1. Log in to www.google.com/webmasters/tools/ with your Google account.

2. Click **Add a site**.

3. Enter your blog URL then click **Continue**.

4. Copy the meta tag, which looks something like `<meta name='google-site-verification' content='dBw5CvburAxi537Rp9qi5uG2174Vb6JwHwIRwPSLIK8'>`.

5. Leave the verification page open and go to your blog Dashboard.

6. Open the **Tools, Tools** page and paste the code in the appropriate field.

7. Click **Save Changes**.

8. Go back to the verification page and click **Verify**.

Yahoo! Site Explorer

1. Log in to https://siteexplorer.search.yahoo.com/ with your Yahoo! account.

2. Enter your blog URL and click **Add My Site**.

3. You are presented with several authentication methods. Choose **By Adding a META Tag to My Home Page**.

4. Copy the meta tag, which looks something like `<meta name='y_key' content='3236dee82aabe064'>`.

5. Leave the verification page open and go to your blog Dashboard.

6. Open the **Tools, Tools** page and paste the code in the appropriate field.

7. Click **Save Changes**.

8. Go back to the verification page and click **Ready to Authenticate**.

9. Go to the main page using the **My Sites** link on the left. In the status column, look for a green check mark indicating your site has been validated.

Bing Webmaster Center

1. Log in to www.bing.com/webmaster with your Live! account.

2. Click **Add a Site**.

3. Enter your blog URL and click **Submit**.

4. Copy the meta tag from the text area at the bottom. It looks something like `<meta name='msvalidate.01'  content='12C1203B5086AECE94EB3A3D9830B2E'>`.

5. Leave the verification page open and go to your blog Dashboard.

6. Open the **Tools, Tools** page and paste the code in the appropriate field.

7. Click **Save Changes**.

8. Go back to the verification page and click **Return to the Site List**.

NOTE: **Authentication Takes Time**

Most authentication with Google, Yahoo, or Bing happens within a few minutes; however, it might take up to 24 hours.

After you've got your site validated, you can use the webmaster tools to leverage the power of these search engines to determine who is linking to your site, what pages are most popular, and other statistics. You can even block the search engines from indexing part of your blog if you have pages you would like to exclude.

Backing Up Your Data

Computers are not perfect. Sooner or later, we all lose data. To reduce your risk, make regular backups of your information including your blog data.

The way to make backups of your WordPress data is to go to **Tools**, **Export** in the side menu. Fortunately, this is one of the easiest things to do in WordPress; there is only one button! (See Figure 7.9.)

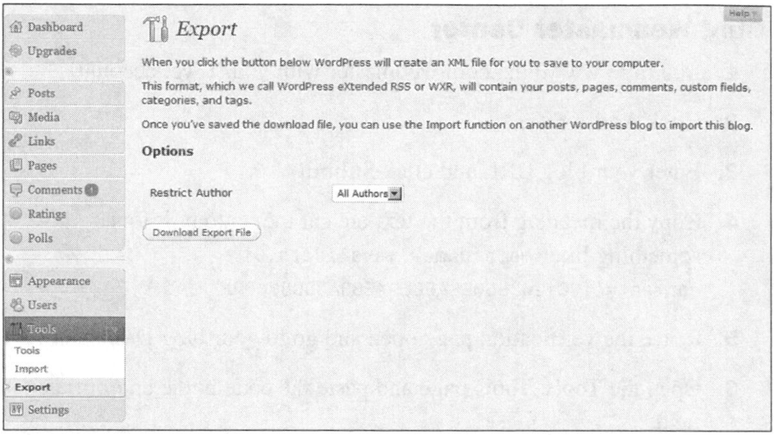

FIGURE 7.9   Use the export feature to back up or migrate your blog data.

When you click the **Download Export File** button, WordPress saves all your information in a file and sends it to your computer. Save the file on your computer. If you ever need to restore the information, you can use the Import feature.

> NOTE: **Take Note Where You Save Your Export File**
>
> Mac OS X automatically saves the file in your Download folder, whereas Windows users need to tell the computer to open or save the file. Be sure you know where your browser is saving the file in the event you ever need to import it.

Migrating Your Blog

There are several reasons why you might want to move your blog data from one WordPress instance to another. You may be starting your own website with its own hosted WordPress blog, or you want to change the name of your blog and keep the content, or you want to transfer owner-ship and control of the blog to another user account. WordPress has a way to address all these requirements.

If you are starting your own hosted website, the process is as follows:

1. Register your domain.

2. Download the software from WordPress.org.

3. Install the WordPress software.

4. Export the data from your current blog (refer to "Backing Up Your Data" earlier in this lesson).

5. Import the data to your new blog (refer to "Importing Data from a WordPress Export in the next section).

The first three steps are covered in greater detail in Lesson 8, "Setting Up Hosting."

If you are renaming your blog or migrating from one WordPress.com blog to another, the process is similar:

1. Register the new blog (refer to Lesson 1, "Introducing WordPress").

2. Export the data from your current blog (refer to "Backing Up Your Data" earlier in this lesson).

3. Import the data to your new blog (refer to "Importing Data from a WordPress Export" in the next section).

NOTE: **Media Not Included**

Creating an export file only exports the posts, pages, comments, categories, and tags. With the exception of migrating between two WordPress.com sites, you need to manually migrate the media files. If you have a large number of files and are migrating from one WordPress.com blog to another, you can contact support at http://en.support.wordpress.com/contact for assistance.

Importing Data from a WordPress Export

If you are importing from a previously exported WordPress (XML) file, follow these steps:

1. Log in to your blog as an administrator.

2. Go to **Tools**, **Import** in the side menu.

3. Choose **WordPress** from the list.

4. Select and import the file. Click the browse button and navigate to your export file. WordPress names the exported file word-press.date.xml, where date is in the *year-month-date* format, such as wordpress.2009-11-30.xml. When you've located the file, select it and click **Open**. On the WordPress page, click the **Upload file and import** button.

5. Map the authors in the export file to users on the blog. For each author, you may choose to map to an existing user on the blog or to create a new user.

6. Check the box marked **Download and import attachments**. This downloads the media library from the original site if possible. This option is only available if you are migrating between two WordPress.com sites.

7. Click **Submit**. A screen is displayed indicating the import has started. You will receive an email when it is complete.

8. WordPress then imports each of the posts, comments, and categories contained in this file into your new blog.

The import could take up to 24 hours, depending on the amount of data in your blog. You will receive an email when the import is complete. If you do not, contact WordPress.com support at http://en.support.wordpress. com/contact. When the import is complete, review your new blog to ensure everything migrated correctly.

Transferring a Blog

WordPress allows you to transfer your blog to another WordPress.com user. You may choose to do this to transfer ownership to someone new, or you may have created a new account for yourself and want all your previously independent blogs under one account. The procedure to transfer a blog is as follows:

1. Log in as an administrator.

2. Go to **Dashboard**, **My Blogs**.

3. Move your cursor over the address of the blog you want to transfer.

4. Click on the **Transfer Blog** link. Note that you do not see this link if you are not the owner.

5. Read and review the Big Important Warning that appears. It is important that you understand all the terms and conditions of the transfer. This procedure cannot be undone (see Figure 7.10).

6. Check the check box on the bottom of the warning.

7. Enter the WordPress.com account or email address of the person you are transferring the blog to and click the **Transfer Blog** button.

8. A confirmation email is sent to your registered WordPress email address. The transfer does not occur until you read the message and click the link in email.

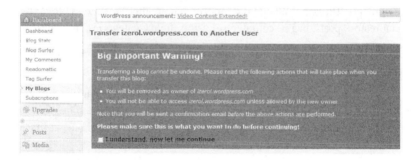

FIGURE 7.10 Transferring a blog to another user cannot be undone.

NOTE: **Upgrades Transfer, Too**

Upgrades to a blog are transferred with that blog to the new owner. A blog with domain upgrades is processed manually by a member of the WordPress.com staff. All other upgrades (space, videopress, and so on) are processed automatically.

Importing from Another Blog

If you have set up a blog on another site, WordPress allows you to import the content from that blog using the **Tools**, **Import** feature (see Figure 7.11). You can import from several other blogging platforms (including other WordPress sites).

Currently, it is possible to import your content from the following blogs:

▶ Blogger

▶ LiveJournal

▶ Movable Type or TypePad

▶ WordPress

▶ Yahoo! 360

Each import tool walks you through the specific steps to import your data from your old blog to your new one. Follow the onscreen instructions for your particular situation. The importer is used only to retrieve the content. It does not import any themes, images, or media files you may have had on your other blog. In some cases, the importer brings in only posts and comments (Blogger). When you import from another WordPress blog, you can restore posts, pages, comments, custom fields, categories, and tags.

In addition, you can also import links and convert WordPress tags to categories and vice versa using **Tools**, **Import** (WordPress.org only).

Importing from Blogger, TypePad, or LiveJournal might seem like a logical thing to do if you are just getting set up with a WordPress blog; however, the WordPress option might not seem like an obvious choice at first. There are a few reasons why you might choose this option:

▶ **Restoring a previous backup of your blog**. Some people like to have two sites. The first is a public site that they want highly available, often called a *production site*. The second is a *sandbox* (or development) site where they can make changes without the public noticing. After they have made the necessary changes in development, they can promote the changes quickly from the development site to the production site. Periodically, they might want to refresh the information in development with the more current information in production. This is done by first creating an export file (covered later in this lesson) and then using the import to update the development site.

▶ **Migrating from the WordPress.com to WordPress.org site**. You might find that WordPress.com's features are too constraining and you would like to host your own blog. Similar to the preceding scenario, you import an existing WordPress export file to bring over the content. The import subpanel is available in the self-hosted software discussed in greater detail starting in Lesson 8, "Setting Up Hosting." To learn more about how to migrate your blog from WordPress.com to WordPress.org, read the sections at the end of this lesson.

▶ **Renaming your blog**. You might find at some point that your blog name and URL do not match the brand of content you are providing. You cannot rename the WordPress.com URL, but you can register a new blog and migrate the information from your old blog to your new blog.

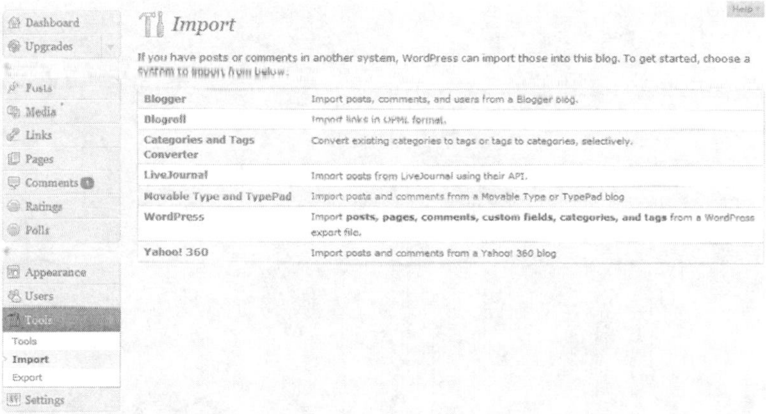

FIGURE 7.11 The Import subpanel allows you to import your blog data from another location.

Summary

Your WordPress.com blog is set up, and you have the skills to create the content you need and make it appear in a variety of formats. Now you have the necessary information to make it easy for readers to get your posts automatically with RSS. When you are ready to move to another WordPress blog or just make a backup to ensure your work's safety, WordPress has you covered there too.

Setting Up Hosting

This lesson discusses why you might want to install your own copy of WordPress, including the advantages and disadvantages of doing that, and what to look for in a web hosting service. You also find out how to sign up for a domain and hosting services.

Why Host Your Own Blog?

WordPress is an amazing piece of software and can really shine when you do your own custom installation. There are a lot of reasons why you may or may not want to install it yourself. Perhaps you would like to install it on your company's internal network as part of an intranet solution, or you would like to use it in a custom fashion that it was not necessarily intended for, or perhaps you cannot find a web host that can offer you the options that meet your personal goals. In any case, when you are installing your own WordPress, there are certainly advantages and trade-offs to keep in mind.

One advantage that you get to exercise right out of the box is control. WordPress is licensed as open source software under the GNU General Public License (GPL). The GPL, in a nutshell, enables you to see, edit, and modify the source code as you see fit. If you have knowledge of PHP, you can have complete control of your code. If you want to make WordPress do something that it does not already do, you can. Keep in mind that learning to program is not necessary to use WordPress, and you can install WordPress without having the intention of modifying the source code.

PLAIN ENGLISH: **Open Source and GPL**

To learn more about open source software or the GPL, you can visit GPL.org at http://www.gnu.org/licenses/gpl.html. Alternatively, you can read the Wikipedia article on Open Source at http://wikipedia.org/wiki/Open_source.

When you use WordPress.com, you save money by using a free hosting service, but you are restricted in what you can to do with your site. WordPress is rich with downloadable themes and plug-ins that allow you to do pretty much whatever you want to do with your site. So hosting your own site gives you a finer degree of control over your entire site, including the ability for you to upload your own themes and plug-ins.

TIP: **Look for Existing Themes and Plug-ins First**

Before you start developing your own theme or plug-in, visit http://WordPress.org/extend/ and do a little searching. You are likely to find hundreds of themes and plug-ins already written for what you are trying to accomplish.

Understanding Your Responsibilities

Although maintaining your own site gives you a larger degree of control, you need to consider the responsibilities. Some of them include providing support, monitoring for spam, maintaining your own backups, and keeping up with software updates. Although plug-ins that can assist in everyday maintenance are available, having your own installation means you need to take an active role in maintaining your site. Is this task overwhelming? Normally not, but it does increase the amount of effort you put into managing your site.

Common maintenance in upkeep with your site is also needed for functions ranging from keeping a look out for spam to approving comments to managing software updates. You can use plug-ins to help maintain your site automatically (which you can read about in Lesson 11, "Customizing Your Site with Plug-ins"). In addition, performing software updates is much easier today than in previous versions of WordPress. As of the last few versions of WordPress, you can upgrade plug-ins and even WordPress itself from your WordPress Dashboard with just a few clicks and no additional software. Historically updates had to be done manually by downloading them to your computer and then uploading all your updates using the File Transfer Protocol (FTP) service where your WordPress site resides.

Finally, you need to keep cost factoring in mind. WordPress.com offers free hosting, but if you go out on your own, you have to pay for hosting. Costs do vary from one hosting company to another so be sure that your hosting costs are manageable. It would be a disappointment to you and your readers if you had to take down the site because of costs.

Setting Up Your Domain Name

Part of setting up hosting for your site is setting up your domain name. Your domain name is your calling card. It is what people will remember, bookmark, or tell others when referring to your site. Therefore, it is important that you choose a name that is unique to you and your site. Several sites can assist you in registering your domain, and several hosting companies not only register your domain, but also walk you through the entire process up to and including setting up your actual web space.

> NOTE: **Finding a Registrar**
>
> You may use any domain registrar you want, and there are hundreds to choose from. To help you start, the following short list includes some of the more well-known services:
>
> Go Daddy—www.godaddy.com
>
> NameCheap—www.namecheap.com/
>
> Yummy Names—www.yummynames.com/
>
> Network Solutions—www.networksolutions.com

When you register your domain name, the registration is set up for annual renewals. You don't actually own the domain name; you rent it. Domain names can cost anywhere from $4 to $30 for an entire year, depending on which service you are using and the domain type (.com, .us, and so on).

CAUTION: **Watch Out for Auto Renew**

Be aware that some registrars also have an Auto Renew setting that automatically drafts the renewal fee annually from your credit card.

To start your search, use your web browser to go to one of the several registrars. For each one, the process is essentially the same:

1. Pick a name that is simple and easy to remember. Again, this is the name that people will link to and tell others about when referring to you. If you are a company, choose wisely and remember you may want to register more than just the .com. You may want to get the .net and .info also to protect your brand. In addition, be prepared with backup domain names in case your first choice is already taken.

2. Start your search at one or several of the registrars (see Figure 8.1). Each one has a search box on the site where you can verify the availability of your domain name and register it. If your domain is taken already, you may be presented with alternatives, or you can try again with your second choice. Also, keep in mind that other top-level names such as .info, .us, and so on, may be available too, so try searching in different ways.

FIGURE 8.1   Searching for a domain using NameCheap.

3. After you find a name that you are happy with, the registrar walks you through the steps in registering your name, which includes payment and email notification after everything is complete.

TIP: **Look for Discounts**

Remember, some registrars offer hosting along with registering your domain. Taking advantage of this service can lower the cost in some cases when you bundle everything together and make it easier for you to manage. Also, registering your name for multiple years may also qualify you for a discount. Shopping around a little before settling on one company is worthwhile.

Setting Up Your Web Hosting Account

After you have your domain name, it is time to set up your web hosting. The hosting service for your site is provided by companies referred to as web hosts. Web hosts provide you with a web server, disk space, and bandwidth, as well other services, including support.

Disk space at a web host is not unlike the hard drive in your computer. It is, in essence, the amount of space you are allowed to use when storing files for your website. Normally, the amount of space provided is, at a minimum, about 5GB. This is more than sufficient for most websites, but if you plan on hosting video and pictures, you will eventually need more space.

Also, be aware of limitations in bandwidth. Bandwidth is the amount of data transferred between your site and your visitors; it is normally tracked over a monthly period. Web hosts generally offer large amounts of bandwidth with the even lower-end packages, but if you are hosting your own video and audio files and perhaps photos, your bandwidth can dwindle quickly and become a big problem.

> TIP: **Plan for Disk Space and Bandwidth**
>
> Try to plan ahead regarding what files you will have on your server, such as pictures or other media that you will offer your visitors. Hosting companies charge for disk space and bandwidth and charge extra if you go over your allotment. Make sure you have room to operate and can expand at a reasonable price in the future.

Requirements for Operating WordPress

Because you want to run WordPress for your site, you need to make sure that your web host provides what you need. The requirements for hosting WordPress are pretty basic when compared to most web applications. It requires PHP (version `4.3 or higher`) and MySQL (version `4.1.2` or higher) as a minimum. Most web hosting companies do support these technologies "out of the box" without your even having to ask for them. Some hosting companies give you an option of which operating system you would like your site to run on. WordPress is operating system agnostic, so any option should be fine.

Also, you should make sure you have FTP access to your site for two reasons. This access makes it easier to upload your files to the remote server and update graphics as needed and makes it much easier to keep your WordPress up to date with patches. FTP access is normally standard for hosting services, but it is something to keep in mind as you are shopping around.

Finding Support

If you choose to maintain your own blog installation, you have several avenues for help with questions or problems you have. As with other open source software projects, WordPress offers support in the form of community, ranging from forums to web pages to online video tutorials on how to perform specific tasks to diagnoses of error codes. For most common problems, someone has likely had the same issue and has written about it.

WordPress is very well documented all over the Internet, and a good place to start looking for help is right at WordPress.org. If you or your company needs more personal support, several companies provide contract services such as help installing, troubleshooting, and even custom coding. More on finding support can be found in Lesson 13, "WordPress Support."

Summary

This lesson examined the advantages and disadvantages of running your own self-hosted WordPress site, as well as setting up your domain name and web hosting in preparation to install your own WordPress.

Installing WordPress

In this lesson, you learn about scripting services that can help you install WordPress, and you walk through installing it manually.

Using Automated Script Services

Installing WordPress can be as automatic or as manual as you would like the process to be. Some web hosts even provide services that install WordPress, among other web applications, for you with little or no hassle.

NOTE: **What You Need to Have**

This lesson assumes that you have chosen a web hosting provider and are able to access your account via File Transfer Protocol (FTP). It is important that you have a hosting service and domain name because you will be uploading and possibly manipulating files and using the database server as part of the installation. You should make sure your web host supports PHP and MySQL.

Using Script Services

Scripting services can make it easy to install WordPress or any number of web applications on your web hosting account and can also assist in keeping you up to date with security patches. The examples of scripting services described here are just two of many options.

NOTE: **Use Your Preferred Scripting Service**

To be clear, you may choose any scripting service you prefer. The services listed here are similar to most other services.

Go Daddy provides a service called Hosting Connection. If you have already purchased and set up a Go Daddy hosting account, or are planning to, the Hosting Connection can assist you in setting up your WordPress site.

After you set up your web hosting account with Go Daddy, visit the list of applications that Go Daddy offers and select WordPress. Go Daddy asks you to complete a form with some information needed to set up your blog, such as title, passwords, and so on. Go Daddy does the rest of the heavy lifting for you and notifies you after the process is complete. From there, you have a functioning blog.

Simple Scripts is a similar service that enables you to install any number of web applications on any web hosting account as long as you have FTP access. You can use the service for up to three installations; however, you can pay for these services and have Simple Scripts install a number of web applications in different places as well as help you keep your system up to date by automating software updates. Some web hosting companies offer Simple Scripts free with your account.

Installing WordPress Manually

Now it's time to put together the pieces to create your own blog using WordPress.

Downloading the Software from WordPress.org

To download WordPress, visit http://WordPress.org/download. From there, you can read the release notes and see the current version available.

> TIP: **Finding Earlier Versions of WordPress**
>
> If you need to install a previous version other than the current release, use the Release Archive link to find what you need.

To download, click the **Download WordPress** button (see Figure 9.1).

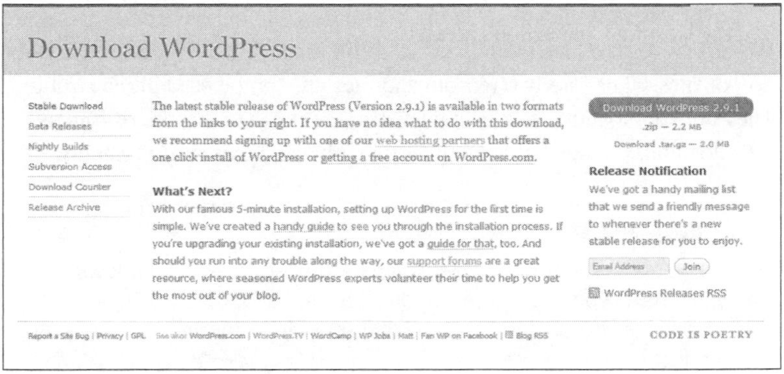

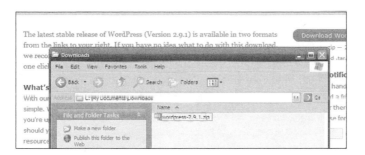

FIGURE 9.1   Downloading WordPress.

Your browser asks you to save the WordPress zip file to a location on your computer. Normally, this is a folder named Download, but sometimes your browser defaults to your desktop. Make a note of the location where your file is being saved so it is easy to find later.

After your download is complete, you see a new file in your download folder. Its name is similar to *WordPress-2.9.zip* (see Figure 9.2).

FIGURE 9.2   The WordPress file in the downloads folder.

Unpacking the Software

Now that you have downloaded the WordPress zip archive from WordPress.org, we need to unpack it. A zip archive is a compressed collection of files. There are two reasons the files are compressed into a zip file. They are kept together in a container, and the file size is reduced for easy downloading. We need to open the zip archive and extract its contents.

> TIP: **Unzipping WordPress**
>
> Mac and Linux include archive software, but if you use Windows, you may not have such software installed to unzip WordPress. If you need software to unzip files, try 7-Zip at www.7-zip.org/ or WinZip at www.winzip.com/.

- ▶ **Mac**—Double-click on the file named WordPress-2.9.zip.

- ▶ **Linux**—Right-click on the WordPress-2.9.zip and select **Extract Here**.

- ▶ **Windows**—Right-click on the file and select **Extract Here**. After the files are extracted from the WordPress zip archive, a newly created folder named wordpress appears in your Downloads folder (see Figure 9.3). Inside the WordPress folder you just created are all the files that will make up your blog. Now it's time to upload them.

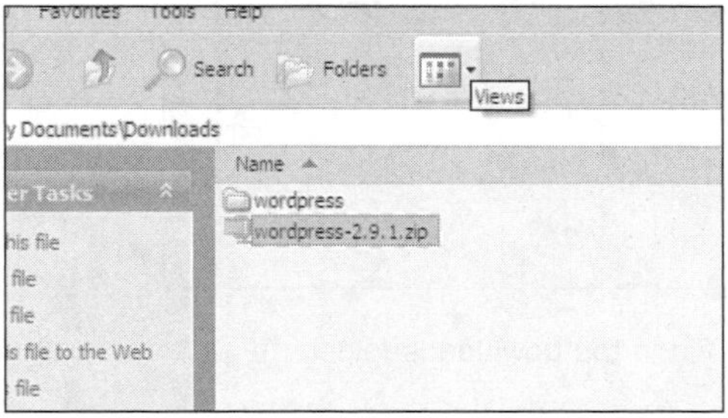

FIGURE 9.3   The WordPress folder after it has been unzipped.

Uploading Your Files

After you have all your files successfully extracted out of the zip archive, you need to move them from your computer to your website. To do this, you need to plan a bit on where you are going to move them to and then you can use an FTP program to physically copy them to your webserver.

Choosing Your Blog Folder

Before you upload your files to your web host, it is important to establish where you are going to put them. If you are adding a WordPress blog to your existing site, it is likely that you already have a main page on your site for visitors and already have a main folder created. If this is the case, you might want to put your blog in a subfolder of your website folder.

For example, you may have a Home page, photo gallery, and some other pages you have created. When you install your blog, you wouldn't want WordPress to interfere with what is already there. So it makes sense to put WordPress in a folder by itself, such as blog. Your blog site address then would be www.yoursite.com/blog.

If you are not concerned about existing content or if your site is completely new, you might want WordPress at the top level of your site so that when visitors come to your website, they are automatically greeted with your WordPress.org installation.

Copying WordPress Files to Your Site

To upload the WordPress files to your site, you need an FTP client. An FTP client provides the functionality to log in to your remote account and upload and manipulate files. You need an FTP program to use FTP. There are many options for FTP clients, including free and pay applications. For this example, I used FileZilla. It is an open source application that costs nothing to download and use. It is available for Windows, Mac, and Linux.

> **Note: Choosing an FTP Client**
>
> If you want to use FileZilla, you can find it at http://filezilla-project.org/.
>
> If you use another FTP client, you should be able to follow the steps with no trouble. FileZilla's settings are similar to other FTP clients.

Your web hosting service should have provided you with file locations, a username, and a password to access your files via FTP. Make sure you have that information handy. Follow these instructions to transfer your WordPress files via FTP to your web host:

1. Start FileZilla.

2. Click **File** and select **Site Manager**.

3. In the window that opens, click on the **New Site** button and add the name of your website on the left side of the window (see Figure 9.4).

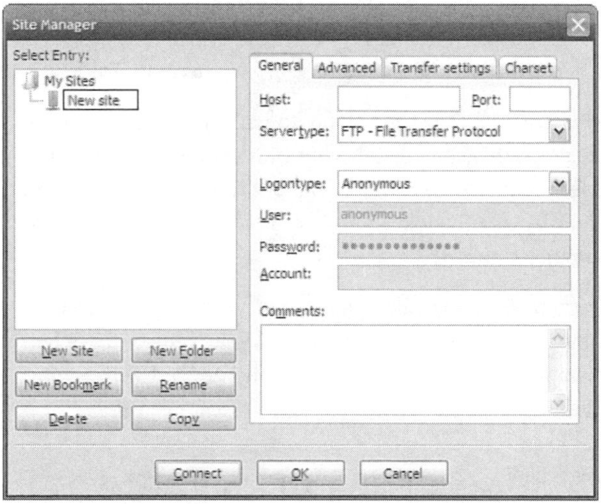

FIGURE 9.4   Creating a new site to transfer files to.

4. On the right side, enter the information provided by your host in the appropriate boxes. In the Host box—type the name of the server that you will be logging in to—for example, **ftp.yoursite.com**. You can leave the Port box empty.

5. Leave FTP as the selection in the Servertype box unless you have another specification from your web host.

6. Further down in the window is the Logontype box. You need to change this setting to **Ask for a Password** or **Normal**.

> CAUTION: **Always Ask for a Password**
> Using the Normal type allows you to specify your username and password one time. Thereafter, you are automatically logged in. In the interest of security, though, I recommend you use the Ask for a Password setting so that a password is required each time you connect.

7. After you add the necessary information, you can click on **OK** or **Connect**. Connect does just that: It saves the settings and connects you right away.

8. Now on the left side, you can view the local files that are on your computer's hard drive, and the remote files on your website are on the right side (see Figure 9.5). Not seeing any files in the remote view could be completely normal if this is a new site.

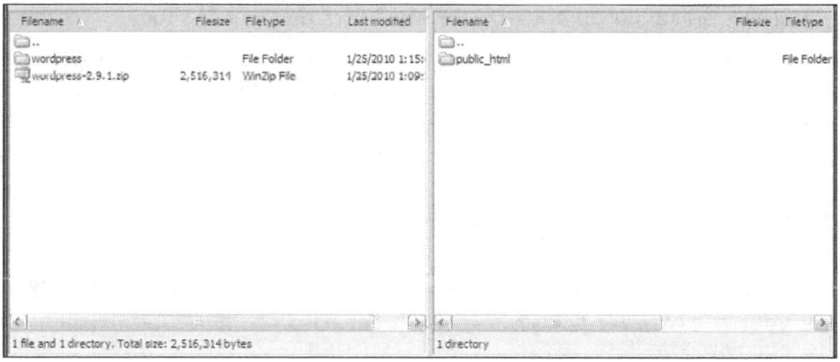

Filename ↗	Filesize	Filetype	Last modified		Filename ↗		Filesize	Filetype
📁..					📁..			
📁wordpress		File Folder	1/25/2010 1:15:		📁public_html			File Folder
📦wordpress-2.9.1.zip	2,516,314	WinZip File	1/25/2010 1:09:					

1 file and 1 directory. Total size: 2,516,314 bytes | | | | | 1 directory

FIGURE 9.5 Viewing local and remote files in your FTP client.

At this point, you are ready to copy over your WordPress files. On the left side of the window, navigate to the WordPress folder you created when you extracted your files from the WordPress zip file (more than likely, this folder is in your download folder). On the right side of the window, you may see a folder named public_html, htdocs, or httpdocs. This is normal. Some hosts, depending on their setup, may have a folder intended for you to put any files that you want to make public to the world, such as your WordPress files. This folder, if it exists, is called your web root folder. This is the place where you put your WordPress files. Not seeing a web root folder also could be normal, so you can just upload your files as they are.

> NOTE: **Creating a Folder for Your Blog**
>
> If you already have a site, or want to put your blog in a folder as mentioned earlier in this lesson, now is the time to create that folder on your remote site. For example, if you want to create a folder called blog, you need to create a blog folder in your web root folder. After you create a folder, double-click it to open it and then proceed to copy files into it.

In your WordPress folder, you should see several files and folders that have "wp_" at the beginning of the filename. Select all of them using the keyboard shortcut Cmd-A on a Mac or Ctrl+A on Windows. When you have them all highlighted, drag and drop them to the right side. At this point, the file transfer starts, and you see activity as the files start to upload.

After this process is complete, your local files on the left should look the same as your remote files on the right side. If they do, congratulations! You have successfully uploaded your copy of WordPress. You are now ready to create the database for WordPress to use.

Creating the Database

WordPress needs a database to store all the posts, comments, and settings for your site. WordPress uses a MySQL database.

To create the database for your web site, you need to use the administration site provided by your web host. There are a lot of different ways your web host can give you access to your database server. No matter which administrative tool your web host uses, the basic steps to create your database for WordPress are the same.

> NOTE: **Required Database Information for WordPress**
>
> When you are done creating your database, you should have a server address, database name, username, and password. You need all that information for the last part of the installation.

1. Log in to your site's management console using the access information provided by your web host.

2. Find the section that says MySQL Server, Database Server, or something similar. Click the link to open it.

3. In the Create Database or New Database field, provide a database name. I recommend that you call your database something that is easy to recognize. For example, if your site domain name is izerol.com, consider using the database name izerol or wp_izerol.

4. You may be asked to create a username and password associated with your database. If so, be sure to make a note of this information. You will need it when running the WordPress install script. Also, make a strong password that includes numbers, uppercase and lowercase characters, and symbols. This is a place where security really matters.

It might take a little while for your database to be created after you complete these steps.

Running the Install Script

If you have come this far, you are doing great. The installation is all downhill from here, but you are not done yet.

To finish the install, you need to run the install script. If you have uploaded all your files and created the database, you have all the tools you need to follow these steps and finish:

1. To run the installer, point your web browser to your blog's URL. You should see the first startup screen (see Figure 9.6).

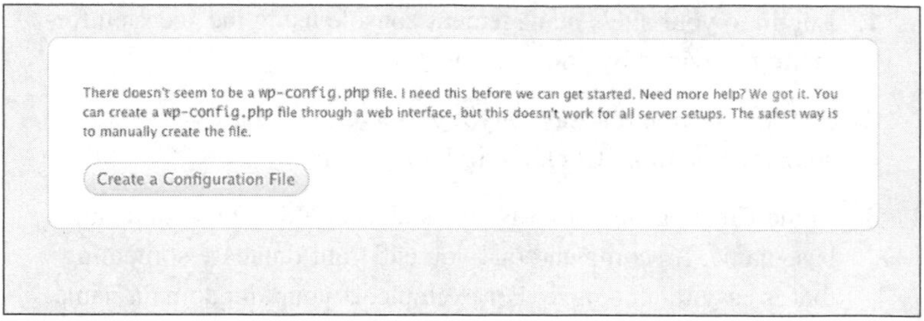

> There doesn't seem to be a wp-config.php file. I need this before we can get started. Need more help? We got it. You can create a wp-config.php file through a web interface, but this doesn't work for all server setups. The safest way is to manually create the file.
>
> (Create a Configuration File)

FIGURE 9.6   Creating your wp-config file.

2. Click **Create a Configuration File**.

3. Gather the following information before proceeding:

    ▶ Database name

    ▶ Database username

    ▶ Database password

    ▶ Database host (the address of the server). Sometimes this can be localhost or an actual name of a server. If you are unsure, check with your web host, who should be able to provide you with that information

    ▶ Table prefix. This is a prefix for the tables in your database. If you want to run more than one WordPress installation with the same database, you can change the prefix. Doing so is not necessary for this lesson, however. On the next page, you see the prefix defaults to "wp_." Use the default.

4. Click **Let's Go**. Again, the resulting screen should look familiar. Fill out these fields with the appropriate information (see Figure 9.7).

FIGURE 9.7 Entering your database credentials. After you have filled out these fields, click **Submit**.

Now WordPress has all the information it needs to proceed. It is ready to create your configuration file and create all the data needed for WordPress to run in the database.

5. Click **Run the install**. If everything works as expected, the next screen asks you for some more information:

   ▶ **Blog title**—Give your blog a title. It could be a phrase, something like your business name, or "My Awesome Blog" for something personal. Feel free to be more creative than that.

   ▶ **Your E-mail**—Your email address is required in case you need to reset your Admin account password within this install of WordPress or for notifications when there are comments or other events on the blog that you need to be made aware of.

▶ Also displayed is a check box asking whether you would like your blog to appear in search engines such as Google and Technorati. Leave the box checked if you would like your blog to be visible to everyone, including search engines. Uncheck the box if you want to block search engines but allow normal visitors. For example, if you make a post about my hometown, Middling Fair, PA, when people search for "Middling Fair, PA," they will more than likely have the chance to find your post. I recommend you leave this box checked, unless you are creating a private blog.

NOTE: **You Can Edit Your Information**

You can change all this information after you've completed your installation by using the Administration panels.

6. Click **Install WordPress**, and you are taken to the final screen with your administrator username and password. The username is admin and the password is a mix of characters, numbers, and symbols. Be sure to write down this information. You need it in a moment after you click **Log In**.

At the login prompt, put in your username and the password for your admin user; then you are taken to the Dashboard for your new blog.

One final step in the completion of your installation appears at the top of your Dashboard: You are alerted that you need to change the password for the user named admin (see Figure 9.8).

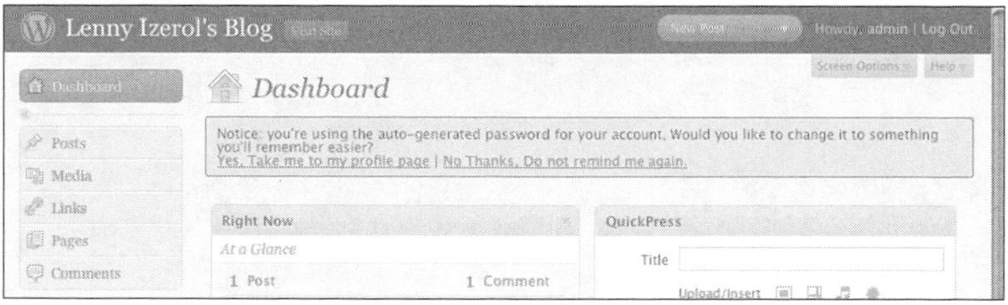

FIGURE 9.8   Warning to change the Admin user password.

I recommend taking this opportunity to change the Admin password right away. The password provided for you is a random set of characters, but you may want to change this to something more meaningful to yourself. I also recommend making your password for Admin something good and secure, including numbers, uppercase and lowercase characters, and a symbol or two.

Summary

In this lesson, you successfully installed WordPress. You uploaded your files, created a database on the database server, and proceeded through the install script to create a functioning blog.

Using Themes on Your Own Site

This lesson covers how themes can affect the form and function of your own self-hosted WordPress site and what types of layouts are available. You also will install a new theme to your newly installed blog.

Changing the Look and Function of Your Site

WordPress was originally intended to be a blogging platform, and it is really good for that purpose. However, you might want to use WordPress for other purposes, too. Are you are a photographer who wants to show-case your images or a cartoonist who wants to start a web comic? These are just two examples illustrating where the standard WordPress design may not suit your needs.

If you are a photographer who wants to show your work as a photo-blog, for example, you might want to display a large photograph on the front page for more of a gallery feel. Then you can include thumbnails on the side for easier navigation so that your readers can find your other works.

In the case of a web comic, you might want to show your latest comic strip at the top of the site until you post the next one and allow the readers to flip through older strips as they view your archive. And, of course, you want to keep a regular blog all at the same time.

Because there are so many WordPress themes in a variety of styles, having a clear idea of what direction you want to go can help you in your decision.

Theme Types

When you start to look at themes, you will notice that there are as many variations of styles as there are themes for WordPress. There are fixed width, variable width, two-column, three-column, free, and premium. Before deciding on a style, first consider your blog content and readers.

If your blog is for a business, you may want something more corporate or business-like. If your blog is for you or someone else's personal site, you may not need to be so straightforward with your theme and therefore can select something more along the lines of your personality.

Finding a unique style for your blog and its voice can be a challenge. It might make sense to hire a web developer and let her design a theme from the ground up, but this task may be as simple as finding the right theme and doing a little customization. Perhaps you or someone in your organization is familiar with cascading stylesheets (CSS) and a little HTML. In that case, you can easily take a theme you find online and change it to meet your needs. Or developing your theme may be as simple as changing a logo and colors.

Free Versus Premium

I don't want to start a debate on why premium themes are better than free themes or vice versa. I will, however, break down this issue to the lowest common denominator: You get what you pay for. There are a lot of high-quality free themes available for WordPress, many of which are available directly from the WordPress Dashboard. On the other hand, there also are a lot of high-quality premium themes for WordPress that you might like and can find simply by doing a little Internet searching.

So what do you get if you go with premium versus free?

Often premium themes come with some level of support in the form of a developer that you can contact with installation problems or even customization help. Perhaps for the cost of your theme or a few dollars more, you can have an exclusive license to use the premium theme and no one else can. This would ensure your unique look.

Alternatively, using free themes means that you can afford to change your look from time to time. You would be on your own to install or customize them, but you do get a little more freedom in return at little or no cost.

Usually, the author asks only that you include a link to his site, which is common courtesy.

Choosing between free and premium themes boils down to what your personal preferences and needs are.

Layouts

Depending on the type of site you are running, you may need room in a sidebar for links and other functionality. Maybe you need more than one sidebar, and that is where columns come in. The number of columns you see when searching for themes refers to the structure and layout of your page.

The default theme that comes with WordPress is a two-column theme in which one column is larger than the other (see Figure 10.1). The larger column is meant to display your blog posts, and the smaller, more narrow sidebar column is meant to display links, search functions, and other widgets that you choose to display. (You can read more about widgets later in this lesson.)

FIGURE 10.1   The default two-column theme.

As you can see, two-column themes offer a lot of flexibility and space. They also don't take up all the browser real estate to allow for readers who have lower screen resolutions and smaller browser windows. Other options for two-column designs include having the narrow column appear on the left or right of the larger content column.

CAUTION: **Be Careful with Resolution**

Browser real estate is the area you can view from left to right and top to bottom when you open a web page. Some people, believe it or not, do run their computers at lower resolutions for a number of reasons, which causes the viewable area to be smaller. So if you run a theme that takes up a lot of space, it could mean that a reader may have to scroll side to side and up and down to view your site. It is common for websites to be designed with a width of between 800 and 1,000 pixels.

Three-column layouts are similar to two-column layouts except that they have one larger content column with two smaller columns for links. Three-column layouts are also good when you're trying to organize data that you do not want pushed below the fold of the site.

PLAIN ENGLISH: **The Fold**

The fold of the site refers to the bottom of your web browser that the users can't see unless they scroll down. Many websites are designed so the main content of the sites is above the fold. That way, users see the important content without having to scroll.

When you use the three-column layouts, it is common to place your two narrow columns either both on the left or right, or split with the content column between them. Some themes give you the option to specify how the columns are arranged, whereas others do not, so you get what you get.

Fluid Versus Fixed Layouts

With all types of layouts, you have to decide if there is going to be extra space on either side of the content area or if your site will fill the full width of the screen. How much space the site fills is determined by fluid or fixed themes.

Using themes with fluid styles means that as you resize your browser, your site expands and contracts to fill up the space. Additionally, as visitors come to your site, they are presented with your site that fits their browser. With a fluid design, your site does not look odd with a small, fixed-width column or a compact content area if the viewer has room to display.

Fixed themes are the most predictable. Unlike fluid themes, fixed designs are essentially the same size design on anyone's browser, which offers you the advantage of having your graphics and text in a predictable format. This format is especially important if you have a theme that is image based, meaning the background and other parts of the site are made up of a series of images that need to line up correctly to look right.

Searching for and Installing a Theme

Now that you have an understanding of the options that are available when beginning your search, you can start sorting through the large assortment of themes, choose one, and install it.

Locating Themes

Finding a theme is probably the hardest part of installing a theme for your site. As mentioned earlier, hundreds and thousands of themes are available to you, free or otherwise, and they come in just about every color in the spectrum.

The main source for finding a theme you like is the Internet itself, and another is the WordPress.org site. Free themes are the easiest to download and try on your site, but the directions for installing a theme are the same whether the theme is free or premium.

CAUTION: **Don't Download from Just Anywhere**

Be careful downloading themes from just anywhere. The WordPress Themes directory is probably the safest place to find themes. There are reports of malicious WordPress themes that can hide links to known spam sites and run malicious code, compromising the security of your site.

Browsing Themes at WordPress.org

You can access the WordPress database of free themes in two ways. You can access the site by pointing your browser to http://wordpress.org/extend/themes/ or you can use your WordPress Dashboard to search for and download themes directly into WordPress itself.

When you open http://wordpress.org/extend/themes/ in your web browser, you are presented with several site features that help you start looking for themes (see Figure 10.2):

- ► **Search Box**—You can search for tags or keywords that you think describe what you are looking for, such as *green* and *two-column*.

- ► **Featured Themes**—These themes are chosen randomly and change periodically.

- ► **Most Popular**—This list includes themes that get a lot of down-loads and are used by a lot of users of the WordPress Themes directory.

- ► **Newest Themes**—These themes have recently been added to the Themes directory.

- ► **Recently Updated**—These themes have been recently updated by the author.

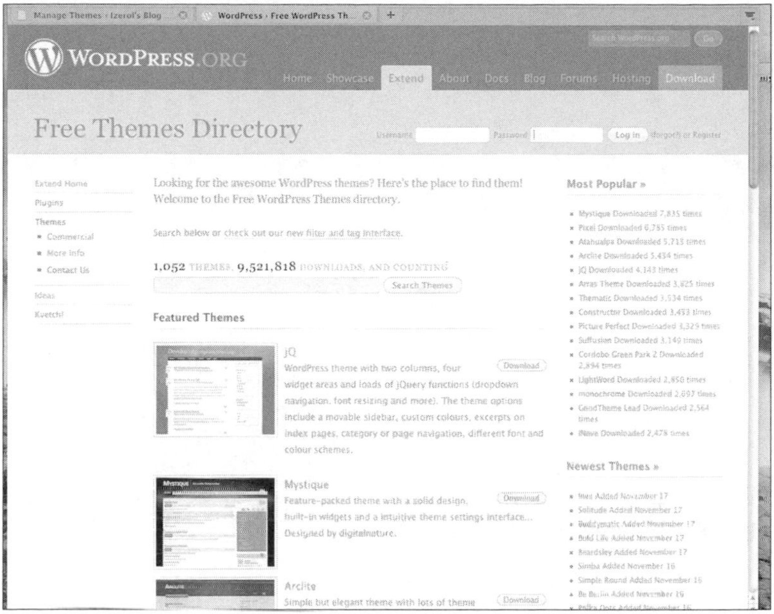

FIGURE 10.2   The WordPress Themes directory.

The WordPress Themes Directory is a good start and gives you several options to start browsing themes right away. All themes on the site are tagged with keywords that make them easy to search for. For example, if you search for *Photo* or *Picture*, you find WordPress themes that mostly relate to photography themes or galleries. Themes are also tagged with keywords about their layout and main color scheme.

If you are looking for a fixed-width theme that is mostly green, search for *fixed* and *green* and you see a selection of mostly fixed-width, green themes.

Additionally, when you click **Check Out Our New Filter and Tag Interface** on the main page at WordPress.org's Themes page, you are presented with a set of check boxes where you can click the keywords that you are looking for and continue your search (see Figure 10.3).

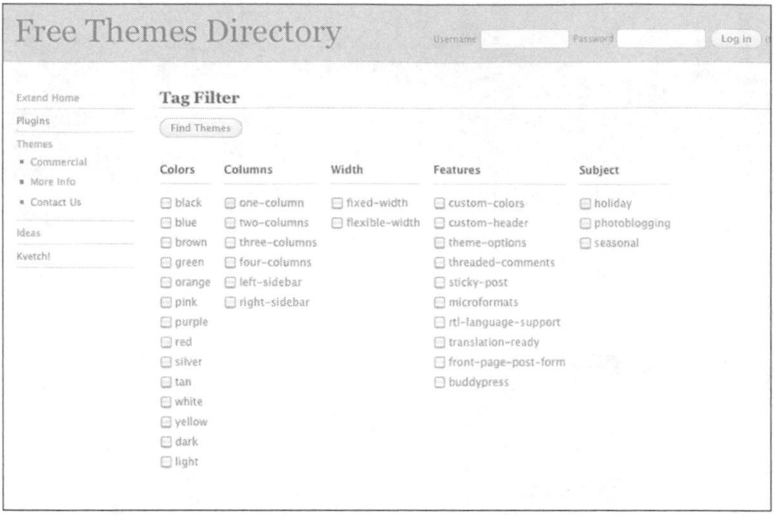

FIGURE 10.3   Searching for themes with tag selection.

After you click on a theme and view its profile, you can see the theme's description and a link to its stats (see Figure 10.4). The stats provide you with some information on how many times it has been downloaded over time. This information might or might not be of interest to you. You might want a popular theme, which would be one that is downloaded a lot. However, you might prefer to have a unique theme, in which case you can steer clear of themes that are downloaded frequently and choose something else instead.

The description tells you a bit about this theme, providing the layout along with a thumbnail image. If you click the thumbnail or the green Preview button to the right of the page, you are presented with a large preview of the theme in action to see whether it is what you're looking for. This feature makes it much easier to shop around for a look you like.

Instead of using the WordPress site, you can also browse the same themes from inside your WordPress Dashboard (see Figure 10.5). Go to your Dashboard (www.yoursite.com/wp-admin) and log in. While you're viewing your Dashboard, on the left side there is a block that has the title Appearance. Inside the block is a link called Add New Themes. Clicking this link takes you to a search that is similar to what's on the WordPress site.

FIGURE 10.4   Viewing a theme's details.

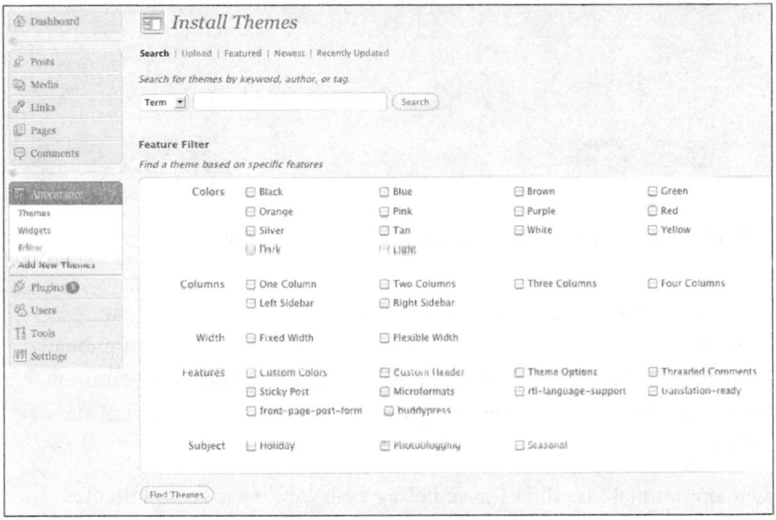

FIGURE 10.5   Installing themes from inside your own WordPress.

The main differences between searching for themes on the WordPress site and searching from your Dashboard are that on your Dashboard, your search results (see Figure 10.6) are displayed in a grid fashion with thumbnails and descriptions, and you have a couple of additional options.

FIGURE 10.6   Theme search results on your Dashboard.

Clicking **Details** gives you details on the author of the theme, ratings from other users, and the last time it was updated. Clicking on the thumbnail image or the **Preview** link brings up a larger preview, just as before on the WordPress site. To close the preview, click the **X** in the top left of the new window.

One option that you didn't have before is the ability to install themes directly from your search. To install themes directly from your search, follow these steps:

1. Click the **Install** link, which opens the dialog box shown in Figure 10.7.

FIGURE 10.7 Ready to install a theme from your WordPress.

> TIP: **Where's the Install Now Button?**
> You may have to scroll down a little to see the Cancel and Install Now buttons.

2. Click **Install Now**.

3. Enter your File Transfer Protocol (FTP) credentials. You should have this information from an earlier lesson, or your Internet service provider (ISP) can provide that information for you.

4. Fill in this form with your username, password, hostname, and the connection type (see Figure 10.8). Usually, the Connection type is FTP unless otherwise specified by your ISP. When you are ready, click **Proceed**.

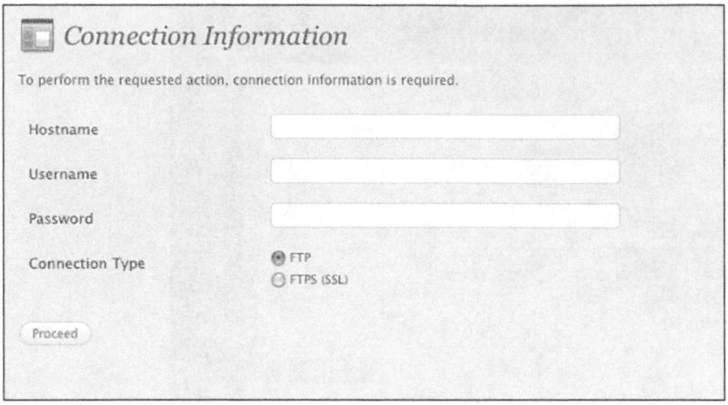

Connection Information

To perform the requested action, connection information is required.

Hostname

Username

Password

Connection Type   ● FTP
                  ○ FTPS (SSL)

Proceed

FIGURE 10.8   Enter the connection information.

On the following screen, you see that your theme was downloaded, unpacked, and installed (see Figure 10.9). At this point, you can preview your theme and actually see what it looks like with information from your site. If you do preview it after installation, you also see the X at the top left to close the window, and on the right side you can activate the theme. If you click **Activate**, the theme is immediately enabled on your site.

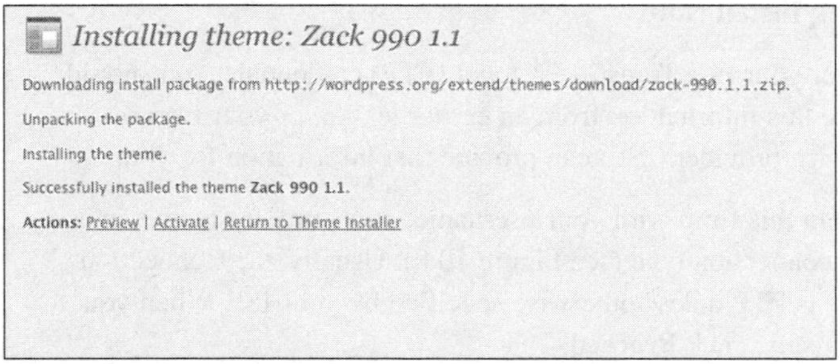

Installing theme: Zack 990 1.1

Downloading install package from http://wordpress.org/extend/themes/download/zack-990.1.1.zip.

Unpacking the package.

Installing the theme.

Successfully installed the theme **Zack 990 1.1**.

Actions: Preview | Activate | Return to Theme Installer

FIGURE 10.9   WordPress's installation confirmation screen.

Downloading and Installing Themes

If you do not have access to automatically install themes on your site, you have found a theme on another website, or you have purchased a premium theme, installing a theme is still easy.

NOTE: **Using FTP**

In this section, you access your site with an FTP client. If you don't already have an FTP client, refer to Lesson 9, "Installing WordPress," to find out more about using one.

On the WordPress.org themes site (http://wordpress.org/extend/themes), select a theme that you think will work on your site and you are happy with. After you choose a theme and are looking at its profile page (refer to Figure 10.4), click on **Download**.

Most WordPress themes you download are in the form of a zip file that you must save and unzip; this includes premium themes also. Your browser asks you where you want to download your zip file. Save it to a location on your computer that you will remember, such as a download folder or your desktop.

When the download is complete, go to the folder where you downloaded your theme. In that folder, you need to unzip your theme file; it creates a folder. The folder it creates should be named the same as the theme. For example, if your zip file is called AwesomeTheme-2.2.3.zip, your new folder should be called AwesomeTheme.

Use your FTP client and connect to your hosting account. On the right side of your client, you should see the remote files. Double-click on the folder named wp-content. Now double-click on the folder named Themes. You should see two folders: classic and default. These two standard themes come with WordPress out of the box. The folder name's default is the theme you see on your WordPress site as soon as the installation is complete.

In the left pane of your FTP client, navigate to the download folder that has the new theme you downloaded.

To upload your theme properly, upload the entire folder to your website. In this example, you would upload AwesomeTheme to your site. After the upload is complete, you should have three folders: classic, default, and AwesomeTheme.

Now that your theme is uploaded, it's time to turn it on.

Applying Themes

Changing between themes, now that they are installed, is fairly straight-forward.

1. Using your web browser, go to your Dashboard (http://www.yoursite.com/wp-admin).

2. On the left side of your Dashboard is a block called Appearance. Open that block and select Themes.

3. On the Managing Themes page, all the themes you have installed are listed. The theme listed at the top is your current one. Activate the theme you want to use by clicking the **Activate** link.

4. If you want to see how a theme is going to look before turning it on, click the **Preview** link or click the thumbnail.

   As you have seen before (refer to Figure 10.7), a preview appears. From the top-right corner of the preview, you can activate the theme if you are happy with its appearance.

TIP: **Deleting Themes**

If you have a theme you do not care for any longer, you can delete it from the Manage Themes page by clicking on **Delete** just below its description.

Widgets

With your new theme installed and running, you might want to move things around a little bit. Perhaps you have a two- or three-column layout and want to move some of the items in those columns around a little bit or possibly put something in a column of your own. You can use widgets, which are similar to small plug-ins designed so that you can move them easily from place to place on your site, specifically in the sidebars.

From your Dashboard, go to **Appearance, Widgets**. On the resulting page, you see a list of available widgets in the center of the page and the columns available to your theme on the right (see Figure 10.10).

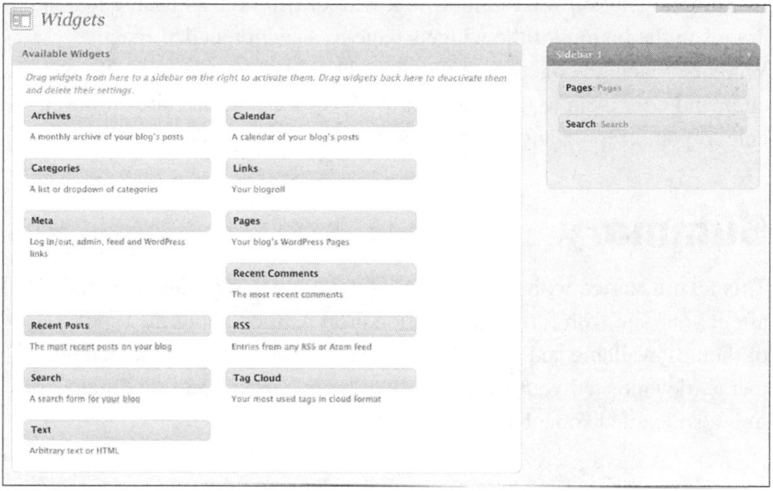

FIGURE 10.10 Available widgets with a one-column theme.

Below each widget is a quick description of its function. To move a widget to a column—in this case, Sidebar 1—do the following:

1. Click your mouse on a widget and hold it.

2. Now drag and drop it over the column where you want it to appear.

3. When you drop the widget where you want it, usually it asks you for a title. This title is optional. If you want to call the Search widget Find It, for example, this is the place where you would assign it a name. Leave the field blank, and it defaults to the name of the widget.

Other widgets have more options than just the title. So be prepared if the one you choose asks for something more than just a title.

If you want to change a title or other options for a widget, click the small, downward-pointing arrow on the right of the title bar for the widget. It then expands, showing all the options available.

Additionally, if you want to remove a widget from the sidebar, click and drag it to the bottom of the widgets page to a section called Inactive Widgets. Placing widgets here removes them and their settings. If you click and drag them to the Available Widgets section, they are still available to you, keeping any settings that you may have added.

Summary

This lesson started with a discussion of what themes are and how they affect your site with form and function. You learned about the types of themes available and their layouts. You also started with the default theme, downloaded your own, installed it, and customized it a little. You also learned some basic Widget skills.

LESSON 11

Customizing Your Site with Plug-ins

Plug-ins make all the difference in how your WordPress.org site runs. This lesson discusses how you can use plug-ins to change the function of your self-hosted site and how to install some of the more popular plug-ins.

What Are Plug-ins?

In a nutshell, plug-ins are bits of code designed to extend the functionality of your site to do almost anything. WordPress itself is designed to be lean and functional out of the box, but with plug-ins you add the extra functionality you need. Everyone has different needs, so the capability to add plug-ins keeps the WordPress core code clean and uncluttered, while at the same time allowing you the flexibility to easily add on features that make your site what you need.

For example, if you want to create a podcasting site with WordPress, two plug-ins help with that task: PodPress and PowerPress. They provide similar functions. They take a link to an MP3 (your podcast file) and add a Flash Audio player on your site to each post with an MP3 link so you can play and listen to the episode and also add a download link and other information for your readers. These plug-ins also perform certain functions, such as notifying Apple iTunes that you have a new episode when you post one. With plug-ins, the possibilities for customizing your site become nearly endless.

Using the Plug-ins Dashboard

The Plug-ins Dashboard is designed to give you complete access to manage the plug-ins installed on your site. From here you can install, activate, deactivate, and permantly remove plug-ins as you see fit. You can get to the Plug-ins Dashboard by opening your web browser and pointing it to your Dashboard (for example, http://www.yoursite.com/wp-admin). When you get there, click on **Plug-ins**. You then are presented with a list of all your plug-ins (see Figure 11.1). At this point, if you haven't added any plug-ins, you should see only two listed; they are the default plug-ins that come with WordPress: Akismet and Hello Dolly.

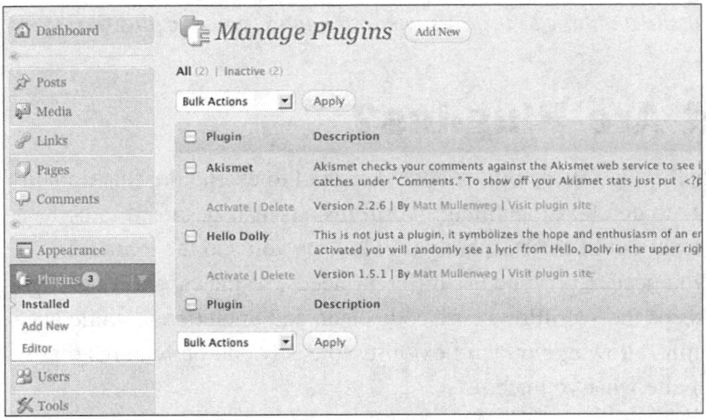

FIGURE 11.1 Plug-ins page displaying the default plug-ins.

This screen shows you all you need to know about your plug-ins. At the top, just below Manage Plug-ins, you may see several links that give you several group views of all your plug-ins and each link allows you to toggle between the category groupings. The categories are as follows:

- ▶ **All** displays all the plug-ins you have installed.

- ▶ **Active** displays all the plug-ins you have installed and currently in use on your site.

- ▶ **Inactive** shows a list of plug-ins you have available on the system but not currently activated.

▶ **Upgrade Available** gives you a list of plug-ins you have on the system that need an upgrade. Plug-in authors release upgrades to plug-ins when adding new features or possibly addressing security issues.

▶ **Recently Active** shows the plug-ins you recently deactivated. This list is handy if you accidentally deactivate a plug-in and need to quickly turn it back on.

NOTE: **Some Categories Are Missing**

You may not see all these categories until you start adding some plug-ins or depending on the state of your plug-ins. For example, if you don't have any plug-ins that need an upgrade, you do not see the Upgrade Available view, or you may not see Inactive if all your plug-ins are active.

All your plug-ins are listed in the middle portion of the page. Each one displays its name and a description. Just below the name and description are Activate and Delete links for each one. If a plug-in is already activated, you see Deactivate instead. To the right of the Activate, Delete, and Deactivate links are the current version of the plug-in and possibly links to the author and the plug-in's site.

To the left of each plug-in listed is a check box. The check boxes are used in conjunction with the Bulk Actions list box. If you select all the plug-ins or a couple, you can then select an action from the list and perform that action on all selected plug-ins. This capability can save time if you are changing the status of several plug-ins at once.

CAUTION: **Deleting Permanently**

Deleting a plug-in *permanently* removes all the files associated with the plug-in. If you do not want use a plug-in now and possibly try it later, I suggest just deactivating it. If plug-ins are cluttering your workspace and you don't plan on using them anymore, there is nothing wrong with deleting old plug-ins.

Below the Plug-ins menu item are the following options:

- ▶ **Installed** takes you to a list of all installed plug-ins (active or inactive), or if upgrades are available, this option takes you to the list of plug-ins that have an upgrade available.

- ▶ **Add New** takes you to the search screen to start looking for plug-ins that you might want to install. This option allows you to search the list of plug-ins available on the WordPress plug-ins directory, directly from your WordPress site. (More details on this in the next part of this lesson.)

- ▶ **Editor** lets you edit the code of your plug-ins. If you're not familiar with PHP, you might not need to use the editor.

NOTE: **File Permissions for Plug-ins**

To edit files properly and be able to save them, you might need to check your file permissions on the files to make sure you have access to write to them.

CAUTION: **Be Careful When Editing**

Editing your plug-ins can cause them to become unstable unless you know what you are changing. Use the Editor option with caution.

Finding Plug-ins

There are several places to start your search for WordPress plug-ins, and I recommend starting with the "official" plug-ins repository for a couple of reasons.

Anyone can submit a plug-in for inclusion in this repository, but not all will be listed. A few restrictions and standards must be met for inclusion in the plug-ins repository:

- ▶ The plug-in must be GPL-compatible. This means, in the simplest terms, you are free to download and use the plug-in. If you modify it and release it as a new plug-in, you must release it under the same license.

▶ The plug-in must not do anything illegal or immoral.

▶ The plug-in cannot add any external links unless the user explicitly gives permission to do so.

These restrictions as well as other standards that WordPress enforces only make your decision a little easier if you choose plug-ins from the WordPress repository:

▶ There is no cost, and licensing isn't an issue.

▶ You can modify the code if you want with no restrictions if you have some programming skills or know someone who does.

▶ These plug-ins do not have malicious code that can be harmful to your site.

If you do not find the plug-ins you are looking for here, there are other alternatives. Simply search for "WordPress plug-in" on Google or your favorite search engine, and you will find a lot of other sites that also host WordPress plug-ins. Keep in mind that much of what you are looking for can be found in the WordPress repository.

CAUTION: **Not All Plug-ins Are Created Equal**

Take caution where you download plug ins from. The plug-ins are just PHP code that can do anything, even something malicious. So, download with care.

As with themes, premium plug-ins are also available for a fee. There are not as many premium plug-ins as there are premium themes, but this is starting to become a larger business. The main advantage for you is if you are looking for support in the form of someone to contact in case you need installation help or modifications. Costs can range from $4 to more than $60. Again, at the time of this writing, there are a lot more free plug-ins than premium.

Because there are so many places from which you could possibly download WordPress plug-ins, I focus on the Official WordPress repository here. Keep in mind that wherever you download plug-ins, the basic steps are the same.

There are two ways to access the plug-ins directory at WordPress: You can access plug-ins from the WordPress Dashboard or by visiting http://wordpress.org/extend/plug-ins/.

NOTE: **Writing Your Own Plug-in**

You can write your own plug-in or hire someone to write a plug-in for you. Writing plug-ins is not difficult if you have some programming skills, some knowledge of PHP, and some extra time. Writing plug-ins for WordPress is very well documented on the WordPress site as well as other sites across the Internet.

However, lots of plug-ins are already available, and likely there is one already written that does what you need. So be sure to do a thorough search first because it could save you time in the long run.

Searching from Your Dashboard

To search from the Dashboard, click on **Plug-ins**, **Add New**. If you are viewing your plug-ins from the Managing Plug-ins page, you also can click the **Add New** button at the top of the page. It takes you to the same search page.

At the top of the Install Plug-ins page is a list of views that will assist you in finding and installing plug-ins:

- ▶ **Search** allows you to search through the plug-ins directory on the WordPress site and also allows you to navigate through all the plug-ins via the tags assigned to them—for example, Comments, Twitter, and Stats.

- ▶ **Upload** walks you through uploading a zip file that contains a plug-in that you downloaded manually.

- ▶ **Featured** shows you the plug-ins showcased by WordPress. They are chosen based on user activity and popularity.

- ▶ **Popular** highlights the plug-ins with the highest ratings and number of users.

- ▶ **Newest** shows the newest plug-ins added recently to the directory.

▶ **Recently Updated** also shows the plug-ins recently updated either for functionality or security reasons.

Click on **Search**, and you see the page shown in Figure 11.2.

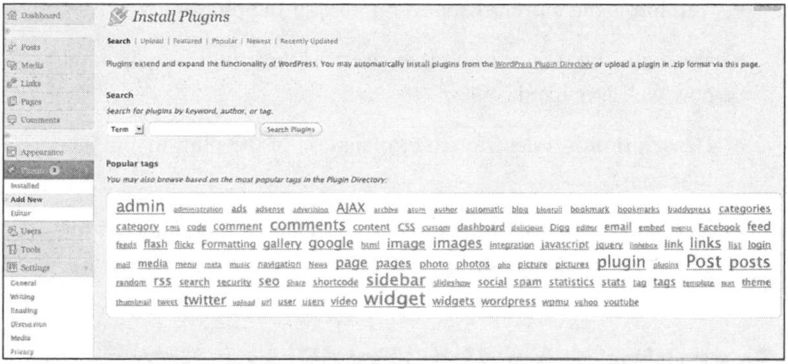

FIGURE 11.2 Starting the search for plug-ins.

On the Install Plug-ins page, you are presented with a search box where you can search for plug-ins by keyword, author, or *tag*. Also, you are presented with a *tag cloud* full of keywords that you can click on and instantly find plug-ins associated with the tag you choose.

PLAIN ENGLISH: **Tag**

A *tag* is a word or set of words associated with an item that helps identify it. In this instance, tags are associated with plug-ins. A *tag cloud* is a view of all the tags in the database. In the tag cloud, larger and bolder tags represent more items, and smaller, less bold tags indicate fewer items.

Type in a search word or click on a tag word from the tag cloud. You then are presented with a list of plug-ins that match your search results in a grid list. This list is composed of five columns:

- ▶ **Name** is, of course, the name of the plug-in.

- ▶ **Version** is the current version number of the plug-in.

- ▶ **Rating** is the rating from other users of this plug-in indicating how well it is liked.

- ▶ **Description** is a descriptive explanation of the plug-in and its functions.

- ▶ **Actions** shows what functions you can take on the plug-ins listed, and it will say **Install**.

Searching from the WordPress Site

Searching for plug-ins on the WordPress repository site is similar, but results are displayed a little differently (see Figure 11.3).

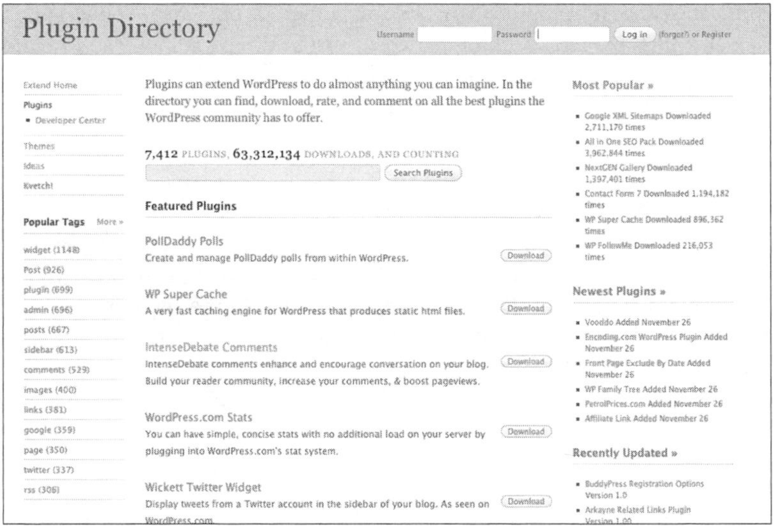

FIGURE 11.3   Searching for plug-ins on the WordPress repository site.

On the left side of the site, below the links to other places on the site, is the title Popular Tags. This is a shorthand representation of the tag cloud. You can see the popular tags and the number of plug-ins associated with them. Clicking **More** shows you the tag cloud much like you saw in your Dashboard.

Among other features here, again mimicking Dashboard searching, is a search box in the center with Featured Plug-ins below. To the right are Most Popular, Newest Plug-ins, and Recently Updated.

If you choose to install from the WordPress site, you have to download the plug-in yourself and upload it to your site using the automated installation functions of WordPress or the manual installation method using your FTP client.

When you find a plug-in that you would like to use and are looking at its profile on Wordpress.org, you see the orange Download button. When you click **Download,** you are asked to download a zip file. After you download it, note where you saved it.

Installing a Plug-in

There are several things you should know before you start installing plug-ins:

▶ Some plug-ins require changes to permissions of files and folders on your website.

▶ Some plug-ins may require changes or additions to your site's themes to work properly.

▶ You should make backups of your site's files and its database. If you lose the files and database and don't have a backup, you lose your website.

TIP: **Good Practices for Editing Code**

If you're a programmer who is making modifications to your theme or other files, follow these guidelines for good code management: Put in a comment with your initials and a date so you will know what you changed. Also, avoid deleting lines but use comments in the code to hide old lines. Or simply copy the file you are about to edit and rename it for easy identification if you need to roll back a change.

Generally, there are three methods for installing plug-ins. They are described next.

Fully Automatic

The easiest way to install plug-ins is to use the fully automatic option. If you have searched for a plug-in through your Dashboard, an Install link (mentioned previously) appears in orange.

After you click **Install**, you are asked for your FTP credentials much like you have seen previously in other lessons. After you fill out the form, click **Proceed**. If all works correctly, you see a status page with the option to activate the plug-in right away, or you can choose to go back to the plug-ins page and activate it later (see Figure 11.4).

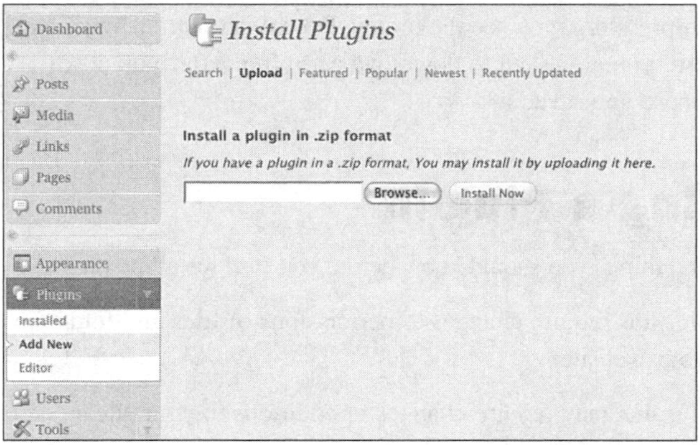

FIGURE 11.4   Installing from a zip file.

NOTE: Folder Permissions

If you get an error installing from the WordPress Dashboard, your permissions may not be set correctly on your web server. If you do not know how to set permissions on folders, contact your web hosting support for assistance.

Automated Installation

If you choose not to use the fully automatic installation method, or you are installing a plug-in that you got from somewhere other than the official WordPress repository, the steps to install it are nearly as easy.

1. Open your web browser and navigate to your Dashboard; then go to **Plug-ins**, **Add New**.

2. On the Dashboard page, below the title **Install Plug-ins** at the top of the page, notice the Upload option to the left of Search. Upload takes your zip file, copies it to the web server, expands it, and places all its files into the correct place.

3. Click **Browse**. Navigate to the download folder where you placed your plug-in zip file and select the zip file to upload. When you have the filename in place, click the **Install Now** button.

4. You are prompted for your FTP credentials. Make sure these fields are correct and click **Proceed**.

5. If the upload performs correctly, you see page that displays the status of what is occurring or has occurred with a link to a couple of actions. You can immediately activate your new plug-in from here or simply return to the plug-ins page if you are not ready to take action on your new plug-in (see Figure 11.5)

You can activate your new plug-in later if you choose, but it is installed and ready to use now.

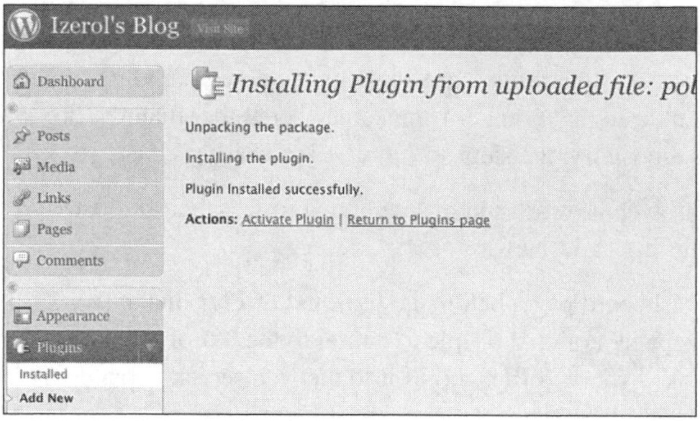

FIGURE 11.5   Installation complete.

Manual Installation

The zip file that you downloaded is the plug-in itself. To proceed, you need to upload the plug-in files to your webserver:

1. Go to your download folder where you saved the plug-in and expand the zip file.

2. Once expanded, the zip file is ready for upload. Open your FTP program and log in to your site.

3. After you open it, navigate to the wp-contents folder, where you see a plug-ins folder. Open the plug-ins folder and upload your expanded plug-in zip file here.

4. After you successfully upload your plug-in into the wp-content, plug-ins directory, you need to activate your plug-in by visiting your Dashboard at http://yoursite.com/wp-admin and click on **Plug-ins**.

5. On the plug-ins page, an additional link called **Inactive** appears just below the Manage Plug-ins title.

6. If you click on **Inactive**, you see all the plug-ins that you currently do not have enabled. The new plug-in you uploaded is shown here. As you did earlier with the Hello Dolly plug-in, click **Activate** below Title on the plug-in column.

That's it. Your new plug-in is now activated.

Upgrading Plug-ins

As time goes on, upgrades, security releases, or new features will be added to the plug-ins that you accumulate. It is important that you are able to keep up and make sure that your system is up to date.

There are several reasons for keeping your code up to date, and chief among them is security of your site. Plus, upgrading plug-ins is not as hard as you may think.

One of the advantages of downloading your plug-ins from the WordPress repository is that your copy of WordPress will let you know that upgrades are available. This is not true of plug-ins you have downloaded from other sites.

Two notifications alert you that updates are available. On the menu to the left in your WordPress Dashboard, notice that the Plug-ins menu header has a number highlighted in a circle (see Figure 11.6). This circle shows you the number of updates you have.

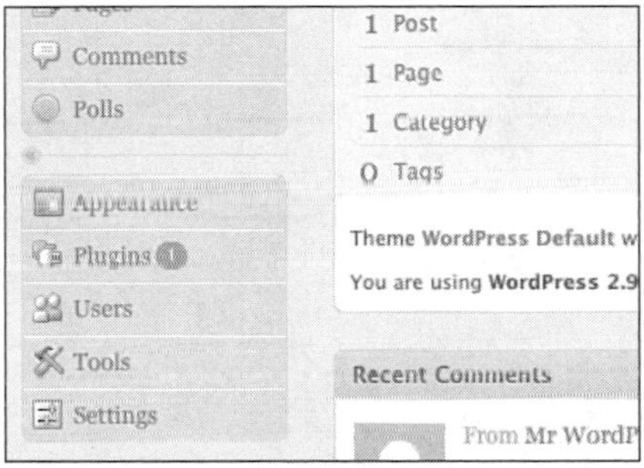

FIGURE 11.6   Upgrades available.

Additionally, if you visit your plug-ins page by clicking on **Plug-ins**, each plug-in that has an update available has a highlighted area associated with it that gives you a little information about the update.

If you click on **Details,** you see a pop-up window much like you saw when searching for plug-ins with details on the update and an **Install Update Now** option. If you click on **ChangeLog** at the top of the pop-up window, you see a list of changes that have been implemented since the last released version.

> NOTE: **Check ChangeLog**
>
> I recommend looking at the ChangeLog to see if the changes being made will affect any of the reasons you use this plug-in. It is good to be aware of what is happening in case questions come up later.

After you click on **Install Update Now,** you are asked to confirm your connection information with your FTP credentials. Fill out this page and click **Proceed**.

The next page shows you the progress as it downloads the plug-in and upgrades the code (see Figure 11.7).

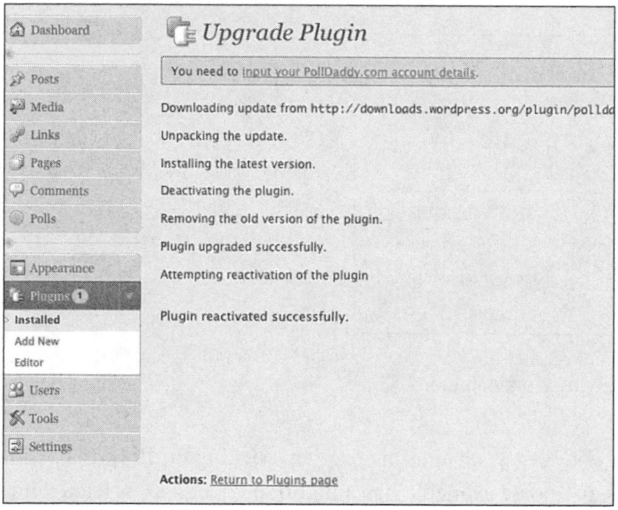

FIGURE 11.7   Upgrade complete.

> NOTE: **Notification Reminders**
> Plug-ins you have installed that are not in the WordPress repository do not notify you that you have updates waiting.

Removing a Plug-in

It is inevitable that eventually you will have plug-ins you no longer use and want to disable or even delete entirely. This is very common, so WordPress makes it simple to remove old plug-ins.

1. Navigate to the Plug-ins panel in your Dashboard.

2. Under the title Manage Plug-ins is your list of plug-ins. Under the plug-in you want to remove, you should see the Deactivate button.

3. Click **Deactivate** and you will then see two new options: Activate and Delete.

4. After a plug-in is deactivated, you can remove it for permanently by clicking **Delete**.

5. You are taken to a Delete Plug-in confirmation page. From here, if you choose **Yes, Delete These Files**, your plug-in is removed from your website permanently.

If you select **No, Return Me to the Plug-in List**, nothing happens, but you are returned to the plug-in list. Your plug-in will still be there if you choose to activate it later.

> CAUTION: **Deactivate and then Delete**
> Keep in mind that some, not all, plug-ins have dependencies on others. Deactivating one and deleting it may have adverse effects on your site. I recommend deactivating first; then check your site to make sure it is in good shape and delete only after you verify everything is okay.

Popular Plug-ins

Following are some popular plug-ins that you might find useful. They are all found in the WordPress.org plug-ins directory.

Ads

▶ **Google Adsense for feeds**—This plug-in puts Google RSS ads in your feed. Make sure you fill in your publisher ID by editing the plug-in file.

▶ **Advertising Manager**—This plug-in manages and rotates Google Adsense and other ads on your Wordpress blog. It automatically recognizes many ad networks, including Google Adsense, AdBrite, Adify, AdGridWork, Adpinion, Adroll, Chitika, Commission Junction, CrispAds, OpenX, ShoppingAds, Yahoo!PN, and WidgetBucks. Unsupported ad networks can be used as well.

Spam

▶ **Akismet**—This default plug-in is available in your WordPress site. This plug-in helps curb spam by comparing it to a database of other spam messages that WordPress.com collects to determine if it is in fact spam. (This plug-in requires a WordPress.com account.)

▶ **WP-SpamFree Anti-Spam**—This extremely powerful WordPress antispam plug-in eliminates blog comment spam, including trackback and pingback spam.

Getting the Word Out

▶ **Wp-pubsubhubbub**—This plug-in contacts and sends notification of changes on your site to pubsubhubbub hubs so that new posts are known and available to search engines.

Statistics

▶ **Wordpress.com Stats**—This plug-in was created by the company Automattic to collect your site's visitor data and statistics to create easy-to-understand graphs and dates of your site's visitation traffic. (This plug-in requires a WordPress.com account.)

▶ **Google Analyticator**—This plug-in adds the necessary JavaScript code to enable Google Analytics to keep statistics on visitors to your site. It includes widgets for Analytics data display.

Social Networking

▶ **Sociable**—This plug-in enables you to automatically add links to your favorite social bookmarking sites on your posts, pages, and in your RSS feed. You can choose from 99 different social bookmarking sites.

▶ **Social Bookmarks**—This plug-in for WordPress adds a list of XHTML-compliant graphic links at the end of your posts and/or pages. These links allow your visitors to easily submit them to a number of social bookmarking sites.

▶ **Twitter Tools**—This plug-in creates a complete integration between your WordPress blog and your Twitter account.

Podcasting

▶ **Blubrry PowerPress**—This plug-in brings the essential features for podcasting to WordPress. Developed by podcasters for podcasters, PowerPress offers full iTunes support, the Update iTunes Listing feature, web audio/video media players, and more. PowerPress is designed as an upgrade to PodPress.

Summary

In this lesson, you learned what plug-ins are and what they do. You also explored the Plug-ins Dashboard and used the search functions in WordPress to find and install plug-ins using the fully automatic, automated installation, and manual methods. Finally, you looked at the process of upgrading and removing old plug-ins.

LESSON 12

Blogging on the Go

You can't always be on your computer. With a smart phone and the avail-ability of Wi-Fi, you can take the blogging experience with you almost anywhere you go. There are several ways to get posts to your blog, from email to iPhone apps. This lesson describes the various ways you can blog on the go.

Setting Up Your Blog for Remote Access

Blogging can be fun, and with wireless technology there's no reason you can't do it while you are out and about. Perhaps you are at a conference or on a special vacation, and you would like to blog about your experiences as they happen. WordPress can make that a very real possibility. Capturing your thoughts and blogging them right away can be very captivating for readers of your site.

To remotely access your blog, you have to turn on the WordPress feature to allow outside applications to connect and interact with your site. By default, this feature is turned off. There are two ways that outside applications can interact with WordPress:

▶ Atom Publishing

▶ XML-RPC

> NOTE: **WordPress.com Versus WordPress.org**
>
> If you are using a WordPress.com account, the Remote Publishing feature is turned on by default as opposed to your WordPress.org install.

Use the following steps to turn on an option for remote access:

1. Open your site's Dashboard.

2. Select **Settings**, **Writing**.

3. In the Remote Publishing section, select the **XML-RPC** option.

4. Click **Save Changes**.

CAUTION: **Enable Only What You Need**

I recommend turning on only the options you believe you are going to use. Turning on features you are not using could be a security risk.

NOTE: **XML-RPC or Atom Publishing?**

I cannot say that one publishing protocol is better than another; however, the applications that are discussed in this lesson support XML-RPC for remote operations, so that's the protocol used in this lesson. Of course, if you come across an application that supports Atom Publishing, you can come back here and easily turn it on.

Now, to use your remote blogging capabilities, you need to know only your site's URL, username, and password, and you are set.

NOTE: **Finding the XML-RPC Script**

Some sites and applications are smart enough to figure out where your XML-RPC script is, and others want a complete URL to your site, including the XML-RPC script. If that is the case, use http://www.yoursite.com/xml-rpc.php instead of http://www.yoursite.com.

Posting from Other Websites

Some websites offer interaction with other sites using remote publishing. This can be very beneficial by allowing you to create more compelling content on your site by including material from other places across the internet.

Flickr

Flickr, a popular photo-sharing site, offers support for a variety of websites.

Say you upload a picture from your camera phone to Flickr, and you want to also post that image on your blog. Flickr allows you to set up several blogs to publish to, not just one.

> NOTE: **Flickr Accounts**
>
> To use Flickr to post photos, you need a Flickr account. It is free, and you get a generous amount of space to store images. Flickr does offer Pro accounts with a few more features and more storage space.

1. After you set up your Flickr account and are logged in, click the arrow directly to the right of **You** and select **Your Account**.

2. Now you see a tab labeled Extending Flickr, Click it.

3. On that tab, you see Your Blogs, Click it.

4. Click the **Configure-Flickr-to-Blogs Setting** link.

5. Flickr walks you through the process with a wizard that will eventually ask for your URL, username, and password.

After you configure your blog, you can go directly back to the same location and edit the settings for your blog, including the default layout, and even post a test post.

The layout allows you to set the default image site and text flow, so it looks correct on your blog each time (see Figure 12.1).

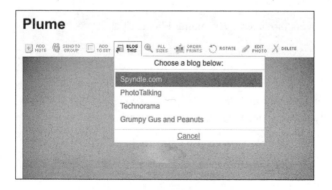

FIGURE 12.1   Using Flickr to configure the default layout of your blog.

After you set up your blog, above any picture in your photostream that you have marked as public is a **Blog This** icon. The Blog This icon is also available for any photo that is on Flickr that is marked as public and the photographer has allowed allow blogging of his or her photos.

After you click **Blog This**, as shown in Figure 12.2, Flickr asks which blog (you can configure more than one) and prompts you for a title and text body. After you submit this information, it is published to your site.

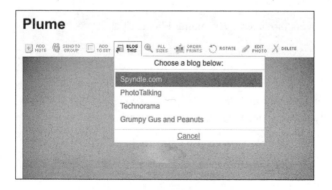

FIGURE 12.2   Blogging a picture from Flickr.

Posterous

The Posterous service enables you to send emails to your Posterous account, and it creates a blog for you. Posterous not only creates a blog for you (non-WordPress), but also directs your messages to several services on your behalf, including Twitter, Facebook, WordPress, and others.

The Posterous page tells you that you don't have to set up an account to start using the services; however, to add your WordPress blog for posting, you need to set up one.

To set up a page, visit the Posterous site at http://posterous.com and click on the login in the top-right corner.

1. You can create an account using your Facebook credentials if you want or click on the **Sign up with Posterous** button.

2. The service asks what you want your site's name to be and your email address (for your account login) and a password. When this setup is complete, you can email post@posterous.com, and the service routes your message wherever you have it set to go.

3. After creating your account, log in. You see Manage at the top of the page. From there, you can set up where your messages will be routed.

Setting up WordPress autoposting is easy

1. Click on the **Autopost** heading on the left side.

2. Click on the large green **Add a Service** button (see Figure 12.3). The resulting pop-up shows you all the services that Posterous uses.

3. In the Blogs section on the pop-up window, select **WordPress**, and you are presented with the familiar settings that you have been using, including your site's URL, username, and password.

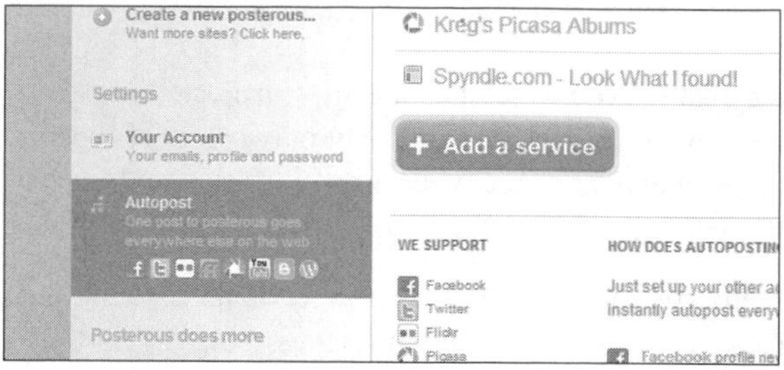

FIGURE 12.3   Setting up autoposting in Posterous.

NOTE: **Post to Multiple Sites with Posterous**

What is nice about Posterous is that anything you send in is sent to all the services you have set up. So, one post is posted to many sites, or Posterous can provide you with a special email address so you can post to just one site at a time.

Now you are all set. You can post text, pictures, and video to your WordPress site and other services, all at the same time, through one email message.

Using Mobile Applications

There are lots of mobile applications for either the iPhone or BlackBerry. There are also applications for other mobile devices, such as Android, but not an official one as of yet. Here we focus on the Official WordPress application written by Automattic, Inc., the company behind WordPress.

There are versions for the iPhone and the BlackBerry; they both work similarly and both support a WordPress.com account as well as your own self-hosted WordPress.org site.

Using the iPhone App

The WordPress application is available through the App Store. You can install it by opening the App Store and searching for WordPress. The App Store walks you through the installation process.

To configure the iPhone app with your first blog:

1. Click on the app's icon to open it.

2. You are prompted for your username, password, and URL.

3. After you have entered your credentials, click **Save**.

4. A pop-up window tells you that the app is being validated. Let the validation process complete.

5. After the app is installed, you see content from your site starting with comments.

Now that you are viewing your blog, at the top left of the screen is a link to go back to your blog's list, and a button on the right has an edit button (see Figure 12.4). This is the place where you make new posts.

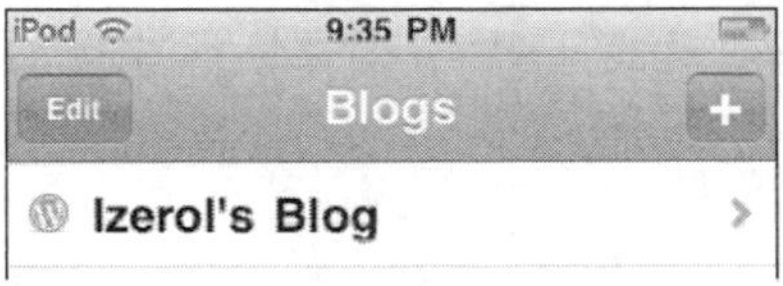

iPod 🛜	9:35 PM	
Edit	**Blogs**	**+**
Ⓦ **Izerol's Blog**		>

FIGURE 12.4   WordPress functions on the iPhone and iPod touch.

At the bottom, you see three buttons:

▶ **Comments**—Allows you to moderate comments as they come in

▶ **Posts**—Enables you to create and edit posts

▶ **Pages**—Enables you to create pages on your site

You can perform any blogging function from this application. Creating a post is intuitive. You can even add media; for example, you can upload pictures that you have taken with your cell phone camera or even take one at that moment.

Clicking Blogs will take you back to your Blog List. An Edit button appears at the top left, and a + button is on the right (see Figure 12.5).

Clicking **Edit** changes to edit mode and allows you to delete any blogs that you have listed, and clicking + prompts you to add a new blog, if you have another to add. While in Edit mode, you can click on your blog and change any settings for it, such as your username and password.

FIGURE 12.5   Using your blog on your iPhone or iPod touch.

If you're not in Edit mode, clicking on the blog's title takes you to the screen where you can view the content and work with your selected blog.

BlackBerry

If you are a BlackBerry user, an application is also available for that platform.

> CAUTION: Something to keep in mind before you install the BlackBerry app is that at press time of this book, the Blackberry application is in beta and not a final release version. Options and features could change by the time you read this and, as with all beta/pre-release software, you should be aware that you could run into bugs that might cause you trouble.

To install the BlackBerry application:

1. Open your web browser and navigate to http://blackberry.word-press.org.

2. Click the download link on the top-right side.

3. Your BlackBerry asks if you want to install the application and walks you through the rest of the installation process.

After installing the BlackBerry application, you can start adding blogs that you write for and start posting.

The main difference between this and the iPhone application is that the BlackBerry relies on the context menu (by clicking the BlackBerry Menu button) to perform many of its functions.

To start adding a blog, click the BlackBerry Menu button. You then can perform several functions:

▶ **Show Blog**—Shows you the options for the blog you have high-lighted (if you already have one set up on the main page).

▶ **Add Blog**—Allows you to create and set up a blog for posting or managing.

▶ **Delete Blog**—Will remove a blog that you have highlighted (if you already have one set up on the main page).

▶ **Setup**—Allows you to set various options regarding how this application talks to the Internet and so on. Most likely, the defaults will work for you.

▶ **Check Update**—Checks to see whether you have an update to your WordPress mobile application.

▶ **About**—Displays version and other information about this appli-cation.

Select **Add Blog**. You are asked for the familiar credentials described ear-lier in the lesson. Once set, your BlackBerry application tries to authenti-cate you and download information, such as the last 10 posts and any comments that need approving.

Now you are set and ready to blog from your BlackBerry. You can add posts and media from your cell phone's camera and moderate comments as you would on your blog from your computer.

> TIP: **Why Can't I See My Posts?**
>
> If posts have been made since you last opened your BlackBerry application—for example, posts you made from your computer—you might have to click the **Refresh** menu option to see the newer posts (see Figure 12.6).

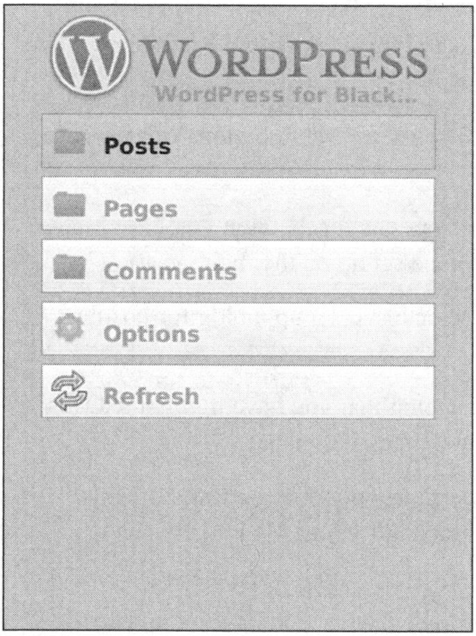

FIGURE 12.6 WordPress functions for a blog on the BlackBerry.

Using Email to Post

I like to blog from my mobile device, but there are some issues to consider when you do so, especially while you're on vacation. Usually I vacation with my family, and they tend to frown on my monkeying around on my BlackBerry. And to be honest, trying to make a quick post with the

BlackBerry, iPhone, or iPod Touch using the mobile applications can take a little longer than shooting off an email.

The mobile apps are great, but sending an email to your blog can be a quick and effective way to blog. You can add pictures or media, and everything is picked up on the other end. This approach is quicker and less cumbersome and will score some points with whomever you are vacationing with.

Email Posting with WordPress.com

If you want to set up your WordPress.com blog for email posting, visit WordPress.com and log in with your account.

1. Along the menu at the top of your screen, click **My Dashboards** to see a drop-down menu with all the blogs you have configured.

2. At the bottom, click **Manage Blogs**.

3. You now see a page titled Blogs You're a Member Of.

4. To the right is a column called Post by Email. For each blog listed, you see an Enable button.

5. Clicking **Enable** generates a secret email address for your blog.

That's it; now you're ready to post by email to your WordPress.com blog.

TIP: **My Secret Email Isn't Secret Anymore!**

If you hover your mouse cursor over the email address, you see the Regenerate and Delete options. If your secret email address becomes public, or you need to change it for another reason, you can regenerate it by clicking **Regenerate**, and you create a completely new address to post to.

Email Posting with WordPress.org

To set up your WordPress.org blog for email posting:

1. Open your Dashboard in your web browser and navigate to **Settings**, **Writing**.

2. You then see a section called Post via E-mail. It is recommended that you create a special email address to use as your publishing email.

   You can create an email address for posting to your blog through your web host, or you can create one through one of the free email services offered by Yahoo!, Google, and others.

CAUTION: **Don't Share This Email Address**

WordPress recommends posting via email using an email address that is secret—for example, hr22ma@yourdomain.com. It is a good idea not to share this email address with anyone because anyone who has the address is able to post to your blog.

---

3. After you have your secret email address, you need the URL of the email server, your username, and your password to proceed (see Figure 12.7).

TIP: **SSL on Email Servers**

Some services, such as Google's Gmail, use SSL to secure your connection to your email. If you use a service that requires SSL, you might have to indicate that as part of the email server's URL—for example, ssl://pop.gmail.com (see Figure 12.7).

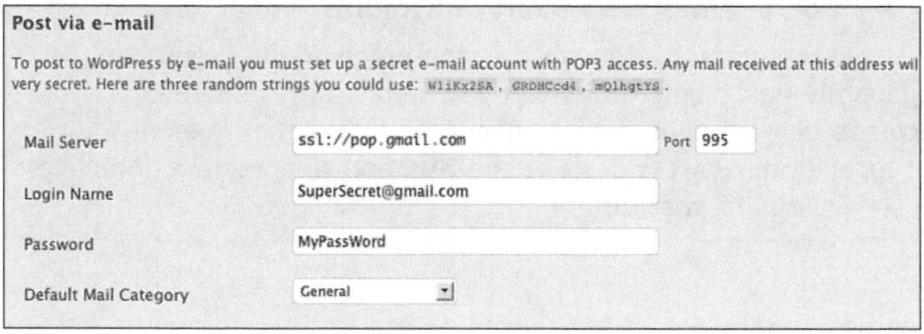

Post via e-mail

To post to WordPress by e-mail you must set up a secret e-mail account with POP3 access. Any mail received at this address will very secret. Here are three random strings you could use: W1iKx2SA , GRDHCcd4 , mQlhgtYs .

Mail Server	ssl://pop.gmail.com	Port 995
Login Name	SuperSecret@gmail.com	
Password	MyPassWord	
Default Mail Category	General ▾	

FIGURE 12.7   Settings for email publishing.

4. After filling out your information, click **Save Changes**.

There is one caveat with posting in this manner: When you are running
your own WordPress.org site much like you have to check your email,
your WordPress blog has to check for email, too. Unfortunately, this
process is not automatic. Each time you send an email to your secret
email address, you have to visit the URL http://yourdomain.com/wp-
mail.php for it to pick up your posts.

For WordPress.com sites, this is automatic.

This procedure can be automated with a CRON job for your
WordPress.org site. CRON is a UNIX application that runs jobs at a certain time and date of your choosing. Some web hosts allow you to create
a CRON job and automate the process of having WordPress check for
messages.

CAUTION: **Setting the Frequency of CRON Jobs**

Don't set your CRON job to have WordPress check your email too
often. Some email providers may frown on that. I recommend setting
up your CRON job to check once an hour or perhaps twice a day,
depending on your expected use.

Now that you have your settings in place, you are ready to email your
blog messages and pictures as you travel around.

NOTE: **Formatting in Emails**

If you send emails with HTML formatting, be aware that
Wordpress.com and .org strip unnecessary HTML from your messages while retaining some of the formatting. When your emails
appear on your blog, they might not look exactly as you created
them.

Also, be aware that any email signature you have on your outgoing
email (including disclaimers) could show up on your blog posts.

Using ScribeFire

ScribeFire is a free plug-in for Firefox that allows you to post directly
from your web browser. If you're wondering why you would use a plug-in
instead of just using the Dashboard to make a post, the reason is that
ScribeFire makes it extra easy to reference other pages or blog posts in
posts you write. You can cut and paste from the page you are viewing, as
well as create links and add pictures from the plug-in, all without having
to open your blog to switch between tabs or open windows to gather your
information.

To install ScribeFire in Firefox, visit the plug-in's page at
http://scribefire.com.

1. On the right side of the page, click the **Install ScribeFire Now**
   link. This link takes you to the ScribeFire page at the Firefox
   Add-ons page.

2. Click on the **Add to Firefox** button, and Firefox walks you
   through the rest of the process. If you have installed plug-ins
   previously in Firefox, this process will be familiar.

3. After the plug-in is installed, an orange icon appears on the bottom-right side of Firefox's status bar (see Figure 12.8).

4. Clicking this icon opens a window that overlays about one third
   of the viewing area of your browser.

FIGURE 12.8   The ScribeFire button in Firefox.

This window should look familiar in the sense that there is an editor in which you can view the WYSIWYG editor, the source, or a preview of what your post will look like.

On the right side is a button labeled Launch Account Wizard. If this is your first time running ScribeFire, the wizard might start automatically. If not, click Launch Account Wizard, and ScribeFire walks you through the process of adding your blog or blogs. First, you add your blog's URL and click **Continue**.

The wizard identifies the software you are using for your blog; in this case, it is WordPress. The wizard also automatically supplies the API URL. Click **Continue** again. Then you are asked for the username and password for your blog. After entering this information, click **Continue**.

The wizard logs in to your website and then asks you to confirm the addition. Click **Continue**. On the last wizard screen, ScribeFire tells you it has added the account. Click **Done**. Now you are ready to blog from ScribeFire.

> NOTE: **Adding More Than One Blog**
>
> If you have more than one blog you want to configure, clicking the **Add** button below your list of blogs also launches the Account Wizard.

Before you create a post, look at the options on the right. Clicking on the orange ScribeFire icon opens an area on the right with tabs. These tabs are as follows:

- **Blogs**—Provides a list of all the blogs you have configured.

- **Entries**—Offers you a view into the content on your site. There are three tabs under the Entries tab: Posts, Notes, and Pages. This is content on your site. You can select any of these tabs and edit your content directly from here without having to visit your site's Dashboard.

▶ **Categories**—Lists all the categories you have configured on
your site for your content. ScribeFire reads them in and makes
them available for you to use as you create posts. It also lists
your tags at the bottom.

▶ **Options**—Provides options for the post you are creating; for
example, you can change some of the settings, including changing the time stamp of a post so it will show in the future. You
can also set tags and turn on pinging if you want.

To create a post, you can just open ScribeFire by clicking the orange icon
in Firefox (refer to Figure 12.8). You can also right-click on a page in
Firefox that you want to reference, and you can use the ScribeFire options
in the context menu.

Try opening any web page and highlighting some text. Then right-click
and select **Blog This Page** (see Figure 12.9). ScribeFire opens, and a link
to the blog is created with the text that you highlighted shown in the editor.

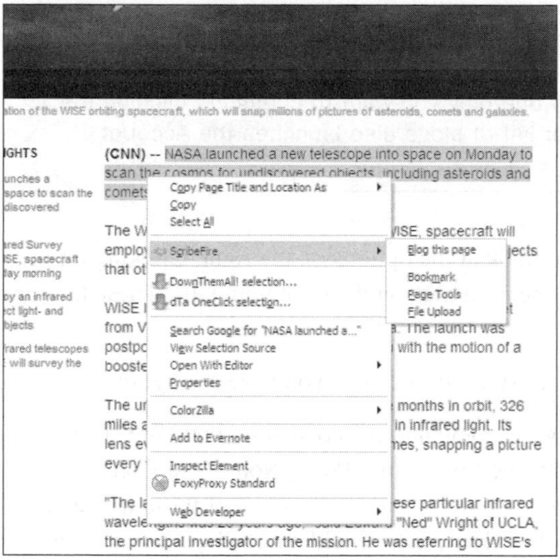

FIGURE 12.9   Using the context menu to blog about the page you are on.

From here, you can add your own commentary into your post, or you can cut and paste more quotes from the page you are viewing.

After you create your post and are happy with it, be sure to assign it a category. On the right side is a tab called Categories, beside the Entries tab. This is a list of the categories you have on your site set up for categorizing your posts.

Click **Publish to (Your Blog)**, and a small pop-up window asks if you want to publish as new posts or page. Select the appropriate choice for your post, normally **Post**. Then click **Publish**. When the item is successfully published, click **OK** to clear the editor. Alternatively, you can click **Keep Content** or **View this Blog**. When finished, close the window.

You can also save a draft of your post if you like. Select the check box, and when you publish as a draft, the post is not live, but you can edit it and continue with it later from your Entries, Posts tab (see Figure 12.10) or from your WordPress Dashboard. Drafts are shown in Red.

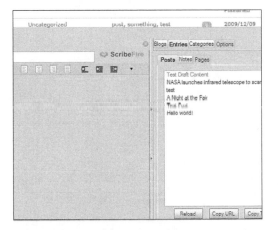

FIGURE 12.10 Viewing existing content and drafts in ScribeFire.

> NOTE: **Editing in ScribeFire**
>
> If you are editing content that already exists, you see the pop-up windows that ask you whether you want to post as an edit.

ScribeFire provides many more options, including using bookmarking services to share content with other social networks, creating notes for research on posts you want to make, and uploading media to your site.

Summary

In this lesson, you discovered how powerful remote publishing to WordPress can be, yet this lesson only scratched the surface with a few convenient services and applications. You set up WordPress to allow remote publishing, configured it to accept email submissions, and configured several websites to interact with your site, making publishing easy and flexible for yourself.

WordPress Support

Sometimes you might have to look for help while working with WordPress. The knowledge of friends and family may take you only so far. In this lesson, you look at the various support options you have with WordPress whether you self-host or use WordPress.com.

Looking for Help

WordPress is open source software. It is free for you to download and use, and you can even modify the code for your needs. As is the nature of open source software, you can find help in a many places.

One advantage of WordPress support is that it has such a large user base; therefore, it is inevitable that someone else has had the same problem as you and has already solved it. Because WordPress is a blogging tool, often you will find that people post their solutions to problems through their blogs.

Blogs are not the only area for help with WordPress. There are many free support channels, and there are those you can pay for and be able to contact someone.

Free Support

You can find free support for WordPress in many different formats, such as using WordPress documentation, searching the Internet, and reading WordPress forums.

WordPress Documentation

Before you start searching the Internet high and low for instructions on how to do something, consulting the WordPress.org documentation is a good place to start. Visit http://codex.wordpress.org to read the documentation.

The official WordPress documentation is very well organized and well written. It is a *wiki* that is set up so that anyone can add documentation; you get input from a lot of sources on how things work with WordPress. The reason it is such a good resource is that you get input from lots of individuals. If you have knowledge about a particular subject and you would like to share, you, too, can participate. To do so, just create an account at http://codex.wordpress.org.

> PLAIN ENGLISH: **Wiki**
>
> A wiki is a website set up so that anyone can view and edit the information on the site. This capability might sound strange at first, but wikis have real value. If you come to a wiki such as this, you can add information that you know about and someone else can do the same. Eventually, you have knowledge from several sources and a quality set of source material.

The WordPress documentation is organized from beginner topics to advanced.

- ▶ Getting Started with WordPress—Installing and upgrading WordPress
- ▶ WordPress 2.9 Information—Compatibility, feature lists, and so on
- ▶ Working with WordPress—Administration, themes, plug-ins, and spam
- ▶ Design and Layout—Installing and creating themes
- ▶ Advanced Topics—WordPress MU (multiuser), backing up
- ▶ Troubleshooting—Support forms and FAQs
- ▶ Developer Documentation—How-to documentation on creating themes and plug-ins

▶ About WordPress—General information about WordPress

A lot of information is available in the WordPress documentation. As you grow and learn more about WordPress, this should be your first resource online.

Contact WordPress Directly

WordPress offers support, but it is directed to those who use the WordPress.com service, and not the self-hosted WordPress. You can reach the support team at http://en.support.wordpress.com/contact/.Before contacting WordPress support, make sure to perform some basic troubleshooting. Try looking in the WordPress documentation before reaching out to the support team.

Search Engines

As mentioned previously, because WordPress is a blogging system, blogs are often a support form. When bloggers have trouble with WordPress and find a solution, there is a good chance they will blog about their experience.

Yahoo!, Google, Ask, and Bing are all great places to start your search for issues you have.

If you are doing searches about a particular feature, and not so much a problem, be sure to use the word *WordPress* in your search terms. For example, search "WordPress edit time stamp," and you get more results for exactly what you are looking for than if you just search for "edit time stamp."

Also, when you're searching for a solution to a specific error message you received, be sure to put the text of the error message in the search box, too. Adding this extra text can help narrow your search results to those that address exactly the error you are having an issue with.

Of course, searching with your favorite search engine will find not only pages and blog posts, but also forum results.

Forums

WordPress hosts Official Support forums at http://wordpress.org/forums. These forums provide another great starting point. Usually, especially when you're starting out, you find other people have had the same or similar issues.

The big attraction to using the WordPress forums is that other users here share a common interest (WordPress) and are willing to help solve your problem. I have found other users to be friendly and generous.

The forums are free to read and search, but to participate in conversations, you need to create an account. It is quick and easy, and I highly recommended it.

After you register, you are sent an email with a password as a confirmation of your account.

Topics are logically laid out based on function from installation to troubleshooting to theming and plug-ins.

Before you start posting, here are some tips to get the most out of your forum experience:

- ▶ Search first. Spending a few minutes can save you and others time trying to figure out your issue. Often you can find an answer right away.

- ▶ Be descriptive. Describing your issue thoroughly can make the difference in explaining yourself three times and getting an answer right away. Be sure not to ask something like "Why doesn't my plug-in work?" Instead, explain which plug-in you are using and what you are trying to do. Also include version numbers, such as your WordPress version and the version of your plug-in. And use clear subject titles when creating a forum post.

- ▶ Show your issue. If the problem you are experiencing is visible on the Internet, include a URL or link to a screenshot. Diagnosing your issue is much easier if others can see it.

▶ Be patient and courteous. Remember the other users of the forums are there to help you at no cost. Often you might not get a response right away. You are on the other person's time if someone engages you to help with an issue.

Paid Support

Regarding the nature of the issue you are having, an appropriate course of action may be to contact someone at your hosting company. If you are having trouble viewing your website or having other hosting matters not related to WordPress directly, contacting paid support should be covered under your monthly costs for web hosting.

Some companies and individuals prefer to rely on someone they can call and ask for support, and that is certainly available. Depending on your web host, it may provide services that assist in the installation or maintenance of your site for a fee, or perhaps it can recommend someone who can.

Automattic (the company behind the hosting of WordPress.com) offers a list of WordPress consultants from around the world at http://codepoet.com/.

In addition, Automattic offers tiered levels of enterprise support for companies. The cost for this paid support service ranges from $15,000 to $150,000. Automattic states that this support provides

▶ Access to several members of the WordPress development team to help you solve problems with your WordPress system

▶ Unlimited number of support incidents

▶ Software updates and upgrade notices

▶ Personal introductions to recommended third-party WordPress consultants and companies that offer custom development, design, and training

Automattic offers four tiers of support, each offering more features, better response times, and even site monitoring.

See Automattic's site for details at http://vip.wordpress.com/support/.

Other Learning Resources

The following sources of support shouldn't be the places where you start searching for information, but they still provide excellent sources of information on what is happening in the world of WordPress.

WordPress.tv

As stated on its site, WordPress.tv is "your visual resource for all things WordPress." This site has a lot of excellent videos posted that include how-tos, interviews, talks, and also videos featuring specific plug-ins.

If you navigate to http://wordpress.tv/category/how-to/, you can find lots of videos broken out into categories, which makes it easy to find videos on the specific topic you need.

WordPress Lessons at the WordPress Codex

WordPress Codex offers a subset of some of the topics listed at the official WordPress documentation. These lessons range from installing WordPress to writing themes and plug-ins. You can find this site at http://codex.wordpress.org/WordPress_Lessons.

NetTuts

If you are working on being a web developer, NetTuts is a valuable resource. On the NetTuts site, you can find articles regarding HTML, Ajax, JavaScript, PHP, and WordPress.

NetTuts offers tutorials for web developers and designers to help improve your work.

You can find the tutorials pertaining to WordPress at
http://net.tutsplus.com/category/tutorials/wordpress/.

I have found these articles and screencasts to be very helpful in the past.

Sams Teach Yourself WordPress in 10 Minutes 10 Minute Podcast

Chuck Tomasi and Kreg Steppe (the authors of this book) expand on
some of the topics presented in this book and also keep you up to date on
what's new in the world of WordPress, including releases, new features,
and interviews.

Visit http://www.chuckchat.com/wpin10 to keep current on WordPress.

Summary

There is no shortage of WordPress help to keep you going when you need
it. In this lesson, you learned many levels of support are available to you,
ranging from forums, to blog posts, and even some paid support options.
In addition, you were exposed to a lot of resources to continue your education in the world of WordPress.

Index

A

A Comment Is Held for Moderation option (Discussion Settings screen, Email Me Whenever section), 68
A Static Page option (Reading Settings screen, Front Page Displays setting), 63
About Yourself section (profiles)
  Biographical Info area, 21
  completing, 25
  passwords, 22-23
accounts
  activating, 12
  passwords, creating, 9
  profiles, updating, 11
  setting up, 9
  user names, creating, 9
Active category (Plug-ins Dashboard), 170
Add New option (Plug-ins Dashboard), 172
Add New Post page, 28
Add This to the (Current) Theme's CSS Stylesheet option (CSS Stylesheet Editor page), 110
adding
  RSS feeds, 116
  widgets to blogs, 102
Admin Color Scheme, 17
Admin passwords, 151
Administrative Dashboard
  managing comments, 82
  Recent Comments Dashboard widget, 83-84
Advertising Manager plug-in, 184
advertising plug-ins, 184
Akismet spam filtering plug-in, 184
Akismet spam filtering software, 80-81
All category (Plug-ins Dashboard), 170
Allow Link Notifications from Other Blogs (Pingbacks and Trackbacks) option (Discussion Settings screen), 78
Allow People to Post Comments on New Articles option (Discussion Settings screen), 78
allowing comments, 77
alternate text image descriptions, 46
Anyone Posts a Comment option (Discussion Settings screen, Email Me Whenever section), 68
API (Application Programming Interface)
  defining, 17
  Personal API keys, profiles, 16
App Store, WordPress application, 192-193
applying themes, 97, 166
approving comments
  comments list, 86-88
  Recent Comments Dashboard widget (Administrative Dashboard), 84
archives widget, 101
articles
  Attempt to Notify and Blogs Linked To from the Article option (Discussion Settings screen), 78
  comments, changing settings for individual articles, 79-80
  posting, Press This feature, 120
Atom Publishing, remote publishing, 188
Attempt to Notify any Blogs Linked To from the Article option (Discussion Settings screen), 78
audio, adding to pages, 51-52
authentication, 123
Author column (comments list), 86
Auto Renew setting (registrars), 134
Auto-embeds option (Media Settings screen), 71
automated script services, WordPress installations, 139
Automatically Close Comments on Articles Older Than __ Days setting (Other Comment Settings section (Discussion Settings screen), 67
Automattic, paid technical support via, 209
avatars. *See also* gravatars
  Avatar Display option (Discussion Settings screen), 69

Blog Picture/Icon area (General
  Settings screen), 58
Default Avatar option (Discussion
  Settings screen), 69
Maximum Rating option
  (Discussion Settings screen), 69
uploading images as, 58

B

backups, 123-124, 128
bandwidth, web hosting, 136
Before a Comment Appears setting
  (Discussion Settings screen), 68
Bing Webmaster Center, webmaster tools
  verification, 123
Biographical Info area (profiles, About
  Yourself section), 21
BlackBerry
  remote publishing from, 194-195
  viewing posts, 196
Blog Pages Show at Most option
  (Reading Settings screen), 64
Blog Picture/Icon area (General Settings
  screen), 58
Blog Title setting (General Settings
  screen), 56
blogs
  activating, 12
  comments, configuring settings,
    78-80
  configuring settings
    comments, 78-80
    discussion settings, 65-69
    formatting settings, 60-61
    general settings, 55-58
    media settings, 70-71
    privacy settings, 71-72
    reading settings, 62-65
    writing settings, 58-59
  customizing
    CSS Stylesheet Editor page,
      108-111
    Extras page, 103
    header images, 107
    header images, 107
    lateral navigation, 105-106
    mobile browsers, 104

mShots preview links, 103
    Related Links option
      (Extras page), 105-106
    themes, 93-97
    widgets, 100-102
databases, creating, 146
deleting, 72
development strategies, 9
domains, choosing, 10
finding, 77
folders, creating, 146
folds, 156
hosting
  bandwidth costs, 136
  bandwidth requirements, 136
  costs of, 133
  disk space costs, 136
  disk space requirements, 136
  finding support, 137
  Go Daddy web hosting
    service, 140
  maintenance, 132-133
  plug-ins, 132
  pre-existing themes, 132
  reasons for hosting, 131
  registering domain names,
    133-135
  requirements, 139
  responsibilities of, 132-133
  uploading files to web hosts,
    143-145
  WordPress operational
    requirements, 136
importing content from other blogs,
  128
migrating, 124-125
  content to WordPress, 13
  importing data from exported
    WordPress (XML) files, 126
  transferring blogs, 126-127
  WordPress.com blogs to
    WordPress.org sites, 129
naming, 10, 56, 129
OpenID, 73
personalizing
  CSS Stylesheet Editor page,
    108-111
  Extras page, 103
  header images, 107

lateral navigation, 105-106
mShots preview links, 103-104
Related Links option (Extras page), 105-106
themes, 93-97
widgets, 100-102
Primary Blog setting (profiles, Personal Options section), 18
remote publishing
   Atom Publishing, 188
   BlackBerry, 194-195
   technical support, 200-205
   configuring, 187-188
   email, 196-199
   Flickr, 189-190
   iPhone, 192-193
   mobile applications, 192-195
   Posterous, 191
   ScribeFire plug-in, 200-204
   WordPress.com email posts, 197
   WordPress.org email posts, 197-199
   XML-RPC, 188
renaming, 129
taglines, 56
themes, 153
   applying, 166
   browsing at WordPress.org, 158-159
   deleting, 166
   downloading, 158, 164-165
   finding, 157
   fixed layouts, 157
   fluid layouts, 157
   free themes, 154-155
   installing, 162-165
   premium themes, 154-155
   resolution and, 156
   three-column themes, 156
   two-column themes, 155
   types of, 154
   viewing details of, 160
transferring, 126-127
upgrades, transferring blogs, 127
widgets, adding/removing, 102
BluBrry PowerPress plug-in, 185

branding (corporate) themes, 95
browsers
   connections
      Always Use HTTPS When Visiting Administration Pages dialog, 18
      encryption, 18
   remote publishing from, 200-204
Bulk Actions drop-down list (comments list), 88
Bulk Edit menu, Quick Edit option, 39

C

calendars
   calendar widget, 101
   Week Starts On option (General Settings screen), 57
categories widget, 101
categorizing posts, 36
ChangeLog, plug-in upgrades, 182
code, editing, 177
comments
   A Comment Is Held for Moderation option (Discussion Settings screen, Email Me Whenever section), 68
   allowing, 77
   Anyone Posts a Comment option (Discussion Settings screen, Email Me Whenever section), 68
   approving
      comments list, 86-88
      Recent Comments Dashboard widget (Administrative Dashboard), 84
   Automatically Close Comments on Articles Older Than __ Days setting (Discussion Settings screen), 67
   Before a Comment Appears setting (Discussion Settings screen), 68
   best practices, 90
   blog settings, configuring, 78-80
   bulk actions, making to comments list, 88
   checking, 90

Comment Author Must Fill Out Name and Email setting (Other Comment Settings section, Discussion Settings screen), 67

Comment Blacklist setting (Discussion Settings screen), 68

Comment Moderation setting (Discussion Settings screen), 68

Comment Reply via Email setting (Discussion Settings screen), 68

comments list
  approving comments, 86-88
  Author column, 86
  deleting comments, 87-88
  filtering comments, 88-89
  In Response To column, 86
  making bulk actions, 88
  replying to comments, 87
  searching comments in, 88
  spam filtering, 86-89
  unapproving comments in, 88

Comments Should be Displayed with the _ Comments at the Top of Each Page (Discussion Settings screen), 67

deleting
  comments list, 87-88
  Recent Comments Dashboard widget (Administrative Dashboard), 85

denying, 77

Discussion Settings screen, configuring, 78-80

editing
  Quick Edit link (comments list), 87
  Recent Comments Dashboard widget (Administrative Dashboard), 84

email
  email aliases, 91
  receiving notifications, 90

Enable Threaded (Nested) Comments _ Levels Deep setting (Discussion Settings screen), 67

filtering in comments list, 88-89

leaving, 76-77

moderating
  Administrative Dashboard, 82-84
  comments list, 85-88
  Recent Comments Dashboard widget (Administrative Dashboard), 83-84

Notify Me of Follow Up Comments via Email option, 77

Other Comment Settings section (Discussion Settings screen), 66

page index (comments list), 89

replying to, 91
  comments list, 87
  Recent Comments Dashboard widget (Administrative Dashboard), 84

searching in comments list, 88

spam filtering, 68, 80-81
  comments list, 86-89
  Recent Comments Dashboard widget (Administrative Dashboard), 85

Subscribe to Comments setting (Discussion Settings screen), 69

unapproving in comments list, 88

Users Must Be Registered and Logged In to Comment setting (Discussion Settings screen), 67

viewing all, 85

configuring
  blog settings, 55
    discussion settings, 65-69
    formatting settings, 60-61
    general settings, 55-58
    media settings, 70-71
    privacy settings, 71-72
    reading settings, 62-65
    writing settings, 58-59
  comment settings, 78-80
  discussion settings, 78-80
  remote publishing, 187-188
  RSS feeds, 114-116

Contact Info section (profiles), 20
copying WordPress files to websites, 143-145
copyrighted material, adding to pages, 52
corporate branding themes, 95
CSS Stylesheet Editor page
    customizing blogs, 108-111
    previewing changes in, 110
    saving changes in, 110
customizing
    blogs
        CSS Stylesheet Editor page, 108-111
        Extras page, 103
        header images, 107
        lateral navigation, 105-106
        mobile browsers, 104
        mShots preview links, 103
        Related Links option (Extras page), 105-106
        themes, 93-97
        widgets, 100-102
    header images, 107
    themes (blogs), 153
        applying, 166
        browsing at WordPress.org, 158-159
        deleting, 166
        downloading, 158, 164-165
        finding, 157
        fixed layouts, 157
        fluid layouts, 157
        free themes, 154-155
        installing, 162-165
        premium themes, 154-155
        resolution and, 156
        three-column themes, 156
        two-column themes, 155
        types of, 154
        viewing details of, 160

D

Dashboard
    browsing themes in, 160
    Plug-ins Dashboard

Active category, 170
Add New option, 172
All category, 170
Editor option, 172
Featured view, 174
Inactive category, 170
Installed option, 172
Newest view, 174
plug-in searches, 174-175
Recently Active category, 171
Recently Updated view, 175
Search view, 174
Upgrade Available category, 171
Upload view, 174
    widgets, 167
data backups, 123-124
databases, creating, 146
Date Format setting (General Settings screen), 57
deactivating plug-ins, 183
Default Article Setting (Discussion Settings screen), 66
Default Avatar option (Discussion Settings screen), 69
Default Link Category (Writing Settings screen), 61
Default Post Category (Writing Settings screen), 61
deleting
    blogs, 72
    comments
        comments list, 87-88
        Recent Comments Dashboard widget (Administrative Dashboard), 85
    plug-ins, 171
    themes, 166
denying comments, 77
descriptions (blogs), taglines, 56
development strategies, 9
disabling mShots preview links, 104
Discussion Settings screen, 65, 79-80
    Allow People to Post Comments on New Articles option, 78
    Avatar Display option, 69

Before a Comment Appears
    setting, 68
Comment Blacklist setting, 68
Comment Moderation setting, 68
Comment Reply via Email setting, 68
Default Article Setting, 66
Default Avatar option, 69
Email Me Whenever section, 68
Maximum Rating option, 69
Other Comment Settings section, 66
Subscribe to Comments setting, 69
discussions, setting post options, 34
disk space
    web hosting costs, 136
    web hosting requirements, 136
Display a Mobile Theme When This
    Blog Is Viewed with a mobile browser
    option (Extras page), 104
Display Name Publicly As list
    (profiles), 20
documentation, WordPress documenta-
    tion as free support, 206-207
domain names, registering, 133-135
Domains section (Settings section), 73
domains, choosing, 10
downloading
    plug-ins, 173
    themes, 158, 164-165
drafts (posts)
    changing status of, 34
    saving, 34

E

Edit button (Add New Post page), 28
editing
    code, best practices, 177
    comments
        Quick Edit link (comments
            list), 87
        Recent Comments Dashboard
            widget (Administrative
            Dashboard), 84
    pages, 41
    plug-ins, 172
    posts, 36-39
        HTML editing, 32
        Visual Editor, 29-31

WYSIWYG (what you see is
    what you get) editing, 32
Editor option (Plug-ins Dashboard), 172
email
    comments
        email aliases, 91
        receiving email notifications, 90
    email address field (General
        Settings screen), 57
    Email Me Whenever section
        (Discussion Settings screen), 68
    Notify Me of Follow Up Comments
        via Email option, 77
    Post by Email option (Writing
        Settings screen), 61
    Posterous, remote publishing, 191
    remote publishing from, 196
        WordPress.com, 197
        WordPress.org, 197-199
embedded content
    Auto-embeds option (Media
        Settings screen), 71
    Maximum Embed Size option
        (Media Settings screen), 71
Enable mShots Site Previews on This
    Blog option (Extras page), 103
Enable Threaded (Nested) Comments __
    Levels Deep setting (Other Comment
    Settings section, Discussion Settings
    screen), 67
Encoding for Pages and Feeds
    setting (Reading Settings screen), 65
encrypted browser connections, 18
Excerpt view (Edit list), 39
excerpts, 33
export files
    creating, 125
    media and, 125
    saving, 124
Extras page
    customizing blogs, 103
    Display a Mobile Theme When This
        Blog Is Viewed with a Mobile
        Browser option, 104
    Enable mShots Site Previews on
        This Blog option, 103
    Related Links option, 105-106

F

Featured view (Plug-ins Dashboard), 174
file permission plug-ins, 172
filtering comments in comments list, 89
finding
    blogs, 77
    plug-ins, 172-173
        Plug-ins Dashboard searches, 174-175
        WordPress site searches, 176-177
    profiles, 15
    themes, 95-96, 157
    web hosting support, 137
Firefox, ScribeFire plug-in, 200-204
First Name, Last Name fields (profiles), 19
fixed layouts, 157
Flickr, remote publishing, 189-190
fluid layouts, 157
folds (layouts), 156
For Each Article in a Feed, Show setting (Reading Settings screen), 65
For Each Article in an Enhanced Feed, Show setting (Reading Settings screen), 65
formatting
    Date Format setting (General Settings screen), 57
    Formatting option (Writing Settings screen), 60
    Post by Email option (Writing Settings screen), 61
    Time Format setting (General Settings screen), 57
forums, finding support via, 208
free themes versus premium themes, 154-155
Front Page Displays setting (Reading Settings screen), 63-64

G

Gallery (media library), adding images to pages, 49
Gears (Google), Turbo mode, 118-120

General Settings screen, 55
    Blog Picture/Icon area, 58
    Blog Title setting, 56
    Date Format setting, 57
    email address field, 57
    Language field, 56
    taglines, 56
    Time Format setting, 57
    Timezone setting, 57
    Week Starts On option, 57
GNU GPL (General Public License), 131-132
Go Daddy web hosting service, Hosting Connection script service, 140
Google
    AdSense for feeds plug-in, 184
    Analyticator plug-in, 185
    Gears, Turbo mode, 118-120
    webmaster tools verification, 122
GPL (General Public License), 131-132
gravatars, 23-24. *See also* avatars
grouping posts, 36

H

header images, customizing, 107
help
    free support, 205
        forums, 208
        search engines, 207
        WordPress documentation, 206-207
        WordPress website, 207
    NetTuts website, 210
    paid support, 209
    Sams Teach Yourself WordPress in 10 Minutes 10 Minute Podcast, 211
    web hosting, 137
    WordPress Codex website, 210
    WordPress.tv website, 210
hosting blogs
    bandwidth, 136
    costs of, 133, 136
    disk space, 136
    domain names, registering, 133-135
    finding support, 137
    Go Daddy web hosting service, 140
    maintenance, 132-133
    plug-ins, 132

pre-existing themes, 132
reasons for hosting, 131
requirements, 139
responsibilities of, 132-133
uploading files to web hosts
    choosing blog folders, 143
    copying WordPress files to
      websites, 143-145
WordPress operational
  requirements, 136
Hosting Connection script service, 140
HTML (Hypertext Markup Language),
  editing in posts, 32
hyperlinks
  adding to pages, 42-44
  Default Link Category (Writing
    Settings screen), 61
  images, 51
  lateral navigation, 105-106
  links widget, 101
  Related Links option (Extras page),
    105-106

I

I Would Like My Blog to Be Visible
  Only to Users I Choose option (Privacy
  Settings screen), 72
I Would Like to Block Search Engines,
  but Allow Normal Visitors option
  (Privacy Settings screen), 71
icons
  Blog Picture/Icon area (General
    Settings screen), 58
  uploading images as, 58
images
  adding to pages
    alternate text descriptions, 46
    images from computer, 44-46
    images from Gallery (media
      library), 49
    images from media library, 50
    images from URL, 46-48
    storage limitations, 46
  Blog Picture/Icon area (General
    Settings screen), 58
  Flickr, remote publishing, 189-190
  header images, customizing, 107
  hyperlinks, 51

Large Size option (Media Settings
  screen), 71
Medium Size option (Media
  Settings screen), 71
Thumbnail Size option (Media
  Settings screen), 70
uploading, 58
importing
  content from other blogs, 128
  data from exported WordPress
    (XML) files, 126
In Response To column (comments list),
  86
Inactive category (Plug-ins Dashboard),
  170
Installed option (Plug-ins Dashboard),
  172
installing
  plug-ins, 177
    automated installations, 179
    fully automatic installations,
      178
    manual installations, 180
  themes, 162-165
  WordPress
    automated script services, 139
    creating blog folders, 146
    creating databases, 146
    initial logins, 150
    manual installations,
      140-142
    running install scripts, 147-151
    uploading files to web hosts,
      143-145
Interface Language setting (profiles,
  Personal Options section), 18
iPhone, remote publishing from, 192-193

J - K - L

keyboard shortcuts, 17, 32
Language field (General Settings screen),
  56
languages
  blogs, selecting language for, 56
  Interface Language setting (profiles,
    Personal Options section), 18

Large Size option (Media Settings screen), 71

Last Name, First Name fields (profiles), 19

lateral navigation, 105-106

layouts
    fixed layouts, 157
    fluid layouts, 157
    folds, 156
    resolution and, 156
    three-column themes, 156
    two-column themes, 155

Limit Width option (CSS Stylesheet Editor page), 110

links (hyperlinks)
    adding to pages, 42-44
    Default Link Category (Writing Settings screen), 61
    images, 51
    lateral navigation, 105-106
    links widget, 101
    Related Links option (Extras page), 105-106

List view (Edit list), 39

logins
    login names versus nicknames, 20
    WordPress, 150

M

maintenance, blog hosting, 132-133

manual WordPress installations, 140-142

Maximum Embed Size option (Media Settings screen), 71

Maximum Rating option (Discussion Settings screen), 69

media
    audio, adding to pages, 51-52
    export files, creating, 125
    video, adding to pages, 53-54

media library
    adding media library images to pages, 50
    Gallery, adding images to pages, 49

Media Settings screen
    Auto-embeds option, 71
    Large Size option, 71
    Maximum Embed Size option, 71
    Medium Size option, 71
    Thumbnail Size option, 70

Medium Size option (Media Settings screen), 71

meta widget, 101

migrating blogs, 13, 124-125
    importing data from exported WordPress (XML) files, 126
    transferring blogs, 126-127
    WordPress.com blogs to WordPress.org sites, 129

mobile applications, remote publishing
    BlackBerry, 194-195
    iPhone, 192-193

mobile browsers, 104

mobile themes, 104

moderating comments
    Administrative Dashboard, 82
        Recent Comments Dashboard widget, 83-84
    comments list, 85, 88
        Author column, 86
        In Response To column, 86

moving blogs, 13, 124-125
    importing data from exported WordPress (XML) files, 126
    transferring blogs, 126-127
    WordPress.com blogs to WordPress.org sites, 129

mShots preview links
    customizing blogs, 103
    disabling, 104

N

naming
    blogs, 10, 56, 129
    Display Name Publicly As list, 20
    domain names
        registering names, 133-135
        registrars, 133
    First Name, Last Name fields (profiles), 19
    nicknames, 20
    usernames, 19

NetTuts website, technical support via, 210

New Post button, 27

Newest view (Plug-ins Dashboard), 174

nicknames versus login names, 20

Notify Me of Follow Up Comments via Email option, 77

O - P

open source software, 131-132
OpenID section (Settings section), 73
organizing posts, 36
Other Comment Settings section (Discussion Settings screen), 66

page index (comments list), 89
pages
    Add New Post page, 28
    audio, adding, 51-52
    copyrighted material, adding, 52
    creating, 40-41
    editing, 41
    hyperlinks, adding, 42-44
    images, adding
        alternate text descriptions, 46
        images from computer, 44-46
        images from Gallery (media library), 49
        images from media library, 50
        images from URL, 46-48
        storage limitations, 46
    video, adding, 53-54
pages widget, 101
passwords
    account passwords, creating, 9
    Admin passwords, 151
    copying WordPress files to websites, 145
    profiles, 22-23
performance, improving via Turbo mode (Gears), 118-120
permissions, plug-in files, 172
Personal API keys, profiles, 16
Personal Options section (profiles)
    Admin Color Scheme, 17
    Always Use HTTPS When Visiting Administration Pages dialog, 18
    Interface Language setting, 18
    Keyboard Shortcuts, 17
    Primary Blog setting, 18
    Proofreading section, 19
    Visual Editor, 17

personalizing
blogs
    CSS Stylesheet Editor page, 108-111
    Extras page, 103
    header images, 107
    lateral navigation, 105-106
    mobile browsers, 104
    mShots preview links, 103
    Related Links option (Extras page), 105-106
    themes, 93-97
    widgets, 100-102
    header images, 107
pictures
    adding to pages
        alternate text descriptions, 46
        images from computer, 44-46
        images from Gallery (media library), 49
        images from media library, 50
        images from URL, 46-48
        storage limitations, 46
    Blog Picture/Icon area (General Settings screen), 58
    Flickr, remote publishing, 189-190
    header pictures, customizing, 107
    hyperlinks, 51
    Large Size option (Media Settings screen), 71
    Medium Size option (Media Settings screen), 71
    Thumbnail Size option (Media Settings screen), 70
    uploading, 58
pingbacks, 78-79
plug-ins
    Advertising Manager plug-in, 184
    advertising plug-ins, 184
    Akismet spam filtering plug-in, 184
    blog hosting plug-ins, 132
    BluBrry PowerPress plug-in, 185
    creating, 174
    defining, 169
    deleting, 171
    downloading, 173
    editing, 172

file permissions, 172
finding, 172-173
    Plug-ins Dashboard searches,
    174-175
    WordPress site searches,
    176-177
Google AdSense for feeds plug-in,
    184
Google Analyticator plug-in, 185
installing, 177
    automated installations, 179
    fully automatic installations,
    178
    manual installations, 180
Plug-ins Dashboard
    Active category, 170
    Add New option, 172
    All category, 170
    Editor option, 172
    Featured view, 174
    Inactive category, 170
    Installed option, 172
    Newest view, 174
    plug-in searches, 174-175
    Recently Active category, 171
    Recently Updated view, 175
    Search view, 174
    Upgrade Available category,
    171
    Upload view, 174
podcasting plug-ins, 185
promotional/publicity plug-ins, 184
publicity/promotional plug-ins, 184
removing, 183
ScribeFire plug-in, remote
    publishing via, 200-204
Sociable plug-in, 185
Social Bookmarks plug-in, 185
social networking plug-ins, 185
spam filtering plug-ins, 184
statistics plug-ins, 185
Twitter Tools plug-in, 185
upgrading, 181-182
Wordpress.com Stats plug-in, 185
Wp-pubsubhubbub plug-in, 184
WP-SpamFree Anti-Spam plug-in,
    184
writing, 174

podcasts
    plug-ins, 185
    Sams Teach Yourself WordPress in
        10 Minutes 10 Minute Podcast,
        technical support via, 211
Post by Email option (Writing Settings
    screen), 61
Posterous, remote publishing, 191
posts
    Add New Post page, 28
    BlackBerry, viewing on, 196
    categorizing, 36
    creating
        Add New Post page, 28
        discussion options, 34
        excerpts, 33
        New Post button, 27
        tags, 35-36
        trackbacks, 33
        Visual Editor, 29-31
    Default Post Category (Writing
        Settings screen), 61
    discussions, setting options, 34
    drafts
        changing status, 34
        saving, 34
    editing, 36-39
        HTML editing, 32
        Visual Editor, 29-31
        WYSIWYG (what you see is
        what you get) editing, 32
    excerpts, 33
    lateral navigation, 105-106
    New Post button, 27
    Post by Email option (Writing
        Settings screen), 61
    Press This feature, 120
    previewing, 34
    publishing, 34-35
    saving drafts, 34
    Size of the Post Box setting
        (Writing Settings screen), 59
    summaries, 65
    tags, 35-36
    trackbacks, 33
    visibility of, changing, 35
Posts Page option (Reading Settings
    screen, Front Page Displays setting), 63

premium themes versus free themes, 154-155

Press This feature, posting articles via, 120

previewing
    CSS changes in CSS Stylesheet Editor page, 110
    posts, 34
    themes, 96
    websites, mShots preview links, 103

Primary Blog setting (profiles, Personal Options section), 18

Privacy Settings screen
    I Would Like My Blog to Be Visible Only to Users I Choose option, 72
    I Would Like to Block Search Engines, but Allow Normal Visitors option, 71

profiles
    About Yourself section
        Biographical Info area, 21
        completing, 25
        passwords, 22-23
    Contact Info section, 20
    Display Name Publicly As list, 20
    finding, 15
    First Name, Last Name fields, 19
    gravatars, 23-24
    nicknames, 20
    passwords, 22-23
    Personal API keys, 16
    Personal Options section
        Admin Color Scheme, 17
        Always Use HTTPS When Visiting Administration Pages dialog, 18
        Interface Language setting, 18
        Keyboard Shortcuts, 17
        Primary Blog setting, 18
        Proofreading section, 19
        Visual Editor, 17
    saving changes, 25
    updating, 11, 25
    usernames, 19

promotional/publicity plug-ins, 184

Proofreading section (profiles, Personal Options section) and Visual Editor, 19

publicity/promotional plug-ins, 184

publishing
    posts, 34-35
    remotely
        Atom Publishing, 188
        BlackBerry, 194-195
        browsers, 200-204
        configuring, 187-188
        email, 196-199
        Flickr, 189-190
        iPhone, 192-193
        mobile applications, 192-195
        Posterous, 191
        ScribeFire plug-in, 200-204
        XML-RPC, 188

Q - R

Quick Edit link (comments list), 87

Quick Edit option (Bulk Edit menu), 39

Reading Settings screen
    Blog Pages Show at Most option, 64
    Encoding for Pages and Feeds setting, 65
    For Each Article in a Feed, Show setting, 65
    For Each Article in an Enhanced Feed, Show setting, 65
    Front Page Displays setting, 63-64
    Syndication Feeds Show the Most Recent setting, 65

Recent Comments Dashboard widget (Administrative Dashboard), 83-84

Recently Active category (Plug-ins Dashboard), 171

Recently Updated view (Plug-ins Dashboard), 175

redirected RSS feeds, 117-118

registrars
    domain names, 133
    renewals, 134

Related Links option (Extras page), 105-106

remote publishing
    Atom Publishing, 188
    browsers, 200-204
    configuring, 187-188

email, 196
  WordPress.com, 197
  WordPress.org, 197-199
Flickr, 189-190
mobile applications
  BlackBerry, 194-195
  iPhone, 192-193
Posterous, 191
ScribeFire plug-in, 200-204
XML-RPC, 188
removing
  plug-ins, 183
  widgets from blogs, 102
renaming blogs, 129
renewals, registrars, 134
replying to comments, 91
  comments list, 87
  Recent Comments Dashboard widget
    (Administrative Dashboard), 84
resolution, themes, 156
restoring backups, 128
RSS (Really Simple Syndication) feeds,
  8, 113
  adding feeds, 116
  configuring, 114-116
  For Each Article in a Feed, Show
    setting (Reading Settings screen),
    65
  For Each Article in an Enhanced
    Feed, Show setting (Reading
    Settings screen), 65
  redirected feeds, 117-118
  RSS Links widget, 115-116
  Syndication Feeds Show the Most
    Recent setting (Reading Settings
    screen), 65

S

Sams Teach Yourself WordPress in 10
  Minutes 10 Minute Podcast, technical
  support via, 211
saving
  CSS changes in CSS Stylesheet
    Editor page, 110
  exported files, 124
  post drafts, 34
  profile changes, 25

ScribeFire plug-in, remote
  publishing via, 200-204
script services (automated), WordPress
  installations, 139
scripts (install), running, 147-151
Search view (Plug-ins Dashboard), 174
searches
  comments in comments list, 88
  plug-ins
    *Plug-ins Dashboard searches,
    174-175*
    *WordPress site searches,
    176-177*
  search engines, finding support via,
    207
  search widget, 101
  themes, 157
security
  browser connections, 18
  privacy settings, configuring, 71-72
Settings section
  Discussion Settings screen, 65
    Avatar Display option, 69
    *Before a Comment Appears
    setting, 68*
    Comment Blacklist setting, 68
    *Comment Moderation setting,
    68*
    *Comment Reply via Email
    setting, 68*
    Default Article Setting, 66
    Default Avatar option, 69
    Email Me Whenever section, 68
    Maximum Rating option, 69
    *Other Comment Settings
    section, 66*
    *Subscribe to Comments
    setting, 69*
  Domains section, 73
  General Settings screen, 55
    Blog Picture/Icon area, 58
    Blog Title setting, 56
    Date Format setting, 57
    email address field, 57
    Language field, 56
    taglines, 56
    Time Format setting, 57
    TimeZone setting, 57
    Week Starts On option, 57

Media Settings screen
    Auto-embeds option, 71
    Large Size option, 71
    Maximum Embed Size option, 71
    Medium Size option, 71
    Thumbnail Size option, 70
OpenID section, 73
Privacy Settings screen
    I Would Like My Blog to Be Visible Only to Users I Choose option, 72
    I Would Like to Block Search Engines, but Allow Normal Visitors option, 71
Reading Settings screen
    Blog Pages Show at Most option, 64
    Encoding for Pages and Feeds setting, 65
    For Each Article in a Feed, Show setting, 65
    For Each Article in an Enhanced Feed, Show setting, 65
    Front Page Displays option, 63-64
    Syndication Feeds Show the Most Recent setting, 65
Writing Settings screen
    Default Link Category, 61
    Default Post Category, 61
    Formatting option, 60
    Post by Email option, 61
    Size of the Post Box setting, 59
Short Link button (Add New Post page), 29
shortcuts (keyboard), 17, 32
Sign Up screen, 9
Simple Scripts script service, 140
Size of the Post Box setting (Writing Settings screen), 59
Sociable plug-in, 185
Social Bookmarks plug-in, 185
social networking plug-ins, 185
spam filtering
    comments, 80-81
        Comment Blacklist setting (Discussion Settings screen), 68

        comments list, 86-89
        Recent Comments Dashboard widget (Administrative Dashboard), 85
    plug-ins, 184
Start from Scratch and Just Use This option (CSS Stylesheet Editor page), 110
statistics plug-ins, 185
status
    filtering comments by (comments list), 88
    post drafts, changing, 34
strong passwords, 22-23
subscriptions, RSS feeds, 8
summaries (blog posts), 65
support
    technical
        free support, 205-208
        NetTuts website, 210
        paid support, 209
        Sams Teach Yourself WordPress in 10 Minutes 10 Minute Podcast, 211
        WordPress Codex website, 210
        WordPress.tv website, 210
    web hosting, 137
syndication (RSS feeds), 8, 113
    adding feeds, 116
    configuring, 114-116
    For Each Article in a Feed, Show setting (Reading Settings screen), 65
    For Each Article in an Enhanced Feed, Show setting (Reading Settings screen), 65
    redirected feeds, 117-118
    RSS Links widget, 115-116
    Syndication Feeds Show the Most Recent setting (Reading Settings screen), 65

T

tag clouds, 175
taglines, 56
tags, 35-36, 175
technical support

free support
  forums, 208
  search engines, 207
  WordPress documentation,
   206-207
  WordPress website, 207
NetTuts website, 210
paid support, 209
Sams Teach Yourself WordPress in
  10 Minutes 10 Minute Podcast,
  211
WordPress Codex website, 210
WordPress.tv website, 210
text, alternate text image
  descriptions, 46
text widget, 102
themes, 93, 153
  applying, 97, 166
  blog hosting themes, 132
  branding (corporate) themes, 95
  browsing at WordPress.org, 158-159
  changing, 97
  deleting, 166
  downloading, 158, 164-165
  finding, 95-96, 157
  fixed layouts, 157
  fluid layouts, 157
  free themes, 154-155
  header images, customizing, 107
  installing, 162, 165
  mobile themes, 104
  premium themes, 154-155
  previewing, 96
  resolution and, 156
  three-column themes, 156
  two-column themes, 155
  types of, 154
  viewing details of, 160
three-column themes, 156
Thumbnail Size option (Media Settings
  screen), 70
Time Format setting (General Settings
  screen), 57
Timezone setting (General Settings
  screen), 57
titles, blogs, 56
trackbacks, 33, 78-79
transferring blogs, 126-127

Turbo mode (Gears), improving blog
  performance via, 118-120
Twitter Tools plug-in, 185
two-column themes, 155

U

unapproving comments from
  comments list, 88
updates
  profiles, 11, 25
  Recently Updated view
   (Plug-ins Dashboard), 175
upgrades
  CSS customizations, 109
  plug-ins, 181-182
  transferring blogs, 127
  Upgrade Available category (Plug-
   ins Dashboard), 171
  WordPress.com, 18
  WordPress.org, 18
Upload view (Plug-ins Dashboard), 174
uploading
  files to web hosts
   choosing blog folders, 143
   copying WordPress files to
    websites, 143-145
  images, Blog Picture/Icon area
   (General Settings screen), 58
URL (uniform resource locators)
  images from URL, adding to pages,
   46-48
  OpenID, 73
user names (accounts),creating, 9
user profiles
  About Yourself section
   Biographical Info area, 21
   completing, 25
   passwords, 22-23
  Contact Info section, 20
  Display Name Publicly As list, 20
  finding, 15
  First Name, Last Name fields, 19
  gravatars, 23-24
  nicknames, 20
  passwords, 22-23
  Personal API keys, 16

Personal Options section
  Admin Color Scheme, 17
  *Always Use HTTPS When
    Visiting Administration
    Pages dialog, 18*
  Interface Language setting, 18
  Keyboard Shortcuts, 17
  Primary Blog setting, 18
  Proofreading section, 19
  Visual Editor, 17
  saving changes, 25
  updating, 11, 25
usernames, 19
Users Must Be Registered and Logged
In to Comment setting, Other
Comment Settings section (Discussion
Settings screen), 67

V

verifying webmaster tools
  Bing Webmaster Center, 123
  Google webmaster tools, 122
  Yahoo! Site Explorer, 122-123
video. *See also* embedded content
  adding to pages, 53-54
  export files, 125
viewing
  comments, 85
  posts on BlackBerry, 196
visibility of posts, changing, 35
Visual Editor, 17
  editing posts, 29-31
  keyboard shortcuts, 32
  Proofreading section (profiles,
    Personal Options section) and, 19
voice, export files, 125

W

web hosting
  Go Daddy web hosting service, 140
  requirements, 139
  uploading files to web hosts
    choosing blog folders, 143
    *copying WordPress files to
      websites, 143-145*

webmaster tools verification
  Bing Webmaster Center, 123
  Google webmaster tools, 122
  Yahoo! Site Explorer, 122-123
websites
  Automattic, paid technical
    support via, 209
  folds, 156
  NetTuts website, technical
    support via, 210
  previewing, mShots preview links, 103
  themes, 153
    applying, 166
    *browsing at WordPress.org,
      158-159*
    deleting, 166
    downloading, 158, 164-165
    finding, 157
    fixed layouts, 157
    fluid layouts, 157
    free themes, 154-155
    installing, 162-165
    premium themes, 154-155
    resolution and, 156
    three-column themes, 156
    two-column themes, 155
    types of, 154
    viewing details of, 160
  WordPress Codex website,
    technical support via, 210
  WordPress website, finding
    support at, 207
  WordPress.tv website, technical
    support via, 210
Week Starts On option (General Settings
screen), 57
widgets, 100, 166-167
  archives widget, 101
  blogs, adding to/removing from, 102
  calendar widget, 101
  categories widget, 101
  links widget, 101
  meta widget, 101
  pages widget, 101
  RSS Links widget, 115-116
  search widget, 101
  text widget, 102

width, Limit Width option (CSS
Stylesheet Editor page), 110
WordPress, 5
    Admin passwords, 151
    development of, 8
    features of, 7
    history of, 8
    installing
        automated script services, 139
        creating blog folders, 146
        creating databases, 146
        initial logins, 150
        manual installations, 140-142
        running install scripts, 147-151
        uploading files to web hosts,
            143-145
    logins, 150
    migrating outside blog content to
        WordPress, 13
    operational requirements, 136
    support
        documentation, 206-207
        WordPress website, 207
WordPress application (App Store), 192-193
WordPress Codex website, technical
    support via, 210
WordPress MU (multiuser), 6
WordPress.com, 6
    email posting, 197
    feature comparison table, 7
    profiles, differences from
        WordPress.org profiles, 15
    remote publishing
        configuring, 187
        via email, 197
    Sign Up screen, 9
    Stats plug-in, 185
    upgrades, 18
WordPress.org, 6
    email posting, 197-199
    feature comparison table, 7
    manual WordPress installations
        downloading software, 140
        unpacking software, 142

profiles, differences from
    WordPress.com profiles, 15
remote publishing
    configuring, 187
    via email, 197-199
themes, browsing, 158-159
upgrades, 18
WordPress.tv website, technical
    support via, 210
Wp-pubsubhubbub plug-in, 184
WP-SpamFree Anti-Spam plug-in, 184
Writing Settings screen
    Default Link Category, 61
    Default Post Category, 61
    Formatting option, 60
    Post by Email option, 61
    Size of the Post Box setting, 59
wsers, 204
WYSIWYG (what you see is what you
    get) editing, 32

X - Y - Z

XML (Extensible Markup Language)
    exported WordPress (XML) files,
        importing data
        from, 126
    XML-RPC, remote publishing, 188

Yahoo! Site Explorer, webmaster tools
    verification, 122-123

FREE Online Edition

Your purchase of **Sams Teach Yourself WordPress in 10 Minutes** includes access to a free online edition for 45 days through the Safari Books Online subscription service. Nearly every Sams book is available online through Safari Books Online, along with more than 5,000 other technical books and videos from publishers such as Addison-Wesley Professional, Cisco Press, Exam Cram, IBM Press, O'Reilly, Prentice Hall, and Que.

SAFARI BOOKS ONLINE allows you to search for a specific answer, cut and paste code, download chapters, and stay current with emerging technologies.

Activate your FREE Online Edition at www.informit.com/safarifree

> **STEP 1:** Enter the coupon code: FLHJZAA.

> **STEP 2:** New Safari users, complete the brief registration form. Safari subscribers, just log in.

If you have difficulty registering on Safari or accessing the online edition, please e-mail customer-service@safaribooksonline.com

Safari
Books Online

Addison Wesley · Adobe Press · ALPHA · Cisco Press · FT Press · IBM Press · lynda.com · Microsoft Press · New Riders

O'REILLY · Peachpit Press · PRENTICE HALL · QUE · Redbooks · SAMS · SAS · Sun · WILEY